China's Socialist Rule of Law Reforms Under Xi Jinping

Under the direction of the Communist Party of China (CPC), key legal challenges have been identified which will shape the modernization of China's legal and administrative institutions. An increasingly complex set of legal actors now seek to influence this development, including securities regulators, bankers, accountants, lawyers, local-level mediators and some of China's newly rich. Whilst the rising middle class wants to voice its interests and concerns, the CPC strives to maintain its leading role.

This book provides a critical appraisal of China's deepening socialist rule of law and looks ahead to the implications of the domestic reforms for the international legal domain. With contributions from leading Chinese law specialists, it draws on specific illustrations from judicial reform, constitutional law, procedural law, anti-corruption, property law and urban development, socio-economic dispute resolution and Chinese macroeconomics. The book questions how China's domestic law reforms will impact international legal systems, and how international law can be used in managing key regional and bilateral relationships and in dispute resolution, such as in the South China Sea and international trade.

Assessing the state and direction of domestic law reform and including debates around the legal implications of some of China's most pressing foreign policy challenges today, this volume will be of huge interest to students, scholars and practitioners with an interest in Asia law, Chinese law, international law, comparative law and law reform.

John Garrick is an attorney of the Supreme Court of New South Wales, Australia. He is an author and editor of publications including *Law, Wealth and Power in China: Commercial Law Reforms in Context* (Routledge 2014) and *Law and Policy for China's Market Socialism* (Routledge 2015).

Yan Chang Bennett is a lawyer and Manager for the Center on Contemporary China at Princeton University. From 2009 to 2015 she was the Assistant Director for the Princeton–Harvard China and the World Program. Before coming to Princeton, she was a Foreign Service Officer with the U.S. Department of State having served as Vice Consul in China.

Routledge Contemporary China Series

1 **Nationalism, Democracy and National Integration in China**
Leong Liew and Wang Shaoguang

2 **Hong Kong's Tortuous Democratization**
A comparative analysis
Ming Sing

3 **China's Business Reforms**
Institutional challenges in a globalised economy
Edited by Russell Smyth, On Kit Tam, Malcolm Warner and Cherrie Zhu

4 **Challenges for China's Development**
An enterprise perspective
Edited by David H. Brown and Alasdair MacBean

5 **New Crime in China**
Public order and human rights
Ron Keith and Zhiqiu Lin

6 **Non-Governmental Organizations in Contemporary China**
Paving the way to civil society?
Qiusha Ma

7 **Globalization and the Chinese City**
Fulong Wu

8 **The Politics of China's Accession to the World Trade Organization**
The dragon goes global
Hui Feng

9 **Narrating China**
Jia Pingwa and his fictional world
Yiyan Wang

10 **Sex, Science and Morality in China**
Joanne McMillan

11 **Politics in China Since 1949**
Legitimizing authoritarian rule
Robert Weatherley

12 **International Human Resource Management in Chinese Multinationals**
Jie Shen and Vincent Edwards

13 **Unemployment in China**
Economy, human resources and labour markets
Edited by Grace Lee and Malcolm Warner

14 **China and Africa**
Engagement and compromise
Ian Taylor

15 **Gender and Education in China**
Gender discourses and women's schooling in the early twentieth century
Paul J. Bailey

16 **SARS**
Reception and interpretation in three Chinese cities
Edited by Deborah Davis and Helen Siu

17 **Human Security and the Chinese State**
Historical transformations and the modern quest for sovereignty
Robert E. Bedeski

18 **Gender and Work in Urban China**
Women workers of the unlucky generation
Liu Jieyu

19 **China's State Enterprise Reform**
From Marx to the market
John Hassard, Jackie Sheehan, Meixiang Zhou, Jane Terpstra-Tong and Jonathan Morris

20 **Cultural Heritage Management in China**
Preserving the cities of the Pearl River Delta
Edited by Hilary du Cros and Yok-shiu F. Lee

21 **Paying for Progress**
Public finance, human welfare and inequality in China
Edited by Vivienne Shue and Christine Wong

22 **China's Foreign Trade Policy**
The new constituencies
Edited by Ka Zeng

23 **Hong Kong, China**
Learning to belong to a nation
Gordon Mathews, Tai-lok Lui, and Eric Kit-wai Ma

24 **China Turns to Multilateralism**
Foreign policy and regional security
Edited by Guoguang Wu and Helen Lansdowne

25 **Tourism and Tibetan Culture in Transition**
A place called Shangrila
Åshild Kolås

26 **China's Emerging Cities**
The making of new urbanism
Edited by Fulong Wu

27 **China–US Relations Transformed**
Perceptions and strategic interactions
Edited by Suisheng Zhao

28 **The Chinese Party-State in the 21st Century**
Adaptation and the reinvention of legitimacy
Edited by André Laliberté and Marc Lanteigne

29 **Political Change in Macao**
Sonny Shiu-Hing Lo

30 **China's Energy Geopolitics**
The Shanghai Cooperation Organization and Central Asia
Thrassy N. Marketos

31 **Regime Legitimacy in Contemporary China**
Institutional change and stability
Edited by Thomas Heberer and Gunter Schubert

32 **U.S.–China Relations**
China policy on Capitol Hill
Tao Xie

33 **Chinese Kinship**
Contemporary anthropological perspectives
Edited by Susanne Brandtstädter and Gonçalo D. Santos

34 **Politics and Government in Hong Kong**
Crisis under Chinese sovereignty
Edited by Ming Sing

35 **Rethinking Chinese Popular Culture**
Cannibalizations of the canon
Edited by Carlos Rojas and Eileen Cheng-yin Chow

36 **Institutional Balancing in the Asia Pacific**
Economic interdependence and China's rise
Kai He

37 **Rent Seeking in China**
Edited by Tak-Wing Ngo and Yongping Wu

38 **China, Xinjiang and Central Asia**
History, transition and crossborder interaction into the 21st century
Edited by Colin Mackerras and Michael Clarke

39 **Intellectual Property Rights in China**
Politics of piracy, trade and protection
Gordon Cheung

40 **Developing China**
Land, politics and social conditions
George C.S. Lin

41 **State and Society Responses to Social Welfare Needs in China**
Serving the people
Edited by Jonathan Schwartz and Shawn Shieh

42 **Gay and Lesbian Subculture in Urban China**
Loretta Wing Wah Ho

43 **The Politics of Heritage Tourism in China**
A view from Lijiang
Xiaobo Su and Peggy Teo

44 **Suicide and Justice**
A Chinese perspective
Wu Fei

45 **Management Training and Development in China**
Educating managers in a globalized economy
Edited by Malcolm Warner and Keith Goodall

46 **Patron–Client Politics and Elections in Hong Kong**
Bruce Kam-kwan Kwong

47 **Chinese Family Business and the Equal Inheritance System**
Unravelling the myth
Victor Zheng

48 **Reconciling State, Market and Civil Society in China**
The long march towards prosperity
Paolo Urio

49 **Innovation in China**
The Chinese software industry
Shang-Ling Jui

50 **Mobility, Migration and the Chinese Scientific Research System**
Koen Jonkers

51 **Chinese Film Stars**
Edited by Mary Farquhar and Yingjin Zhang

52 **Chinese Male Homosexualities**
Memba, Tongzhi and Golden Boy
Travis S.K. Kong

53 **Industrialisation and Rural Livelihoods in China**
Agricultural processing in Sichuan
Susanne Lingohr-Wolf

54 **Law, Policy and Practice on China's Periphery**
Selective adaptation and institutional capacity
Pitman B. Potter

55 **China–Africa Development Relations**
Edited by Christopher M. Dent

56 **Neoliberalism and Culture in China and Hong Kong**
The countdown of time
Hai Ren

57 **China's Higher Education Reform and Internationalisation**
Edited by Janette Ryan

58 **Law, Wealth and Power in China**
Commercial law reforms in context
Edited by John Garrick

59 **Religion in Contemporary China**
Revitalization and innovation
Edited by Adam Yuet Chau

60 **Consumer-Citizens of China**
The role of foreign brands in the imagined future china
Kelly Tian and Lily Dong

61 **The Chinese Communist Party and China's Capitalist Revolution**
The political impact of the market
Lance L.P. Gore

62 **China's Homeless Generation**
Voices from the veterans of the Chinese civil war, 1940s–1990s
Joshua Fan

63 **In Search of China's Development Model**
Beyond the Beijing consensus
Edited by S. Philip Hsu, Suisheng Zhao and Yu-Shan Wu

64 **Xinjiang and China's Rise in Central Asia, 1949–2009**
A history
Michael E. Clarke

65 **Trade Unions in China**
The challenge of labour unrest
Tim Pringle

66 **China's Changing Workplace**
Dynamism, diversity and disparity
Edited by Peter Sheldon, Sunghoon Kim, Yiqiong Li and Malcolm Warner

67 **Leisure and Power in Urban China**
Everyday life in a medium-sized Chinese city
Unn Målfrid H. Rolandsen

68 **China, Oil and Global Politics**
Philip Andrews-Speed and Roland Dannreuther

69 **Education Reform in China**
Edited by Janette Ryan

70 **Social Policy and Migration in China**
Lida Fan

71 **China's One Child Policy and Multiple Caregiving**
Raising little Suns in Xiamen
Esther C.L. Goh

72 **Politics and Markets in Rural China**
Edited by Björn Alpermann

73 **China's New Underclass**
Paid domestic labour
Xinying Hu

74 **Poverty and Development in China**
Alternative approaches to poverty assessment
Lu Caizhen

75 **International Governance and Regimes**
A Chinese perspective
Peter Kien-Hong Yu

76 **HIV/AIDS in China – The Economic and Social Determinants**
Dylan Sutherland and Jennifer Y.J. Hsu

77 **Looking for Work in Post-Socialist China**
Governance, active job seekers and the new Chinese labor market
Feng Xu

78 **Sino-Latin American Relations**
Edited by K.C. Fung and Alicia Garcia-Herrero

79 **Mao's China and the Sino-Soviet Split**
Ideological dilemma
Mingjiang Li

80 **Law and Policy for China's Market Socialism**
Edited by John Garrick

81 **China–Taiwan Relations in a Global Context**
Taiwan's foreign policy and relations
Edited by C.X. George Wei

82 **The Chinese Transformation of Corporate Culture**
Colin S.C. Hawes

83 Mapping Media in China
Region, province, locality
Edited by Wanning Sun and Jenny Chio

84 China, the West and the Myth of New Public Management
Neoliberalism and its discontents
Paolo Urio

85 The Lahu Minority in Southwest China
A response to ethnic marginalization on the frontier
Jianxiong Ma

86 Social Capital and Institutional Constraints
A comparative analysis of China, Taiwan and the US
Joonmo Son

87 Southern China
Industry, development and industrial policy
Marco R. Di Tommaso, Lauretta Rubini and Elisa Barbieri

88 State–Market Interactions in China's Reform Era
Local state competition and global market building in the tobacco industry
Junmin Wang

89 The Reception and Rendition of Freud in China
China's Freudian slip
Edited by Tao Jiang and Philip J. Ivanhoe

90 Sinologism
An alternative to Orientalism and Postcolonialism
Ming Dong Gu

91 The Middle Class in Neoliberal China
Governing risk, life-building, and themed spaces
Hai Ren

92 The Chinese Corporatist State
Adaption, survival and resistance
Edited by Jennifer Y.J. Hsu and Reza Hasmath

93 Law and Fair Work in China
Sean Cooney, Sarah Biddulph and Ying Zhu

94 Guangdong and Chinese Diaspora
The changing landscape of Qiaoxiang
Yow Cheun Hoe

95 The Shanghai Alleyway House
A vanishing urban vernacular
Gregory Bracken

96 Chinese Globalization
A profile of people-based global connections in China
Jiaming Sun and Scott Lancaster

97 Disruptive Innovation in Chinese and Indian Businesses
The strategic implications for local entrepreneurs and global incumbents
Peter Ping Li

98 Corporate Governance and Banking in China
Michael Tan

99 Gender, Modernity and Male Migrant Workers in China
Becoming a 'modern' man
Xiaodong Lin

100 **Emissions, Pollutants and Environmental Policy in China**
Designing a national emissions trading system
Bo Miao

101 **Sustainable Development in China**
Edited by Curtis Andressen, Mubarak A.R. and Xiaoyi Wang

102 **Islam and China's Hong Kong**
Ethnic identity, Muslim networks and the new Silk Road
Wai-Yip Ho

103 **International Regimes in China**
Domestic implementation of the international fisheries agreements
Gianluca Ferraro

104 **Rural Migrants in Urban China**
Enclaves and transient urbanism
Fulong Wu, Fangzhu Zhang and Chris Webster

105 **State-Led Privatization in China**
The politics of economic reform
Jin Zeng

106 **China's Supreme Court**
Ronald C. Keith, Zhiqiu Lin and Shumei Hou

107 **Queer Sinophone Cultures**
Howard Chiang and Ari Larissa Heinrich

108 **New Confucianism in Twenty-First Century China**
The construction of a discourse
Jesús Solé-Farràs

109 **Christian Values in Communist China**
Gerda Wielander

110 **China and Global Trade Governance**
China's first decade in the World Trade Organization
Edited by Ka Zeng and Wei Liang

111 **The China Model and Global Political Economy**
Comparison, impact, and interaction
Ming Wan

112 **Chinese Middle Classes**
China, Taiwan, Macao and Hong Kong
Edited by Hsin-Huang Michael Hsiao

113 **Economy Hotels in China**
A glocalized innovative hospitality sector
Songshan Sam Huang and Xuhua Michael Sun

114 **The Uyghur Lobby**
Global networks, coalitions and strategies of the World Uyghur Congress
Yu-Wen Chen

115 **Housing Inequality in Chinese Cities**
Edited by Youqin Huang and Si-ming Li

116 **Transforming Chinese Cities**
Edited by Mark Y. Wang, Pookong Kee and Jia Gao

117 Popular Media, Social Emotion and Public Discourse in Contemporary China
Shuyu Kong

118 Globalization and Public Sector Reform in China
Kjeld Erik Brødsgaard

119 Religion and Ecological Sustainability in China
Edited by James Miller, Dan Smyer Yu and Peter van der Veer

120 Comparatizing Taiwan
Edited by Shu-mei Shih and Ping-hui Liao

121 Entertaining the Nation
Chinese television in the twenty-first century
Edited by Ruoyun Bai and Geng Song

122 Local Governance Innovation in China
Experimentation, diffusion, and defiance
Edited by Jessica C. Teets and William Hurst

123 Footbinding and Women's Labor in Sichuan
Hill Gates

124 Incentives for Innovation in China
Building an innovative economy
Xuedong Ding and Jun Li

125 Conflict and Cooperation in Sino-US Relations
Change and continuity, causes and cures
Edited by Jean-Marc F. Blanchard and Simon Shen

126 Chinese Environmental Aesthetics
Wangheng Chen, translated by Feng Su, edited by Gerald Cipriani

127 China's Military Procurement in the Reform Era
The setting of new directions
Yoram Evron

128 Forecasting China's Future
Dominance or collapse?
Roger Irvine

129 Chinese Migration and Economic Relations with Europe
Edited by Marco Sanfilippo and Agnieszka Weinar

130 Party Hegemony and Entrepreneurial Power in China
Institutional change in the film and music industries
Elena Meyer-Clement

131 Explaining Railway Reform in China
A train of property rights re-arrangements
Linda Tjia Yin-nor

132 Irony, Cynicism and the Chinese State
Edited by Hans Steinmüller and Susanne Brandtstädter

133 Animation in China
History, aesthetics, media
Sean Macdonald

134 Parenting, Education and Social Mobility in Rural China
Cultivating dragons and phoenixes
Peggy A. Kong

135 Disability Policy in China
Child and family experiences
Xiaoyuan Shang and Karen R. Fisher

136 The Politics of Controlling Organized Crime in Greater China
Sonny Shiu-Hing Lo

137 Inside Xinjiang
Space, place and power in China's Muslim far Northwest
Edited by Anna Hayes and Michael Clarke

138 China's Strategic Priorities
Edited by Jonathan H. Ping and Brett McCormick

139 China's Unruly Journalists
How committed professionals are changing the People's Republic
Jonathan Hassid

140 The Geopolitics of Red Oil
Constructing the China threat through energy security
Andrew Stephen Campion

141 China's Socialist Rule of Law Reforms Under Xi Jinping
Edited by John Garrick and Yan Chang Bennett

142 Economy, Emotion, and Ethics in Chinese Cinema
Globalization on speed
David Leiwei Li

China's Socialist Rule of Law Reforms Under Xi Jinping

Edited by John Garrick and Yan Chang Bennett

Routledge
Taylor & Francis Group
LONDON AND NEW YORK

First published 2016
by Routledge
2 Park Square, Milton Park, Abingdon, Oxon OX14 4RN

and by Routledge
711 Third Avenue, New York, NY 10017

First issued in paperback 2017

Routledge is an imprint of the Taylor & Francis Group, an informa business

British Library Cataloguing in Publication Data
A catalogue record for this book is available from the British Library

Library of Congress Cataloging in Publication Data
China's socialist rule of law reforms under Xi Jinping / edited by John Garrick and Yan Chang Bennett.
pages cm. – (Routledge contemporary china series ; 141)
Includes bibliographical references and index.
ISBN 1-138-95573-6 – ISBN 1-315-66612-X 1. Law reform–China. 2. Rule of law–China. 3. Law and socialism. 4. Law and economic development. 5. China–Politics and government–2002- I. Garrick, John, editor. II. Bennett, Yan Chang, editor.
KNQ470.C473 2016
349.51–dc23 2015034031

ISBN 13: 978-0-8153-8698-8 (pbk)
ISBN 13: 978-1-138-95573-8 (hbk)

Typeset in Times New Roman
by Wearset Ltd, Boldon, Tyne and Wear

Contents

List of figures xvi
List of tables xvii
Notes on contributors xviii
Preface xxii
Acknowledgments xxiv
List of abbreviations xxv

Introduction: China's deepening socialist rule of law 1
YAN CHANG BENNETT AND JOHN GARRICK

PART I
China's socialist law reform agenda 15

1 Judicial reform in China: an overview 17
QIANFAN ZHANG

2 An assessment of socialist constitutional supervision models and prospects for a constitutional supervision committee in China: the constitution as commander? 30
KEITH J. HAND

3 China's socialist rule of law: a critical appraisal of the relationship between the Communist Party and comprehensive law reform 45
CHONGYI FENG

4 Reform directions for China's socialist market economy: a macroeconomic perspective 59
QIYUAN XU

PART II
Major challenges for China's socialist rule of law 75

5 **The law and growth nexus in China** 77
LINDA YUEH

6 **Efforts towards procedural justice in post-Mao China** 94
JIANFU CHEN

7 **Addressing corruption and the trial of Bo Xilai: historical continuities, rule of law implications** 109
NORMAN P. HO

8 **China's land use and urbanization: challenges for comprehensive reform** 122
RICHARD HU

9 **Individual rights protection or social management? Equal employment laws and policies in China** 134
SU LIN HAN

PART III
China's socialist rule of law and international legal re-ordering 149

10 **Sovereignty vs rights: China's reasons for rejecting the Rome Statute of the International Criminal Court** 151
JING TAO

11 **The impact of Chinese legal reform on WTO dispute resolution** 167
JI LI

12 **China's maritime interests and the law of the sea: domesticating public international law** 179
ISAAC B. KARDON

13 **Screening the 'dragon's gift'? National security review of China's foreign direct investment** 197
WEITSENG CHEN

14 Conclusion: China's socialist rule of law reforms under Xi Jinping 208
JOHN GARRICK AND YAN CHANG BENNETT

Bibliography 222
Index 250

Figures

4.1	China's potential growth rate has been slowing down	59
4.2	The contribution of net exports, fixed asset investment and final consumption to GDP growth	60
4.3	The contributions of final demands to GDP growth rate	61
4.4	Structure of employment in the service sector: comparing China and the United States	66
4.5	Forecasts of China's growth rate in the 2020s: two scenarios	68
4.6	Structural problems in China's labor market	68
4.7	China's employment in the service sector is inhibited	69
4.8	Divergent thinking on the sequencing of financial reforms: across different *financial* institutions	70
4.9	Divergent thinking on the sequencing of financial reforms: across *different types of institutions*	71
4.10	The structure of authorized patents: China and Japan	72
11.1	Frequency of litigation as a function of disputing state's domestic social norms	171

Tables

5.1 Rule of law 81
5.2 Regulatory quality 82
5.3 Investor protection 83
5.4 Property rights and freedom from corruption 84

Contributors

Yan Chang Bennett is a lawyer and Manager for the Center on Contemporary China at Princeton University. Before coming to Princeton, Yan was a Foreign Service Officer with the US Department of State and served overseas in China and Bosnia-Herzegovina. In China she served as Vice Consul and reported on US corporate labor practices and intellectual property issues. She received several awards for superior performance from the State Department, including a personal commendation from the Secretary of State. From 2009 to 2015, she was the Assistant Director for the Princeton–Harvard China and the World Program of the Woodrow Wilson School of Public and International Affairs at Princeton University. She graduated *cum laude* from the Syracuse University College of Law, with her BA in Political Science and MA in International Affairs from the Elliott School of International Affairs at George Washington University.

Jianfu Chen, LLM (Hon I, Sydney), PhD (Sydney), is Professor of Chinese Law and Legal Globalisation at La Trobe University, Melbourne. He has authored, co-authored and co-edited many volumes on Chinese law including *From Administrative Authorization to Private Law: A Comparative Perspective of the Developing Civil Law in the PRC* (1995); *Chinese Law: Towards an Understanding of Chinese Law, Its Nature and Development* (1999); *Chinese Law: Context & Transformation* (2008) .

Weitseng Chen is an Assistant Professor at the National University of Singapore (NUS) Faculty of Law. He specializes in comparative Asian law with an emphasis on property law and financial institutions in East Asia. He received his JSD from Yale Law School where he was a Fulbright scholar, and thereafter worked for Stanford University as a Hewlett Fellow of the Center on Democracy, Development and the Rule of Law. Immediately before he joined NUS, Weitseng Chen worked as a corporate lawyer at Davis Polk & Wardwell LLP, specializing in cross-border capital market transactions in the greater China area and Southeast Asia. Weitseng's recent research focuses on property rights transition in China, China–Taiwan comparisons in terms of law and economic development, and China's outbound foreign investment and global capital markets.

Chongyi Feng, elected one of the top 100 Chinese public intellectuals in the world in 2005 and 2008, is Associate Professor in China Studies, University of Technology, Sydney and Adjunct Professor of History, Nankai University, Tianjin. His current research focuses on intellectual and political development in contemporary China. He has over 90 published articles in academic journals and edited volumes, numerous articles in newspapers and on the Internet and is author of several books including *From Sinification to Globalisation*, *The Wisdom of Reconciliation: China's Road to Liberal Democracy* and *Liberalism within the Chinese Communist Party: From Chen Duxiu to Li Shenzhi.*

John Garrick LLB (Hon 1, UTS), M.Soc Stud (Sydney), PhD (UTS), is an attorney of the Supreme Court of New South Wales specializing in commercial law. He is convenor of postgraduate Competition and Consumer Law at Macquarie University (Sydney) and author and co-editor of a wide range of scholarly publications including *Law, Wealth & Power in China: Commercial Law Reforms in Context* (2011), *Law and Policy for China's Market Socialism* (2012) and several well-known Routledge books on power relations. He has worked extensively in both legal practice and academia in China, the Middle East, North America and Australia, and currently sits on the editorial board of the *Universiti Utari Malaysia Journal of Legal Studies* (UUMJLS).

Su Lin Han is a Research Scholar in Law and Senior Fellow in Residence at Yale University's China Law Center. A native of Beijing, she has lived in the United States since graduation and has extensive experience and expertise in numerous aspects of Chinese and American law. After receiving a JD from the Boalt Hall School of Law at the University of California, Berkeley, she worked as a corporate attorney at Wilmer, Cutler & Pickering in Washington, DC, and then at the Hong Kong office of Cravath, Swaine & Moore. More recently, she has worked as a legal consultant to the World Bank and the Asian Development Bank on legal reform projects in China and was the editor and co-founder of the *China Law and Governance Review.*

Keith J. Hand is Professor of Law and Director of the East Asian Legal Studies Program at the University of California, Hastings College of the Law. Prior to joining the UC Hastings faculty, Professor Hand served as Senior Counsel to the US Congressional-Executive Commission on China and as Beijing Director and Senior Fellow at Yale Law School's China Law Center. Professor Hand has worked with Chinese courts, legislatures and government agencies to implement cooperative legal reform projects and his research focuses on constitutional law, legislation and citizen efforts to use the law to promote legal, social and political change in China. He is the author of several recent publications on constitutional law in China, including *Resolving Constitutional Disputes in the People's Republic of China* and *Understanding China's System for Addressing Legislative Conflicts: Capacity Challenges and the Search for Legislative Harmony.*

Norman P. Ho is Assistant Professor of Law at Peking University School of Transnational Law. His research and writing focuses on Chinese legal history, legal philosophy and comparative jurisprudence. He is a non-resident research fellow at the Netherlands China Law Centre and has taught as a lecturer at the University of Hong Kong Faculty of Law. He received his AB and AM degrees from Harvard University and JD from New York University School of Law. Prior to joining the Peking University School of Transnational Law faculty, he practiced law at the law firms of Slaughter and May and Morrison & Foerster LLP.

Richard Hu is Associate Professor and Director of Globalisation and Cities Research Program at the University of Canberra. With academic and professional experience in China, America and Australia, he is a member of the Planning Institute of Australia (PIA) and its certified planner (CPP), a member of the American Planning Association (APA) and its certified planner (AICP), and has received two divisional PIA Awards for Excellence in research and scholarship. In both English and Chinese, Richard has published widely on the history and theory of built environment, urban analysis and development and urban design, including contemporary Chinese urban affairs.

Isaac B. Kardon, at the time of writing, was Fulbright-Hays Fellow and Visiting Scholar at the National Institute for South China Sea Studies (南海研究院), PRC, researching for his doctorate in Government at Cornell University. He is an Affiliated Scholar at NYU Law's US–Asia Law Institute, and was a Research Analyst with the Center for the Study of Chinese Military Affairs at the National Defense University in Washington, DC, continuing at NDU as an Adjunct Fellow. He holds an MPhil in Modern Chinese Studies from Oxford University (St Antony's College) and a BA in History from Dartmouth College. He studied Mandarin at Peking University, Taiwan Normal University and Tsinghua University.

Ji Li is an Associate Professor at Rutgers Law School. He received his PhD in political science from Northwestern University and his JD from Yale Law School where he was an Olin Fellow in Law, Economics and Public Policy. He joined the Rutgers faculty in 2011 after practicing law for several years at the New York office of an international firm. Professor Li's research and teaching interests include taxation, international and comparative law (with a focus on China), property and empirical legal studies.

Jing Tao (陶靖) specializes in Chinese foreign policy, international law and organization and East Asian security. During 2014–15 she was a 'China and the World Program' Research Fellow based at Princeton University focusing on China's approach to legalized dispute resolution in international treaties. This project uses different types of 'hard laws' with legalized dispute settlement mechanisms to examine the depth of China's socialization in international legal regimes and the changes and continuities of China's approach to state sovereignty. She holds a PhD in Political Science from

Cornell University, an MA in International Relations from Peking University and double BA degrees in International Relations and Economics.

Qiyuan Xu is Senior Research Fellow at the Chinese Academy of Social Sciences (CASS) in Beijing. He was a visiting fellow from April to September 2013 at the European think-tank *Bruegel* where he worked on global economic governance, especially on interactions and cooperation between China and Europe. His research interests include the internationalization of the renminbi and its exchange rate and issues related to Chinese macroeconomics and policies. His 2008 doctorate is from Northeast Normal University, China, and he completed his postdoctoral research at the Institute of World Economics and Politics (IWEP), Chinese Academy of Social Sciences by 2010. In 2012, he was appointed Advisor to the International Department within China's Ministry of Finance. He sits in the work team of China's External Economic Environment in IWEP, which issues quarterly reports on global macroeconomics. He is responsible for research on China and Renminbi issues.

Linda Yueh is Fellow in Economics at St Edmund Hall, Oxford University, Adjunct Professor of Economics at the London Business School and Visiting Professor of Economics at Peking University. She directs the China Growth Centre (CGC) at St Edmund Hall, Oxford, serves on the Policy Committee of the Centre for Economic Performance (CEP) and is an associate of the International Affairs, Diplomacy & Strategy (IDEAS) research centre, both at the London School of Economics (LSE). Previously, she was an attorney at Paul, Weiss, Rifkind, Wharton & Garrison resident in New York, Beijing, Hong Kong, and Economics Editor at Bloomberg TV in London. She is very widely published, including the award-winning *The Economy of China* and *China's Growth: The Making of an Economic Superpower* (2013). She serves on the Advisory Board of the Official Monetary and Financial Institutions Forum (OMFIF), and has advised the World Bank, European Commission, Asian Development Bank and World Economic Forum, among others. Dr. Yueh is Chief Business Correspondent for the BBC and presenter of *Talking Business with Linda Yueh.*

Qianfan Zhang is Professor of Law at Peking University's Law School where he is Director, Center on the People's Congress and Parliamentary Studies and Senior Deputy Director, Center on Administrative and Constitutional Law. Professor Zhang obtained his PhD in Government from the University of Texas at Austin (1999) and taught comparative constitutional law and administrative law at Nanjing University Law School in China from 1999 to 2003 before joining the law faculty at Peking University. He is Vice-President of the Chinese Constitutional Law Association and has published several books and numerous articles in Chinese and comparative public law.

Preface

The Eighteenth Central Committee of the Communist Party of China (CPC) met in October 2014 with 'rule of law' as its central theme. This followed General Secretary Xi Jinping's (2013) explanation of the *Decision* of the CPC Central Committee on deepening reform that had made it clear that China will continue to prioritize 'economic reforms'. In keeping with past pronouncements, there is also the familiar insistence on the CPC's leading role, with Western notions of judicial independence and separation of powers rejected. This book interprets the meanings and directions of China's deepening socialist rule of law and questions whether success on the economic front may lay the groundwork for more ambitious legal, social and political reform to come. It further questions whether ongoing economic success can be sustainable without the required legal, social and political reforms.

China is now in a state of transition from a lower-middle-income to an upper-middle-income country. This transition is accompanied by many predictable problems associated with increased pluralism, movement and competition in Chinese society as more informed communities demand a better life, with higher expectations for social and legal fairness. There are competing conceptions of legal development, pressing socio-economic and environmental issues, wealth disparity, rural–urban coordinated development and inequality, and ongoing concerns about corruption. What has worked in the past may not work as well in future. In fact there is a growing consensus among economists, both within and outside China, that the state-investment-led, export-oriented model of development will not be sustainable. Economic issues directly affect many other facets of social development such as the nature and type of law reform, multi-level governance, social welfare programs, urban and rural property rights and environmental protection. New challenges await Beijing and overcoming entrenched interests will not be easy.

Here we have identified a number of key challenges for China's broad law reform program. These include major ideological developments such as the promotion of theories of socialist rule of law and their incorporation into the constitution; implementation issues associated with the promulgation of many thousands of new laws and regulations; and challenges to the development of modern legal institutions including the legislature, judiciary and administrative agencies. There is also an increasingly complex set of other legal actors who seek to influence development such as securities regulators, bankers, accountants, lawyers and local-level mediators. Furthermore, some of China's new rich seek to directly influence law-making in China through their political participation. The rising middle classes want to voice their interests and concerns through various channels. China's legal reform agenda is indeed connected to a nexus of political, economic, cultural and power-related influences.

The theoretical standpoints of Chinese socialist law reform, comparative law, government, macroeconomics, finance, political economy and legal practice are all used to critically examine the future of legal reform in the People's Republic. Specific illustrations are drawn from the fields of judicial reform, constitutional law, alternative legal ideologies, procedural law, anti-corruption, property law and urban development, socio-economic dispute resolution and Chinese macroeconomics. Throughout, there is a paradox related to China's growth model that is explored – the development of a market within an essentially state-controlled property system in which state-owned enterprises receive favorable policies and treatment in terms of accessing financing and market opportunities.

In addition, the book examines influences of the global rules-based system on China's law reform including PRC participation in international courts and tribunals. The emerging global system has gained prominence around the same time as China's integration into the international legal framework after years of relatively inward-focused development. How will a socialist rule of law with Chinese characteristics adapt international best practices to local conditions? Numerous limitations in the reach of the fledging international legal system are noted, but certain aspects of that legal infrastructure have some influence on China's domestic reforms. This system is, however, two-way. China, and its firms, should be expected to seek out where advantage may be found, while at the same time they are operating in those evolving global legal and financial systems. The international market share of yuan (¥) usage in trade finance, or Letters of Credit and Collection is now second only to the US dollar ($). At least, this is true according to available data. At the same time, the surge in market share of yuan trade finance has increased in abnormal ways and the trend is likely to be unsustainable. This book aims to accurately represent China's growth rate and relate the implications of this to law reform.

China aims to lift the global clout of the yuan and reduce its reliance on the US dollar. So, how will China assert its vast and growing power over international legal and financial institutions? How will international law be used to help manage key regional and bilateral relationships, such as between the United States and China? How will China's domestic law reforms interact with the international legal domain? These questions and others are all explored in this book, which aims to contribute to several fields, including Chinese and international business and commercial law, Asian legal studies, comparative law, the political economy of law reform, rule of law promotion and international studies more generally.

Acknowledgments

In addition to the contributors themselves, this volume received the valuable feedback of specialists, generously shared knowledge and ideas from each of the following: Marc K. Chan, Minglu Chen, Michael Dowdle, Matthew Erie, John Garnaut, Judith Gibson, Yingjie Guo, Shoumei Hou, Zhigang Li, Randall Peerenboom, Renee Stevens, Wenli Tian, Laurelle Wishart and Ming Zhang. The editors sincerely thank each of them. This publication was made possible in part by a grant from the Carnegie Corporation of New York and the John D. and Catherine T. MacArthur Foundation. The statements made and views expressed herein are solely the responsibility of the authors.

Abbreviations

AB	Appellate Body
ADR	alternative dispute resolution
AML	*Anti-Monopoly Law*
BCS	Budgetary Contracting System
CBRC	China Banking Regulatory Commission
CCDI	Central Commission for Discipline Inspection
CFIUS	Committee on Foreign Investment in the United States
CIRC	China Insurance Regulatory Commission
CNOOC	China National Offshore Oil Corporation
CPC	Communist Party of China
CPD	Congress of People's Deputies
CRS	Contract Responsibility System
CSRC	China Securities Regulatory Commission
DSM	Dispute Settlement Mechanism
ECS	East China Sea
EEOC	Equal Employment Opportunity Commission
EEZ	exclusive economic zone
EPL	*Equal Employment Promotion Law*
FIA	*Foreign Investment Act*
FINSA	*Foreign Investment and National Security Act*
FTZ	free trade zone
GDP	gross domestic product
HRS	Household Responsibility System
ICC	International Criminal Court
ICCPR	International Covenant on Civil and Political Rights
ICESCR	International Covenant on Economic, Social and Cultural Rights
IPO	Initial Public Offerings
LPC	Local People's Congress
MLE	Naval and Maritime Law Enforcement
MOHRSS	China's Ministry of Human Resource and Social Security
MSR	Marine Scientific Research
NPC	National People's Congress
NPCSC	National People's Congress Standing Committee

NSRC	National Security Review Committee
POE	privately owned enterprises
PPP	purchasing power parity
RTL	re-education through labor
SASAC	State Asset Supervision and Administration Commission
SCB	state-owned commercial bank
SCNPC	Standing Committee of the NPC
SCS	South China Sea
SEC	Securities and Exchange Commission
SPC	Supreme People's Court
TVE	Township and Village Enterprises
UN	United Nations
UNCLOS	UN Convention on the Law of the Sea
UNSC	United Nations Security Council
VCP	Vietnamese Communist Party
WTO	World Trade Organization

Introduction

China's deepening socialist rule of law

Yan Chang Bennett and John Garrick

China's socialist rule of law

The fourth plenary session of the Communist Party of China's (CPC) Eighteenth Central Committee met in October 2014 with 'rule of law' as its central theme. Chaired by General Secretary Xi Jinping, this was the first time a CPC plenary session had set rule of law center stage.[1] The meeting also reviewed the CPC's 'mass line' campaign to boost ties between officials and the public. This followed Xi's (2013a) explanation of the earlier CPC 'Decision on Major Questions about Deepening Reform' (*quan mian shen hua gai ge*). Xi made it clear that 'ideological unity continues to be forged around Deng Xiaoping's "two-hands" formula: a market-based economy and uncompromising political control'.[2] The explanation emphasized that rule of law should be advanced under the CPC leadership, in line with socialism with Chinese characteristics. This book provides a critical appraisal of China's deepening socialist rule of law and, looking ahead, what the implications of the domestic reforms are for the international legal domain.

Of the many factors influencing China's legal system developments, three broad organizing principles have been established for this book. First are *ideological* factors shaping the People's Republic of China's (PRC) law reform agenda, including contested notions of 'socialist rule of law' and associated constitutional implications. At issue are the boundaries around the power of the Party and the law, and of the proper relationship of the Party and state with regard to the judiciary and the administration of justice more generally. Do we see emerging a broader 'rule of law' (法治), or a narrowing 'rule by law' (法制) that emphasizes rules and regulations? Or, does an unstable mix emanate from the CPC's pledge to a virtuous rule of law *and* guarantee of the Party's leading role?

Second are *economic* influences on reform implementation, which include political economy, legal and judicial practice and procedural fairness. Third are external or *international* influences that impact on the comprehensive deepening of reform. Permeating each of these organizing principles or categories are forces of history, culture and, critically, politics or political imperatives. Rather than treating these powerful influences as separate, we agree with Peerenboom (2011: 283) that history and culture 'should not be uncritically accepted as determinative of future outcomes'. The crux of the matter is the function and reach of law in the PRC and primary questions as to whether the power of the Party-state (and its multiple agents) should be constrained and, if so, how and to what extent?

Three further theoretical assumptions helped shape the conceptual framework of the book:

1 That there is no single 'correct' or 'one best way' legal model for the PRC. There is no idealized Western legal order underpinning this collection of chapters. We are mindful of Ruskola's (2013) admonitions against 'legal orientalism' and avoid presupposing any specific direction of law reform that favors Western conceptions of, for example, Chinese courts, judicial independence, legislative drafting or local-level interpretation and enforcement of regulations.
2 That the PRC government is aware of many of the problems associated with promoting rule of law concepts and views rule of law development as a very high priority that will take a long time to achieve. At times, there will be more progress on some fronts than on others.
3 That it is difficult to achieve a completely impartial evaluation of different legal systems. As Li (2013a: 120) puts it, 'consciously or not, researchers tend to select or emphasize facts that support their theory or hypothesis and neglect those otherwise. As a result, theories derived from studying a single law often cannot be applied more broadly'. It is thus valuable to bring together different perspectives, including disaggregated analyses of key legal and economic issues that underpin China's deepening reforms.

Under Xi's leadership, the power structure of China's one-party autocracy remains intact. The CPC retains its tight grip on legal reform through its leading role in the polity and economy. The political leadership, although less technocratic in character than in previous generations, is still exclusively recruited by the regime, with an emphasis on political loyalty. Despite a growing disjunction between official ideological claims and market realities, the Party-state's justifying narrative of the CPC's leading role defines most aspects of society. Under socialist market conditions, China's ideological and institutional changes are being made to accommodate a socialist rule of law. What this means for reform directions and practice is not always clear. In part this is because 'socialist rule of law' is rhetorical. What the *Decision* on deepening rule of law actually states is:

> What is most important is to uphold the leadership of the Party, adhere to the Party's basic line, reject both the old and rigid closed-door policy and any attempt to abandon socialism and take an erroneous path, firmly take the socialist road and ensure that our reform is in the right direction.[3]

Within China, while Marxism–Leninism–Mao Zedong Thought is maintained as 'the right direction', that is, official ideology, the agenda policies of reform and opening to the outside world have been largely guided by the pragmatic strategies of Deng Xiaoping Theory, the Three Represents and the Scientific Concept of Development. According to the *Decision*, the most important achievement of reform and opening up is 'the establishment and development of socialism with Chinese characteristics' (Point One of the *Decision*). The cult of personality, over-concentration of power, lawlessness, obscurantism and other aspects of despotism have been labeled remnants of feudalism and systematically attacked – notwithstanding the Chongqing experiment in cracking down on organized crime and corruption and the rise and fall of powerful former Chongqing party boss, Bo Xilai (see Ho 2012: 202), and other so-called Party-tigers.

Contributors address the implications and key challenges of China's pragmatic approach to its socialist legal reform agenda. Following over 35 years of reform, major ideological developments are emerging and at the heart of these is the promotion of theories of socialist rule of law and their incorporation into the Constitution. At the same time, as shown in previous volumes,[4] there is the promulgation of thousands of new laws and regulations, such as the new trademark law of the PRC (*NTL*),[5] and a continual strengthening of China's legislative framework. There are major challenges for rule-making, rule-application and rule-adjudication with development of modern legal institutions, including the legislature, judiciary, regulators, mediators, police, prisons, and other legal actors, being extended. As China follows its two-track approach to reform, it is economic reform that is prioritized over political and legal reforms. Advocates hoping for political reform may be disappointed at this stage, but there is no surprise that economic reform has top priority over personal or individual liberties, with a central, legitimizing narrative about pursuing a stable, 'harmonious' society (see deLisle 2014).

Given the scale and pace of China's rise to power, there is relatively little debate around the critical issues associated with such significant law reforms. The aim of this volume is to bring fresh perspectives to analyzing the legal, economic and political underpinnings of China's comprehensive widening and deepening of reform (全面深化改革) that follows the earlier policies of 'opening up' (开放) and 'going out' (走出去). Policy-wise, given the political system, the level of economic and institutional development and the traditional, civil and socialist origins of China's legal system, it is hardly surprising, nor necessarily inappropriate, that we see a more centralized, coordinated approach under Xi's leadership. The longer-term pathway of a socialist rule of law is far less clear.

Forging a socialist rule of law with Chinese characteristics

The following chapters cover a range of topics and adopt various perspectives and methodological approaches. Contributors sometimes reach similar, sometimes differing, conclusions. Essentially the book addresses the three central sets of issues regarding China's law reform agenda, the first relating to ideology and competing conceptions of legal development and these are examined in Part I. In Part II, the second set of issues focuses on the relationship between economic and legal reform and implementation challenges for both theory and practice. In Part III, the third set relates to how China's domestic law reforms may influence global legal systems and how international legal infrastructure (such as the World Trade Organization, United Nations and so on) may interact with China's domestic and foreign policy settings. Here, contributors probe how the management of key regional, bilateral and global relationships are assisted, or otherwise, by international legal institutions as China exercises its role as one of the world's great powers.

Opinions about the fate of China's legal system are as diverse as those about China's economic future. Depending on the issue, some see legal reforms as stalled, while others see progress – though often a two-steps-forward, one-step-back affair. More fundamentally, some see (or hope to see) China evolving toward a 'Chinese variant of democracy' based on rule of law (Lin 2011: 251; Xu 2014). Others see China as mired in the remnants of Marxist–Leninist rule-by-law; while opportunities for participation in the policy-making process may have increased, the political system as a whole remains authoritarian and dominated by the CPC. Others see a 'hybrid form of non-democratic socialist rule of law' as the most likely outcome in the short term, and possibly even in the longer term (Guo 2011: 53).

While some commentators portray socialism in the context of marketization as increasingly incoherent, ideology *has* played a key role in recent debates over many important law reforms (see Minzner 2011; X. Zhang 2012: 39; Hu 2012: 90; Bennett 2012: 70; Hurst *et al.* 2012: 118; Fan 2012: 198; Peerenboom and Ginsburg 2014). For example, ideology is central to current debates over judicial reforms. Taking note of the 'color revolutions' in the former Soviet Republics, where foreign governments supported international and domestic non-governmental organizations that used courts to push for democratization and political reforms, party leaders have expressed concern that legal institutions can be used to undermine the Party's power. As a result, the CPC has been adamant that Chinese courts will not simply mimic courts in Western liberal democracies. The infamous 'Document No. 9', which refers to an internal Party circular on the current state of ideological development, even warns that Western anti-China forces and domestic dissidents are trying to foster the type of color revolutions that occurred in the former Soviet Republics and more recently in the Middle Eastern 'Arab Spring' (see Feng in Chapter 3). There have thus been ongoing efforts to shore up loyalty in the courts and public security institutions. Under the deepening reform agenda, it is the 'Three Supremes' – the supremacy of the interest of *the people, the Party* and *the constitution and laws* – that continue to shape directions.

Following the *Decision* and recent Supreme People's Court reform plans, we now have good indicators of where legal and judicial reforms are heading in the short–medium term. The Supreme People's Court agenda seeks, on the one hand, to ensure that courts are under sufficient political control to prevent them from undermining the regime. On the other hand, efforts are continued to enhance professionalism, efficiency and justice. The agenda emphasizes that courts must be consistent with China's political structure, yet simultaneously strive for technical reform to reduce wrongful convictions and improve criminal, civil and administrative law, procedural fairness and enforcement. A challenge will be to ensure the country's emerging legal elite does not become too out of touch with the common people they are appointed to represent.

How China's legal institutions reflect their socialist or civil law origins is considered by the contributors with the force of history evident in much of China's cautious approach to allowing foreign investors access to its internal markets and in its concern for sovereignty in human rights cases. It is also reflected in its reluctance to allow foreign pressure to influence the way courts handle some controversial cases: for example, those involving foreign passport holders embroiled in serious criminal matters or implicated in commercial disputes. These issues may be difficult to understand without at least some reference to history. For example, the 1894 Sino-Japanese War that saw Taiwan ceded to Japan, and later Japanese incursions into the Middle Kingdom in the 1930s and 1940s, are painful memories that are difficult to forget, as is 100 years of national humiliation when foreign powers compelled China to sign unequal treaties. Trade ports and foreign concessions were forced open in major cities such as Shanghai. Indeed, under the principle of extraterritoriality, Chinese courts were 'denied jurisdiction over foreign citizens charged with crimes, and foreign entities dominated economic opportunity (arguably) resulting in stagnant growth and deteriorating living conditions' (Peerenboom 2011: 283).

As Linda Yueh shows in Chapter 5, resources (or lack of resources) underpin law reform in China. The relative strength of legal institutions generally corresponds with levels of wealth. In China, even in richer provinces, the lack of resources remains evident in how socio-economic claims are handled (see Su Lin Han in Chapter 9). In economic downturns, the decline in resourcing is generally exacerbated by the expansion of need, with established ways of determining the truth, resisting injustice, holding people to account and securing redress less accessible or effective. In many cases, courts that are not able to provide an adequate remedy face protests by disgruntled parties. Courts have thus tried to push such cases into political and administrative channels or to mediation (Fan 2012: 199).

Fan (2012: 200) describes a variety of political, legal and policy factors as clearly having an impact on China's 'modern approach to alternative dispute resolution [with] signs the people are becoming more aware of the value of drawing on traditional culture to resolve disputes'. Hand (2011) further argues that shifting focus from the individual-legal to the collective-political dimension of constitutional law, a dimension dominant in China's one-Party state, will enhance our understanding of the Constitution in China and patterns of bargaining, consultation and mediation across a range of both intrastate and citizen–state constitutional disputes. At the same time, a central issue for most middle-income countries, including China, is not lack of resources, but how resources are allocated (see Peerenboom and Ginsburg 2014; deLisle 2014; Xu in Chapter 4; Yueh in Chapter 5). Thus, it is not simply economics shaping directions, but political economy and ideology. Even when there is general agreement about basic principles, the wide variation in institutions, rules and practices can lead to controversy. Current debates over judicial reform provide one clear illustration of this: What will be the judiciary's relationship with other political organs? Will there be a judicial role in policy making? Will the People's Congress continue to be able to review final court decisions? How much say will the judiciary have in promotions and appointments? What roles will be played by the Party organs and political-legal committees in judicial decision making and legal appointments?

Ideology, implementation and international factors shaping the 'decisive role of the market'

Part I deals with China's major legal ideological developments and how these may impact upon the trajectory of law reform. The promotion of a socialist rule of law is contested with not only opposing views on interpretation, but also clashes of interest. It becomes clearer that Western notions of liberal democratic rule of law, based on a separation of powers doctrine, is rejected for deepening development. But just what constitutes the meaning of 'rule of law' under such ideological conditions? What are the implications for *implementing* and deepening socialist rule of law? How will Chinese macroeconomic modeling affect the trajectory of these developments? Closely related to these questions is, of course, the relationship of the Party and the state. Peerenboom (2014a: 3) describes this relationship as a *fault line* appearing in the 'interplay between the unwritten constitution, which includes the reality of Party organizations governed primarily by the Party constitution and other Party regulations, and the written constitution which governs state institutions'. The fault line may be exaggerated, however, as the PRC is called a Party-state for a reason. The written constitution of the PRC says the state is a people's democratic dictatorship led by the proletariat. The people's democratic dictatorship is now under the guidance of Marx–Xi-isms and thoughts and the four cardinal principles, one of which is the leadership of the CPC.

Part II focuses on the relationship between economic and legal reform, highlighting particularly pressing challenges for implementation. For example, some of China's law reforms face problems associated with how best to deal with all legitimate socio-economic disputes, as citizen demands rise along with their increased wealth and consumption patterns. At the local level, Keith *et al.* (2013) refer to a rebalancing and updating of the 'mass line' with professionalism.[6] The mass line is still used in the court system and 'the plan of two thousand people' (2千人计划) has come into effect to raise standards in the system and ensure courts are able to immediately respond to public needs.[7] Challenges also include some of China's most controversial and contested reforms such as the pivotal role in the socialist market economy of new rural property laws, critical developments in urbanization and environmental law, issues around socio-economic disputes including discrimination, judicial and procedural reforms, and the ongoing need for vigilance over corruption.

The major reforms in procedural law – criminal, civil and administrative litigation – are highly significant in a country where, historically, justice has tended to be perceived in terms of substantive law, not procedural matters. Whether viewed separately or collectively, these reform issues have significant local *and* global implications. As such, the question arises as to whether China will follow a master plan for law reform, developed by the central authorities, such as a top-down comprehensive blueprint as indicated by Xu Xin (2014).[8] Xu argues that constitutionalism, democracy and rule of law are inevitable for China's development and notes changes in the reform approach:

> Previously it often followed from the peripheries to the centre, the local to the national, and the grassroots level to elite levels; from now on, the reform approach should emphasize the other way around: from the top to the bottom, the state to society, the centre to the periphery.

Xi's Explanation of the *Decision* (2013a) puts economic structural reform at the center of deepening reform more generally: 'The core issues are dealing with the relationship between the government and the market well, ensuring that the market has a decisive function in resource allocation, and giving better rein to the function of government.' What, precisely, the 'decisive function' of the market will be remains to be seen. Pettis (2014a) claims Beijing will unlock greater productivity potential in the Chinese economy 'by improving the capital allocation process so that capital will be diverted from SOEs, real estate developers, local governments and other inefficient users of capital'. Constraints that prevent productive use of resources will also need to be eliminated, including weak legal enforcement of legitimate legal claims and better protection of managerial and technological innovation. As Pettis (2014a) points out, correctly in our view, implementation of such reforms is uncertain. Even assuming they are forcefully implemented, higher productivity will not necessarily lead to higher reported GDP growth. Pettis (2014b) further asserts:

> It is impossible to find a single relevant case in history in which the adjustment following a 'growth miracle' did not include an unexpectedly sharp slowdown in growth … I would propose that we can judge the forceful implementation of the reforms inversely with GDP growth. If China is able to impose an orderly adjustment quickly, its GDP growth rate will slow substantially for several years. GDP growth rates of 7% or more, on the other hand, will suggest that credit is still rising too quickly and that China has otherwise been unable to implement the [economic] reforms, in which case China is likely to reach debt capacity constraints more quickly. Growth of 7% for the next few years, in other words, is almost prima facie evidence that China is not adjusting.

Plenum decisions of 2013–14 to deepen reform all but guarantee that China's growth rates will slow down and the implications of an economic slowdown for progressing the rule of law agenda are examined in Chapters 4 and 5.

Part III then critically examines the interactions of China's domestic law reforms and international legal ordering. Several themes have been identified to illustrate this dialectical relationship, including how domestic social norms impact on international trade dispute resolution, regulating foreign investment and interpretations of laws of the sea. There are, clearly, significant international tensions emanating from reforms to China's domestic maritime law enforcement bureaucracy. What precisely is being conveyed by the PRC's stern reaction to the Philippine government's pursuit of international arbitration of disputed islands and waters? Given the numerous foreign and security policy actors within China who favor Beijing taking a more forceful foreign policy stance, will regional stability be at risk if China's leadership merely reacts as events unfold? To what extent can/should international legal systems such as UNCLOS arbitration and the WTO Dispute Settlement Mechanism (DSM) help manage the example disputes cited?

Contributors raise questions about the effectiveness of formalized international dispute resolution and arbitration; indicators are examined informing us about what is anticipated over the next 5–10 years and beyond. The available evidence, in respect of China's participation in international organizations such as the International Criminal Court (ICC), UNCLOS the WTO and international legal domain more generally, is reviewed to seek insights into the interactions of the PRC's domestic law reform and the international legal system. Is a platform being laid that may produce more ambitious political, social and legal reforms in future? What challenges to the existing international legal framework should be anticipated?

Chapters commence with Qianfan Zhang's overview of judicial reform since 1999, when the Supreme People's Court (SPC) published the First Outline for a Five-Year Reform of the People's Court. He highlights impediments that have for decades prevented China's courts from developing into a modern professional judiciary and then describes the main initiatives of the new judicial reform, providing a brief analysis on prospects of success. While scholars on the right have criticized judicial reform for not doing enough in creating an independent judiciary, some scholars on the left have blamed it for going too far and encouraging judicial corruption. After early reform efforts toward a more professional, less politicized judiciary, Zhang notes that direction was reversed in the third phase of judicial reform from 2008 to 2013, when the new president of the SPC highlighted 'the leadership of the party' as one of the 'Three Supremes' (*sange zhishang*) to be followed by courts in adjudicating cases. With a new blueprint for comprehensive solutions directed against the evils within the existing judicial system, reforms announced in the Third and Fourth Plenums of the Eighteenth Party Congress are again championed by the CPC. Zhang questions how much ought to be expected of new judicial reforms when the political environment is fundamentally the same.

In Chapter 2 Keith Hand views the Constitution as being more than a political document, discussing parts of the Constitution that can be directly applied and assessing prospects for a concrete enforcement/review mechanism that would help to accomplish this task. Hand's analysis is set against the October 2014 context of the CPC's Fourth Plenum of the Eighteenth Central Committee call for 'the perfection of constitutional interpretation, implementation, and supervision systems'. The prominence of these statements has generated speculation that the Party may consider concrete institutional reforms to strengthen review of the constitutionality of legislation. Events since 2000 demonstrate that China's leaders are unlikely to turn to the courts, but one alternative to judicial review is review by a constitutional supervision committee under the National People's Congress.

The socialist world provides a range of models for constitutional committees that are structured to uphold the unity of state power in supreme socialist legislatures. Here Hand argues that there are significant obstacles to such a committee in China, including historical inertia, likely capacity limitations, the experience of failed socialist states and the importance of flexibility in the Party's governance model. For a conservative Party leadership that places a premium on flexibility to maintain its leadership status and to address political-legal tensions in a rapidly changing society, the perceived risks of establishing a constitutional supervision committee are likely to outweigh perceived benefits.

Chongyi Feng, in Chapter 3, then examines 'rule of law with Chinese characteristics' from theoretical and empirical perspectives. He pays special attention to two key, seemingly contradictory, Party documents about political direction and legal reform. The first is the 'Communiqué on the Current State of the Ideological Sphere' urging the Party to guard against Western liberal-democratic ideals.[9] The second is the 'Decision on Some Major Issues in the Comprehensive Promotion of Ruling the Country According to Law'.[10] This lays down the guidelines and measures for legal reform and proposes technical improvements to the Chinese legal system without contemplating any fundamental reform to the relationship between the legal system and the Party. Feng argues that the CPC's legal reform agenda serves three purposes. First is to enhance the power of the Party, as indicated by the fighting spirit of *Document No. 9* and the overarching principle of 'Party leadership'; second is to boost economic growth by facilitating greater legal protection for the operation of the semi-market economy; and third is to improve the image of the Party among the masses by countering local protectionism and reducing corruption in the court system at the grass-roots level.

For Qiyuan Xu in Chapter 4, 'structural reform' is *the* key for China's policy and reform directions for a socialist market economy. From a macroeconomic perspective, Xu argues that sustainable economic growth must be driven by labor input, capital input, technical progress and institutional reforms. Unfortunately, China also faces an aging population and overcapacity issues. Furthermore, the gap between the PRC and the global technical frontier is much smaller now than it once was. This means limited space for China to make technical progress through an imitation strategy. In relation to inputs and outputs Xu sees structural reform as essential to sustainable growth. With regard to outputs, a balanced structure in aggregate demand and supply, more public goods in social welfare and environmental protection, more justice and less corruption are all required. Xu's perspective anticipates policy tools will be adopted in the following three aspects: resource allocation and business cycle stabilization, policies for efficiency and income redistribution policies for justice.

Linda Yueh argues in Chapter 5 that an enduring paradox of China's remarkable economic growth has been the lack of a well-established legal system. Her thesis proposes that legal and economic reforms give rise to, and reinforce, each other. Once a market is created by law or more informally through institutional reform, then interested constituencies and stakeholders will push for more formal and explicit legal reforms to protect their interests. Better legal protection promotes market development by providing greater security of economic transactions and the complementary processes can explain the paradox of strong growth within an underdeveloped system of law with potential lessons for developing countries.

Jianfu Chen in Chapter 6 overviews efforts in post-Mao China to reintroduce procedural justice into Chinese law. Specifically, it focuses on the development and reform of the three principal procedural laws: *Criminal Procedure Law*, *Civil Procedure Law* and *Administrative Litigation Law*. The chapter argues that 'procedural justice' is a notion that was reintroduced to Chinese law in the post-Mao reforms. Not surprisingly, the establishment and consolidation of such a notion in Chinese law has faced some difficulties. Some of these difficulties are identified in Chapter 7, where Norman Ho examines China's crackdown on corruption from the time of the organized crime clean-up in Chongqing (2009–11). This chapter situates Bo's downfall and trial in an historical context and, specifically, in the context of Xi Jinping's 'tigers and flies' anti-corruption campaign. Ho argues that the role of the CPC in Bo's downfall, prosecution and trial should be viewed as part of Xi's anti-corruption campaign more generally. Ho shows that, historically, there is a continuity in anti-corruption measures in China, with little having changed as to how the CPC seeks to eradicate corruption and, indeed, dissent. Ho reveals how Party-led crackdowns and mass movements have remained favored methods.

Richard Hu investigates China's new land-use and urbanization reforms in Chapter 8, analyzing how the new reforms differ significantly from previous generations. His land-use and urbanization analysis dissects two key policy documents: (1) Section Six of the *Decision* that relates specifically to 'improving integrated urban–rural development systems and mechanisms', and (2) the National New-type Urbanization Plan, released in March 2014 as a policy follow-up to the *Decision*. Looking ahead at China's comprehensive land-use and urbanization reforms, Hu's chapter is particularly concerned with the interaction of development and changing land rights in both rural and urban areas.

Currently the impact of employment laws and policies on women's rights is underdiscussed, or rather missing in main discussions. In Chapter 9, Su Lin Han seeks some redress, providing a general picture of employment rights in China with respect to equality and non-discrimination principles. Han argues that China has, at this stage, not yet implemented equal employment laws despite various policies aimed at protecting specific disadvantaged groups such as women and people with disabilities. She refers to the lack of clear judicial and legislative guidance for courts to handle discrimination claims and lax enforcement by government regulators, arguing that these issues are perceived to be low policy priorities. China's leadership now turns to rule of law as a strategy for improving governance and bolstering its legitimacy in leading an increasingly 'rights conscious' populace. For Han, key questions relate to how to improve delivery of the benefits of rule of law to citizens by strengthening enforcement of individual rights protection. She probes an alternative enforcement model that could enhance both public and private enforcement of individual rights protection, seeking a workable compromise between the government's strong desire to control social management issues *and* citizens' needs to realize the protection of their rights.

Jing Tao, in Chapter 10, provides a critical appraisal of China's rejection of the Rome Statute of the International Criminal Court as a window into PRC reasoning behind its policy choices on international human rights. The relative weight China accords to sovereignty issues compared to human rights norms is revealing in that some long-held anti-Western sentiments remain pervasive. The legalized Rome Statute sets up an independent court with mandatory jurisdiction and grants the Prosecutor *ex officio* rights to investigate a crime. Tao explains why China voted resolutely against this Statute with sovereignty costs perceived as far too high.

Ji Li, in Chapter 11, argues that while many previous reforms could be characterized as indiscriminate legal and institutional transplantation from the West or, as some have argued, a systematic 'turn against law',[11] the CPC intends the current law reforms to take root in the Chinese political and value system. Hence, the Chinese legal culture is to remain unchanged. Li discusses how an essential component of the Chinese legal culture, the norm governing dispute resolution, will impact upon the international legal order for trade disputes. He examines how China's growing power, and its non-litigious social norm, will help sustain the international structure for informal dispute resolution despite the trend to litigate under the WTO DSM. Indeed, it may be readily argued that his theory applies broadly to developments in other areas of the international legal order for dispute resolution.

Critical questions are then asked by Isaac Kardon in Chapter 12 as to whether China complies with all its international legal obligations with regard to the law of the seas, whether international laws influence China and, if so, through what mechanisms? Specifically, he explores China's relationship to international legal rules and norms by analyzing the *internalization* of the law of the sea into Chinese domestic law and policy. The rights and duties created by the 'exclusive economic zone' (EEZ), a key component of the law of the sea, provide an ideal case study to evaluate international legal influences upon Chinese institutions. Crucial observations are made of how this new regime enables previously unclaimed international legal rights to be transformed into domestic Chinese law and policy, including the incorporation of the EEZ into PRC national legislation, administrative regulations and departmental rules. Kardon's chapter describes this internalization process in terms of (1) the *function* of the EEZ in creating new tasks for the state, (2) the *content* and *scope* of the rights and duties created, and (3) the changes required for state actors to have sufficient *capacity* (resources and personnel) to execute those rights and duties.

Weitseng Chen in Chapter 13 analyzes the most recent developments in both the United States and China regarding the national security review of foreign investment. Since the *Foreign Investment and National Security Act 2007* amended the 'Exon–Florio' statute, making several significant changes to the process by which foreign investments are screened for national security risks, the Obama administration has generally increased scrutiny. Cases filed by Chinese firms for approval increased so rapidly that, as of 2012, they accounted for the second-largest source of transactions reviewed by the Committee on Foreign Investment in the United States (CFIUS). Over the years since 2007, the CFIUS blocked only two cases. Both involved Chinese firms. In 2014, however, an unprecedented case saw the US Court of Appeals side with the Chinese firm suing the CFIUS for violation of due process. Notwithstanding the outcome of this case, and in response to the perceived 'hostile attitude' of foreign governments toward China's inbound foreign direct investment (FDI), in January 2015 China's Ministry of Commerce published the draft *Foreign Investment Act* for public comment, aiming to establish a comprehensive national security review process of its own. The new procedure is set to be immune from judicial review and this chapter forecasts an increase in disputes in the years to come.

Garrick and Chang Bennett conclude by reflecting on the significance of the contributions in this volume with respect to how China's domestic law reforms interact with the international legal order. As China asserts its power in new ways, what follows has both domestic and global ramifications. Nation-states remain central to international legal ordering as we do not live in a post-national world despite the extent of globalization and transnational legal influence. But even the great powers cannot, on their own, define the territorial boundaries of legal ordering – as the following chapters reveal.

Notes

1 Xinhua News Agency (2014). The statement added: 'rule of law is "a must" if the country wants to build a prosperous society in an well-rounded way, rejuvenate the nation, comprehensively deepen reform, improve socialism with Chinese characteristics and the Party's governance capability.'

2 An English translation is available at: http://news.xinhuanet.com/english/china/2013-11/15/c_132891949.htm.

3 Decision of the Central Committee of the Communist Party of China on Some Major Issues Concerning Comprehensively Deepening the Reform at: China.org.cn, January 16, 2014.

4 See Garrick (2011, 2012).

5 Amended and passed by the Standing Committee of the Twelfth National People's Congress on August 30, 2013, the *New Trademark Law* came into force on May 1, 2014. The advent of the *NTL* seeks to redress many of the perennial concerns of

international brand owners, including 'improving the efficiency of trademark application and opposition practice and procedure, significantly increasing fines against infringers and introducing the good faith concept to applications' (Green 2014: 56).

6 The 'mass line' refers to 'the Party doing everything for the masses, relying on the masses – from the masses to the masses, bringing the correct position of the Party into the conscious action of the masses' (Lu 2013). The mass line campaign was officially launched at a meeting of the Political Bureau of CPC Central Committee in June 2013. Xi Jinping said in his speech at the meeting that the campaign will be a 'thorough clean-up of undesirable work styles [and] a crackdown on the four forms of decadence, that is, formalism, bureaucratism, hedonism and extravagance'. To adhere to the mass line, Party members have been asked to 'take a long look in the mirror, groom themselves, take a bath and seek remedies' (see: 群众路线 [*qun zhong lu xian*] at www.chinadaily.com.cn/opinion/2013-07/19/content_16797277.htm).

7 In 2014, 1,000 legal experts, selected from the law schools, were sent to the local courts, and 1,000 judges sent to the law schools with the experts to become involved directly in legal cases in the courts, and judges to teach at the law schools. This educational process aims to raise policy levels and consciousness and is an updated aspect of the historical mass line process of 'going down', i.e., to local level (see note 6 above). For a full definition (in Chinese), see Yunliang and Xiaoya (2013); for general discussion, see Keith *et al.* (2013: 2–12).

8 Xu (2014) points out that 'top level design of reform', first adopted by the Fifth Plenary Session of the Seventeenth Central Committee, referred originally to large project planning, but later to broader strategies for development in much wider fields. The term can be broken down as 'top-level' and 'comprehensive' reform: 'top level' in its commitment to a main purpose, aiming high and managing from the top down; 'comprehensive' in its commitment to overall planning, a holistic view, systematic structuring and comprehensive design.

9 Issued by the General Office of the Central Committee of the CPC in April 2013.

10 Promulgated by the Fourth Plenum of the Eighteenth Central Committee of the CPC in October 2014.

11 For instance, see Minzner (2011), Clarke (2013).

Part I

China's socialist law reform agenda

1 Judicial reform in China

An overview

Qianfan Zhang

Introduction

In 2003, I wrote that:

> It is perhaps impractical to expect that the current judicial reform, ambitious as it is, will make the Chinese judiciary truly independent by western standards. Even if the on-going judicial reform is successful otherwise, it will still be limited by the ultimate political bottom-line: a party that is essentially above the law.
>
> (Zhang 2003: 100–1)

Over a decade has now passed, and China's judicial reform has gone through three phases with turns and twists, which largely confirmed the above expectation. Since 1999, when the Supreme People's Court (SPC) published the First Outline for a Five-Year Reform of the People's Court, judicial reform has been a spotlight in China's legal community, but the achievements in judicial practice have fallen far short of academic and social expectations. While scholars on the right (i.e., the liberals) criticized judicial reform for not doing enough in creating an independent judiciary, a few scholars on the left blamed it for going too far and encouraging judicial corruption. Despite the lack of substantial progress, judicial reform in the first decade was rather consistent in working toward a more professional and less politicized judiciary, but that direction was reversed in the third phase of judicial reform from 2008 to 2013, when the new president of the SPC highlighted 'the leadership of the party' as one of the 'Three Supremes' (*sange zhishang*) to be followed by courts in adjudicating cases.

Now the curtain has been raised for the new phase of judicial reform, which signifies a return to the initial path of professionalization. A new blueprint has been put forward, with comprehensive solutions directed against the evils in the existing judicial system. However, the reform is championed, once again, by the ruling party as a part of its overall reform program announced in the Third and Fourth Plenums of the Eighteenth Party Congress. How much can we expect the new judicial reform to achieve in a fundamentally similar political environment?

This overview highlights the major impediments that have for decades prevented China's courts from developing into a modern professional judiciary, and reviews the previous judicial reforms aimed at removing some of these impediments. It then describes the main initiatives of the new judicial reform and provides a brief analysis of the possibility of its success.

The judicial syndrome

China's judicial reform cannot properly be understood without awareness of the historical context that made the reform necessary. The Maoist revolutionary movements, culminating in the Great Cultural Revolution (1966–76), had disrupted normal social life and destroyed regular government functionaries. It would be rather unthinkable that a working judiciary could be sustained in a revolutionary society where rule of law and human rights were discarded as reactionary 'bourgeois' values. This situation began to change since the economic reform initiated in 1978, when the legislations and government functionaries, including the courts, were quickly restored. But the structural reform of the judiciary had to wait for another two decades (Cohen 2014a). Due to the lack of basic separation of powers, China's courts were, and to a large extent still are, plagued by the so-called judicial syndrome. There are four key aspects to this syndrome, summarized as follows: (1) low professional quality; (2) lack of institutional independence and heavy reliance on local party-governments; (3) lack of individual independence of judges within the courts; and (4) rampant judicial corruption that adds constraints to the judicial reform.

For a large part of Chinese history, the judiciary has been a neglected branch of the government, subordinate to and often directly exercised by the executive officer. The problem became exacerbated after the Communist takeover in 1949, when the judiciary was treated purely as a political instrument of the Party-state. For almost half-a-century since then, China's judiciary fulfilled the same function as the police and the armies – the 'knife's handle' (*daobazi*) of the proletarian dictatorship (He 1999). Since a 'judge' in China hardly had a different meaning from an 'ordinary cadre' in the bureaucratic echelon under the party leadership, he or she was supposed to perform a variety of public functions. Sitting in the court, hearing cases and delivering legal decisions is only one of the many roles – perhaps not even the major role – a Chinese judge is supposed to play.

The current judicial body was the result of rapid expansion after 1979, in response to the need for regulating rising social conflicts during the economic reform. Judicial personnel were largely 'borrowed' from social and political organizations that previously had little to do with work of a judicial nature. A significant portion of 'judges' was made up of military veterans, who were assigned 'political and legal work' (*zhengfa gongzuo*) without prior legal training. Some of them have become the court presidents or heads of divisions who control judicial decision making. Perhaps the best example is Wang Shengjun, president of the SPC between 2008 and 2013, who had not received formal legal training. Judicial appointments were made by party leaders – mainly according to their political loyalty rather than professional qualifications. In the same vein, factory workers and high school graduates were assigned to courts as 'judges'. Court secretaries (*shujiyuan*) might become judges within a few years after having been promoted to 'assistant judges' (*zhuli shenpanyuan*), without having to go through any formal academic training and extensive legal practice (Feng and Su 2000).

As a result, until recently, China's judges have been a large, amorphous category with very low, if any, professional qualifications. In the early 1990s, China had twice as many judges as lawyers, though only a small proportion of them heard any cases.[1] Over time, a large number with low remuneration and low professional quality formed a 'stable equilibrium' in the Chinese judiciary. The first step toward a more effective judicial system has been to break this 'equilibrium', or vicious cycle, by adopting a rigorous definition of 'judges', reducing the existing pool of judges and improving the social and economic status of this more selective group. A key to the success of this judicial reform is to make the judiciary a more appealing vocation for China's young talent.

Second, Chinese courts are institutionally and financially dependent on local governments. Until now, all levels of local courts have depended on local governments at the corresponding level – in terms of both appointments and funds. Judges' salaries and funds for court operations have come mostly from the local government budget, with leaders of the courts selected by the Local People's Congress (LPC) at the corresponding level. According to Art. 101 of the Constitution and Art. 11 of the *Judges Law*, the president of a local court is elected and dismissed by the LPC at the same level. Vice presidents, heads of divisions and ordinary judges are appointed and dismissed by the corresponding standing committee of the LPC upon recommendation of the court president. As a result, a judge failing to carry out the instructions of local leaders can be remonstrated with or even removed (Cai 1999). The local party or government leader(s) often instruct the court as to how a case is to be decided.

This institutional and financial reliance has seriously undermined the independence of the court as a whole, despite Art. 126 of the 1982 Constitution which requires courts to 'exercise judicial power independently, in accordance with the provisions of the law, and ... not be subject to interference by any administrative organ, association or individual'. Unable to shield judges from the various pressures exerted by local government, the current institutional arrangement has failed to protect the most basic aspects of judicial independence. The problem is most obvious in administrative litigation where the defendant is an administrative agency or the local government itself. In this scenario, the agency or local government as a litigant can, at the same time, affect the fate of the deciding judges and leaders of the court. An unfriendly decision may well trigger serious retaliation against those key players in the court. This conflict of interest has the effect of controlling the judiciary, which, in turn, cannot then be expected to be truly independent and impartial.

The lack of institutional independence of the court can, in part, be attributed to the lack of independence of individual judges within the court. The *Organic*

Law of the People's Courts establishes the so-called 'president responsibility system' (*yuanzhang fuzezhi*). In this system the president, assisted by the judicial committee (*shenpan weiyuanhui*), is held responsible for all judgments made by the court. Partly owing to the low professional quality of judges and the need to reduce judicial errors, the final decision for an 'important', 'complex' or 'sensitive' case is made not by its hearing judge(s), but by the judicial committee. The judicial committee does not actually hear cases, but 'gets the gist' of the facts from the report of the hearing judge(s). Every court decision must also be approved by the president or head of division to which the case belongs. Such a procedure of judicial administration not only removes personal responsibility from judges for their cases, but facilitates interference from other institutions or powerful figures. For instance, the local party leader or government can simply give instructions on a case to the president of the court, and the latter will then coordinate the court to reach the desired decision.

Third, the lack of judicial independence has greatly exacerbated local protectionism and undermined the uniform application of national laws and regulations. The supposedly unified judicial system in China has become the 'courts of local governments' in the sense that they naturally lean toward local interests at the expense of the uniform application of law. It is not uncommon that, in a dispute involving litigants from different localities, the judge would distort an obvious interpretation of law or ignore the preponderant evidence in order to decide in favor of the litigant from his or her own jurisdiction. Even if all the parties are local, the court may still apply a local regulation despite its conflict with a national norm, as illustrated in the *Corn Seed Case* (Zhang 2012: 96).

In calculating compensation for selling bad seed, the city court of Luoyang, Henan province, declined to apply the Henan Provincial Regulation on Crop Seeds as it conflicted with the *Seed Law* enacted by the Standing Committee of the National People's Congress. The seemingly reasonable judgment, which defended the supremacy of the national Seed Law against a local regulation, sparked unexpectedly strong reactions from the Standing Committee of Henan People's Congress. This committee had the power to supervise the Henan provincial high court and the Luoyang People's Congress, both authorized to supervise the Luoyang city court. Denouncing the court judgment as a 'serious illegal act' that 'essentially constituted legality review of the local regulation enacted by the provincial LPC Standing Committee, and violated the People's Congress institution of our country and the authority properly belonging to the organ of state power', it pressured the provincial high court and the city People's Congress to take actions against the 'directly responsible judge and leaders in charge'.[2] Only following sharp national criticism, particularly from the legal community, did the city court withdraw its decision to penalize the presiding judge. This case reveals the pressure put on a judge who refused to give in to 'regional protectionism' (*difang baohu zhuyi*).

Fourth, a poor and dependent judiciary can also mean a corrupt judiciary. In turn, this limits the depth of judicial reform. Judicial independence presupposes a minimum degree of professional and moral integrity on the part of the judiciary itself. 'Independence' usually implies the weakening of external controls and deterrence of self-seeking behavior among judges. As many have sensibly argued, Chinese courts seem to be corrupt enough even when they are supposedly under close scrutiny. If further independence only served to aggravate corruption, it is thus worth asking: 'Can China afford to maintain an independent judiciary?' The following sections examine this rhetorical question in historical context.

The judicial reforms (1999–2013) and their assessments

In order to remedy China's judicial syndrome, the SPC published in October 1999 the Outline of a Five-Year Reform of the People's Court ('Outline'). Consistent with the analysis above, the Outline recognized that judicial independence and impartiality in China have been impeded by four types of problem: (1) local protectionism that seriously undermined the uniformity of law; (2) the overall low professional and moral quality of Chinese judges, which makes them prone to corruption and unfit for impartial administration of justice; (3) the bureaucratic management model that is at odds with judicial independence and efficiency; and (4) the lack of material provisions (e.g., funding and working conditions) necessary for effective court functioning, especially of basic-level courts. Aiming to resolve these problems, the Outline sought to achieve the following reform measures in the five years from 1999 to 2003. The program will be summarized below as a response to the four types of problem outlined above.

Toward a more professional judiciary: the First and Second Outlines of judicial reform

The First Outline was a result of academic criticism and local experimentations over several years. It vowed to improve China's existing judicial structure, enhance the power and autonomy of individual judges and guarantee judicial efficiency and fairness. Undertaking to make China's judges 'real judges',[3] this ambitious program aimed to professionalize the heavily politicized courts. And it did manage to change the judicial outlook from *army uniform and starred epaulets* to *gavel and black robe*. Judges would be more carefully selected from existing judicial tribunals and lawyers who had established good performance records. At the same time, judges unable to meet professional standards would be laid off.

The reform also aimed to improve the quality of judicial reasoning. Chinese judicial decisions had been notoriously brief on legal reasoning. Indeed, the absence of reasoning often served as a pretext for prejudicial decisions (see Wang 2000). The lack of legal reasoning as a potential source of prejudice is further exacerbated by a lack of transparency in China's judicial opinion-making. For instance, opinions are normally available only to the specific parties rather than society at large. This shield from public examination is perhaps the best protection for shoddy opinions and secret deals. To remedy this problem in criminal trials, the SPC drafted in 1999 the 'Model Format for Judicial Opinions in Criminal Trials'. This emphasized the importance of legal reasoning in all types of judgments (Yahong Li 2000). From June 2000, the SPC also began to publish judicial opinions of 'particularly important and typical' cases in the *SPC Gazette*, the *People's Court Daily* and on the Internet (Supreme People's Court 2000). The publication of opinions has so far been highly selective, however, making it appear that it will take a long time for ordinary opinions to be publicly accessible.

The First Outline did relatively little with respect to the institutional structure of the courts, local protectionism and judicial corruption. It did modernize the trial process by explicitly separating the filing, trial, judgment, enforcement and supervision stages of cases. This separation helped prevent *ex parte* contacts with judges and eliminate the egregious 'three-together' (*santong*) phenomenon, in which a judge would travel, dine and lodge with the plaintiff – at the latter's expense – to conduct an investigation outside his jurisdiction (Wan 1999). The SPC also fashioned an institutional mechanism to reduce local protectionism by requiring provincial high courts to establish a special enforcement division or bureau. This mechanism was expected to streamline the overall enforcement process and reduce the pervasive 'enforcement difficulty' (*zhixing nan*), which became even more conspicuous when a unfavorable judgment was to be enforced in another province, where the losing party could easily collude with the local authority to evade enforcement. Rather than making the court directly enforce its judgment outside its jurisdiction, the new mechanism delegated the task to the Enforcement Bureau of the province in which the judgment was to be enforced. Further, to root out local protectionism, the court finance structure needed to be overhauled so that local courts would receive their funding directly from the national treasury rather than their local administrative branch.[4]

The First Outline aroused many expectations of judicial reforms as they were so badly needed. In retrospect, however, its achievements were limited. It did change the outlook of the judiciary, but improvements to the quality of judicial opinions were far less than hoped. The rapid rise in the number of law schools and law graduates has largely resolved the professional quality problem for courts in urban centers such as Beijing and Shanghai. But this has not relieved the shortage of legal talent in less developed areas, particularly poor rural areas. More fundamentally, in the same institutional structure that used to stifle free inquiry and independent reasoning, legal knowledge and techniques can easily be used to conceal corrupt practices rather than serve justice. A trained legal mind can easily manipulate judicial jargon to cover up traces of political or administrative interference. This was well illustrated in the infamous trial of Li Zhuang, a defense attorney victimized in the 'strike-mafia' (*dahei*) campaign in Chongqing (see Ho 2012: 211–12). Some of the presiding judges, who defended what appeared to be obviously defective criminal procedure in their judgment, had earned doctoral degrees in law and had well-reasoned articles published in law journals (Zhao Lei 2010). Like other forms of power, legal knowledge can be gravely misused in the wrong institutional context.

What the First Outline left unaccomplished should have been picked up by the next waves of reform. The reform momentum generated by the First Outline subsided considerably, however, by 2005 when the Second Outline of Five-Year Reform of the People's Courts (2004–8) was published and implemented by the SPC – under the same President, Xiao Yang. Compared to its predecessor, the Second Outline was more cautious in goal-setting, limiting itself to technical improvements such as the establishment of a unified bar examination scheme and 'case guidance system', the prohibition of extortion for confession and extended detention and the recentralization of the power to review death-sentence judgments by the SPC.

The Third Outline: 'judicial populism' or back to political control?

After more than ten years since its inauguration, China's judicial reform had reached a crossroads. It appears to have lost momentum *and* direction. By the end of the second judicial reform in 2008, the SPC was led by a new president with a new philosophy of reform. While professionalization was the goal over a decade ago, the new SPC allied with several legal scholars in advocating the 'judicial populism' (*sifa dazhonghua*) of the People's Courts and a return to an outdated mass-trial model once practiced in the Communist base (Yan'an) during the 1940s. In effect, far from inviting ordinary people to participate in the 'People's Court', this so-called line of 'judicial reform' only undermines judicial fairness and invites even more political interference in activities that properly belong to courts. If the revocation of the legal effect of the Qi Yuling decision at the end of 2008 indicated a departure from the Western line of judicial reform initiated by the previous SPC, the Li Zhuang case (2009) served to remind the Chinese people of the damage a retreat to the old revolutionary days can do to rule of law.

The main thrust of 'judicial populism' is to ensure that judgments will 'satisfy the people' (*rang renmin manyi*) and reduce social conflict in order to 'maintain stability' (*weiwen*). The 'maintenance of stability' is a common narrative of the Central Politburo Standing Committee to legitimize its approach to reform. The official position is supported by a minority of 'leftist' legal scholars who advocate 'popular trials' (*minyi shenpan*) and insist that judicial decisions should be made by the people rather than judges (Zhang 2008; He 2008). These propositions confuse the judicial process with law-making; a democratic process that ultimately 'satisfies' public interest. In China, where the democratic law-making process has been institutionally impaired, however, such a proposal has considerable popular appeal. It is popular, in part, because neither the NPC, nor its Standing Committee, keeps up with amending laws and making them adaptable to the changing demands of a fast-developing society. In other words, it is an easy way out to leave some things to popular opinion rather than to leave legal decision making to professional judges.

The Xu Ting case provides telling evidence on this point. In April 2006, Xu Ting extracted money over 170 times from a malfunctioning ATM in

Guangzhou, illegally obtaining ¥170,000 (roughly $25,000). This constituted an 'extraordinarily large sum' under a provision of the 1979 *Criminal Law*. As a result, Xu was sentenced to life imprisonment. Like the Sun Zhigang case, the judgment excited strong public protest. Although the sum involved may have appeared to be 'extraordinarily large' three decades ago, it is unthinkable today that this amount would warrant such a disproportionate penalty as life imprisonment. The failure of the NPCSC to update the law, or more precisely, of the SPC to update its interpretation of the law, has obliged the people to step in, express their disapproval for an outdated law and demand the court adjust its application to a specific case. After requesting instructions from the SPC, which was apparently concerned with mounting public pressure, the middle-level court of Guangzhou, on appeal, changed the sentence to five years' imprisonment (Li 2008).

Although the Xu Ting case can be counted as a victory for 'judicial populism', the downside is that it may invite inadequate interference by the media and society at large through exerting pressure on the government. In turn, it can then easily order a court to render a judgment that will preserve its image and appease the public. Nor can ad hoc popular intervention promise any consistency of judgments in similar cases. For example, a similar case occurred in Yunnan province, where an undergraduate illegally obtained over ¥400,000 and was sentenced to life imprisonment – even though he had returned the money to the authority. He had already been imprisoned for seven years by the time of Xu Ting's case in 2008 (Editor 2008). Even more importantly, 'the people' are not always right. In April 2002, Liu Yong, a rich merchant and leader of a gang responsible for one killing and 16 serious injuries in Shenyang city, was sentenced to death for murder. The judgment was quashed on appeal for lack of evidence and suspicion that the confession was obtained by torture. Although most jurists in criminal law approved of the appellate judgment, the decision excited strong social protest out of hatred against gang crimes. In December 2003, the SPC unprecedentedly took over the retrial and changed the judgment back to a death sentence – in order to appease public anger (Editor 2003). In April 2008, the new SPC President expressed in a public speech that a court shall consider the nature of an unlawful act, its social harm and 'the people's feelings' in deciding whether a death sentence should be given. Such an arbitrary standard undermines justice and the rule of law, and invites arbitrary political interference from a desire to 'maintain stability' and 'satisfy the people'. In effect this is the same as when courts were used as a 'knife handle' for pursuing political ends. It is 'justice' from the pre-reform past.

The 'results-oriented' approach was unable to 'satisfy the people' in Deng Yujiao's famous 2009 case (Editor 2009). Deng, a 21-year-old hotel servant in Badong county, Hunan province, killed a local official. She alleged she was resisting the official's attempt to rape her. The case excited enormous public attention at the time.[5] The Badong authority denied the rape attempt, harassed the defendant's family and attorneys and refused to disclose the exact details of the event. At the end of the trial, Deng was acquitted by the court, which apparently yielded to public pressure. Many bloggers subsequently speculated that the decision reflected 'public pressure'. Indeed, comments on the killing at the time inundated blogs and bulletin boards, and news of the 21-year-old's release from custody was widely welcomed. Deng's case – and its handling by police – became emblematic of the struggle of ordinary people against abusive officials, but it did not earn any respect for the court from the public.

The retreat of the third 'reform' illustrates inherent limits that are, to an extent, common to all judicial reforms. Ambitious as it was, the first reform failed to change the power structure both within and outside the courts. Nor did it change judges' thinking. At the heart of the matter is the relationship between the courts and the ruling party. As judges are under the leadership of their court president, so too is the president under the leadership of the party. This makes the judicial structure as a whole prone to political interference. The First Outline declared 'party leadership' as the guiding principle of reform. On the one hand, this might divert political challenges from the conservatives, but on the other hand it highlights a line beyond which no reform may proceed.

The ruling party may intervene in a judicial process in many ways. First and most obviously, court presidents and vice presidents are usually party members and thus subject to party discipline. Since the president is held responsible for the whole court, the party can easily 'control the entire court through the presidential responsibility and the judicial committee system' (Nathan 1997: 240–2). In this way it can supervise any judicial judgments that involve 'important', 'complicated' or 'difficult' cases (Nathan 1997: 240–2). Second, it is common for the party secretary of the Politics and Law Committee (*zhengfawei*), usually the same person as the chief of the public security bureau, to coordinate the policies and case works of the public security bureau, procuratorate and court at the same level. They can thus ensure conformity of all three institutions to party principles. Finally, the party is responsible for initiating and carrying out all major reforms. The constitutional amendment on 'rule of law', for example, was first enacted in the CPC Charter during the Fifteenth Party Congress before it was copied, verbatim, to the Constitution. Judicial reform simply could not be launched without the approval of the major party leaders. Since judicial reform is initiated by the party itself, it is inherently limited by the party's own imperatives. This is especially so when 'impartial justice' conflicts with the personal interests of party leaders. Hence the question: 'Is it too much to expect that substantial progress in judicial reform can be achieved by a ruling party that essentially puts itself above the law?'

The new reform (2014–present)

The Third Plenum of the Eighteenth Congress of the CPC opened a new era for judicial reform in China. The *Decision* issued at the end of the Third Plenum rehabilitated the 1999 'professionalization' reform. There are three major aspects of the reform (CPC Central Committee 2013). First, the objectives of the new reform is to:

> Guarantee independent and fair exercise of judicial and procuratorial powers according to law, to reform the judicial administration system, to promote uniform administration of the personnel, property and assets of local courts and procurator offices below the provincial level, to explore the establishment of jurisdictional arrangements adequately separate from the administrative zonings, and to establish the uniform application of the state laws.
> (CPC Central Committee 2013)

Second, and more specific, the above objectives are to be realized by:

> improving the mechanism of exercising judicial powers,… reforming the judicial committee, improving the accountability of the trial judge or the panel of judges in adjudicating cases, so as to make the trial judges decide the cases and the deciders accountable [to the judgments].
> (CPC Central Committee 2013)

Third, the *Decision* vows to 'promote the openness of judicial process, improve the persuasiveness of the legal judgments, and promote publication of court judgments that have taken legal effect' (CPC Central Committee 2013).

The Third Plenum also established the Central Leading Group of Comprehensively Deepening the Reform, chaired by the General Secretary Xi Jinping. Its third conference, held in June 2014, issued the 'Framework Opinion Concerning Several Issues of Judicial Institutional Reform Experiments' and 'Working Plan for Shanghai Judicial Reform Experiment'. The conference highlighted several aspects of the forthcoming judicial reform, including the classification of judicial personnel, improvement of judicial accountability and enhancement of the leading role of trial judges and procurators (Xiao 2014).

The Central Government has selected Shanghai municipality and five provinces as venues for the pilot judicial reform projects (*shidian*).[6] The crux of the Shanghai project is to:

- establish a judicial classification system centered on judges and procurators;
- promote the professional development of the judiciary;
- establish the system of uniform nomination;
- separate appointment and removal at each level for all municipal judges and procurators; and
- reduce external interference in the judicial process.

The Shanghai pilot project will also establish a mechanism for the uniform municipal administration of court finance and adjust the income of judicial personnel at the three levels of the judiciary within the municipality (Editor 2014).

After five years of retrogression, it appears that China's judicial reform has suddenly accelerated. In July 2014, the SPC announced an outline of the Fourth Five-Year Reform Plan of the People's Court (2014–18). This includes as many as 45 reform measures in eight major areas, which can be summarized in four aspects: (1) improving the classification system of judicial personnel; (2) establishing judicial accountability by reducing the administrative powers of the court presidents and judicial committees; (3) realizing the occupational protection of judicial personnel; and (4) establishing the vertical administration of courts and procurator offices below the provincial level (Yuan 2014). These measures are elaborated in the full-length plan published near the end of February 2015. The Supreme People's Court Opinion on 'Comprehensively Deepening the People's Court Reform' contains 65 points of judicial reform, focusing on the establishments of a jurisdictional system that is adequately detached from the administrative zones, and a litigation system centered on adjudications, the optimization of functional distribution within the courts and the operational mechanism of judicial power, the construction of an open and transparent judicial system, promotion of professional development of judges, and the independent and impartial exercise of judicial power.

The measures adopted by the new judicial reform lay the foundations for establishing a more professional judiciary, and are directed against the judicial syndrome that has plagued China's courts for decades. The crux of China's judicial problems has, to an extent, been the lack of professionalization – despite three decades of legal development since the end of the Cultural Revolution. Not only are there too many judges, but many of them, particularly the court leaders who are often preoccupied with various 'administrative matters', adjudicate very few cases during their whole career. In a professional judiciary, they belong to the category of 'redundant workforce' that is best laid off to enable the court to move ahead more effectively. The Shanghai project is an illustration that current judicial personnel are to be 'streamlined'; judges or procurators will constitute only one-third of existing personnel, over one-half of them will be categorized as 'auxiliary judicial staff' (*sifa fuzhu renyuan*). The remaining one-sixth will be 'administrative managers' (*xingzheng guanli renyuan*) (Xinhua News 2014a).

The last category reserved for 'administrative managers' has left some suspense over the judicial reform in that it avows to reduce administrative and political control over courts. The Shanghai pilot project highlights the strengthening of the individual role of judges, and the elitist personnel reform points in the same direction. The cryptic category, however, still casts doubt on the capacity of the current reform to substantially reduce political and administrative interference in judicial processes. It is unrealistic to expect that the courts of the PRC can maintain independence and impartiality in politically sensitive cases. The best reform scenario at this stage is probably for judges to be enabled to maintain independence in most ordinary cases and make impartial decisions.

The centralization of judicial power, a conspicuous aspect of the current reform, is expected to reduce, if not eliminate, judicial interference from the party and government at the same level. These have dogged the uniform application of national laws and regulations. The centralization reform is therefore being coupled with a reduction in political and administrative control inside the courtroom at the same time as enhancing the role of individual judges in deciding cases. It is possible that improving judicial independence may exacerbate judicial corruption by hampering supervision by political and administrative means. But there is an adequate remedy by making judicial procedure more transparent by opening up the trial process and improving the reasoning of judicial opinions. Surely this is superior to turning the clock back to the old days of a highly politicized judiciary. These requirements are reflected in the new judicial reform plan (see Bo 2014 for details).

Although the new reform plan has been widely applauded for setting up a more enlightened path for judicial reform (Lubman 2014), the legal community (and society at large) has shown some skepticism about whether it can be carried through effectively. What will these reforms produce in reality? Such questions are commonplace in China. The people have seen many good laws and plans end up producing poor performance. The new judicial reforms too may be hampered by powerful vested interests that do not support the creation of an independent and impartial judiciary. Even if the current plan is successfully implemented, it is too early to predict its effects. The trimming and classification of the judicial structure may move ahead with some difficulty. But the Shanghai plan still reserves the category of 'administrative managers' and it is not clear how this will play out. The main concern is, of course, that as the plan has not clearly explained its function nor the scope of its power, the so-called 'management' (*guanli*) may easily turn itself into the new form of interference (*ganyu*).

The new reform plan also vows to improve the financial condition of judges. Again, it remains to be seen whether dramatic improvement is feasible before judicial performance (and social reputation of that office) has been significantly improved. Although China's courts recruit thousands of law graduates every year, it is common knowledge they have not been an attractive place for the most outstanding talent. Past attempts of the SPC to open recruitment have failed to attract senior lawyers and legal scholars even though a judicial appointment is, supposedly, a high point of legal practice (He 2000). If the responsibility of individual judges is enhanced without corresponding improvements in remuneration, or a deeper sense of honor, the courts will experience new difficulties in retaining competent judges simply because they can earn more by moving *from* court *to* private practice.[7]

Finally, the centralization of judicial administration may help reduce local protectionism below the provincial level, but it cannot reduce political interference coming from the province itself. Indeed, it may even facilitate provincial interference. The 2003 *Corn Seed Case* illustrates precisely how interference came from the Henan provincial People's Congress. It also remains to be seen whether the local courts can be sufficiently detached from local pressure. Local judges simply cannot be cut off from local connections and interests. The establishment of several 'circuit courts' (*xunhui fating*) as SPC branches should help to improve uniform application of national laws. But their jurisdiction is limited to important administrative, civil and commercial cases (see Ma 2015 for details). It remains to be seen how these courts will intervene in ordinary adjudications as China's appellate process normally ends at the middle (i.e., county) level or, under extraordinary circumstances, high (provincial) level courts.

Conclusion

The new judicial reform illustrates the direction of China's judicial reform over the next five years. It highlights two key areas: (1) a limited deregulation of the courtroom, which will reduce judicial bureaucracy and enable individual judges to assume more responsibility in deciding cases; and (2) centralization of judicial administration to reduce local protectionism. While the former operates within the existing legal framework, and needs only the approval of the SPC, the latter goes beyond this and arguably may run into conflict with the People's Congress regime in the 1982 Constitution. The authorization of the Standing Committee of the NPC, or even a constitutional amendment, may thus be required before it can be legitimately executed (Xiao 2014).

Procedural problems aside, the new judicial reform is substantively limited by a political regime in which the ruling party alone has the final say on how far reforms can proceed. A high degree of social skepticism has been identified as looming large in this matter – especially when citizens are intimidated by the state machinery when it comes to exercising their rights as defined in the Constitution and law. At the time of writing this overview, the civil movement activist Xu Zhiyong is serving a prison sentence; rights lawyer Pu Zhiqiang is still awaiting trial after he was arrested over 18 months ago; and five women's rights activists who were simply advocating gender equality were detained the day before International Women's Day in 2015 (Lubman 2015). At the moment, there seems little a Chinese judge can do to prevent or remedy these egregiously unlawful political actions. The *Decision* of the Fourth Plenum, progressive as it is in promoting rule of law, highlights 'leadership of the party' as many as 13 times! The first among the 65 measures in the most recent Outline of judicial reform again insists on the leadership of the party. It therefore remains unclear how the party leadership can be reconciled with 'rule of law', as this rests upon the principle that all private individuals, as well as public institutions, submit themselves to the impartial application of laws.

Notes

1 In 1991, there were 138,000 persons above the rank of assistant trial member, with only 47,000 lawyers. In 1997, the number of lawyers in China increased to 100,000, but the number of judges above the assistant rank increased to 247,000 due to the local expansion of capacity (Wang, Chengguang 1998). On the other hand, one need not be a judge in order to decide a case. It used to be common for the court secretaries to be in charge of investigating a case and even writing its decision (Fu and Wei 2000).

2 See China Law and Governance Review (2004).

3 Words as expressed by the former SPC president, Xiao Yang, who was instrumental in achieving the first five-year judicial reform plan.

4 For supporting arguments made by the former president of the SPC, see Zheng (1999).

5 For example, see Guardian (2009).

6 The five provinces are Guangdong, Jilin, Hubei, Hainan and Qinghai; see Xinhua News (2014).

7 Sun (2015) reports that Beijing and Shanghai municipalities have already begun to witness a 'tide of resignation' (lizhichao) of judges.

2 An assessment of socialist constitutional supervision models and prospects for a constitutional supervision committee in China

The constitution as commander?

Keith J. Hand

Introduction

Recent official statements have renewed discussion of constitutional supervision in China. In a Politburo speech, Xi Jinping emphasized the supremacy of the PRC Constitution and the importance of implementing the Constitution (Xinhua 2013a). In October 2014, the Fourth Plenum of the Communist Party of China's Eighteenth Central Committee issued a major decision on the socialist legal system (CPC Central Committee 2014). The Fourth Plenum Decision called for the perfection of constitutional interpretation and supervision systems. The prominence and specificity of these statements suggest that Chinese leaders may be considering concrete reforms to strengthen constitutional supervision.[1]

They will not turn to judicial institutions. In China's unitary system, the National People's Congress (NPC) is the supreme organ of state power. The NPC and its Standing Committee (NPCSC) interpret and supervise enforcement of the Constitution. The establishment of an independent constitutional court would require a major constitutional realignment.[2] Over the past decade, the people's courts shelved limited efforts to apply the Constitution (see Zhang, Chapter 1). Recent domestic commentaries attacking 'constitutionalism' and separation of powers (Creemers 2014) reinforce the conclusion that judicial review is not feasible in the current political environment. Instead, the Fourth Plenum Decision emphasized the development of NPC and NPCSC constitutional supervision.

What types of reforms might be feasible? Chinese experts have long argued that the most realistic approach would be to establish a constitutional supervision committee within the NPC structure. Opinion differs on whether such a committee should take the form of an NPC organ with status equal to the NPCSC, a special committee that is subordinate to the NPCSC, or some variation on the above (Cai 1995; Zhu 2010). The Fourth Plenum Decision revived these discussions (*Beijing News* 2014). Former Supreme People's Court (SPC) President Xiao Yang encouraged them when he endorsed a constitutional supervision committee (*Beijing Youth Daily* 2014).

This chapter assesses current prospects for a constitutional supervision committee in China. I conclude that for a conservative Party leadership that places a premium on flexibility to maintain its supremacy, the perceived risks of such a committee are likely to outweigh the perceived benefits. Chinese leaders have emphasized the socialist characteristics of China's legal system. In the second half of the twentieth century, communist regimes in Europe established a range of specialized constitutional supervision organs. This experience demonstrates that China could establish a constitutional supervision committee that upholds core socialist legal principles and one-party rule. However, several factors, including precedent, the association of this model with failed communist regimes, problems of political sensitivity and capacity, and the importance of flexibility and adaptation in the Party's governance posture, are likely to limit the willingness of Chinese leaders to experiment with such a reform.

Socialist constitutional supervision models

China's current system manifests core elements of socialist constitutionalism. Soviet legal theory firmly rejected the concept of separation of powers. Instead, all state power was unified in a supreme people's legislature. The supreme legislature enacted a Constitution, which sat at the apex of the legislative hierarchy. Statutes gave concrete legal effect to constitutional provisions. In theory, statutes conformed to the Constitution, and lower-level legislation conformed to the Constitution and statutes.[3]

Stalin's leading legal theorist denounced judicial review as a bourgeois institution. Extra-parliamentary review of the constitutionality of legislation was considered an improper limitation on the sovereignty of the people's legislature and in turn a violation of the people's will. Consistent with the theory of unified state power, ultimate authority to supervise the constitutional order was vested in the supreme legislature or its sub-units (the Presidium of the Supreme Soviet in the USSR and standing committees in other socialist legal systems) (Ludwikowski 1991). State organs were presumed to work harmoniously under ruling party leadership, and legislative organs did not actively police constitutional violations in practice (Garlicki 1988). The basic components of this system are easily recognized in China's constitutional structure.

De-Stalinization catalyzed new discussions on constitutional supervision. Communist regimes began to experiment with limited judicial review of administrative acts (Ludwikowski 1991), a path that China would follow in the 1980s. Socialist legal scholars also recognized that statutes could conflict with Constitution and that more effective constitutional supervision mechanisms might be necessary to discipline bureaucracies. Such mechanisms would preserve the supremacy of people's legislatures by ensuring consistency in the unified legislative hierarchy and the implementation of central policies (Kuss 1986).

Communist regimes experimented with a range of institutions to strengthen constitutional supervision. These institutions can be divided into three basic categories: parliamentary committees with advisory powers; parliamentary committees with a mix of advisory and binding review powers; and quasi-judicial organs with a mix of advisory and binding review powers.[4] In each case, the institutions were designed to uphold the principle of legislative supremacy.

In 1965, Romania created a Constitutional Committee with advisory powers. The National Assembly elected its own deputies and leading jurists to serve as Committee members. The Committee was empowered to advise the National Assembly on the constitutionality of statutes, but the National Assembly exercised ultimate authority on this issue. It was not an effective institution (Kuss 1986; Garlicki 1987).

Hungary established a committee with a mix of advisory and binding review powers in the early 1980s. The Council on Constitutional Law consisted of National Assembly deputies and legal experts. It was empowered to review the constitutionality and legality of statutes, administrative regulations and other normative documents. If the Council determined that an administrative regulation was unconstitutional or unlawful, it could suspend the regulation and direct the promulgating organ to amend it. If the promulgating organ failed to amend the regulation, the Council could petition the National Assembly to annul it. In contrast, if the Council found a statute, Presidential Council decision, or Supreme Court directive unconstitutional, it could not suspend the provision. Instead, it could only submit its finding to the National Assembly for a final determination (Kuss 1986; Garlicki 1987).

Poland adopted a third variant in the mid-1980s. The Polish regime's decision to create a Constitutional Tribunal was in part a response to public demands for constitutional review and control of arbitrary administrative action. Brzezinski (1993: 162) observed that Polish authorities sought to 'present the illusion of constitutional legality without challenging its most fundamental assumptions'. The Polish parliament (the Sejm) adopted a constitutional amendment providing for the Tribunal in 1982, but implementing legislation was delayed until 1985. The Sejm elected 12 Tribunal judges that met the existing qualifications for senior judges, and the Tribunal held public, adversarial proceedings. Scholars characterized the Tribunal as a quasi-judicial organ and a de facto constitutional court (Kuss 1986; Brzezinski 1993).

Similar to the Hungarian Council, the Tribunal exercised a mix of advisory and binding review powers. The Tribunal was empowered to review the constitutionality of Sejm statutes, Council of State administrative decrees and other central administrative rules. If the Tribunal determined that an administrative provision conflicted with the Constitution or a statute, its determination was binding. If the promulgating organ failed to amend the offending provision, the legal effect of the provision was canceled. In contrast, if the Tribunal determined that a Sejm statute conflicted with the Constitution, it could only submit its finding for Sejm consideration. The Sejm was obliged to review the finding, but could nullify it with a two-thirds vote.

Although Soviet scholars actively participated in expanded discourses on constitutional supervision, the USSR did not create a new constitutional supervision organ until the late 1980s. As a component of Mikhail Gorbachev's constitutional reforms, the Soviets established a Constitutional Supervision

Committee under a reconstituted supreme legislature (the Congress of People's Deputies or CPD) in 1989.[5] The Committee commenced operations in 1990. The CPD elected a Committee of over 20 members from the fields of politics and law. The Committee's implementing statute provided that the Committee was 'subordinate only to the USSR Constitution'.[6]

The Committee was empowered to review the constitutionality and legality of a range of state acts of the USSR and its republics. Its jurisdiction included CPD laws, decrees of the Supreme Soviet's Presidium, union republic constitutions and laws, some central administrative decrees, Supreme Court explanations and other central normative documents. In most cases, if the Committee found that legislation conflicted with the USSR Constitution or a USSR law, it could suspend the legislation. If the promulgating agency refused to amend the legislation, the Committee sent its opinion to the CPD. Ultimately, the CPD could reject the Committee's opinion with a two-thirds vote. Otherwise, the challenged legislation lost legal force.

The Committee's powers with respect to CPD laws and union republic constitutions were weaker. If the Committee determined that these acts violated the Constitution, it generally could not suspend them. Instead, the Committee reported its opinion to the CPD. The CPD was obliged to discuss the opinion and could reject it with a two-thirds vote. In addition, while the Committee was empowered to review certain administrative acts on its own initiative, it could review other legislation only at the request of certain state organs.[7]

Each of these constitutional supervision organs incorporated features to preserve legislative supremacy. People's legislatures enacted constitutional amendments or statutes to create the supervision organs, appointed the members of the organs and supervised their operation. In Romania and Hungary, legislators themselves served on constitutional committees. Most importantly, review authority over statutes was limited. Either constitutional supervision organs exercised only advisory powers with respect to statutes, or legislatures could overturn a finding of unconstitutionality.

One exception to this approach can be found in the operation of the Soviet Constitutional Supervision Committee. The Committee exercised the power to invalidate CPD laws if it determined that a law violated 'basic human rights and freedoms consolidated in the USSR Constitution or international acts to which the USSR is a party'.[8] This provision gave the Committee more expansive powers than its Hungarian and Polish cousins exercised.

In practice, these constitutional supervision organs did not challenge communist regimes. Continued party control over state institutions, limitations on citizen petition rights and the scope of review, the power of supreme legislatures to overturn constitutional decisions and other constraints ensured that supervision organs would not pose such threats. As Ludwikowski (1988: 107) noted, socialist institutions 'have a real chance at political survival only if they do not directly challenge the rudiments of power of the communist elite'. Brzezinski (1993: 175) concluded that the Polish Constitutional Tribunal 'fail[ed] to substantially modify the totalitarian political framework'. Although supervision organs issued some rights-reinforcing decisions on economic issues and equal protection of the law, they avoided sensitive political questions, exercised caution in reviewing statutes and generally worked in system-reinforcing manner (Kuss 1986; Garlicki 1988; Brzezinski 1993; Schwartz 2000).

Again, the Soviet Constitutional Supervision Committee presents a somewhat more complex picture. As discussed below, the Committee invalidated some legislation that violated fundamental rights. The Committee's broad authority in rights cases was a product of the expansive liberalization program of the late USSR (Feldbrugge 1993). In this respect, it can be viewed as an outlier that emerged under special political conditions. Overall, procedural limitations, a lack of enforcement power and legitimacy deficits limited the Committee's effectiveness (Hausmaninger 1992; Schwartz 2000). Some state organs simply ignored its decisions and continued to apply suspended legislation (Blankenagel 1992). As its own chairman acknowledged, the Committee was the product of 'deceit and falsification embodied in state bodies and institutions' (Maggs 1991: 1061).

Committee decisions were not an important factor in the collapse of the USSR. If anything, the Committee worked against this outcome by invalidating some republic legislation that weakened central state, military and party power. In addition, the Committee issued only a weak response when party conservatives attempted to depose Gorbachev (Maggs 1991; Hausmaninger 1992). It was eventually swept aside when the USSR dissolved in late 1991.

Constitutional courts in East Asian authoritarian states faced constraints similar to those in socialist legal systems. Both South Korea and the Republic of China established constitutional courts under their post-war constitutions. Authoritarian governments used a range of tools to marginalize these institutions for decades (Ginsburg 2003). Constitutional courts in some authoritarian states have managed to enhance rights on the 'margins of political life', but only by avoiding challenges to core regime interests (Ginsburg and Moustafa 2008: 18). The record of constitutional supervision organs in socialist and East Asian authoritarian states demonstrates that such institutions are unlikely to catalyze fundamental political transformations on their own.

The application of socialist constitutional supervision models in China

Experience in the socialist world demonstrates that it is possible to create specialized constitutional supervision organs that uphold core socialist legal principles and one-party rule. These innovations have shaped discourse in China. For example, Ji Weidong's (2003) proposal that China establish a constitutional committee made up of judges, political figures and legal scholars to issue advisory opinions to the NPCSC clearly incorporates socialist models. Ji views such a committee as an interim step toward a constitutional court.[9] Qianfan Zhang (2013) argues that a constitutional supervision committee would be consistent with China's socialist system. As in Eastern Europe, the establishment of a constitutional supervision committee in China would require a modest relaxation of socialist legal orthodoxy. But the Party has demonstrated that it is quite capable of such ideological dexterity when it serves the Party's political interests.

Beyond considerations related to constitutional structure, it is unlikely that a constitutional supervision committee would threaten Party power. The Party controls appointments through its *nomenklatura* system, and it closely monitors the work of political-legal institutions. While the Fourth Plenum Decision renewed China's commitment to legal reform, it also strengthened the Party's emphasis on control of political-legal institutions. A constitutional supervision committee under the NPC would not be an exception. China's leaders have plenty of tools to control the operation of a specialized constitutional supervision organ in practice.

The creation of a committee could generate modest legitimacy dividends for the regime. While the NPC and NPCSC implement parts of the Constitution through the adoption of concrete legislation (Lin and Ginsburg 2014), the NPCSC largely has failed to carry out its formal constitutional supervision duties in practice. Chinese scholars have proposed a specialized constitutional supervision organ for decades, and the perception of stagnation in China's legal reforms weakens the Party narrative that China is building a rule of law state. The Constitution is fundamental law, and the Party's Charter makes clear that the Party must act within the Constitution.[10] As such, failure to implement the Constitution opens Chinese authorities to criticism. The creation of a constitutional supervision committee would temper such criticism and demonstrate that the reform process is progressing.

A constitutional supervision committee would also reinforce current efforts to discipline China's bureaucracy. Xi Jinping has acknowledged that corruption poses an existential threat to the Party. Corruption and local protectionism also create obstacles to Xi's economic reform agenda. As I have argued elsewhere, conflicts in legislation at all levels undermine the ideology of a unified socialist legal system, create barriers to economic growth and the implementation of central policies and generate unnecessary disputes that weaken stability. In the current system, most state organs file legislation with higher-level organs, which in theory review the legislation. In practice, this filing and review system lacks the organizational and political capacity to address legislative conflicts in an effective manner (Hand 2013). A constitutional supervision committee could help to address some of these deficiencies.

The socialist record is instructive here. In practice, supervision organs in Poland and Hungary primarily reviewed administrative measures that conflicted with statutes or national constitutions. As such, they acted to strengthen the authority of supreme legislatures and promote the implementation of central policies (Garlicki 1987; Brzezinski 1993). Kuss (1986) concludes that constitutional supervision organs in both countries eliminated bureaucratic obstacles to economic reforms.

Despite the modest legitimacy and governance dividends that a constitutional supervision committee might generate, Chinese leaders have repeatedly rejected proposals for such a committee. As discussed below, leaders shelved proposals for a constitutional supervision committee during the drafting of the 1982 Constitution. Over the following decade, the Party and the NPC considered proposals for a committee on multiple occasions (Cai 1995; Liu 2011). Reformers again proposed a constitutional supervision committee in discussions on drafts of the 2000 *Legislation Law* and the 2006 *People's Congress Standing Committee Supervision Law*, in both cases without success (Li Yahong 2000; *Southern Weekend* 2002).

In 2004, China did establish an NPCSC Filing and Review Office. The Filing and Review Office is a department within the NPCSC Legislative Affairs Commission that manages review of some legislation for consistency with the Constitution and law. It is only a work organ, however, and it does not exercise any formal authority to interpret the Constitution or annul conflicting legislation. It is hobbled by capacity deficits. Cai Dingjian (2007) concluded that the work of this office should not be considered formal 'constitutional review', and it is difficult to envision the office evolving into an authoritative constitutional supervision organ in the current system.

The recent amendment of the PRC *Legislation Law* provided an opportunity to change this dynamic and implement concrete reforms on constitutional supervision. The revised *Legislation Law* incorporates some internal filing and review procedures into national law and strengthens them in minor respects. For example, the law now explicitly references 'work organs' of the NPCSC and their role in analyzing legislative conflicts, provides that unresolved conflicts 'should' (rather than 'may') be referred to the NPCSC and states that review organs 'should' provide feedback to citizens who raise review proposals.[11] On paper, the amendments enhance the legal foundation for the Filing and Review Office's work and promote transparency.

However, the limited amendments also strongly suggest that Chinese leaders will not establish a constitutional supervision committee in the near future. The *Legislation Law* is the principal piece of national legislation that addresses review of the constitutionality and legality of legislation, and the NPC has amended the law only once since it was enacted in 2000. If Chinese leaders were prepared to create a constitutional supervision committee, it would be natural for them to provide for it in the *Legislation Law*. They chose not to do so.

Obstacles to a constitutional supervision committee

If a constitutional supervision committee would be consistent with China's socialist legal system, generate legitimacy dividends and promote governance goals without posing a threat to Party power, why would Chinese leaders decline to pursue this modest reform? This section discusses four interrelated factors that generate uncertainty and discourage action on a committee.

Precedent

Leadership judgments made early in the reform era are one obstacle. Beginning in late 1980, the Secretariat of the PRC Constitutional Amendment Committee engaged in a broad discussion of constitutional supervision mechanisms, including constitutional supervision committees, centralized constitutional courts, constitutional review by the people's courts and other mechanisms.[12] Discussions on constitutional review were percolating in the socialist world at this time, and the Secretariat clearly was aware of them. From February to July 1981, the Secretariat provided for a constitutional supervision committee in its amendment discussion drafts. However, the Secretariat suddenly dropped these proposals in August 1981. Although discussion of a constitutional supervision committee revived briefly in the fall of 1981 and again after draft constitutional amendments were circulated for public comment, the final version of the amendments retained NPC supervision and simply added the NPCSC as a supervisory organ.

A number of factors contributed to this outcome. First, participants could not reach consensus on whether a constitutional supervision committee should be equal in status to the NPCSC or subordinate to it (a debate that continues today). Second, as NPCSC Chairman Peng Zhen later explained, the development of constitutional supervision was closely connected to political system reform and could not be addressed until fundamental political questions were settled (Liu 2011). Most importantly, Deng Xiaoping and Hu Yaobang firmly opposed such a committee (Liu 2010). In this context, it was politically expedient to shelve consideration of a constitutional supervision committee and instead promote more effective supervision by adding constitutional supervision to the NPCSC's functions (Cai 1995).

The 1982 amendment process generated path-dependent effects with respect to constitutional supervision. A Chinese leader advocating for a constitutional supervision committee must be prepared to reverse Deng's apparent judgment that such a committee is not appropriate for China. While leadership thinking on this issue might have evolved had broader discussions on political reform in China progressed, domestic unrest in 1989 and the collapse of communist regimes in Europe derailed those discussions. In the wake of the stability challenges of the 2000s, Xi Jinping has renewed the Party's commitment to Deng's basic formula of economic liberalization, complementary legal reforms and Party political supremacy. In this context, Deng's early opposition to a constitutional supervision committee has particular salience.

Political sensitivity and capacity

The Party's sensitivity to even modest citizen constitutional claims has intensified over the past 15 years. In the late 1990s and early 2000s, Chinese leaders also emphasized the need for concrete constitutional enforcement mechanisms, and they undertook limited reforms related to constitutional review. For example, when the NPC adopted the *Legislation Law* in 2000, it gave citizens a concrete statutory right to submit proposals to the NPCSC for review of the constitutionality and legality of regulations. In 2001, the SPC authorized a provincial court to apply the Constitution as a source of law to decide a civil dispute (the *Qi Yuling* case). By the mid-2000s, the NPCSC had established the Filing and Review Office and revised internal procedures for review of legislation.

These and other reforms generated a wave of citizen constitutional activism. Chinese scholars argued for judicialization of the Constitution and raised numerous constitutional claims in the people's courts. Citizens filed hundreds of review proposals with the NPCSC and pressed for the development of what they considered to be an embryonic constitutional review mechanism. The apparent success of some of these efforts catalyzed the refinement of citizen rights defense strategies and new constitutional claims (Hand 2007, 2011). The wave of activism crested in 2008, when thousands of citizens signed a broad call for constitutional government called 'Charter 08'.

Chinese leaders viewed these developments as threats and acted to contain them. In the second half of the 2000s, the Party tightened control over political-legal institutions and prioritized political loyalty and stability maintenance over legal professionalism and process (Minzner 2011). It took specific steps to contain citizen constitutional argument. Courts reportedly were ordered not to take *Qi Yuling* as a precedent, and the SPC eventually repealed its *Qi Yuling* decision (Zhang 2011). Although the government responded indirectly to some constitutional review proposals, the NPCSC refrained from issuing public rulings on any of them, and some sensitive review proposals were suppressed. Party leaders identified rights defense lawyers as a threat and emphasized that China should not blindly copy Western constitutional models.

As Feng details in Chapter 3, many of these dynamics have intensified under Xi Jinping. While the Fourth Plenum Decision renewed the Party's commitment to legal professionalism and process in certain respects, it also strengthened emphasis on Party leadership as the defining principle of China's constitutional order. Chinese leaders have intensified repression of rights activists and tightened control over political-legal discourse. As Feng notes, *Party Document No. 9* identified discussion of Western constitutionalism and press freedom as ideological threats, and subsequent directives chilled discourse on constitutional governance in the education system and media. Calls for improved institutions and procedures to address constitutional issues have been met with rhetorical hostility and repression (Creemers 2014).

The creation of a constitutional supervision committee would run counter to these trends. First, it would encourage citizens to raise the types of politically sensitive claims that the Party seems determined to contain. Even the limited and largely ineffective reforms to the filing and review system in the early 2000s generated a wave of citizen constitutional activism that the Party found threatening. While the Party could control the operation of a constitutional supervision committee, the establishment of a committee would provide a new public platform for citizens to raise difficult constitutional questions. It might also invite arguments that a committee should be only an interim step toward an independent constitutional supervision organ with stronger powers.

Second, the creation of a constitutional supervision committee would elevate the role of a state institution in resolving constitutional issues. China's political culture emphasizes consultation and the unity of state organs under Party leadership. Consistent with these conventions, the NPCSC has refrained from issuing public decisions to forcibly annul conflicting legislation (Hand 2013). The issuance of public decisions on the constitutionality of legislation by a constitutional supervision committee would weaken the narrative of state organs working harmoniously under Party leadership. It would also diminish the Party's central role in mediating intrastate disputes. The creation of a constitutional supervision committee would signal that there is a new and important locus of constitutional decision making outside the Party.

Finally, Chinese leaders may be reluctant to create a specialized organ that would lack the political capacity to carry out its basic functions. Fundamental questions related to allocations of power among state organs and the tension between constitutional provisions on Party leadership and provisions on citizen rights and the Constitution's legal supremacy are the subjects of ongoing contention. Many citizen constitutional review proposals touch on these sensitive political questions in some way.[13] A committee might also face difficult questions about its authority to review Party documents. China's legislative organs simply do not have the political capacity to resolve these questions on their own. The establishment of an impotent supervision organ could generate citizen disenchantment and undermine Party legitimacy.

Association of constitutional committees with failed communist regimes

The failure of communist regimes that experimented with specialized constitutional supervision organs likely reinforces Party concern about the wisdom of establishing a committee. The Party has engaged in systematic study of the fall of the communist regimes in Europe. It draws lessons from its analysis of failed regimes to avoid their mistakes and proactively shape its own reform agenda (Shambaugh 2008). Xi Jinping has emphasized the importance of learning lessons from the Soviet collapse, combating 'peaceful evolution' and strengthening Party control of the state and military (Buckley 2013). A recent *Red Flag Manuscript* commentary explicitly connected these concerns to implementation of the Fourth Plenum Decision, arguing that as China proceeds with the next stage of legal development, it must avoid Gorbachev's mistake of relaxing party power through constitutional and legal reforms (Zhu 2015).

As discussed above, experience in socialist legal systems suggests that a constitutional supervision committee would not challenge one-party rule in China. Nonetheless, elements of this experience may create uncertainty for Chinese leaders. For example, the Soviet Constitutional Supervision Committee exhibited flashes of independence in several sensitive cases.[14] In one case, the Committee reviewed the constitutionality of provisions on the Soviet internal residence registration system. Like China's residence registration (*hukou*) system, the Soviet system was designed to prevent mass migration of peasants into cities and gave security agencies significant discretion to punish violators. In several decisions, the Committee found that provisions establishing the system violated fundamental rights enshrined in the USSR Constitution and international treaties.

In a second case, the Committee declared a Gorbachev presidential edict unconstitutional. The edict empowered the Soviet Council of Ministers to exercise jurisdiction over a growing wave of mass demonstrations in Moscow.[15] Gorbachev issued the edict because the Moscow municipal government refused to prohibit the demonstrations. To Gorbachev's displeasure, the Committee held that the edict was an unconstitutional exercise of executive authority and suspended it. As Middleton (1998) notes, the Committee demonstrated considerable political courage in striking down a normative act of the head of the state and the Communist Party.

Chinese leaders obsessed with the Soviet experience and lessons to be learned from the relaxation of party power there may be reluctant to consider an institutional model associated with Gorbachev's failed reforms. Moreover, while constitutional supervision organs in Eastern Europe did not challenge ruling parties, communist regimes in all of the countries that experimented with such reforms eventually collapsed. In contrast, none of the surviving communist regimes, including those in Vietnam, North Korea, Laos and Cuba, have established specialized constitutional supervision organs (Wise 2013; Chang *et al.* 2014). While causal relationships cannot be drawn between the establishment of specialized constitutional supervision organs and the collapse or survival of communist regimes elsewhere in the world, the association of this innovation with failed regimes gives Chinese leaders further cause for concern and delay.

Vietnam's recent rejection of a weak constitutional council may reinforce this stance. Vietnam's constitutional structure, development and discourse closely mirror China's (Sidel 2009). Over the past decade, Vietnamese scholars and officials engaged in an expansive discussion of constitutional supervision. When the Vietnamese government released draft constitutional amendments in March 2013, the draft amendments provided for the establishment of a Constitutional Council with advisory powers under the National Assembly. Bui (2014) argues that this concrete proposal was the product of rising rights consciousness and the Vietnamese Communist Party's (VCP) interest in promoting socialist rule of law by controlling corruption and ensuring the uniformity of legislation. He notes that while Vietnamese reformers pressed for an independent supervision organ with binding powers, they viewed the council as an interim step toward a future constitutional court.

Ultimately, the VCP rejected the proposal and retained the existing system of National Assembly constitutional supervision. Opponents feared that the creation of a Constitutional Council would encourage claims that would undermine public security. They also argued that such a reform would be incompatible with VCP leadership and the principle of the unity of state power (Bui 2014). The VCP's decision to reject the modest proposal for a Constitutional Council after years of careful study will not go unnoticed in Beijing, and it is likely to reinforce the reticence of Chinese leaders already disinclined to enact similar reforms in China.

The party's adaptive posture

Finally, Chinese leaders may fear that a constitutional supervision committee would constrain their governing flexibility. The Party attaches great importance to maintaining a flexible and adaptive posture to address governance challenges in a rapidly evolving political-legal environment. As Shambaugh (2008: 4) observes, 'the party finds itself coping with a constant cycle of reform–readjust–reform–readjust ... whereby each set of reforms triggers certain consequences (some expected, some unexpected) that in turn cause readjustment and further reforms'. Adaptations are shaped in part by consultative processes that help Chinese leaders assess public sentiment, identify governance problems and develop solutions (Dowdle 2002; He and Warren 2011). The Party's capacity to learn from practical experience and adapt has been a crucial source of its strength and resilience in the face of significant stability challenges (Nathan 2003; Shambaugh 2008; Heilmann and Perry 2013).

The Party's adaptive posture may limit its willingness to establish a constitutional supervision committee in two respects. First, to the extent Party attitudes are shaped by lessons drawn from failed communist regimes and the unintended consequences of earlier legal reforms, these lessons discourage action. Xi Jinping's apparent goal is to contain corruption and support new economic reforms by revisiting and modestly expanding on some of the legal reforms of the 1990s and early 2000s while containing perceived threats that the earlier reforms generated. In this respect, creating a new constitutional supervision organ poses unnecessary risks.

More importantly, a Party intent on maintaining an adaptive posture is well served by the existing system of NPCSC supervision. To domestic reformers and outsiders, this system appears dysfunctional because the NPCSC ignores many constitutional violations, never forcibly annuls lower-level legislation and fails to issue responses to citizen constitutional review proposals. But for Chinese leaders, this 'dysfunctional' system is useful because it provides an information channel and preserves discretion. Chinese leaders have responded indirectly to some citizen constitutional arguments on property rights, repatriation of rural migrants and discriminatory policies with modest reforms (Hand 2011). But they need not do so. The current system gives Chinese leaders the discretion to respond to claims when appropriate and useful, to suppress them when necessary and to ignore them when expedient. When they do respond, they have the flexibility to craft policy compromises that not only address constitutional arguments but also incorporate non-legal considerations such as stability maintenance, economic impacts and local political authority.

The recent decision to abolish the re-education through labor (RTL) system provides an example of these dynamics. For nearly two decades, citizens challenged the constitutionality and legality of the RTL system by filing constitutional review proposals with the NPCSC, raising arguments in court and issuing open letters (CECC 2012). RTL was an important stability maintenance tool, and these claims were ignored or suppressed. However, after Xi Jinping took the reins of the Party apparatus in 2012, Chinese leaders determined that RTL repeal was in their political interest. When they announced the reform, official media acknowledged RTL's constitutional infirmities and cast the decision as a step to protect constitutional rights (*Xinhua* 2013b).

The creation of a constitutional supervision committee could limit some of this governing flexibility. One way the Party maintains flexibility is by avoiding binding legal obligations and prioritizing informal dispute resolution (Heilmann and Perry 2013). While the Fourth Plenum's renewed emphasis on legal process suggests that the Party is refining this approach in certain respects, grappling with the sensitive political questions at the core of many constitutional claims requires maximum flexibility. A constitutional supervision committee that issues formal decisions through a public process would be forced to address difficult constitutional issues that the regime may prefer to shelve. Moreover, it is unlikely that a committee would interpret constitutional rights in an expansive fashion. Conservative decisions could trigger public disenchantment and shine a spotlight on the gap between the text of the Constitution and political reality. They could also establish precedents that could complicate policy changes when and if political conditions make changes desirable, as was the case with RTL.

Conclusion

A conservative Party leadership determined to maintain flexibility and minimize political risk is likely to conclude that the safer choice on constitutional supervision is to maintain the status quo. Experience in the socialist world demonstrates that it is possible to create constitutional supervision organs that uphold the supremacy of people's legislatures and operate in a manner consistent with ruling party interests. However, the modest benefits of establishing a constitutional supervision committee in China could be discounted in several respects. While a specialized committee could help to address issues of organizational capacity that have hampered NPCSC efforts to address legislative conflicts, it would not resolve basic problems of political capacity. Moreover, legitimacy dividends could turn to deficits if a committee failed to carry out its basic functions. On the other side of the equation, leadership precedents, lessons derived from earlier stages of political-legal reform and the collapse of other communist regimes, current political messaging and the Party's governance posture all weigh against moving forward with this reform.

This assessment brings the contours of China's deepening socialist rule of law into sharper relief. Over the past two decades, citizens have used constitutional argument and legal mechanisms to pressure the Party and promote constitutional interpretations that incorporate some constraints on Party power. The Fourth Plenum Decision itself can be viewed as a constitutional interpretation intended to stifle such citizen efforts and emphasize that Party leadership is the core of the socialist rule of law state. While the legal system may be a useful tool to discipline lower levels of the bureaucracy, ensure the implementation of economic policy and protect rights within limits, the Party, not the NPC or its sub-units, is the final arbiter of the fundamental political questions implicit in most constitutional claims. The Party may fear that even the modest step of establishing a weak constitutional supervision committee could generate ideological confusion.

In closing, it is notable that one of the principal arguments advanced by proponents of a constitutional supervision committee in the early 1980s was that China needed a specialized organ to prevent a repeat of the constitutional violations of the late Mao era. This history resonates in the current political-legal environment. As the Party has emphasized its supremacy in China's constitutional order, Xi Jinping has asserted his dominance over the Party. Many observers believe that Xi has emerged as China's most powerful leader since Deng Xiaoping and possibly Mao himself. As Feng (Chapter 3) suggests, current ideological campaigns are raising uncomfortable memories of the Mao era. A Party decision to create a constitutional supervision committee would be a symbolic step that could reassure observers both inside and outside China about Xi's governance intentions. Conversely, continued reticence will reinforce anxiety about those intentions. More than three decades after the adoption of the 1982 Constitution, the fate of constitutional supervision in China still appears to be tied to political system reform that seems as distant as ever.

Notes

1 Constitutional supervision in China includes constitutional review of legislation, review of the unconstitutional acts of state leaders and the resolution of jurisdictional disputes among state organs (Cai 1995).
2 Jiang Shigong (2013) argues that constitutional adjudication would amount to a 'constitutional revolution'.
3 For core features of Soviet legal theory, see Butler (1988) and Ludwikowski (1991).
4 Yugoslavia established a federal constitutional court. The Yugoslav experiment was a product of its federal system (Garlicki 1987). It is not assessed here.
5 For the operation of the Soviet Constitutional Supervision Committee, see Maggs (1991), Hausmaninger (1992), Blankenagel (1992) and Middleton (1998).
6 USSR *Law on Constitutional Supervision*, adopted December 23, 1989, Arts 24, 25, translated in W.E. Butler (1991: 185–94).
7 Ibid., Art. 12.
8 Ibid., Art. 21.
9 Ji argues that after political reform, China should establish a constitutional court with binding review powers.
10 *Zhonghua Renmin Gongheguo Xianfa* [PRC *Constitution*], adopted December 4, 1982, last amended March 14, 2004, Art. 5, at www.gov.cn/gongbao/content/2004/content_62714.htm, and *Zhongguo Gongchandang Dangcheng* [CPC *Charter*], amended November 14, 2012, General Program, at http://news.xinhuanet.com/18cpcnc/2012-11/18/c_113714762.htm.
11 *Zhonghua Renmin Gongheguo Lifa Fa* [PRC *Legislation Law*], adopted March 15, 2000, amended March 15, 2015, Arts 99–101, at http://news.xinhuanet.com/politics/2015lh/2015-03/18/c_1114682142.htm.

12 Liu Songshan's (2010, 2011) excellent accounts of these debates draw on archival sources and the constitutional histories of key participants. Cai's (1995) discussion is also notable.
13 Huang (2010). My own review of more than 120 citizen review proposals reinforces this point.
14 For accounts of these cases, see Maggs (1991), Hausmaninger (1992) and Middleton (1998).
15 Chinese commentators cite unrest in Moscow as an example of the dangerous dynamics that late Soviet reforms generated (Zhu 2015).

3 China's socialist rule of law

A critical appraisal of the relationship between the Communist Party and comprehensive law reform

Chongyi Feng

Introduction

China's socialist rule of law is examined in this chapter in the context of the comprehensive deepening of reforms undertaken by the leadership of Xi Jinping. Both theoretical and empirical perspectives are used, with special attention paid to two key and seemingly contradictory Party documents about political direction, on the one hand, and the deepening legal reforms, on the other. The first is the 'Communiqué on the Current State of the Ideological Sphere'. Issued by the General Office of the Communist Party of China (CPC) Central Committee (April 2013), the Party is urged to 'guard against Western liberal-democratic ideals'.[1] The second is the 'Decision on Some Major Issues in the Comprehensive Promotion of Ruling the Country According to Law'.[2] This was the first-ever plenary session devoted to legal issues, laying out the scope and guidelines for legal reform (CPC Central Committee 2014). These pivotal documents are set against the backdrop of major ideological and political trends in the Party-state. Some 'market reforms' are tolerated, yet other liberal reforms such as freedom of expression, freedom of assembly, free speech and so on are repressed. The chapter identifies the principal institutional and ideological gaps preventing the Party from embracing an independent and impartial rule of law.

The Fourth Plenum *Decision*: a dashed hope for a rule of law breakthrough?

The United Nations (2004) states that 'rule of law' in the contemporary world consists of three key principles: (1) the supremacy of law, with all persons, entities and institutions, including the State, being accountable to publicly promulgated laws; (2) equality before the law, with laws being equally enforced and independently adjudicated; and (3) consistency with international human rights norms and standards. This view of rule of law is concerned not only with judicial procedures and other formal legal aspects, but also with the substantive contents of law. Rule of law in this sense is not narrowly confined to judicial issues, but is concerned with the fundamental issues related to the interrelations of law, politics and the broader social system.

The CPC leadership has viewed law as essential to Party ideology since the beginning of the reform era, the late 1970s, not least because the rule of man (人治) and lawlessness (无法无天) were identified as key factors contributing to the catastrophic ten years of the Cultural Revolution. In 1997, the political report delivered by Jiang Zemin to the Fifteenth National Congress of the CPC 'established *socialist rule of law* as a state objective'. In 1999, 'ruling the country according to law and establishing a socialist rule of law state' was inscribed as an amendment to the PRC's Constitution. Since the 1990s, and for the first time in Chinese history, the legal discourse in China has clearly distinguished the rule of law (法治), whereby rulers are subject to and limited by law for justice and the protection of human rights, from rule by law (法制), where law is an instrumental 'tool', a stick to control the population by rulers who monopolize institutional power, and from rule of man. It has been convincingly argued in legal theories over time that rule of law and rule by law occupy a single continuum. But they are distinguishable concepts. They are distinguished not by the inherent nature of law, but by the power-system in which laws respond and the power-structure through which institutional power is distributed among social groups. Holmes (2003) makes the general argument that an autocracy exists where one political force monopolizes institutional power and this entails rule *by* law rather than rule *of* law. This chapter argues that Holmes' general description applies to contemporary China.

The 'Decision on Some Major Issues in the Comprehensive Promotion of Ruling the Country According to Law'

The *Decision* pooled many proposals that had been forwarded in recent years for specific legal reforms and general improvements to rule of law. Three particularly salient reforms in the package are: (1) to reduce interventions in court decisions by local Party and government officials (see Qianfan Zhang in Chapter 1); (2) the emphasis on legal professionalism; and (3) measures to protect the rights of citizens and defendants.

The package targeting local protectionism and intervention of local officials is part of the anti-corruption drive to address common mistrust of the Party-state–legal system nexus. To prevent improper interference in court cases by officials, the *Decision* calls for the establishment of 'a system for recording, reporting and investigating the responsibility of instances wherein leading cadres interfere in judicial activities or get involved in the handling of certain cases … [and] the establishment of "circuit courts" operating across jurisdictions'.

In theory, these reforms aim to make courts less dependent on local political authorities at the same administrative level. At the same time, they attempt to curb local protectionism which is often applied at the expense of justice.

Reiteration of legal professionalism in the *Decision* represents a policy change that appears to reverse what liberal reformers have called a 'retrogression' in recent years. For example, in the 1950s the CPC had established a practice of turning ex-servicemen into police, procurators and judges – even though they had no prior legal training. This situation was changed after the 1980s when the threshold was raised for legal personnel, requiring them to have some legal training – ideally at the tertiary education level. Senior positions, such as judges of higher courts, required sufficient legal qualifications and experience. Since the late 1990s, however, the appointment of ex-servicemen and other unqualified personnel as procurators and judges has staged a comeback. As Minzner (2011: 935) puts it, this sees 'political loyalty being put above professional competence'. The *Decision*'s stress on professional qualifications and legal expertise, and the establishment of 'gradual selection and progression systems for judges and prosecutors', appears to signal a move towards legal professionalism.

The measures in the *Decision* to protect legal rights of citizens and defendants also warrants particular attention as the presumption of innocence is a new and fragile principle in China. Some authorities do not, at this stage, regard it as a principle at all. A common practice gives extensive power to the police, procurators and Party disciplinary personnel authorized to detain and interrogate citizens without legal representation. This process has often, in the past, been accompanied by torture and blackmail (Ho 2012: 211–12). Guilty verdicts have frequently been decided even before the case has been to court! Of the 1.16 million people put on trial in 2013, Chinese courts returned a guilty verdict for all but 825. This represents a 99.93 per cent conviction rate.[3] Wang Cailiang, director of Beijing's Cailiang Law Firm, referred to 2013 as 'the darkest year in the history of China's rule of law' (cited in McCoy 2014). Indeed, between 2008 and mid-2013, nearly 150,000 were investigated for corruption alone and the acquittal rate for those charged was less than 0.1 per cent.

Decision guidelines, however, pledge to 'promote structural reform in litigation, placing trials at the centre'. Facts and admissible evidence related to cases under investigation, examination and prosecution must 'stand the test of law'. Such guidelines seek to protect the innocent from punishment in cases where there is insufficient evidence or reasonable doubt. The exclusion of illegal evidence such as 'confessions extracted through torture' is welcomed by jurists domestically and internationally. However, the *Decision* does not establish the supremacy of law; rather it insists on the 'leading role' of the CPC. This is enshrined as the number one principle in carrying out 'rule of law' in China.

The *Decision* declares the supremacy of the Party as the defining feature of 'rule of law with Chinese characteristics' in three ways. First, it states that 'the leadership of the Party is the most essential trait of socialism with Chinese characteristics and the most fundamental guarantee of socialist rule of law'. Second, the *Decision* allows the Party leadership to 'penetrate the entire process and all aspects of ruling the country, with the socialist rule of law being a central element'. Third, the *Decision* insists that Party leadership is basic to socialist rule of law. That is, this is where the

> foundations and the life-line of the Party and the State lie; the interests and happiness of the people of all ethnicities in the entire country are tied to it, and it is a proper element of moving the country according to the law forward.

The concern here is that the authority of the Party is placed above the law despite the *Decision* asserting repeatedly that 'Party leadership and socialist rule of law are *identical*'. It adds that 'socialist rule of law must persist in Party leadership, Party leadership must rely on socialist rule of law'. The *Decision* crystallizes the Party's instrumental take on rule by law in that it is to serve its interests 'in implementing Party leadership over the country and society through State political bodies'. In this view, the role of law must be good at utilizing democratic centralist principles 'to safeguard the authority of the Centre, the unity of the entire Party and the entire country'. Ultimately, it follows that what the *Decision* really means is socialist rule of law with Chinese characteristics equates to 'rule of the Party, legitimized by law'.

The Party does not accept professional recommendations or popular demand for abolishing, or even reforming, its widely denounced CPC Political-legal Committees. The CPC regards legal issues as political in nature. In this sense, Political-legal Committees, at both central and local levels, are required to oversee China's entire government branch of law enforcement. This includes the domestic security apparatus and courts. The Committees enable the Party to take over these functions of government on any matter perceived to be 'sensitive'. According to Zheng (1997: ch. 1), this merely thwarts normal state-building in China.[4] This institutional device gives the Party committee political and institutional control over the judicial apparatus, as well as the nomenclature through which all cadres (including judges) are appointed and managed by the Party (党管干部). Judicial independence is thus compromised. Handling legal cases according to legal principles and the integrity of the law – without prioritizing the interests of the Party – is out of the question. Since the early 2000s there have been growing calls in both the legal profession and among the general public for Political-legal Committees to be abolished. This is especially so since Zhou Yongkang, China's former 'security tsar', was brought down early in 2015 on charges of corruption, abuse of power and leaking state secrets. His political power had been based on his positions as Secretary of the Central Political-legal Committee and member of the Standing Committee of the Politburo. In answering this particular call for change, however, the *Decision* has actually strengthened the Party's control over law and legal institutions. It reaffirms that 'political-legal committees are the organizational form through which Party committees lead political-legal work. This is to be maintained for the long term', appearing to rule out legal institutions acting impartially and independently of the Party leadership any time soon.

The *Decision* reiterates that the country is to be 'governed according to the constitution' (see Hand in Chapter 2). This is a narrative intended to generate strong associations with constitutional rule, implying China has a spirit of constitutionalism. However, the current Chinese Constitution does not clearly define state–society relations or central–local relations. Nor does it define the functions of the different branches of government, or stipulate constitutional remedies for its own violation. Rather than providing institutional limits on the untrammelled exercise of power, it is more typical of a Stalin-era constitution. A Stalinist constitution guarantees monopoly power of the ruling communist party. Essentially, it renders individual human rights meaningless. 'Rights' are conceived collectively and this Stalinist principle is repeated in the *Decision*. As it now stands, the current Chinese Constitution is one of just two constitutions in the world that contains the expression 'dictatorship of the proletariat' (Cao 2005). The other is North Korea. This classic communist definition comes from Lenin (1972), who held that 'dictatorship' means nothing other than power unlimited by any laws and based directly on the use of violence. Indeed, Mao (1938: 224) famously held that 'every communist must grasp the truth; political power grows out of the barrel of a gun'.[5] If the Chinese leadership chooses to use a hard-line Maoist-Leninist interpretation of the preamble to the Chinese Constitution – about 'the people's democratic dictatorship' and 'the leadership of the Communist Party' – there are no institutional impediments as to how that interpretation may be applied.

The reason this preamble clause remains a concern is the above interpretation is actively used in practice. For instance, under Xi's leadership China has witnessed systematic deprivation of legal rights and suppression of dissenting groups such as rights lawyers, liberal intellectuals, Internet advocates and, most recently, women's rights activists. The criminal detention of human rights activists rose from 80 in 2012 to 233 in 2013 and then 442 in 2014.[6] The administrative detention of human rights activists rose from 137 in 2012 to 224 in 2013 and 358 in 2014. In 2014, 11 rights lawyers were detained or imprisoned for 'political crime', including Pu Zhiqiang and Xu Zhiyang (Li and McKenzie 2014). Many liberal intellectuals and high-profile NGO leaders previously tolerated by the security apparatus are no longer tolerated. For example, 70-year-old journalist, Gao Yu, 81-year-old writer, Tie Liu, and Transition Institute for Social Economic founder, Guo Yushan, were all recently detained on the spurious charges of, respectively, 'leaking state secrets' (accused of sending *Document No. 9* to an overseas website), 'picking quarrels and provoking troubles' and 'illegal business activity' (Chinese Human Rights Defenders 2015). Moderate Uyghur economics scholar, Ilham Tohti, was sentenced to life in prison after being charged with 'separatism' (Freedom House 2015). The comprehensive assault on Internet activists and online opinion leaders, in the name of strengthening China's 'Internet sovereignty', has also been ruthless. In February 2014, Xi established the 'Central Internet and Informatization Leading Group', with himself as head and the prime minister and propaganda chief as deputy heads. The Xi leadership has not only removed content deemed as 'political dissent' from Weibo (a Chinese equivalent of Twitter), it has shut down Virtual Private Networks that had been used by Chinese netizens for accessing information blocked by Chinese authorities (i.e. the Great Fire Wall). This has been extended to blocking overseas Chinese websites and international web services such as Google, Facebook and Twitter. By silencing public intellectuals, NGO leaders, critical journalists, Internet opinion leaders and other rights activists, the Xi leadership characterizes itself by stifling the embryonic, but vibrant, civil society that had emerged as the Party-state withdrew from some areas of the public sphere.

Xi's approach to rule of law is further reflected in the ongoing anti-corruption campaign. Rather than using state legal institutions and formal legal processes to deal with economic crimes, Xi continues to rely on the extrajudicial mechanism of '*shuanggui*' (双规) run by the Party's 'Central Commission for Discipline Inspection'. The Commission operates at central and local levels to purge corrupt elements. However, in resorting to *shuanggui*, the Commission and its lower-level counterparts can exercise power without legal restraint. This includes the power to detain suspects without due legal process, and put relatives or other associates of suspects under round-the-clock surveillance. The Commission can tap telephone conversations, access personal files held by any institution, summons anyone to give evidence and, in certain circumstances, use torture and blackmail in interrogation. Indeed, 'discipline inspection' can be very effective in taking down corrupt officials, including senior officials in the domestic security apparatus and People's Liberation Army. As the earlier statistics show, criminal prosecutions rarely fail. The argument for *shuanggui* is that corruption in such powerful state-owned enterprises and state regulators requires commensurate power to overcome it. But this is a shallow argument as the extrajudicial power has the negative side effect of damaging legal institutions, including the central tenets of rule of law. No legal or procedural assurances are provided that protect the rights of suspects and prevent the abuse of power. At the heart of these concerns is that *selective* law enforcement can result in the persecution of political rivals rather than punish criminals. Indeed, the anti-corruption campaign has been accompanied by a crackdown on independent activists, such as lawyers seeking a system of asset disclosure by public officials and a measure of judicial independence in line with standards in virtually all developed countries.

The words and deeds of the Xi leadership thus far have strengthened the 'system of stability preservation' (维稳体制). The 'system of stability preservation' has taken shape in China against a backdrop of communist Party-states losing their ideology-based legitimacy, including the collapse of communist regimes in Eastern and Central Europe. This system consists of measures to preserve the CPC regime 'in the name of maintaining social stability' (Feng 2013: 21). The thesis of the Chinese government is that China can succeed in economic development *only* under conditions of stability and *only* the one-party rule of the CPC can ensure stability. Guided by militant slogans such as 'stability overrides everything' and 'nipping every element of instability in the bud', *stability preservation* extends the authority of the Party-state organs over the security and propaganda apparatuses in particular. These are central to 'preserving stability' and do so by suppressing grievances and dissent, legally or otherwise. Previous administrations have relied on extra-legal measures such as the administrative punishment regime 're-education through labor', 'black jails' to detain petitioners, the detention and interrogation system of *shuanggui*, and comprehensive media censorship. Despite some procedural improvements (see Chen in Chapter 6), what is new is that while most extra-legal practices are continued, the current crackdown on political and ideological dissent is presented as occurring through formal legal processes.

Document No. 9: back to a totalitarian framework or merely a regression?

Document No. 9 refers to the 'Communiqué on the Current State of the Ideological Sphere', an internal document circulated within the Party by the General Office of the Central Committee in April 2013. The Communiqué criticizes neoliberalism for overstating the role of the free market and downplaying the role of regulation and central government oversight. It questions whether 'opening up' and 'going out' reforms have gone too far and warns that Western anti-China forces and domestic dissidents are trying to 'split the nation' by fostering the type of color revolutions that led to the overthrow of authoritarian regimes in the former Soviet Republics.[7] *Document No. 9* and Xi's more recent speeches about ideological dangers theoretically locate 'socialist rule of law with Chinese characteristics' as primarily political and ideological. It directly relates to a strategy for regime survival. Viewed from this perspective, the economic and legal development reforms, and recent repressive measures taken under the guise of maintaining 'social harmony', are designed to strengthen communist rule in China.

When Xi commenced as General Secretary of the CPC in November 2012, he signalled his determination to strengthen the entire Party's 'communist faith', as well as 'self-confidence about the path, the theory and the system'.[8] It was in the context of Xi's speeches and instructions that the Central Office of the CPC Central Committee, headed by Xi's confidante, Li Zhanshu, issued the now infamous *Document No. 9* to guide the ideological and propaganda work of the Party.

Document No. 9 refers to the 'acute struggle in the ideological sphere', identifying eight ideological dangers posing serious threats to the survival of the communist regime, as follows:

- propagating Western constitutionalist democracy, with an attempt to reject the present leadership of the Party and to negate the political system of socialism with Chinese characteristics;
- propagating 'universal values', with an attempt to shake the ideological and theoretical basis for Party rule;
- propagating civil society, with an attempt to deconstruct the social basis for Party rule;
- propagating neoliberalism, with an attempt to change our country's basic economic system;
- propagating the Western concept of press freedom and challenging our country's principle and system that the Party manages the media;
- propagating historical nihilism, with an attempt to deny the history of the Chinese Communist Party and the history of the New China;
- challenging reform and opening up; and
- challenging the socialist nature of socialism with Chinese characteristics.

The above narrative about 'propagating threats and challenges' is based on an assessment that Western anti-China forces and domestic dissidents 'incessantly carry out infiltration activities in the People's Republic, and that Western anti-China forces pressuring us to change will not change'. *Document No. 9* says the 'spearhead of Westernization, separation and "color revolutions" is pointed at us always'. Such a vitriolic, almost paranoid narrative is an attempt to legitimize the tasks *Document No. 9* sets for the entire Party:

> To strengthen its leadership over ideological work at all levels. It is intended to guide Party members and cadres in clearly distinguishing theoretical right and wrong and forbidding opinions that violate the Party's theory, discourses that violate the Party Centre's decisions, and discourses that vilify the image of the Party and the State; to persist unwaveringly in the principle that the Party manages the media; and to realistically strengthen management of the ideological battlefield, to ensure that everyone is responsible to protect the territory, and everyone fulfils their responsibility to protect the territory, strengthening online public opinion guidance, and cleaning up the online public opinion environment.
>
> (General Office of the CPC Central Committee April 2013)

The themes of *Document No. 9* have been repeated many times in Xi's 2013 speeches. For instance, his June 2013 speech at the 'Organizational Work' (组织工作) conference reiterates:

> Firm faith and beliefs are the number one criterion for a good cadre. Anyone without firm faith and beliefs in Marxism and socialism with Chinese characteristics, no matter how strong in terms of ability, is politically disqualified and not needed by the Party, as this kind of cadre will not be able to stand the test of hardships.
>
> (Xi 2013b)

He added that:

> A good cadre has the spiritual strength of revolutionary faith higher than the heaven, whereas those cadres sceptical of communism dare not sheathe sword when facing major matters of principle, such as the leadership position of the Party or socialist system is under threat.
>
> (Xi 2013b)

His August 2013 speech at the national conference on 'Propaganda and Ideological Work' details instructions to the Party in more militant language. 'Propaganda and ideological work' was stated to be extremely important work of the Party with more specific tasks identified as follows:

> Daring to sheathe sword; launching a public opinion struggle to set a clear line between right and wrong; forbidding any space in newspapers, journals, lectures, forums, conferences, films, televisions, radios and theatres for

> discourse that attacks the leadership position of the Party and socialist system, distorts the history of the Party and our country, spread rumours and provoke controversies; blocking this kind of discourse on new media such as online newspapers and journals, websites, mobile phones messaging, WeChat, blogs, and Weibo; punishing by law anyone who dares to stir up troubles; taking the Internet as the principal battlefield and winning the public opinion war which is of vital importance to ideology security and regime security; resolutely resisting change in public opinion guidance by the Party; integrating propaganda and ideology work closely with administrative management and social management; and strengthening the battlefield consciousness in propaganda and ideology to defend ideological territory with strongest sense of mission and upmost efforts.
>
> (Xi 2013c)

Xi's orders have been strictly carried out by the Party since then with a principal focus on the Internet and universities. These were identified by the Party as *the* two most vulnerable links for ideological infiltration by hostile forces at home and abroad. Blogs and micro blogs have been hardest hit. The nationwide 'Internet Cleaning-up Campaign' (净网行动) has resulted in dissenting blogs being shut down and postings blocked or deleted.

In the second half of 2013, a protracted crackdown was directed against online celebrities and opinion leaders who had become known as 'Big Vs' (i.e. verified celebrity, or VIP users). Many were removed from the Internet. For example, venture capitalist and prominent social-media commentator Charles Xue, who had 12 million followers, was spuriously charged with engaging a prostitute. In an act of 'killing the chicken to frighten the monkeys', on 15 September 2013 he was paraded on national TV in a prison vest and handcuffs to confess his crimes. In tactics reminiscent of Cultural Revolution 'struggle sessions', his confession focused specifically on the dangers of 'spreading irresponsible posts online and violating the law' rather than the actual charges made against him (Patience 2013). Also in September 2013, the Supreme Court and the Supreme Procuratorate jointly issued new regulations imposing jail sentences for the publication of 'harmful information' which was reposted more than 500 times.

Showcasing the seriousness of the new rule, the state's media outlets widely reported the case of a 16-year-old middle school student detained on the charge of 'posting a false message'. His message had simply been reposted more than 500 times. Moore (2014) subsequently found 'the number of posts on the hugely successful Twitter-like microblog fell by as much as 70 per cent in the wake of the aggressive campaign to intimidate influential users'. Moore adds that 'a once incalculably important public space for news and opinion – the country's most free-flowing river of information that censors struggled to contain – had been reduced to a wasteland of celebrity endorsements, government propaganda and corporate jingles' (2014). The coordinated crackdown has denied the 'Big Vs' and other opinion leaders any media agenda-setting influence, and Weibo as a forum for political debate and source of information. This has caused an exodus of users towards WeChat, which is a more private communication forum.

Tightening control over the tertiary education sector also started in the second half of 2013, escalating in 2014. One month after the internal circulation of *Document No. 9*, the CPC Central Organization Department, the CPC Central Propaganda Department and the Ministry of Education jointly issued a circular identifying 16 ways to strengthen the ideological and political education of young academics in universities.[9] Chillingly similar to Mao-style ideological and political campaigns of the 1960s, the circular accused some universities of being 'incubators of anti-Party thought' and published this in state media. This was followed by a ban on advocacy of constitutional governance (宪政) and the dismissal of some outspoken scholars, for example, Beijing University professor Xia Yeliang, China University of Politics and Law lecturer Teng Biao, and East China University of Politics and Law lecturer Zhang Xuezhong.

In October 2014, Xi (2014a) encouraged campus Party committees to 'sharpen ideological controls and purge antiparty elements, [and] never allow eating the Communist Party's food and then smashing the Communist Party's cooking pots'. In December 2014, the Party Centre convened a work conference on 'Party-building in Higher Education', at which Xi (2014b) urged universities to 'enhance guidance over thinking and keep a tight grip on leading ideological work in higher education'. Following Xi's instructions, the General Office of the CPC Central Committee and General Office of the State Council, issued a joint decree to guide the ideological battle in higher education institutions. It states that higher education propaganda and ideology work is 'an urgent strategic task of, the management of the higher education propaganda and ideology battlefield to strengthen Party leadership over higher education propaganda and ideology work and insert the Party ideology into textbooks, classrooms and minds' (General Office of the CPC Central Committee and the General Office of the State Council 2015).

In the weeks that followed this decree, many tertiary education sector administrators published pledges of allegiance to the Party in various state media outlets. China's education minister, Yuan Guiren, went so far as to demand 'universities and colleges [should] never let textbooks promoting western values appear in our classes' (Xinhua News Agency 2015a).

The ideological campaign launched by Xi reflects CPC ideology. The current generation of the CPC leadership, brought up in Mao's era and joining the communist bureaucracy under the post-totalitarian, reform-era regime, have had their worldviews framed by an amalgam of Marxism–Leninism–Mao Zedong Thought (Feng 2011). Even through the opening-up period of 'market socialism', the CPC has systematically used education, mass media, mass campaigns and other means to indoctrinate the population through its discourse on truth: that is, that laws governing human society, and the trajectory of Chinese history, legitimize the mission of the CPC, with the Party as the embodiment of Marxism–Leninism–Mao Zedong Thought, the highest form of truth and knowledge.

This meta-narrative holds that the Chinese, with their unique civilization and 5,000-year history, have been humiliated by Western powers for more than a century. The theory is that only under the leadership of the CPC can the Chinese nation stand up to Western hegemony, maintain unity and stability, pursue China's modernization *and* ensure economic prosperity. Constitutional democracy in this discourse is presented as an institutionalization of regular elections, independent judiciary and political and civil rights – features that are merely bourgeois affectations. It is only the 'proletarian dictatorship' (or 'people's democratic dictatorship') under the leadership of the Party that is 'genuine' democracy. In this ideology, the Party represents the interest of the people and serves the people, and *Document No. 9* reflects precisely this ideology in the contemporary era.

Under conditions of market socialism since 1978 and especially in the 1990s, tremendous efforts have been made to emphasize patriotism and the theory of 'building socialism with Chinese characteristics' while obscuring the tenets of Marxism–Leninism–Mao Zedong Thought on the themes of class struggle and communist ideals. With the collapse of communist regimes around the world and consequent loss of ideological credibility, the CPC faced a serious crisis of legitimacy and uncertainty as to direction. The upgrading of patriotic education, in association with rapid economic development, provided the new 'performance legitimacy' to one-party rule. Performance legitimacy was embodied in the 'Theory of Three Represents', the 'Concept of Scientific Development' and the 'Patriotic Education Campaign'. These theoretical innovations were a response to a new global reality. The class-struggle narrative targeting *domestic* people's enemies (exploiting classes) gave way to a patriotic narrative targeting *foreign* 'hostile forces'. Again, the emphasis of that legitimizing narrative is reflected in *Document No. 9*.

Xi's reign has clearly tightened social and political controls and renewed political indoctrination, moral purification and ideological struggle. Xi's rhetoric of the 'China Dream' promises a stronger and wealthier China at the CPC's 100th anniversary in 2021 and 100th anniversary of the PRC in 2049. The so-called China Dream echoes a nationalistic theme of state ideology. In *Document No. 9*, however, Xi's attack on any hopes for a constitutional democracy, civil society and universal rights represents a retrogression and perhaps worse. In terms of China's long march towards rule of law, it is concerning that Xi warns that *the* 'political and legal battlefront' (政法战线) is to ensure 'the handle of the knife' (刀把子) is firmly in the hands of the Party and the people' (Xinhua News Agency 2015b). Xi's use of this Maoist metaphor in particular follows a tradition from Lenin to Stalin to Mao that places the police, procuratorate and courts (公检法) as 'dictatorship organs' (专政机关), with the authority to suppress political dissent – as if it were a crime. Upholding justice is thus reinscribed.

Public thinking in China has come a long way since 1976. Now there is an embrace of much of the liberal concept of the state with regard to public institutions, such as the judiciary, as based on 'social contract theory'.[10] The CPC leadership currently adopts some aspects of a capitalist market economy, but it has not abandoned the state theory of Marxism–Leninism.[11] Historically, communist rulers have always used law as an administrative tool. Even in the most chaotic part of the Cultural Revolution, widely characterized as absolutely lawless, it was in fact governed by very cruel laws issued on 13 January 1967: the *Regulation for Strengthening Public Security during the Proletarian Culture Revolution.* Those Regulations influenced the work of the criminal judicature during that period (CPC Centre and State Council 1996). Commonly known as the 'Six Articles for Public Security' (公安六条), this notorious law provided the legal foundation to persecute and victimize millions of innocent citizens. This systematic persecution showed what can happen when the law functions primarily as a tool or weapon to arbitrarily suppress social activism and civil dissent. Many may argue that this simply could not happen again. But there is no clear impediment to stop it at this stage of China's development.

Conclusion

The CPC's current law reform agenda serves three main purposes. First, to enhance the power of the Party, indicated by *Document No. 9* and the overarching principle of 'Party leadership' in the *Decision.* The *Decision* guarantees the Party power to control legal procedure and outcomes of cases deemed to have 'political significance'. Measures to exercise greater central control over local courts also concentrate power in the Party Centre. Second, to boost economic growth by instilling greater public faith in China's legal system and facilitating better legal protection for the socialist market economy's operations. Third, to improve the image of the Party with the masses by countering local protectionism, reducing corruption of the court system at grass-roots level and upholding justice in ordinary legal proceedings that do not have overt political implications. The CPC views one-party autocracy as *the* defining feature of socialism. The authority of the Constitution and law are essentially subject to the authority of the Party. The Party narrative on law reform is primarily to reinforce the legitimacy of the current political system. Just as 'Socialism with Chinese characteristics' means communist autocracy with Chinese characteristics, 'rule of law with Chinese characteristics' means rule by law under the CPC.

Xi Jinping has carried forward the legacy of predecessors Jiang Zemin and Hu Jintao in maintaining the 'System of Stability Preservation'. The CPC leadership is driven by the 'political imperative of pursuing regime survival at the expense of any other concern, including rule of law' (Feng 2013: 121). While tapping into new sources of wealth and power, the broader pursuit of reform is being largely confined by a Leninist framework. The conflation of the anti-corruption campaign and suppression of dissent to eliminate political opposition is designed to discipline followers and mobilize mass support for the Party. These manoeuvres can be readily viewed as part of an 'end game' for the CPC to retain power.[12] Legal and extra-legal tools are interlocked and there are no institutions to adequately check the authority of the Communist Party in how these tools are used. Xi (2014c) defends CPC domination by exhorting comrades to justify the permanent leadership of the Party, 'boldly and assertively ... with flying banners and beating drums'. Along with *Document No. 9*, an environment is created whereby political and legal development in China is circumscribed by a rejection of universal values related to rights and other freedoms in favour of the overarching authority of the Party-state. In this context, the fruits of world civilization will remain in the higher branches, perhaps out of reach of this socialist construction of 'rule of law'.

Notes

1 An English translation is at: www.chinafile.com/document-9-chinafile-translation.

2 This was promulgated by the Fourth Plenum of the Eighteenth Central Committee of the CPC in October 2014.

3 See McCoy (2014). McCoy cites the report of Zhou Qiang, head of the Supreme People's Court, delivered to the National People's Congress in March 2014 admitting that 'rulings in some cases were not fair ... which harmed the interests of the litigants and undermined the credibility of the law'. The pronouncement taps into a wider debate occurring inside China over the future of the PRC's judicial branch, historically marred by corruption and political infighting. Shen Deyong, the executive vice-president of the Supreme People's Court, wrote in the *People's Court Daily* (2013) that 'it's preferable to release someone wrongfully, than convict someone wrongfully. If a true criminal is released, heaven will not collapse, but if an unlucky citizen is wrongfully convicted, heaven will fall' (as cited in the *South China Morning Post* 2013).

4 In exploring the tensions between the CPC and Chinese state institutions, Zheng (1997) takes a neo-institutionalist approach in suggesting the Party faces an institutional dilemma: 'It cannot live with the state, and it cannot live without the state.' For Zheng, it is not only conceptually constructive, but analytically imperative to distinguish the Chinese state from the Communist Party (see Chapter 1).

5 See Mao Zedong (1938). What Mao then went on to say was that 'our principle is that the Party commands the gun, and the gun must never be allowed to command the Party' (1938).

6 Murray (2015). Murray further reports that China detained 955 human rights activists in 2014, almost as many as the previous two years combined, making it the worst year for such advocacy since the mid-1990s. The detentions came in a turbulent year for rights activists as China marked the twenty-fifth anniversary of the Tiananmen Square 'incident' and thousands of protesters took to the streets in Hong Kong to push for greater democracy.

7 *Document No. 9* describes the ideological situation in China as 'complicated', warning of the dangers of promoting Western liberal democracy, constitutionalism, rule of law, universal human rights, freedom of the press and civil society on the grounds that these 'false ideological trends' undermine Party leadership.

8 In a series of internal speeches in December 2012, Xi reflects on the collapse of the USSR and reminded the Party that 'the belief in Marxism, socialism and communism is the political soul of the Party'. According to his interpretation, vacillation of belief and faith led to the situation where

> no one was manly enough to defend the Soviet Union ... [adding] Why did the Soviet Union disintegrate? Why did the Soviet Communist Party collapse? An important reason was that their ideals and beliefs had been shaken. In the end, the ruler's flag over the city tower changed overnight. It's a profound lesson for

> us! To dismiss the history of the Soviet Union and the Soviet Communist Party, to dismiss Lenin and Stalin, and to dismiss everything else is to engage in historic nihilism, and it confuses our thoughts and undermines the Party's organizations on all levels.
>
> (Xi 2012)

9 The CPC Central Organization Department, the CPC Central Propaganda Department and the Ministry of Education (2013).

10 Social contract theory refers to the Enlightenment theories of Locke, Hobbes, Rousseau and others, whereby an agreement is entered into by individuals that results in the formation of the state, or of organized society, the prime motive being the desire for protection, which entails the surrender of some or all personal liberties. See: www.thefreedictionary.com/Social+contract+theory.

11 This defines *the state* as 'a machine for maintaining the rule of one class over another' or 'simply a machine for the suppression of one class by another' (Engels 1990; Lenin 1964).

12 David Shambaugh (2015) uses the term 'end game' in relation to Xi Jinping's ruthless measures bringing China closer to a 'breaking point'. See Shambaugh (2015).

4 Reform directions for China's socialist market economy

A macroeconomic perspective

Qiyuan Xu

Introduction

China enjoyed very substantial growth from 2000 until the global financial crisis hit in 2009 (see Figure 4.1).[1] In March 2012, for the first time, the Central Government Work Report revised down the GDP growth rate target from 8 percent to 7.5 percent. Again in March 2015, the Central Government Work Report revised the growth target to 7 percent. China's economy has entered into the period of 'New Normal'. The New Normal is a government narrative about the era of double-digit expansion being over. The potential for infrastructure investment has contracted, returns on assets have fallen, export growth is slowing and overcapacity has soared. The old engines of growth, investment and export, are spluttering. Furthermore, China has consecutively suffered from the global

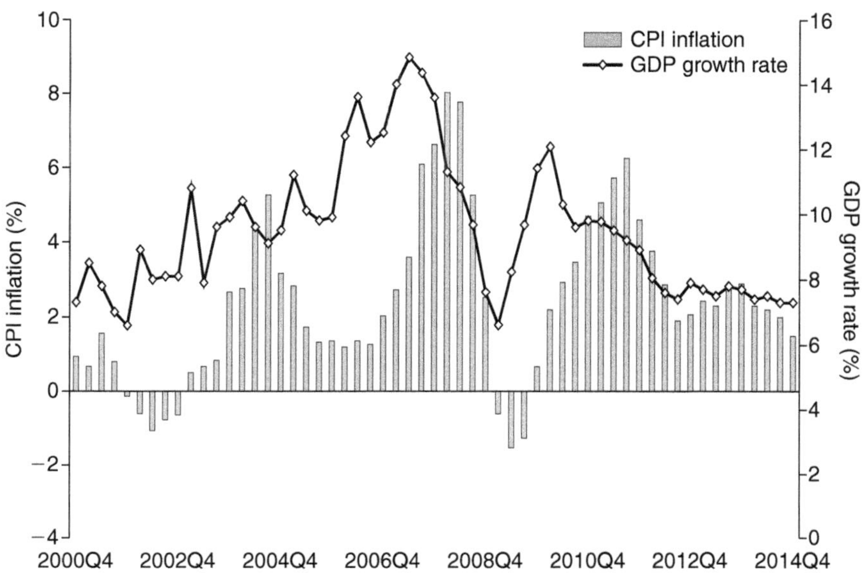

Figure 4.1 China's potential growth rate has been slowing down (source: National Bureau of Statistics of China).

slowdown that followed the US financial crisis, the debt crisis in Europe and then the exit strategies of the Federal Reserve. It is now a factory too big for the world market.

Since 2009, the contribution of net exports to GDP growth has turned from significantly positive to negative – a telling development (Figure 4.2).[2] At the same time, China now has an aging population which undermines population dividends, and faces higher financing costs and deleveraging pressure which deteriorates private investment momentum. Furthermore, the gap between China and the global technical frontier is much smaller now than it once was, which means there is rather limited space for China to make technical progress through an imitation strategy. In other words, China is staring at the 'middle-income trap'; that is, the tendency for countries to stop growing quickly once they reach a certain level of annual per capita income. Although optimists suggest China has a way to go before it falls into the trap, others are not convinced. From a macroeconomic perspective, new sources of growth are urgently needed.

This chapter investigates, from a macroeconomic perspective, new sources of growth as follows: (1) In the short-term view, sources of economic growth can be described from the demand side, such as consumption, investment, net exports and government expenditure. Based on a 'demand framework', reform directions for China are expected to behave in this way: *from* export-oriented *to* domestic demand-oriented; *from* investment-driven *to* consumption-driven. During this transformation, public expenditure could play a 'buffer role'.

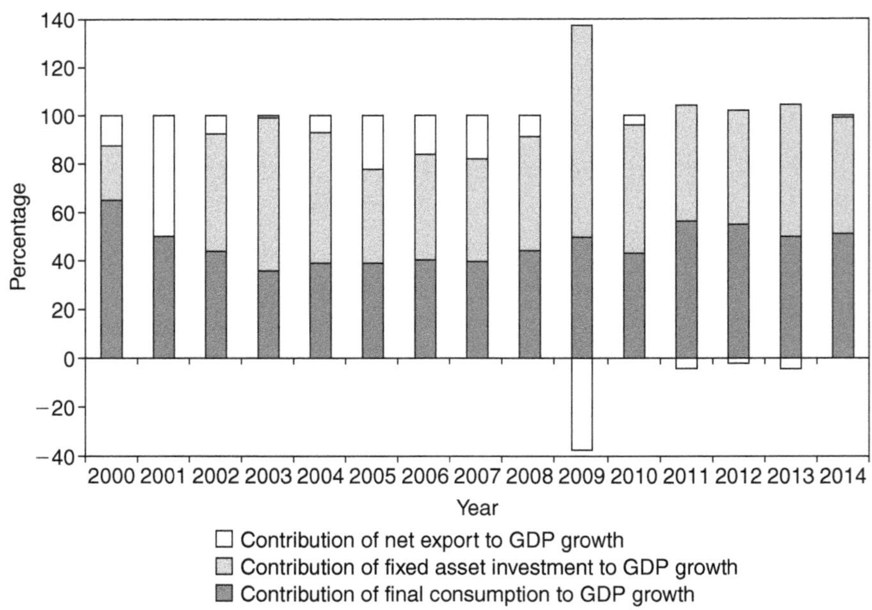

Figure 4.2 The contribution of net exports, fixed asset investment and final consumption to GDP growth (source: National Bureau of Statistics of China).

(2) From the middle–long-term view, the new sources of growth should be analyzed through a 'supply-side' framework. In this sense, production factors like labor, capital and technology constitute the bigger picture from a long-term perspective. The following reform directions could alleviate the decelerating potential growth rate: *from* demographic dividend *to* human capital bonus; *from* technological imitation *to* innovation; and *from* a regulated financial system *to* a market-based financial system that will support the real economy more efficiently. All the above reforms will bring changes for China *from* strong growth *to* sustainable development.

From export-oriented to domestic demand-led

Export and investment have been for some time the two most important engines for China's economy. Since entering the World Trade Organization in 2001, China has become more deeply involved in global affairs. At the same time, the economy had become more dependent on external demand. For instance, between 2005 and 2007, net export contributed approximately 20 percent of China's GDP growth (see Figure 4.2). China's dependence on exports (i.e., export to GDP ratio) ranged from 20 percent in 2000 to 35 percent in 2006 and 2007 at the peak (see Figure 4.3).[3] In 2009, for the first time, China exceeded the United States as the world's largest exporter. Thereafter, in 2014 China's GDP surpassed the United States in terms of purchasing power parity (PPP),

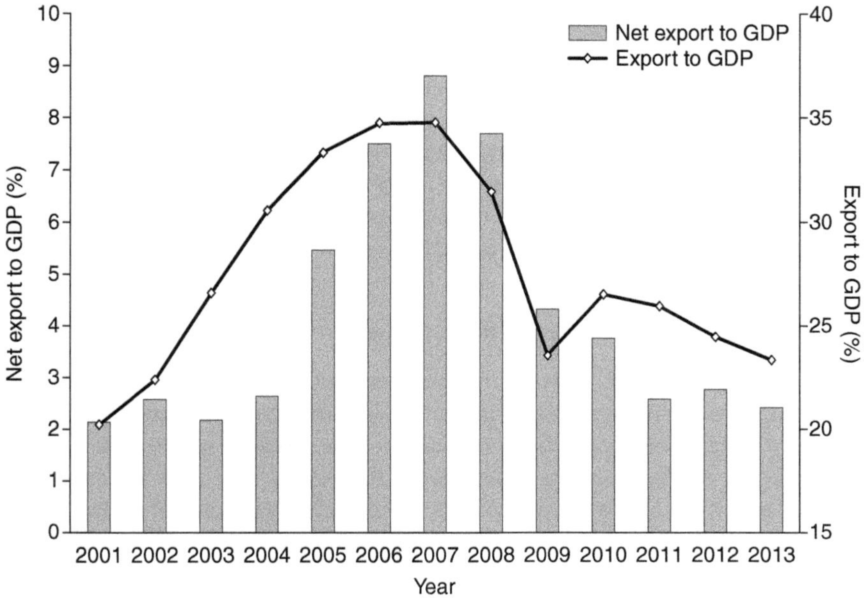

Figure 4.3 The contributions of final demands to GDP growth rate (source: National Bureau of Statistics of China).

becoming the largest in the world. China's economy has shifted from a relatively small economy to a very large one within a short time frame. It has become a factory that is too big for the world market. What it implies is that the export-oriented strategy will become less effective over time.

At an earlier 'takeoff' stage, China enjoyed the benefits of the export-oriented strategy. However, once it became a large economy, external demand seems to have been restricted by global market limitations and imbalances. Under more restrictive conditions, the export-oriented strategy has been confronted by diminishing benefits and increasing costs. Because of its high dependence on exports, China has experienced its own imbalance. Such a growth model is characterized by high vulnerability to external shocks. Another serious problem, emphasized by Premier Li Keqiang in 2014, is caused by excessive foreign exchange reserves accumulated through trade surplus, which is not only wealth but also a burden and a risk (Guo 2014). Compared to the service industry, a typical non-tradable sector, manufacturing is tradable and more capital-intensive. As a result, an economy that is heavily dependent on exports will be more capital-intensive and less labor-intensive. Consequently, the income distribution will incline to capital but not labor. This may result in a widening income gap between capital and labor (Zhang and He 2006). Along the same lines, pollution and general welfare benefit less from the export-oriented strategy.

Due to growing labor costs and currency appreciation, China's export growth rate has declined since 2008. At the same time, net export to GDP ratio also decreased. After the financial crisis, the net export contribution to GDP growth has been negative or near zero.

Although the International Monetary Fund (2012) believes the decrease in China's current account surplus is just periodic and unsustainable, other economists think it indicates a *trend* toward current account balance (Feldstein 2011; Sun and Lu 2012; Zhang Ming 2014). So far, the data in recent years have proved the latter. With such a trend, export and net export will contribute even less in the future. Consistent with the trend, the Twelfth Five-year Plan published in 2011 pointed out that China's growth should change from being 'export-oriented' to 'domestic demand-oriented'.

Three aspects to boost domestic demand

Until domestic demand replaces external demand, how can China manage to realize the transformation and keep growth stable? From the demand side, the answer will be discussed in the next section of the chapter, and includes a solution to boost domestic consumption. From the supply side, it is interesting to find out why there are so many producers who prefer to export rather than doing the same business domestically. Xu (2009) points out three reasons as follows:

- First, *export rebates*. The tax reimbursement for exports can be as high as 17 percent. For example, for tire products, the export rebate ratio is 9 percent, which, although not as high as other items, is still fairly important to the exporter's profit margin. If producers are to sell the precisely same commodities in the domestic market, they will lose their export rebates. Although export rebates should be a 'neutral' policy (to avoid duplicate taxation), the authorities have had a tendency to employ it as a macroeconomic policy tool. For instance, in 2009, when China's exports met difficulties, the export rebate ratios for various commodities were revised up to three times.

- Second, *higher risk premiums in the domestic credit system*. This makes it more difficult for enterprises to run a domestically oriented business. With risks in the credit system, if receivables are not received on time, sometimes this can even cause default. If the borrower lives in another city, the cost of dispute solution will be perceived by the creditor as too high. Producers, therefore, are reluctant to sell commodities in the domestic market, or forced to quote a higher price that includes the risk premium. In contrast, the international trade credit system is supported by bank letters of credit, which facilitates quick and safe settlement. Exporters can enjoy the safer credit system and quick turnover velocity of capital.
- Third, *high transaction costs in the domestic market*. High costs result from local protectionism, corruption and logistics costs. As to logistics costs, in 2011 they account for just 8.5 percent of America's GDP,[4] compared to 17.8 percent for China.[5] For railways, the United States has a track network of 300,000 km, while for China in 2014 it is estimated to be 110,000 km. On a per-capita basis, the length is thus 8.2 cm for the Chinese, shorter than a cigarette! Further differences apply as the American railway has a major function in logistics; China's railway plays a critical role in passenger traffic (see Suo 2014 for details). Suo also claims that the price of road tolls in China is much higher with highway tolls, in general accounting for up to 20 percent of total company transportation costs (2014).

Considering the above constraints, international trade has been boosted while the domestic market has been restricted. To realize the transform to a domestic demand-led economy, China should make reforms to at least the following: (1) restoring export rebates as a neutral policy; (2) constructing a more mature social credit system; and (3) reducing transaction costs in the domestic market through anti-corruption, enhancing the transparency of the fiscal budget of local government and breaking local protectionism through fiscal reforms. In addition, there needs to be reform to officials' evaluation mechanisms.

From investment-driven to consumption-driven

The Twelfth Five-year Plan announced the strategy to transition from investment-driven to consumption-driven economic growth. This is expected to feature again in the next five-year plan. Figure 4.2 shows that the final consumption/GDP ratio has been deteriorating since the financial turmoil in 2008, although the ratio has subsequently improved moderately. The ratio was 51 percent in 2014, 14 percentage points lower compared to the early 2000s. Moreover, government expenditure is included in final consumption. The challenge of realizing the transformation remains arduous for Beijing. Based on existing literature, the following reforms should help set priorities:

Improving the social welfare system

The existing literature (Luo 2004) denotes that 'uncertainty factors', such as unemployment risk, uncertainty of medical expenses and education expenses, have significant negative effects on China's household consumption. A sound welfare system will benefit consumption by reducing such uncertainty. Yet a sound welfare system demands strong support from fiscal budgets. For a country like China that is still developing this is not straightforward and longer-term sustainability issues must be faced. The Eighteenth Party Congress report stressed that China should institute a fully covered, multi-tiered and sustainable system for basic social security provision – for both the urban and rural population. On the one hand, it is a popular decision to expand the welfare system to all households. But on the other hand, this has to be affordable. China can thus draw on lessons from the recent management of the European debt crisis that had to take into account the development level of EU Member States including 'middle-income' countries. The policies to establish a comprehensive welfare system in China will be active in the foreseeable future, but cautious on fiscal sustainability.

Household registration reforms

China's social inequalities are well documented (Sun and Guo 2012). There is a large rural–urban disparity influenced by the household registration institution, or 'Hukou' system. This separates rural migrant workers in cities from access to the urban welfare system. That partially explains why rural migrant workers save more of their wages. Consequently their consumption is restrained. Chen *et al.* (2010) found that the marginal consumption rate of migrants is lower than that of urban residents by about 14.6 percentage points. If Hukou restrictions were removed, it is estimated the the average consumption of migrants would rise by approximately 20.8 percent (Chen *et al.* 2010). Chen *et al.* conclude that the extent to which migrant consumption is constrained by the Hukou system may account for up to half of the decline in household consumption between 2000 and 2005.

China's history reveals a trend associated with economic development whereby the agriculture population (including the population living in rural areas) declines in growth periods. The Hukou system may help slow down this process. But its negative side effect includes a deteriorating household consumption pattern. In terms of political economy, reforms need to be implemented gradually to take account of the various vested interest groups. In 2014, the third plenary session of the Eighteenth Party Congress specifically referred to 'advancing urbanization', emphasizing the need to strictly control the urban population size in megacities like Beijing, Shanghai and Guangzhou. In spite of this, Hukou reforms could be expected in most of the small and middle-sized cities. In 2014, the CPC's Political Bureau of the Central Committee published the *Document on Further Promoting the Hukou System Reforms*. This sets a target of 100 million people immigrating to urban areas who can be registered in the urban Hukou system. Clearly the government is targeting reform of the Hukou system as one way of boosting domestic consumption.

Reducing income disparities

Besides uncertainties in expenditure, income disparity also diminishes the average propensity to consume. The poor may consume with very limited income, while the rich store substantial wealth. Zhu *et al.* (2002), Li Jun (2003) and Yang (2009) show that income disparity plays an important role in China's low consumption share of GDP. For instance, in 2008 and 2009, the income Gini index in China reached 0.49. Then it slowly declined from its peak. In 2014 it was 0.47, still high above what is generally considered 'the danger level' of 0.4, but heading downward. Moreover, comparing with the income Gini index, the wealth Gini index is even higher, recording 0.73 in 2012 – the top 1 percent of households occupied one-third of the national wealth, while the bottom 25 percent of households own 1 percent of the total wealth (Investigation Center of Chinese Social Sciences 2014)! Such income and wealth disparity seriously undermines consumption and has other serious social and legal consequences well documented elsewhere in this book.

Corruption and monopolistic practices are two critical causes of income disparities (Wu 2006). The authorities have cracked down hard on corruption (see Ho in Chapter 7). This has the potential to reduce some income disparity and promote consumption. But this requires a long-term view. Yue *et al.* (2012) also found that there is a more than 50 percent income gap between monopoly and competitive industries. They argue that this is unreasonable. If the implicit welfare costs are included, this level of income gap would likely be even larger. From a macroeconomic perspective it follows that anti-monopoly and state-owned enterprise (SOE) dividend reforms should be expected to make income distribution more equitable. While some well-connected 'princelings' might be unhappy about this, politically it is very likely to be popular.

Reshaping the industry structure

Figure 4.2 shows that investment has contributed approximately half, or even more, to GDP growth for the last decade. Compared to other major economies, this ratio is truly extraordinary. However, the investment-driven model corresponds to the peculiar industry structure in China. For manufacturing, for example, the proportion of the country's potential economic capacity that is 'in use' has declined from around 80 percent before 2008, to around 60 percent in

2012 (IMF 2012). While there may have been overcapacity in manufacturing, the service sector has lacked investment and is therefore in short supply. Finance, education and health care suffer from excessive regulation and lack of competition. Water and environmental conservation, which are important public goods, have not been given sufficient attention including investment for the longer term. All of the above contribute to supply constraints and high prices; shortages in the supply of services inhibits consumption. Medical treatment, education and financial services are often difficult to access and expensive – a very hot topic for many Chinese.

These constraints also contribute to important structural problems in demand. On the one hand, there is oversupply in the manufacturing industry; on the other hand, the service sector is short of supply, and the consumption of services restrained. Figure 4.4 compares employment structures in the service sectors of China and the United States. Compared to the United States, China's employment ratio is lower in education, banking and insurance, scientific research and polytechnic services, and especially in water conservancy, environment and public utility management, health care, social security and social welfare. In order to make these service industries more competitive and increase their capacity, Chinese authorities would do well to free them of excessive regulation and bolster transparency. Again, reforms to establish a sound social welfare system are necessary.

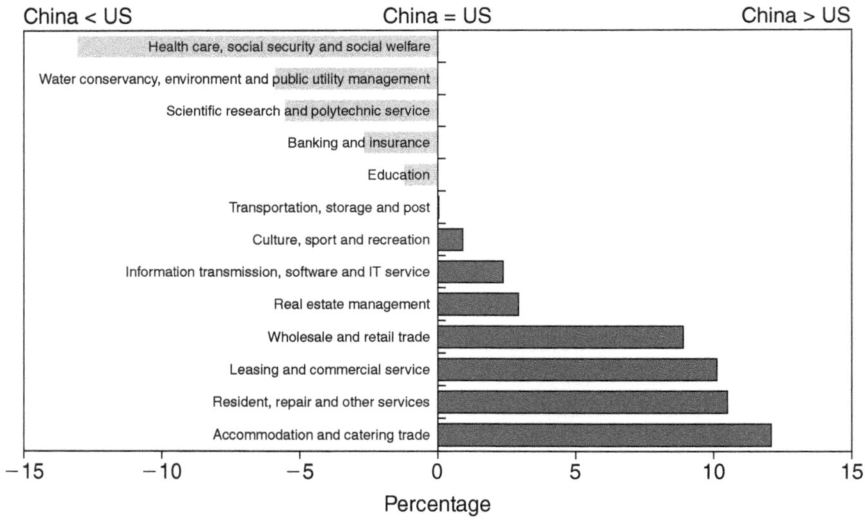

Figure 4.4 Structure of employment in the service sector: comparing China and the United States (source: China's Ministry of Human Resources and Social Security, US Department of Labor).

Note
The data shown in Figure 4.4 is the percentage-point difference in the employment ratio of an industry between China and the United States.

The transformation from an investment-driven to a consumption-driven economy is feasible. In the short term, the high levels of fixed-asset investment (that is, investment in long-term physical assets such as property) could be redirected toward investment in services. This would relieve the shock of currently falling investment levels. Given the supply constraints outlined above, returns on investment could be even higher in services than they have been in the manufacturing industry and perhaps even property. In the long run, the development of services is needed to produce enough supply to match domestic consumer demand. In this model, structural unemployment among university graduates would decrease; their wages would increase; national income distribution could be made fairer; and consumption in innovative services could be fueled. The corollary is less reliance on investment and foreign demand.

From demographic dividend to human capital bonus

From a 'supply-side' perspective, labor, capital and technical progress are *the* resources of economic growth. From the view of labor, China has enjoyed a young demographic structure, 'population dividends', over the past three decades. According to Cai (2009), the decrease of dependency ratio, i.e., the proportion of dependants to people at work, contributed 2.3 percentage points, or a quarter, to per capita GDP growth rate. But a turning point in the population dividend occurs in 2015, whereby the dependency ratio trends unfavorably (Cai 2009). For instance, in 2015 the proportion of the population above 65 years old will rise to nearly 10 percent. Based on an aging population, Cai and Lu (2013) predict that China's growth rate will slow down substantially in the 2020s (Figure 4.5). In this scenario, the growth rate will decline to a level of 5.6 percent. However, it is possible that China's economic growth will be more dependent on generating a 'human capital bonus' and less related to population structure. In this alternative scenario, Liang (2011) forecasts that the economic growth rate will experience a relatively stable trajectory (Figure 4.5).

As Figure 4.5 shows,[6] the actual growth rate is located between the above two scenarios. In March 2015, the Report on Government Work declared 7 percent as the target for GDP growth rate. Again, this target also lies between these two scenarios' forecasts.

The real growth rate is shown to be higher than the demographic dividends scenario but lower than the human capital bonus scenario. This implies human capital may only be partly (or not totally) turned into real productivity. If this is correct, it indicates structural problems in China's labor market. Figure 4.6 shows the coexistence of unemployment for the high-educated labor force and vacancy ratios for the low-educated labor force.[7] In 2014, unemployment among the tertiary-educated labor force (or higher) was 12 percent. The vacancy ratio among the secondary-educated labor force (or lower) was 18 percent. To understand why this is so, it is essential to examine the services industry. Employment here represents only 34 percent of the total workforce, compared with 60 percent in Malaysia and 81 percent in the United States (Figure 4.7).[8] Based on China's

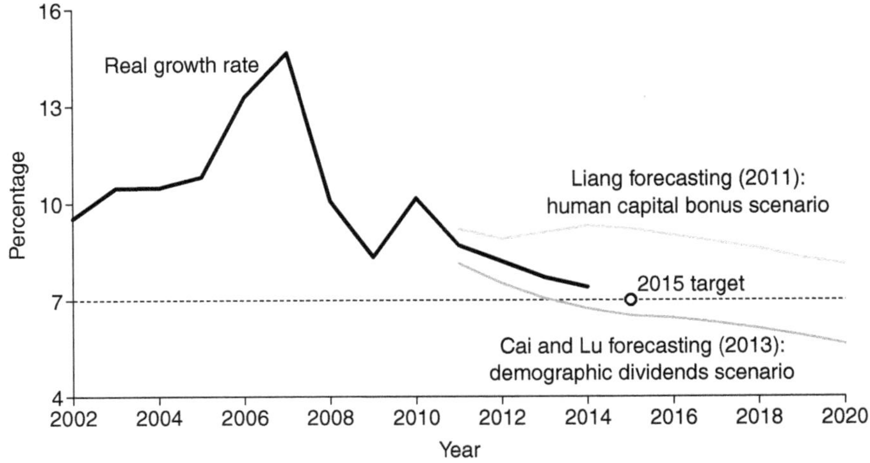

Figure 4.5 Forecasts of China's growth rate in the 2020s: two scenarios (source: National Bureau of Statistics of China; Liang 2011; Cai and Lu 2013).

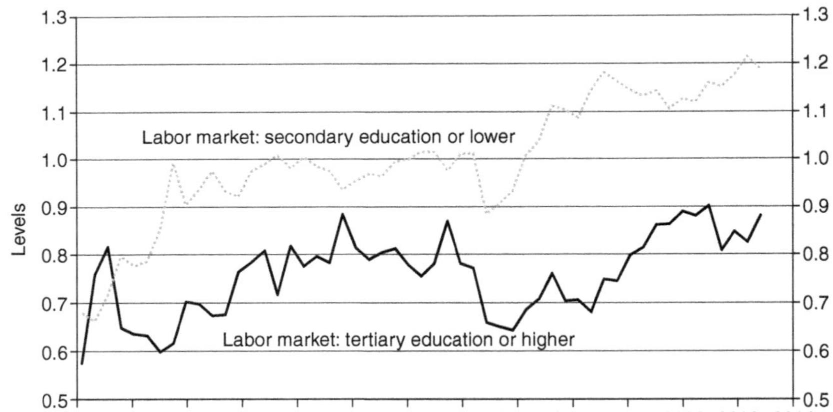

Figure 4.6 Structural problems in China's labor market (source: China's Ministry of Human Resources and Social Security and IWEP).

Note
Calculations by the author.

position on a typical development path, one would expect the service sector to account for about 50 percent of today's jobs. The deficit is particularly apparent in health care, finance and education, as shown in Figure 4.4.

At the same time, it is difficult for university graduates to find work, and their salaries have not risen commensurate with China's growth over the past 20 years or so. In contrast, most factories are short of workers with low levels of

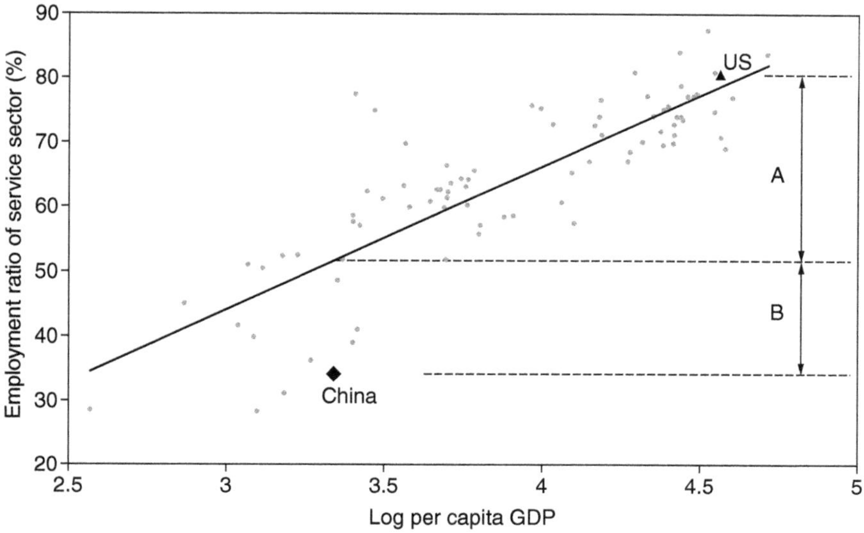

Figure 4.7 China's employment in the service sector is inhibited (source: World Bank, World Development Indicator Online).

education, even migrant workers, and wages for them have increased by more than 10 percent per annum for several years. At this point in time, the development of the service sector will produce more job opportunities, which can then release the human capital bonus, and consequently enhance potential growth. But the transition remains a challenge, as Figure 4.6 shows.

A liberalized financial system to support the 'real economy': the 'middle way' to reform?

In China's economy, capital is as important as labor. But the role of capital is played out through various distortions. For instance, the interest rate system is regulated so as to provide low-cost capital to industries. During the past three decades, the real deposit interest rate by 2012 had averaged around 0 percent. In many years it was even negative: for example, it was –1.1 percent in 2010. As a result, debtors, or the producers and government, benefit, while creditors and households suffer loss. Another distortion has been the renminbi exchange rate regime. For most of the time since 1994, the RMB has been either hard or soft pegged to the US dollar. Since 2002, however, there have been disputes about renminbi undervaluation with many researchers believing the exchange rate undervaluation has contributed to China's current account imbalance.

The control of China's capital account makes the above distortions possible due to the following factors: (1) Because of central controls, depositors could not make asset allocations in the global market. They have had to choose the domestic market and accept the very low yield rate. (2) Due to the controls, the central bank could keep the exchange rate stable and maintain independence in monetary policy within the 'trilemma puzzle'.[9] This puzzle refers to a trade-off among the following three goals: a fixed exchange rate, national independence in monetary policy and capital mobility. The theory is that 'in pursuing any two of these goals, a nation must forgo the third' (Obstfeld *et al.* 2005: 423).

These financial repressions of the past three decades have contributed not only to China's high growth rate, but also to serious structural problems. For example, the fixed exchange rate system and the RMB undervaluation fueled the model of export-driven growth with overdevelopment in manufacturing and a restrained service sector. The regulated interest rate system has undermined consumer welfare and encouraged enterprises to operate inefficiently. Further, capital control separates the domestic financial market from the global market at a cost of achieving a more effective and integrated financial system. In this way, resources have been allocated with distorted capital prices. A consequence is that the sustainability of economic growth is challenged. This reality has reached political circles with a consensus beginning to emerge that the financial system should be reformed with a market orientation. But details such as the reach of reform, sequencing and timing remain controversial. In 2012, a questionnaire was issued to discover how divergent thinking was in relation to sequencing financial reforms and ownership (Xu 2013). Figure 4.8 reflects the different views within financial institutions in terms of ownership. The results show that interviewees from SOEs are more likely to hold a view of 'traditional sequence' (65 percent). From a theoretical perspective this view insists that the proper order of financial reforms should commence with interest rate liberalization, followed by exchange rate regime reforms, and then capital account deregulation. This

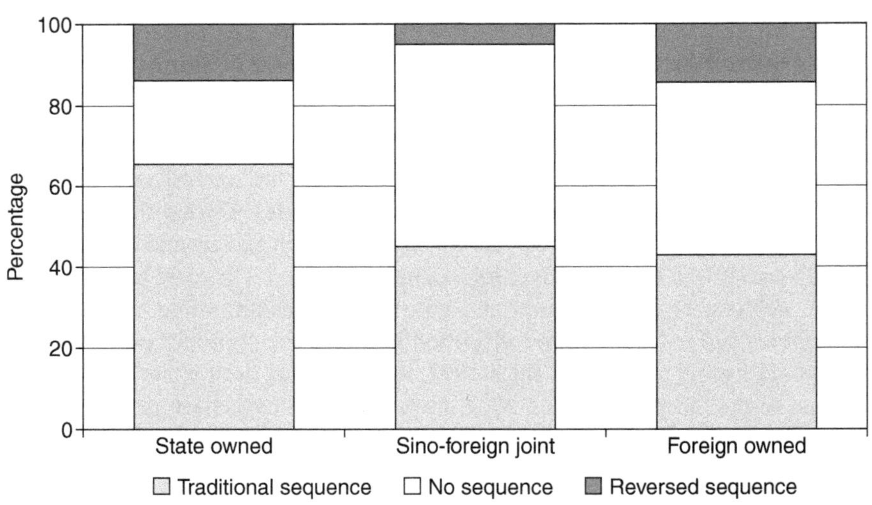

Figure 4.8 Divergent thinking on the sequencing of financial reforms: across different *financial* institutions (source: Xu 2013).

'traditional' view sees any other sequencing as risky, inappropriate and could cause financial instability. Of those interviewed from foreign-owned companies, 43 percent selected 'traditional sequence' and 43 percent selected 'no sequence'. For Sino-foreign joint companies, 50 percent of the interviewees preferred the option of 'no sequence', with 45 percent selecting 'traditional sequence'. While one should not draw too many firm conclusions from this type of survey, it does reveal that SOE financial institutions may tend to support a traditional sequencing of reform whereas Sino-foreign joint and foreign-owned financial institutions may be more inclined to support more radical reform. Here it is worth noting that, in general, SOE institutions are more influential in framing reform plans.

Figure 4.9 shows a subtle variation. Academic institutes stand closer to SOE financial institutions, and are even more conservative, in that 69 percent support traditional sequencing. Most commercial banks are SOEs, and they share similar views to the academic institutes. On the other hand, more investment banks are totally or partly foreign-owned. It is not surprising that investment banks' opinions are similar to Sino-foreign joint and foreign-owned institutions. What is intriguing, however, is that the government's attitude sides with the investment banks. This is best understood from a political economic perspective, as Chinese politicians have tended to make reforms in a trial and error method or, as Deng's famous aphorism put it, by 'crossing the river by feeling for the stones'.

Despite some radical opinions held by government and investment banks, the academic voice and commercial banks' appeal are also influential. My expectation is that the outcome will reflect a compromise. The Research Group of the Financial Survey and Statistics Department of the People's Bank of China (2012) argues that there is no certain sequencing for financial reforms, and it could take place by means of trial and error. But in fact, the implementation

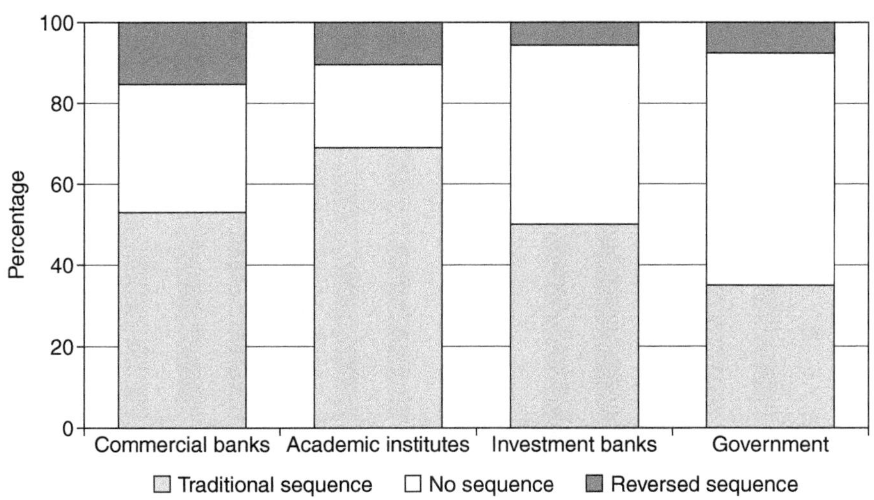

Figure 4.9 Divergent thinking on the sequencing of financial reforms: across *different types of institutions* (source: Xu 2013).

scheme provided by the group is highly consistent with the academic version. Therefore, for financial reform, there is more consensus in practice than disputes in theory! Directions of financial reforms will probably take *the middle way* in the future.

From technological imitation to innovation

In the future, China's economic growth is expected to become more dependent on technological progress. From a macroeconomic perspective, 'technical progress' is best defined broadly and may also include institutional reforms. In terms of technological progress itself, Chinese economists are being asked 'What kind of technical progress could be most helpful for China's economy?' To answer such a question, we need a strong theoretical framework. From the main issues arising in this chapter, answers are needed to help solve the following three 'bottlenecks': (1) labor market problems due to the aging population; (2) the dilemma of environmental degradation and resource needs; and (3) continually upgrading China's technical level. Already, as Veugelers (2011) points out, in specific fields like engineering, chemistry and physics, the gap between China and the European Union and the United States is closing fast. For instance, the number of authorized patents in China reached 1.2 million in 2013, triple that in 2000. But so far, technological progress has evolved by way of imitation. In the past decade, the ratio of inventions in authorized patents rose from 6.5 percent in 2000 to 11.7 percent in 2013 (see Figure 4.10). This compares poorly to Japan's 88.6 percent in the same year. Designs and utility models have been dominant, amounting to 88.3 percent of China's patents. In contrast, the ratio of designs

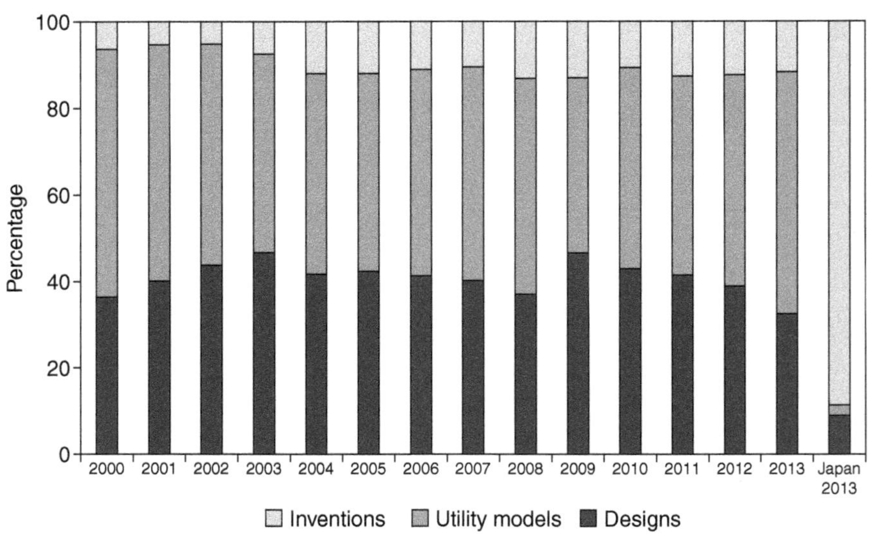

Figure 4.10 The structure of authorized patents: China and Japan (source: NBS of China, Japan Patent Office 2013).

and utility models in Japan's patents is 11.4 percent. This structural characteristic reflects the nature and quality of China's patents. The problem of poor quality is, in part, a result of China's developmental stage. But it is also related to the institutional design of patent law. For example, if a company is recognized as being 'hi-tech', it will enjoy many subsidies and advantages. According to the Guidance on Recognition of Hi-tech Enterprises published by the Ministry of Science and Technology, intellectual property is a weighted index (30 percent). In most provinces, the intellectual property index is measured as one invention equaling six utility models. However, the cost to apply for six utility model patents is fairly low compared to one invention. Consequently, enterprises are encouraged to take advantage of this rule to get a 'hi-tech' recognition.

As the gap between China and the global technical frontier is smaller now than before, there is a net reduction in the space for China to make technical progress through a followed and imitation strategy. It is for this reason that 'independent innovation' has been adopted as a national strategy (see Wen 2012). In this, institutional reform is also considered as 'technical progress' in broad terms. This also contributes to improving the productivity of labor and capital. Premier Li Keqiang underlined the 'reforms dividend' many times as a new resource for China's growth. In this regard, the new leadership has since 2013 started to streamline administration and delegate power. The Shanghai Free Trade Zone and other pilot projects in Tianjin and Shenzhen have also commenced.

Conclusion: *from* strong growth *to* sustainable development

China now faces multiple challenges in transitioning from economic growth to sustainable development. This chapter has argued that structural reforms must address both aggregate demand- and supply-side issues. With regard to the *demand side*, two transformation directions are clear enough: (1) China's growth is to shift from export-oriented to domestic demand-led, and from being investment-driven to consumption-driven. To effect this shift, China will need to make reforms to restore export rebates as a neutral policy, construct a mature social credit system and reduce transaction costs in the domestic market. Anti-corruption measures, greater transparency in the fiscal budget of local government, breaking local protectionism and reforms in officials' evaluation mechanisms will undoubtedly help. (2) To boost consumption, the authorities will have to improve the social welfare system, reform the household registration system, reduce income disparities and reshape the industry structure, especially deregulation of the service sector.

With regard to the *supply side*, sustainable development demands reform in three key areas: (1) The labor factor – from demographic dividend to human capital bonus. The analysis in this chapter reveals the supply of human capital is not in a state of over-supply; rather the problem is related to the need to deregulate the service sector to produce more job opportunities (and thus release the 'human capital bonus'). From this perspective, the following service sectors have the best potential at this stage of China's development: education, banking and insurance, scientific research and polytechnic services, and especially environmental protection, public utility management, health care, social security and social welfare. (2) The capital factor – financial deregulation to liberalize the 'real' economy. This analysis has shown that various views exist as to how reform should be sequenced. It is most likely that a 'middle way' compromise will emerge between sequential and trial and error methods. The likely outcome in terms of policy will be 'gradualism'. (3) Technical progress – encourage a transformation from imitation to innovation. To improve the quality of China's patents, the call to reform the patent law grows louder. The future law and policy system is expected to stress innovation. Reform itself is a kind of technical progress with a so-called 'reform dividend'. From an 'outputs' perspective, this dividend requires a fair distribution in terms of rural and urban provision, better social welfare redistribution, more public goods like environmental protection, a just legal system and less corruption generally.

Notes

1 For full source details, see China's GDP growth rate at: http://data.stats.gov.cn/workspace/index?m=hgjd; CPI inflation at: http://data.stats.gov.cn/workspace/index?m=hgyd.
2 Full source details: http://data.stats.gov.cn/workspace/index?m=hgnd.
3 Full source details: http://data.stats.gov.cn/workspace/index?m=hgnd.
4 Council of Supply Chain Management Professionals (2012).
5 National Bureau of Statistics of China (2013) at: www.stats.gov.cn/english.
6 Also see National Bureau of Statistics of China at: http://data.stats.gov.cn/workspace/index?m=hgnd.
7 Full source details for Figure 4.6 are at: www.mohrss.gov.cn/SYrlzyhshbzb/zwgk/szrs/sjfx/index_1.htm.
8 Full source details, 'employment ratio data' at: http://data.worldbank.org/indicator/SL.SRV.EMPL.ZS; 'per capita GDP data' at: http://data.worldbank.org/indicator/NY.GDP.PCAP.CD.
9 Obstfeld *et al.* (2005: 423) explain that a 'trilemma', or 'impossible trinity' as introduced by Robert Mundell and Marcus Fleming in 1962 and 1963, refers to trade-offs among the following three goals: a fixed exchange rate, national independence in monetary policy and capital mobility. According to the Mundell–Fleming model, a small, open economy cannot achieve all three of these policy goals at the same time.

Part II

Major challenges for China's socialist rule of law

5 The law and growth nexus in China

Linda Yueh

Introduction

One of the enduring paradoxes in China's remarkable economic growth since 1978 is the lack of a well-established legal system supporting the increasingly decentralized marketizing economy (Allen *et al.* 2005; Cull and Xu 2005; Anderson 2011). It is a notable puzzle since it is thought that robust institutions are required to support markets (see Acemoglu and Johnson 2005). The rapid transition experience of many other economies, such as the former Soviet Union, was predicated on establishment of private property rights and removal of the inefficient state in the burgeoning market economy. In China's case, however, many reforms were undertaken without established rule of law and in the absence of a change in ownership from state to private. It raises questions as to how China was able to instill economic incentives in the absence of private property rights and how an imperfect legal system could protect against expropriation that normally limits investment and other private economic activities.

The gradualist and evolutionary nature of both economic and legal reform provides a basis for understanding the relationship between law and growth in China. The Chinese legal tradition is distinct from that of common law (Britain, United States) and civil law (continental Europe) countries; although that does not negate the incrementalist nature of legal reforms that can exist in all legal systems (see Jones 2003 for the modern-day influences of China's dynastic legal system; and Cohen 2014b on prospects for improvements to the legal system under China's deepening socialist rule of law). Perhaps most evident in common law countries, law develops from case law – judicial pronouncements that give meaning and shape the interpretation of the statutory laws. *Stare decisis* and precedent gradually shape rule of law, which develops over time rather than being a wholly formed system.

In law and finance literature regarding China, debate over explanations of this paradox is taking shape. Chen (2003) argues China's financial development follows the '[financial] crash then law path' proposed by Coffee (2001). From a legal perspective, Coffee argues that capital market developments precede, not follow, shareholder legal protection. He offers evidence from the historical development of the United States and United Kingdom, where shareholder ownership arose with the establishment of bourses while legal protection for minority shareholders came afterward (Coffee (2001). His argument is premised on the interests of parties vested into the system: legal reforms are enacted due to a motivated constituency seeking protection from the proposed reforms. Therefore, he argues, the constituency must arise before it can become an instrument for legal change. This runs contrary to the view of economists, namely, La Porta *et al.* (1997, 1998) and Acemoglu *et al.* (2005) who posit that rule of law allows for the development of financial markets.

Chen (2003) applies Coffee's approach to China's capital markets and shows that an interested constituency arose after the two stock exchanges in Shanghai and Shenzhen were established in the early 1990s, which led to the *Securities Law 1999*. La Porta *et al.* (1997, 1998), by contrast, draw a distinction between common law and civil law countries and show that common law countries provide better shareholder protection, which then fosters the development of financial markets. Their argument is legal protection allows markets to develop with legal protections against expropriation and improved contracting security; law, therefore, creates markets. Allen *et al.* (2005) compare China against the La Porta group of countries and conclude that informal institutional arrangements, such as trust-based contracting, supplants the role of law in fostering capital markets.

Aside from the question of the sequence of law and market development, there remains a further mystery as to how markets developed in China in the absence of private property rights, which are typically established by law. Unlike the United States or United Kingdom, and other transition economies that adopted private ownership early in their transition, China's lingering communal property system should have impeded market development. Without property right allocations, transactions should have been hampered and the market stifled.

This chapter proposes that legal and economic reforms give rise to and reinforce each other in China. Also, institutional reform through administrative dictates, such as the Contract Responsibility System that injected market forces into state-owned enterprises (SOEs), was sufficient to instill incentives to create markets in the absence of strong legal protection. Then, once a market is created by law or institutional reform (e.g., administrative dictate or absence of notable prohibition), then interested constituencies and stakeholders will push for more formal and explicit legal reforms to protect their interests. Better legal protection in turn promotes market development by providing greater security of economic transactions. Informal, trust-based relationships supplant the incomplete legal system, particularly in terms of enforcement. In this way, the complementary processes of legal, institutional and economic reform in China can explain the paradox of remarkable growth within an underdeveloped system of law.

This chapter will also argue that legal development in China should be viewed as an evolutionary process alongside incremental economic reforms undertaken during its transition from central planning. This is not dissimilar to the experience of wealthy countries when their legal systems developed alongside financial markets. What makes China unusual is a confluence of factors.

First, it was able to establish markets within a state-controlled property system, highlighting the importance of administrative measures and institutional reforms. Second, its transition and marketization were gradual, such that markets were not always established by law, but developed over time with experimentation of various market mechanisms. Third, it is undertaking reform and global integration at a time of international economic laws and rules that extend beyond trade and into financial regulation and intellectual property rights. The external influence of laws and rules will affect expectations within and without China, particularly in emphasizing regulatory transparency and the enforcement of laws.

The chapter also examines law and market literature and how China appears to be an 'outlier', before providing a comparative view of China's legal system versus common law and civil law countries. The focus will be on China's particular sequence of legal, institutional and economic reform. Enforcement is also briefly examined, with a final section concluding with an assessment of the relationship between law and economic growth in China, positing that China's experience is unusual in the post-war period where the transition and development models are heavily tilted toward formal legal rules. But it is not atypical of the experience of developed countries' legal and economic development during their industrialization phase. The conclusion also assesses the influence of international laws and rules, particularly in shaping the enforcement of laws in China.

Law and markets

There are both theoretical and empirical perspectives on the relationship between law and markets that drives economic growth. Theoretically, the 'invisible hand' of the market works most efficiently when there exists a framework of well-defined property rights and sufficiently low- or zero-transaction costs in which optimizing agents transact (see Coase 1937). A legal system defines property rights and costs of transacting and exchange. For instance, legal ownership establishes the security of the private property to be exchanged. A well-functioning legal and regulatory system ensures transactions involving property provide contracting security to the parties involved. For China, one element of the paradox is the lack of legally protected private property rights (see, e.g., Jefferson and Rawski 2002; Hu 2012: 87). It was not until the *Property Law 2007* that equal protection was granted to both private and public property. Indeed, much of China's growth and reform has taken place with the state retaining ownership of enterprises, land and housing. Privatization of significant SOEs did not occur, but market-oriented reforms have gradually taken place since 1978. The private housing market was established later, marked by the conclusion of the housing privatization reforms in 2001, and the creation of long-term leasehold rather than freehold ownership resulted as land remained largely in state hands (see Ho 2006).

From an empirical standpoint, these theoretical insights have been incorporated into the literature advocating the importance of laws and institutions in explaining persistent economic growth in China (Rodrik *et al.* 2004; Acemoglu and Johnson 2005; Acemoglu *et al.* 2005; Dam 2006). La Porta *et al.* (1997, 1998) emphasize the importance of legal origin in influencing financial sector development and consequently economic development. China does not fit well within this framework, particularly because legal origin was based on the externally imposed legal system of the colonial powers on developing countries. But, for countries such as China, which did not adopt a legal system from a particular colonial power, the legal formalism hypothesis would seem to have minimal explanatory power. Studies of other transition economies conclude that, for economic growth, the effectiveness of laws is more important than the completeness of the written formal law, further reducing the force of the 'legal origins' school. One significant conclusion is that a 'transplanted' legal system into a neophyte transition economy – whereby the wholly formed laws of developed countries, which would presumably encompass the necessary elements for a 'rule of law' – does not work (Pistor *et al.* 2000). Glaeser *et al.* (2004) also emphasize the functional rule of law as relevant for growth. Therefore, the elements of a well-functioning legal system in a legal formalism hypothesis includes an independent judiciary, freedom from executive branch interference and low risk of expropriation (Pistor and Xu 2005; Fan *et al.* 2009).

Institutional development was therefore considered to be important and the focus has shifted away from legal formalism and legal origin to some extent (see Rodrik *et al.* 2004). For instance, Acemoglu and Johnson (2005) emphasize two types of market-supporting institutions that are important for economic growth: property rights institutions that protect against expropriation by government, and contracting institutions that ease contract enforcement. For China, these empirical measures do not measure up well as compared to its impressive growth rate, giving rise to the 'China paradox' (see Cull and Xu 2005; Lu and Yao 2009).

Various measures of the rule of law and institutional development in China suggest its formal legal system is underdeveloped (see Allen *et al.* 2005; Cull and Xu 2005 for a range of indicators). Using the World Bank's Worldwide Governance Indicators for 2006, Table 5.1 shows that China ranked in the bottom 25–50 percentile of all countries surveyed for rule of law. It is also evident from Table 5.1 that China grew more rapidly than comparably sized economies (largest ten economies in the world) in the top half of the table and outpaced the growth of other transition economies from 1990 to 2003. Its growth in per capita GDP exceeded 7.6 percent over this period and was substantially higher than Brazil's, which ranked close to China in the rule of law indicator, and also Estonia, which had a rule of law indicator higher than the United States. No proxy for rule of law is perfect, though nearly all studies conclude China has an underdeveloped legal system (Yao and Yueh 2009; deLisle 2014). When regulatory quality is measured, an indicator of an effective legal system, China fares even worse. Table 5.2 ranks the countries in terms of their regulatory quality, measuring the ability of the government to formulate and implement sound policies and regulations permitting and promoting private-sector development. While China ranked better than Russia and Brazil on rule of law, it only ranked better than Russia for regulatory quality.

Table 5.1 Rule of law

Country	*Percentile rank (0–100)*	*Rule of law score (–2.5 to +2.5)*	*Average annual growth rate of real per capita GDP, 1990–2003 (%)*
China	**45.2**	**–0.40**	**7.61**
Brazil	41.4	–0.48	0.96
France	89.5	1.31	1.47
Germany	94.3	1.77	1.43
India	57.1	0.17	3.95
Italy	60.0	0.37	1.25
Japan	90.0	1.40	0.95
Russia	19	–0.91	–1.27
United Kingdom	93.3	1.73	2.03
United States	91.9	1.57	1.75
Select Eastern Europe and former Soviet bloc countries			
Albania	48.8	–0.14	2.58
Bulgaria	66.3	0.54	1.03
Croatia	61.5	0.35	0.25
Czech Republic	79.5	0.95	0.92
Estonia	92.2	1.42	2.45
Hungary	85.9	1.10	1.72
Poland	69.3	0.64	3.23
Romania	62.0	0.37	0.19
Slovakia	83.4	1.08	1.65

Source: World Bank Worldwide Governance Indicators (2006) (http://info.worldbank.org/governance/wgi/index.aspx#home).

Note
Rule of law measures the extent to which agents perceive that the rules of society, in particular the quality of contract enforcement, the police and the courts, as well as the likelihood of crime and violence, are enforced. The percentile rank places the country on a scale of 0–100 where 100 indicates a country that scored the highest possible value on the rule of law indicator. The governance score is normally distributed with a mean of zero and a standard deviation of one. Governance is better as the value increases. See Kaufmann *et al.* (2007) for a complete definition and discussion. The growth rate of per capita GDP is in 1990 US dollars and calculated from Maddison (2001).

Tables 5.3–5.4 provide more disaggregated measures of rule of law in China, as compared with other countries, namely: investor protection, contract enforcement, security of property rights and freedom from corruption. Table 5.3 measures investor protection, as measured by the World Bank 'Doing Business' survey from 2008, where China ranks 86 out of 175 measured countries in the bottom half. In particular, it obtained the poorest rating on the transparency of related-party transactions (extent of disclosure index), which reflects the lack of arm's-length dealing and transparency in its enterprises. China fares among the worst of selected countries in enforcing property rights, as seen in Table 5.4, as measured by the Heritage Foundation.

Table 5.4 measures the security of property rights, both to obtain and to enforce. China has one of the least secure systems of property rights, likely due to its underdeveloped private property system that only ostensibly existed since

Table 5.2 Regulatory quality

Country	*Percentile rank (0–100)*	*Regulatory quality score (–2.5 to +2.5)*	*Standard error*
Russia	35.0	–0.44	0.17
China	**45.6**	**–0.24**	**0.17**
India	46.1	–0.22	0.17
Brazil	53.4	–0.04	0.17
Albania	55.8	0.09	0.18
Croatia	64.1	0.43	0.17
Romania	66.0	0.48	0.17
Bulgaria	69.9	0.61	0.17
Poland	72.3	0.71	0.17
Italy	74.3	0.81	0.21
Czech Republic	80.1	0.96	0.17
Slovakia	81.1	0.99	0.17
Japan	83.5	1.05	0.21
France	85.9	1.15	0.21
Hungary	86.4	1.15	0.17
United States	90.8	1.45	0.21
Estonia	92.2	1.50	0.17
Germany	92.7	1.50	0.21
United Kingdom	98.1	1.86	0.21

Source: World Bank Worldwide Governance Indicators (2008).

Note
Regulatory quality measures the ability of the government to formulate and implement sound policies and regulations that permit and promote private-sector development. The percentile rank places the country on a scale of 0–100 where 100 indicates a country that scored the highest possible value on the indicator. The indicator score is normally distributed with a mean of zero and a standard deviation of one. Quality improves as the value increases (see Kaufmann *et al.* 2007 for definition and discussion).

the notion was recognized in the Constitution in 2006 and with the passage of the *Property Law 2007*, extending equal protection to private and public property. China performs better in Table 5.4 measuring the extent of corruption. China's degree of corruption is comparable to India and Brazil, while it fares better than Russia and Ukraine. Overall, China ranked 126 out of 157 countries based on these and other indicators exampled in the Heritage Foundation's 2008 Index of Economic Freedoms.

In summary, although no indicators are perfect, across available measures of legal/institutional development, China ranks in the bottom half of countries, despite being the fastest growing major economy in the world. The accumulated evidence suggests that the paradox of fast growth and poor legal system remains after three decades of reform.

Table 5.3 Investor protection

	Rank	*Investor protection index*	*Disclosure index*	*Director liability index*	*Shareholder suits index*
Brazil	64	**5.3**	6	7	3
Canada	5	**8.3**	8	9	8
China	**83**	**5**	**10**	**1**	**4**
France	64	**5.3**	10	1	5
Germany	83	**5**	5	5	5
India	33	**6**	7	4	7
Italy	51	**5.7**	7	4	6
Japan	12	**7**	7	6	8
Poland	33	**6**	7	2	9
Romania	33	**6**	9	5	4
Russia	83	**5**	6	2	7
Slovakia	98	**4.7**	3	4	7
South Africa	9	**8**	8	8	8
Ukraine	141	**3.7**	1	3	7
United Kingdom	9	**8**	10	7	7
United States	5	**8.3**	7	9	9

Source: World Bank Doing Business Database (2008) (www.doingbusiness.org).

Note

The investor protection index (measured from 1–10) calibrates the strength of minority shareholder protection against directors' misuse of corporate assets for personal gain. The indicators, also out of 10, distinguish three dimensions of investor protection: transparency of related-party transactions (extent of disclosure index), liability for self-dealing (extent of director liability index) and shareholders' ability to sue officers and directors for misconduct (ease of shareholder suits index). Countries are ranked out of 175.

A comparative perspective of Chinese law, common law and civil law countries

The legal system in China is in part modeled after the Japanese civil law system (Jones 2003). The Japanese legal system was itself fashioned after the German civil law tradition during the nineteenth-century period of the Meiji Restoration. However, strong elements of China's own legal tradition persist, particularly in emphasizing administrative law and lack of separation between legal and administrative systems. Judicial adjudication was undertaken by administrative officials who acted on behalf of the emperor. The judicial system in China today follows, in part, this tradition (Alford 2000; also see Qianfan Zhang in Chapter 1). As a result, procedural laws are relatively underdeveloped, while administrative law is at the core of the Chinese legal tradition.

This mixed legal tradition renders it difficult to situate China in comparative law and finance literature, which emphasizes the distinction between common law and civil law countries. China does not fit the paradigm of common versus civil law countries; particularly as these cover only roughly 49, or less than one-third, of the countries in the world, virtually all of which are former European

Table 5.4 Property rights and freedom from corruption

Protection of property rights		*Freedom from corruption*	
United States	90	United Kingdom	86
Canada	90	Canada	85
United Kingdom	90	Germany	80
Germany	90	Japan	76
Japan	70	France	74
France	70	United States	73
Slovak Republic	50	Italy	49
South Africa	50	Slovak Republic	47
Italy	50	South Africa	46
Poland	50	Poland	37
Brazil	50	Brazil	33
India	50	India	33
Romania	30	**China**	**33**
Ukraine	30	Romania	31
Russia	30	Ukraine	28
China	**20**	Russia	25

Source: Heritage Foundation Index of Economic Freedom (2008) (www.heritage.org/index).

Note
Property rights are an assessment of the ability of individuals to accumulate private property, secured by clear laws that are fully enforced by the state. The index is from 1–100. Freedom from corruption is based on quantitative data that assess the perception of corruption in the business environment, including levels of governmental legal, judicial, and administrative corruption. The index is from 1–100.

colonies (see Acemoglu *et al.* 2005). China's case is much closer to other transition economies as they had to re-initiate the market during the 1990s after decades of central planning (see, e.g., Pistor and Xu 2005). However, unlike these countries, China did not adopt a legal system transplanted from developed economies (Pistor *et al.* 2000; Berkowitz *et al.* 2003). Instead, it developed its own legal system, which has been influenced by the legal codes of other countries. Nevertheless, the sequence of law and markets remains relevant. The paradox casts doubt on the 'law matters' thesis and has implications for the progress of reform in China some three decades into marketization.

Undoubtedly there has been a push for legal reform in China derived from its global integration and membership in the multilateral rules-based trading system (World Trade Organization) and in response to domestic pressures, which led to the recognition of 'rule of law' in the 1999 Constitution. Given the ongoing primacy of the Communist Party of China (CPC) (see Xi Jinping's 2013a 'Explanation on Deepening Reform'), some argue the amendment is largely symbolic, while others argue it formally incorporates rule of law into China's system of governance. Legal reform, therefore, became prominent at the same time that the private sector was also recognized as part of the socialist market economy in the amended Constitution. The shift culminated in the 2001 embrace of entrepreneurs in the CPC. This move also occurred in the midst of ongoing legal and economic reforms that had taken place since 1978 (such as establishing a *Company Law* in 1993 that accompanied the transformation of SOEs into corporations), adding more credence to the view that legal and economic reforms did not progress in a particular sequence but developed alongside the other.

Therefore, the expectations of the actors in the global economy include rapid implementation of commercial laws and rules to facilitate cross-border transactions, which form an external impetus for China and other developing countries to have a legal framework at an earlier stage of development. Where China lags behind, for example, anti-monopoly and bankruptcy laws, reflects a lack of market need because SOEs make it irrelevant to be concerned with anti-trust policy or bankruptcy. Overall, China appears to have adopted legal reforms at earlier stages of economic development than the United States, making the Chinese paradox – growth without legal development – less of one.

Corporate law and economic necessity

In China, the corporatization process began in the early 1990s when SOEs were in need of reform. By 1992, an estimated two-thirds of all SOEs were thought to be loss-making (Fan 1994, 2003). By creating shareholding companies out of SOEs, the corporatization process transformed these enterprises into joint stock companies owned by shareholders and therefore began the gradual process of privatization, as many SOEs retained the state as their majority shareholder even as it reformed (see Clarke 2003a). The passage of the *Company Law* in 1993 and promulgation in 1994 provided a basis in law for defining the rights and obligations of shareholders. Subsequent laws created other corporate forms, such as partnerships through the *Law on Partnership Enterprises* in 1997 and the *Law on Individual Wholly-Owned Enterprises* in 1999. The coincidence of laws with economic necessity is expected insofar as laws arise to address a specific development in the market, whether it is the growth of firms in the Industrial Revolution or the creation of companies defined by shares to reform the inefficient state-owned sector.

The evolution of corporate law is further complicated in China by its distinct legal tradition that does not rely on the courts as the main institutional source of legal interpretation. Instead, legislative enactments play a larger role, in line with civil law countries such as Germany, although the administrative law tradition in China also plays a part. Nevertheless, its company law has been in existence for less than two decades and the poor scores on the corporate governance indicators, which are seen as representing the effectiveness of a legal regime, likely reflect the nascent stages of its legal development.

However, China's economic development has sped up, particularly with global integration after the 'open door' policy accelerated in 1992. The rapid passage of laws and regulations during the 1990s following the *Company Law*, such as the unified *Contract Law* of 1999, *M&A Law* and *Securities Investment Fund Law* both of 2003, reflect the push to legislate and thus improve the effectiveness of the commercial laws to govern the fast-growing market economy. In a country with a civil law tradition, laws are developed through legislative action, which in turn reflects the needs of the market, much as in a common law system where case laws arise from litigants seeking adjudication of disputes arising from market transactions. For instance, WTO-mandated liberalization of capital markets led to the passage of the *Securities Investment Fund Law* to govern the foreign and domestic firms expected to operate in this opened sector. Similarly, the 'going out' strategy of Chinese firms since the mid-1990s culminated in private firms investing overseas, as witnessed by TCL's purchase of the Thomson brand in 2003, which was followed by Lenovo's purchase of IBM's personal computing business two years later. The acquisition and mergers associated with commercial transactions led to a need for a mergers and acquisitions law. Since the first transactions were dated in the same year as the passage of the law, it is unlikely the law provided a strong basis for M&A transactions as its scope would not have been immediately evident.

Regulatory reform supporting markets: China's CSRC

Regulation plays a role in a legal system through providing measures necessary to implement laws and the apparatus with which to enforce the same. Regulatory agencies, therefore, oversee markets and are the source of regulations governing markets under their remit. In terms of the sequence of law and capital markets for China, it has been argued that capital markets are the most evident place for the '[financial] crash-then-law' hypothesis because they generate a politically powerful constituency to lobby for legal change given the high degree of commonality of interest among the interested parties and the ability to obtain immediately measurable benefits (Chen 2003).

There is evidence that regulatory reforms were adopted in order to better govern markets. The stock markets in Shanghai and Shenzhen were established prior to the regulatory agency, China Securities Regulatory Commission (CSRC), in 1992. China's CSRC was established just a year after the creation of the two exchanges. The China Banking Regulatory Commission (CBRC) was not established until 2003. Both were established to regulate the financial sector, alongside the insurance regulator, the China Insurance Regulatory Commission (CIRC), following the establishment of capital, banking and insurance markets in the 1990s. As discussed earlier, China scores poorly on corporate governance indicators, reflecting the lack of effectiveness of the law and the imperfect oversight of China's trio of regulators. The late establishment of the CBRC in particular suggests the banking sector had developed in the absence of regulation, a paradox partially explained by the dominance of state ownership and state control in bank lending. As the banking sector became increasingly liberalized and the dominance of state banks receded, there was a push – particularly with WTO-mandated opening to foreign banks – for regulation and improved governance. The insurance market also developed after market establishment because insurance was provided by the work unit (*danwei*), so a need for regulation hardly existed. After reform, the market developed and the CIRC undertook a corresponding governance role.

Regarding the CSRC, it can be argued that securities regulations were passed in response to the demands of interested constituents in the capital market (Chen 2003; see also Sun and Tobin 2009). Despite the relatively early establishment of the CSRC, there were no significant securities laws until the *Securities Law* was passed in 1998 six years later. Prior to its enactment, the stock exchanges operated under administrative direction. Provincial governments selected firms to become listed and were in turn allocated a certain quota (Du and Xu 2006). As a result of the incentives of the quota system, provincial authorities selected the better-performing firms for initial public offerings (IPOs) so that the stock market grew throughout the 1990s (Du and Xu 2009). In this way, China's capital markets functioned prior to the establishment of the relevant laws and in the presence of a passive regulator. However, WTO accession changed the picture. As part of its WTO terms, China agreed to open its financial sector to foreign firms. The anticipated opening led to the passage of more securities laws, which rapidly reformed China's financial sector. Foreign firms and governments interested in accessing China's market as well as the *de novo* private sector would be among those clamoring for better-defined rights. The Chinese government's desire to foster its own SOEs as well as safeguard the market from foreign dominance would be among other drivers: for example, the State Asset Supervision and Administration Commission (SASAC) was established in 2003 to oversee state-owned assets when SOEs continued to account for nearly half of China's GDP, while a 25 percent ceiling on foreign equity ownership is maintained in SOEs. The result was a large number of regulations passed since 2002 to improve transparency, increase disclosure requirements, reform non-tradable shares, extend protection to minority shareholders, prevent insider trading and monitor mergers and acquisitions. All of which address the needs of shareholders, investors, debtors and firms in the market (see Chen 2003). In turn, the growth of the market leads to the need for regulation and regulators who, if effective, lead to the further development of the market. The numerous securities laws passed since greater market opening after WTO accession herald significant reform of the stock market in China.

In China's financial sector, the sequence seems to be one of markets preceding laws. Laws appear to develop alongside, and in response to, market needs. As in the United States, laws and regulations were not established in a vacuum to pre-date markets. Instead, some laws (and administrative dictates in China such as the provincial quota system for IPOs) create markets, which gives rise to further laws and regulatory bodies which in turn govern and establish new segments of the market. Therefore, it seems that a more evolutionary process has occurred in China to accompany economic reform such as the *Company Law* and corporatization movement in China, or the passage of IPRs to promote technological advancement. The process is better characterized as complementary rather than sequential or cause and effect.

Complementarities between law and markets

There appears to be a complementary process between law and markets, where law neither entirely precedes market nor vice versa. Formal written law creates property rights in intellectual property, legitimizes corporate forms and establishes capital markets. Informal markets can often also arise through barter or small-scale transactions or in response to market liberalization, for example, privatization of previously state-owned housing. Once the markets are established, then in both common law and civil law traditions, there is a process of interpreting and revising the laws respectively through a judicial or legislative process. This process is driven by interested constituents vested in the markets, which can include holders of IPRs, owners of private firms and shareholders (see Coffee 2001; Sun and Tobin 2009), as well as governments wishing to reform its SOEs (e.g., China in the 1990s) or restore confidence in markets (e.g., U.S. SEC). Countries that produce more effective laws and regulations will have better-functioning markets, which in both the common and civil law traditions occur over time (see La Porta *et al.* 1997, for the finding that better shareholder protection is associated with higher growth rates; see Cull and Xu 2005, for the finding that provinces in China with better legal protection is associated with improved firm performance).

For China, key commercial laws were adopted at comparable levels of development, with China having done so at an earlier stage and with seemingly more impressive economic growth rates. However, the speed of setting up a market or adoption of laws does not equate to effectiveness of the legal system. Undoubtedly, the transition and globalization context increases the complication of this comparison, which will be returned to later in the chapter.

Institutions and transition

The sequence of law and markets is not the only paradox of China's economic success. Markets were created in absence of private property rights as China's transition has been largely undertaken in a state-controlled property system. Law therefore did not play the main role in creating markets during much of China's reform period; instead, administrative dictates and institutional reform were often more crucial. For instance, the passage of the *Company Law* in 1993 occurred after the start of the transformation of SOEs into shareholding companies, just as private firms emerged during the mid-1990s prior to the passage of the *Law on Individual Wholly Owned Enterprises* in 1999 (see Du and Xu 2009, for the argument that administrative arrangements took the place of laws in creating China's capital markets). In numerous examples, Chinese markets began with institutional reform.

Harkening back to the agricultural reforms of the late 1970s and early 1980s, the 'institutional innovations' of the Household Responsibility System (HRS) created property rights by allowing farmers to retain a portion of their earnings under the communal land system (see Lin 1992). Much of China's SOE reform has occurred without an explicit change in ownership from state to private, as the gradual corporatization and the share issue privatization process are ongoing after nearly three decades (see Groves *et al.* 1995).

China's approach has been to pass laws or administrative dictates in an experimental fashion to ultimately achieve successful results. The HRS, responsible for raising agricultural productivity during the early 1980s, was initially banned, then reinstated (see Naughton 1995 for a description of this 'no encouragement, no ban' approach). The same occurred with land tenure rights that led to farmers selling their leaseholds in rural areas, which was initially banned until it became widespread and also pre-dated the passage of the *Property Law* in 2007. Many attribute this flexible approach to 'experimentation' as the source of China's success (see Qian and Xu 1993).

The notable 'institutional innovations' were the HRS for rural residents in the late 1970s and early 1980s, the Budgetary Contracting System (BCS) allowing decentralization of state-owned banks and local authorities in the early 1980s, and the Contract Responsibility System (CRS) instigated in the mid-1980s for SOEs. A more formal set of legal property rights was created for foreign investors in the late 1970s/mid-1980s in the form of joint venture and other corporate laws.

The operation of China's 'dual track' transition, in which one part of the market was liberalized while another was kept under administrative control, depended on generating growth from the marketized part of the economy, which could then subsidize the faltering state-owned sector with the outcome of maintaining economic stability (Lau *et al.* 2001). Prior to the 'institutional innovations', collectivization meant that there was little incentive for farmers to produce output as their work points were allocated on the basis of a day's labor irrespective of effort. Adopted by households gradually in the early 1980s amidst a move to de-collectivize agriculture, the incentives generated from receiving some returns from labor caused agricultural output to increase substantially (Riskin 1987). A significant part of China's growth in agricultural productivity and the overall rural economy can be traced to both the HRS and de-collectivization (Lin 1992; Huang and Rozelle 1996).

Whereas the HRS provided incentives to households, the creation of township and village enterprises (TVEs) is a striking example of how China created a new institution defined by policy and not by private ownership that sufficiently incentivized rural workers that fueled rural industrialization. TVEs grew rapidly and accounted for an impressive one-third of China's total output by the mid-1990s. Growth stemming from these reforms is notable, as rural industrialization helped remove surplus farm labor and significantly reduced rural poverty (see Ravallion and Chen 2007).

With respect to the urban economy, the CRS in the mid-1980s permitted SOEs to pay a fixed amount of taxes and profits to the state and retain the remainder (Koo 1990). In principle, as long as the SOEs delivered the tax and profit remittances, they were free to operate. This resulted in increased SOE productivity in the late 1980s through reorientation of managerial incentives

(Groves *et al.* 1995). However, the decline of SOEs in the 1990s illustrates the limits of institutional innovations as incentive when SOEs receive state support and are not driven by profit and cost. Indeed, many SOEs became stock-holding companies in the 1990s with ownership changing into private hands, despite the positive incentives offered by the CRS (Choo and Yin 2000).

State sector reform was also important. Decentralization has occurred in nearly all areas of decision making in production, pricing, investment, trade, expenditure, income distribution, taxation and credit allocation through the BCS (Riskin 1987). Fiscal decentralization further gave scope for regional experimentation by local governments, a key element to China's gradualist path because it permitted market-oriented activity while limiting the possibility of instability through enabling the fairly autonomous actions of different provinces to act relatively independently.

Since 1985, state grants for operating funds and fixed-asset investments have been replaced by private bank lending. Local governments and SOEs are also allowed to borrow directly from banks and, later, from households and other institutions. The People's Bank of China, was shifted toward becoming a central bank and shed its retail banking functions by reforming it to focus on monetary policy formulation in the mid-1980s. Its banking functions were in turn divided into four state-owned commercial banks (SCBs): Industrial and Commercial Bank of China, China Construction Bank, Bank of China and the Agricultural Bank of China. Three more policy banks were also formed in 1994 to take over the developmental aims of the state banking system: China Development Bank, Export–Import Bank of China and the Agricultural Development Bank of China. There is also a second tier of state-owned banks, which have shares owned by the government and private entities. There are approximately a dozen or so of these joint stock commercial banks, largely set up in the 1990s. A commercial banking law was passed in 1995, though reforms pre-date the law and are driven by governmental institutional reform. Other financial institutions, such as investment banks and other financial intermediaries, made little headway until liberalization sped up in the 1990s in anticipation of accession to the WTO.

Therefore, across all sectors of the economy, marketization, though imperfect, has gradually taken hold in a transitioning China (see, e.g., Young 2000; Anderson 2011: 25; deLisle 2014). Given the gradual reform over three decades whereby the market developed over time, the legal system supporting the market economy was likewise underdeveloped for most of this period. Instead, the development of the market in China can be traced to governmental administrative dictates and institutional reforms (see, e.g., Du and Xu 2009, for the argument that administrative measures creating a quota system across provinces produced a successful stock market in China during the 1990s). Not all of which were initiated by the state, but the system was adaptable, including to economic experiments that often led to the passage of law and regulations by the government, such as the *Property Law* of 2007. Individuals and firms, moreover, responded well to the incentives generated by administrative measures. China's strong administrative law tradition perhaps is one explanation of the willingness of the populace to rely upon such administrative arrangements instead of clearly defined property rights established in law.

Enforcement of laws

Enforcement further points to the continued presence of informal institutions, such as reliance on relational contracting or trust-based relationships in China. There is undoubtedly a cultural element in that interpersonal relationships, such as *guanxi*, play a notable role in economic transactions within and without China, even among the overseas diasporas. Within China itself, this was also perhaps enabled by the reliance on administrative dictates – a legacy of China's administrative law tradition.

Due to the absence of a well-established legal system, developing countries tend to rely on informal institutional arrangements, such as utilization of social capital or relational-based contracting whereby contracting is undertaken with people on the basis of trust. Even developed countries at the start of their marketization relied on such relationships (see, e.g., Franks *et al.* 2009, who studied the development of the UK capital market and found that ownership dispersion relied more on informal relations of trust than on formal systems of regulation). Enforcement, which is often a challenge in an underdeveloped legal system, can be by means of social capital instead of courts. For instance, social sanctions and norms account for the success of microfinance institutions such as the Grameen Bank in Bangladesh. The high repayment rate of loans is not due to threatened legal action, but on account of social capital in the community that acts to enforce the terms of the loan. By overlooking informal institutional arrangements that support the rule of law and other formal institutions, the extent of legal and institutional reform can be misjudged and developing countries could suffer from misfashioned policies as a result. In other words, as countries are increasingly judged on the quality of their institutions, poor legal systems are a common area of criticism of developing countries and aid or technical assistance can hinge on legal reform so leading to adoption of laws that may not suit the country. At the extreme, 'transplanting' legal systems into less developed countries has not been successful (see Pistor *et al.* 2000, for the conclusion that legal systems transplanted into newly transitioning economies were not successful in fostering economic growth).

As the number of arm's-length agreements increases, the ability of informal enforcement arrangements is insufficient and requires the judicial system to develop the ability to enforce contracts and agreements. The development of legal reforms in the West followed a similar pattern, suggesting that greater marketization will require more legal reform to govern relationships that can no longer rely on trust alone. However, relational contracting, i.e., dealing with trusted parties, is much cheaper than litigation if a relationship goes sour, which also explains the continued reliance on social capital in small businesses even in developed economies with more complete but expensive legal systems. China is at a stage where its small businesses and entrepreneurs can still effectively utilize informal institutional arrangements for enforcement alongside the reforming formal legal ones.

Given the necessarily slow pace of creating an independent judiciary, it is likely that informal arrangements, particularly arbitration – when the transactions are more arm's length – will remain in place for some time to come. However, this can also help explain how China has been able to grow and become marketized with a legal system that suffers from weak enforcement and thus lacks effectiveness.

Conclusions

China's economic performance over the past 35 years or so has been the envy of many developing and transition economies, as well as being an 'outlier' with its poor legal system and rapid growth. A key aspect of China's reform is the influence of the international economic system. While China gradually integrated itself into the global economy during the 1990s, the world economy also underwent a transformation, with the emergence of a growing body of international economic laws and rules. In this chapter, several aspects of the relationship between law and economic growth in China have been examined. It assessed the theoretical and empirical relationship between laws and the development of markets across countries, spanning currently developed, developing and recently transitioned economies. The relationship between law and markets appears asynchronous for China. By comparing three Chinese legal reforms – intellectual property protection, corporate law and securities regulation – a pattern shows that law may have created a market in the case of IPRs and enabled corporations, but regulations giving substance to law generally were passed after there was an evident economic necessity, such as abuse of monopoly power or financial sector scandals. Therefore, although a law or administrative dictate (or absence of strict prohibition) may create a market (or an informal one), this factor alone is insufficient to argue that the sequence must be laws preceding markets. By the yardstick of whether an effective rule of law exists, which goes beyond just the provisions that create an IPR or a corporate form, laws appear to develop in response to market demands and needs, which in turn leads to more marketization and economic development.

This perspective reconciles existing views in the literature by arguing that it is the case that laws both precede and follow markets. Thus, this chapter posits that the literature describes different facets of an evolving picture (see, for instance, Chen 2003, who subscribes to the 'crash-then-law' hypothesis, versus La Porta *et al.* 1997, 1998 and Acemoglu *et al.* 2005, who argue that the existence of market-supporting institutions is the cause of subsequent robust growth). It is difficult, if not impossible, to fit China into one paradigm given its history and context.

Exploration of the paradox in China's development of a market within a state-controlled property system shows that a lack of laws clearly defining property rights appears not to be as pertinent as perhaps in other countries. Administrative measures and ensuing institutional reform complete the picture for China, whereby its several-decades-long economic transition has been driven by a series of experiments, trials and 'no encouragement, no ban' policies.

Finally, the chapter concludes by accounting for the influence of the global rules-based system that is gradually emerging and gained prominence around the same time as China's integration into the international system after years of inward-focused development. There are numerous limitations in the reach of the fledgling international legal system, but certain rules such as IPR protection will influence the course of China's domestic reforms. The system, though, is two-way. Particularly in the area of voluntary adherence to rules and norms, China and its firms will seek those which advantage them while at the same time operating in the evolving global financial system. The picture may be more complex, but looks ever more evolutionary as countries gather at various international forums to negotiate and agree everything from liberalization of trade to rules governing risk assessment of banks.

China may continue to be viewed as a paradox, but its path will be enticing for many developing countries in which it is not unusual to have a nascent legal system that will not rate well in terms of effectiveness or enforcement. The success of China, and the prospect of it strengthening laws alongside robust economic growth, has the possibility of being a model to emulate.

6 Efforts towards procedural justice in post-Mao China

Jianfu Chen

Introduction

Procedural justice is seen in the West as a core of democracy. The essence of justice, we are reminded, is largely procedural (Davis 1972: 192, cited in Bayle 1990: 1). 'The history of liberty has largely been the history of procedural safeguards', Justice Frankfurter declared. 'It is procedure that spells much of the difference between rule by law and rule by whim or caprice' (ibid.). Means are thus as important as ends, if not more so. In China, the legal framework providing procedural justice is fragmented and weak, but its importance is increasingly recognized.

Procedural justice necessarily encompasses two kinds of demands: that government decisions will be made under certain procedural principles established for the protection of those affected by such decisions; and that resolution of disputes or the administration of justice will be conducted under procedural safeguards against injustice.

Traditionally, Chinese positive law was mainly conceived of as penal law, operated in a vertical direction and used as a supplementary means for maintaining a hierarchical social relationship. It made no distinctions between public and private law, administration and the judicature and substantive and procedural law. Such distinctions were only introduced into China during the Westernization/modernization processes starting around the turn of the twentieth century (Chen 2008: ch. 1). While modern law reform began to separate procedural law from substantive law and introduce procedural requirements into Chinese law, Communist justice, as practiced in the first 30 years of the People's Republic of China (PRC), destroyed such distinctions and rejected these requirements (Chen 2008: ch. 2). Procedural justice is thus a notion that was reintroduced to Chinese law in post-Mao reforms. Not surprisingly, the establishment and consolidation of such a notion in Chinese law has been difficult.

This chapter overviews efforts in post-Mao China to reintroduce procedural justice into Chinese law. Specifically, it focuses on the development and reform of the three principal procedural laws: *Criminal Procedure Law*, *Civil Procedure Law*[1] and *Administrative Litigation Law*.[2]

The development of the *Criminal Procedure Law*

Many initial studies of post-Mao legal reform focused on civil and commercial law, which were the most prominent areas of legal development at the time. However, procedural law was in fact also among the first laws enacted in post-Mao China. The *Criminal Procedure Law 1979* (CPL), based on drafts prepared in the mid-1950s and early 1960s,[3] was one of the first seven major laws enacted in post-Mao China.[4] The purpose of its enactment was twofold: to elaborate the constitutional provisions regarding the division of powers and responsibilities among the People's Courts, the People's Procuratorates and the public security organs; and to provide working procedures for criminal adjudication. Although the 1979 CPL was supposed to be a comprehensive code, its provisions were short and often ambiguous. Its deficiencies, both on the face and in actual practice, were soon to become apparent and thus attract severe criticism both internally and, in particular, from Western human rights organizations (see e.g. Amnesty International 1991, 1992, 1996; Lawyers Committee for Human Rights 1993). Fundamentally, many important 'due process' principles, such as the presumption of innocence, the right to silence, rules against self-incrimination, judicial independence and adequate right to legal counsel were absent from the 1979 CPL. Many other provisions of the 1979 CPL fell far short of minimum requirements for the administration of justice.[5]

This defective law was made worse by many decisions of the Standing Committee of the NPC (SCNPC) issued during various anti-crime campaigns (see HLR Note 1985; Townsend 1987–8; Traveskes 2007). Many of these decisions were issued specifically for anti-crime campaigns with ad hoc policy orientations and were severely criticized by Chinese scholars as blatant violations of the Chinese Constitution (Cui 1995: 96). Together with the inability, or unwillingness, of the law-enforcement authorities to act within the law, the 1979 CPL (and its practices), instead of providing procedural safeguards, became liabilities to human rights in China (Lawyers Committee for Human Rights 1993: 1).

It should, however, be noted that the 1979 CPL was a product of its time. The 1979 CPL was adopted before the promulgation of the 1982 Constitution which provides general principles for the administration of justice that had been absent from the 1978 Constitution. Further, the promulgation of the 1979 CPL coincided with the re-establishment of law-enforcement institutions: the public security organs, the People's Procuratorates and the courts. The latter two had been 'effectively smashed during the so-called Cultural Revolution of 1966–1976' (Zhao 1990: 368). The inability of law-enforcement authorities and judicial organs to act in accordance with law could be argued as 'to be expected'. The abuse of the criminal process is, however, quite another matter. Finally and most importantly, in the late 1970s, legal research and study had only just resumed after the Cultural Revolution, as had debates on fundamental 'due process' principles. The applicability of these principles in China was unsettled then and hotly contested; the concept of procedural justice was yet to be introduced into Chinese law.

With the development of legal research and the 'open door' policy that brought in foreign influences, Chinese scholars soon recognized deficiencies in their law and began to argue for many Western criminal procedure principles to be included in the CPL (see Chen 1989). Many implementation problems of the 1979 CPL also came to the attention of scholars and officials and the issue of revising the CPL soon became a topic of both academic discussion and official consideration (Gu 1989: 206).

The first major reform of the CPL took place in 1996, a process that could essentially be described as a major 'joint venture' between scholars and law-makers (see Chen Jianfu 2013: ch. 3). The revision was a major one: 70 of the original 164 articles were revised, two articles abolished and 63 articles added to the CPL, thus making the CPL much more comprehensive and precise. Most significantly the revised CPL incorporated certain fundamental 'due process' principles, including a limited version of the presumption of innocence, for the first time in the PRC, representing a moderate progress towards fair administration of law (Chen Jianfu 1997).

While the 1996 reform was significant, it was incomplete, representing compromises rather than clear advances in procedural justice. Further, practical difficulties soon emerged, especially in the roles of lawyer in criminal processes and in the protection of lawyers' rights as incorporated in the 1996 CPL (see e.g. Human Rights Watch 2008; McConville 2011). At the same time, academic studies on the CPL were becoming increasingly sophisticated, focusing on both particular aspects of the law and specific practical issues (see e.g. Chen Guangzhong 2005; Xiong 2004; Xiang *et al.* 2005). These studies helped law-makers and law-enforcement officials to better understand not only the operation of the law, but also specific difficulties and problems in its theory and practice. Thus, when revising the CPL, law-makers accepted that the various compromises that had been made earlier were part of the cause of its generally unsatisfactory operation (Yao 2012: 27–9). In October 2003, the SCNPC formally decided to start a new revision by including the task in its five-year legislative plan. Once again, renewed joint efforts were made by academics and officials towards a comprehensive revision of the CPL (see Chen Jianfu 2013: ch. 3), leading to yet another round of reforms in 2012.

The 2012 revision is once again a major reform. More than half of the 1996 CPL provisions were revised (Yao 2012: 31) and four major chapters/sections were added to the CPL, generally continuing the reform started in 1996. The result is, again, a compromise between academics, law-makers and law enforcement agencies (*Legal Daily* 2011; Yao 2012).

The present CPL is thus far from perfect, but the combined effects of the 1996 and 2012 revisions remain far-reaching.

First, there has been a fundamental ideological shift in the understanding of the functions of the procedural law. Article 1 of the original 1979 CPL provided that the CPL:

> taking Marxism-Leninism-Mao Zedong Thought as its guide and the Constitution as its basis, is formulated in the light of the actual circumstances and concrete experiences of the people of all China's nationalities in carrying

> out the people's democratic dictatorship, led by the proletariat and based on the worker-peasant alliance, that is, the dictatorship of the proletariat, and for the practical purpose of attacking the enemy and protecting the people.

Clearly, it reflected the understanding at the time of law being a weapon for class struggle. This article was revised in 1996, which then provided that the CPL 'is formulated in accordance with the Constitution, in order to ensure the proper enforcement of the *Criminal Law*, to punish crimes, to protect people, to safeguard national security and public safety, and to maintain a socialist social order'.[6] This revision indicates an ideological shift, *from* class struggle *to* maintaining law and order. In March 2004, the 1982 Constitution was revised for the fourth time, declaring that the state respects and protects human rights (para 3, Art. 33 of the revised Constitution). This declaration soon led to 'calls from NPC deputies, academics, lawyers and organizations for the inclusion of human rights protection' in revising the CPL (Liu Wenfeng 2012: 93). While efforts were made to improve human rights protection in criminal processes, the call for an explicit declaration of human rights protection in the CPL encountered considerable resistance. The official line was that Art. 1 already contained the phrase 'protecting the people' and therefore there was no need to add any new human rights provision (*Sina News* 2012). Thus neither the draft issued for public consultation in October 2011, nor the second draft for deliberation by the SCNPC in December 2011, contained any direct reference to human rights protection. A compromise was reached only in the final draft submitted to the full NPC for deliberation and adoption (*Sina News* 2012): instead of declaring human rights protection in Art. 1, the revised Art. 2 added the protection and respect of human rights as one of the tasks of the CPL. While some Chinese scholars were not satisfied that human rights protection provision was not set out in Art. 1 as an underlying principle for the CPL (*Sina News* 2012; Yao 2012: 27–8), it is, nevertheless, a conceptual advance for the CPL.

Second, 'due process' principles or, more precisely, certain elements of these principles such as the presumption of innocence, the right to silence and the rule against self-incrimination, have now been incorporated into the CPL. The right to counsel, including stronger protection for timely access to a defence lawyer, has been significantly improved (for detailed analysis, see Chen Jianfu 2013).

Third, fundamental reforms have been introduced to the Chinese pre-trial and trial processes. These include reforms to the collegiate panel and judicial committee, establishment of stricter time limits for detention and semi-adversary process, stricter rules on investigation and evidence, and abolition of the notorious and often abused 'Shelter and Investigation' and 'Exemption from Prosecution' used widely by the police and prosecutors respectively before its abolition in 1996 (Chen Jianfu 2013).

The development of the *Civil Procedure Law*

The PRC did not have a comprehensive code on civil procedures until 1982, when the *Civil Procedure Law of the PRC (Trial Implementation)* was issued. The 1982 law was, however, interim in nature and soon replaced by the *Civil Procedure Law of the PRC* in 1991. The latter has had two major revisions in 2007 and 2012 respectively.

The reform of the *Civil Procedure Law* has been much less controversial and, mostly, led by the judiciary towards resolving specific practical issues. Put simply, the actual operation of the 1991 *Civil Procedure Law* had been plagued by some major problems in trial processes, evidence rules and the difficulties and problems of enforcing court judgments and rulings (Chen Jianfu 2008: ch. 18). After many years of ad hoc efforts to tackle these problems through judicial interpretations, the *Civil Procedure Law* was revised in 2007. Many more regulations, provisions and measures were also issued by the Supreme People's Court independently or jointly with other state authorities. On the basis of experience of these reforms, a more comprehensive revision of the *Civil Procedure Law* was undertaken in 2012 (see 2012 Decision to Revise the Civil Procedure Law). The 2012 revision is an effort to consolidate many ad hoc reforms that had been undertaken by the Supreme People's Court as well as other law-enforcement authorities. As a comprehensive reform, the revision further improves provisions on mediation, evidence, supervision, trial processes and enforcement.

While many improvements have been made to the 1991 *Civil Procedure Law* through the 2007 and 2012 reforms, the following are particularly noteworthy in terms of procedural safeguards as well as measures to ensure efficiency and effectiveness in civil justice. First, the 1991 *Civil Procedure Law* (before the 2012 revision) did not contain the notion of 'discovery', nor a process of it as practised in many Western jurisdictions. Through the Certain Provisions of the Supreme People's Court on Civil Litigation Evidence (2001), a limited 'discovery' process (called exchange of evidence) was first introduced as a preliminary process before a formal court trial. This judicial initiative has now been formally recognized by the 2012 revised *Civil Procedure Law*.[7]

Second, the evidence rules in the *Civil Procedure Law* are, for practical purposes, far too simplistic and hardly of much usefulness. Not surprisingly, these rules have had to be heavily supplemented, first by Opinions of the Supreme Court on the Implementation of Civil Procedure Law (July 1992), and then more comprehensively by the Certain Provisions of the Supreme People's Court on Civil Litigation Evidence (2001). Together, these rules not only further clarify the meanings of each type of evidence, but also establish rules for proof, evaluation and cross-examination and debate in court.

Third, similar to reforms undertaken in criminal trial processes, the civil trial processes have undergone major reform, again led by the judiciary through the issuance of judicial 'interpretations' such as the Opinions of the Supreme Court on the Application of Civil Procedure Law (July 1992)[8] and the Certain

Provisions Concerning Issues on Reform of Civil and Economic Trial Methods.[9] The overall trend of these reforms is to allow more active roles for lawyers, make judges less interventionist and ensure alternative resolution such as mediation is utilized whenever possible.

The most important and extensive reforms have been in relation to the execution of court judgments and rulings. The 1991 *Civil Procedure Law*, through Part Three, lays down some general principles for execution, provides procedures for application and transfer for execution, defines legal and coercive measures that might be taken by courts to enforce their judgments and rulings, and sets out certain conditions for the suspension and termination of execution. But it has been notoriously difficult to enforce court judgments and rulings (Chen Jianfu 2008: ch. 18).

Extensive reforms have been undertaken, principally led by the Supreme People's Court but often with the collaboration of other authorities and the Party, to address the various problems and difficulties. The most important efforts, prior to the last revision of the *Civil Procedure Law* in 2012, included the Opinions on the Implementation of the Civil Procedure Law of the PRC (1992),[10] the Certain Provisions Concerning People's Court Execution Work (Trial Implementation), the 2007 revision of the *Civil Procedure Law* and the Interpretations on Certain Issues Concerning the Application of Execution Procedures of the PRC Civil Procedure Law (2008). Although these measures do overcome some difficulties, by no means do they solve the problems in the enforcement of the law. These judicial efforts also cause the legal framework governing court execution of judgments and rulings to become complicated, ad hoc and fragmented. Not surprisingly, expectations of the 2012 revision of the *Civil Procedure Law* were high for deep reform and the incorporation of the various judicial measures. In this context, the 2012 revision of the Civil *Procedure Law* was a major disappointment. Although several provisions of the 1991 *Civil Procedure Law* were revised (see Arts 52–57 of the 2012 Decision to Revise the Civil Procedure Law), the real change was minimal.[11] Perhaps the greatest disappointment lies in the failure to incorporate the provisions and rules that had been issued by the Supreme People's Court and practised over the past two decades, thus leaving these rules and practices uncertain as to their continuing validity.[12]

The development of the *Administrative Litigation Law*

Perhaps the most important development in relation to procedural justice has been the adoption of the *Administrative Litigation Law* (ALL) in 1989, which signalled the separation of procedural and substantive administration law and the formal institution of a distinct procedure parallel to the civil and criminal procedures. The ALL, however, is among the most controversial legislation ever enacted in post-Mao China.[13] It is a product of academic effort[14] as well as a compromise between various authorities with vested interests including the courts, bureaucratic authorities and the reformist intellectual constituency.[15]

Yet when the ALL was adopted it was variously described by its opponents as 'a law exceeding historical development [and thus] unsuitable for the Chinese situation' (quoted in Luo 1995: 3), 'a law with a premature birth by twenty years' and 'a result of [bourgeois] liberalisation' (quoted in Pi 1995: 12). The various controversies and compromise solutions have hounded the implementation of the ALL since its 1990 implementation.

The 1989 ALL, while historically important in that it changed the conception of administration law in the PRC, was generally a weak law plagued by many problems in both theory and practice. Of the ALL, Wang Zhenyu and Wang Jingcheng (1997: 79) say:

> There are operational barriers in the system. Its ability to settle administrative disputes is limited. Its efficacy in achieving justice by subjecting administration to rules of law is not good. It is incapable of regulating the relationship between an individual and the government. Its function in promoting democracy and constitutionalism is weak.

The implementation problems of the ALL are often described in terms of 'three kinds of difficulties', in (1) filing a case, (2) adjudication and (3) enforcement of judgments and decisions (see ALL Explanations, NPC Standing Committee 2013). Although the Explanations did not elaborate on the 'three kinds of difficulties', the *China Youth Daily* summarized them in this way:

> First, the total number of cases is relatively low. Published statistics indicates that, from 1990 when the ALL was implemented, to 2012 Chinese courts had only adjudicated 1.91 million administrative litigation cases, or on average 83,168 cases a year. At the moment, Chinese courts accept about 120,000 cases annually. Secondly, the rate of success [for complainants] is low. At the end of 2008 the success rate for the previous three years was below 30%, but this rate has decreased and at the moment it is under 10%. Thirdly, once complainants have won the case, it is difficult to enforce the judgements or decisions. If the administrative authorities refuse to comply with court decisions, there is little that the courts can do, nor is there any compulsory measure that the courts can take [against the administrative authorities]. Law thus becomes empty words.
>
> (Yan 2013)

Chinese NPC deputy, Gu Shengzu, further contextualizes the above statistics thus:

> The Chinese courts now accept about 100,000 administrative litigation cases annually. This amounts to about 1% of the total caseload of 12 million accepted by courts annually.... [Meanwhile], and taking 2011 as an example, the appeal rate for administrative litigation was 72.85%, which is 6 times that in criminal law litigation and 2.4 times that in civil litigation.

> And the petition rate in administrative litigation is 8.5%, which is 6 times that in criminal cases and 6.3 times that in civil disputes.
>
> (Cited in Ma 2013)

Clearly, the implementation of the ALL is perceived as problematic by lawmakers and the general public, and in-depth analyses of reasonably systematic statistics undertaken by scholars in and outside China suggest that the implementation of the ALL has been generally disappointing (see Zhu 2012: 129–36, analysing most comprehensive and systematic national statistics; He 2012, analysing national statistics; and Li 2013b, analysing provincial-level statistics).

Defective as the ALL might be, it remained unrevised for more than 20 years – unusual in post-Mao China. Some of its deficiencies were, for practical purposes, indirectly revised at various times by rules issued by the Supreme People's Court. For adjudication purposes at least four sets of important general rules have been issued by the Supreme People's Court in recent years,[16] many containing more detailed provisions than originally contained in the ALL, and some clearly inconsistent with the provisions of the ALL (thus practically revising the ALL).[17]

It was the failure of the Law to perform as an external control mechanism as had been hoped for, however, that prompted strong calls for its formal revision. Advocacy for reforming the ALL emerged not long after the implementation of the Law, principally from academics and practising lawyers. These voices have become stronger in the last decade or so.[18]

While there had been no disagreement on the need for the ALL to be revised and updated, there were major disagreements as to the extent of and approach to revising the Law, and on specific issues such as the conceptual foundation of the law, structure, applicable scope of the law, court jurisdiction, public interest litigation and the use of mediation in administrative litigation (for a summary of disagreement on these issues, see Jiang 2011; Mo 2011; Ying and Yang 2011). As is often the case in dealing with controversies about revising laws, the SCNPC decided to take an approach of gradual improvement. According to the 2013 ALL Explanations, revision work was to be guided by four principles: (1) addressing the urgent practical problems; (2) ensuring access to judicial remedies; (3) approaching reform through gradual improvement; and (4) incorporating judicial experience into the law. In other words, the ALL was not to be rewritten, but practical difficulties identified would be addressed.[19] The 2014 revision thus focused primarily on the 'three difficulties' through expanding the scope of application and strengthening of court processes.

In relation to applicability, the scope of the original ALL was narrow, being first limited by an abstract notion of 'concrete administrative acts',[20] further limited by the enunciation of types of reviewable concrete administrative acts (see Art. 11 of the 1989 ALL), and finally limited by specific exclusions (see Art. 12 of the 1989 ALL). Among the limiting factors, the distinction between abstract and concrete administrative acts, which leaves a huge area of administrative discretion without legal remedies, had caused major controversy in China ever since the enactment of the ALL. Not surprisingly, and increasingly, more and more scholars have called for revisions to allow the court to review the validity of 'abstract administrative acts' such as *guizhang* (i.e. departmental and governmental rules) and other 'normative documents'.[21] Others have also suggested that the establishment of a specialized administrative court system is needed to address the problems in the scope of law and jurisdiction issues (Mo 2011; Li 2013c; Lang and Lang 2014). Expanding its applicability then became, according to Chinese scholars, a most important, most critical and most sensitive issue for the revision of the ALL (NPC 2013).

The revised ALL now has the list of reviewable acts expanded,[22] incorporating reviewable acts that have already been declared by other administrative laws as well as providing new grounds, such as land acquisition/requisition decisions, or government inactions or non-responses to requests.[23] Further, most of the original eight reviewable acts have been revised by making such review grounds even more specific, hence difficult for court to refuse litigation cases.[24] The revised ALL now replaces the phrase 'concrete administrative acts' with the simple phrase 'administrative acts'.[25] While it is doubtful whether this phrase change actually expands the scope of ALL, it can also be argued that some limited progress has been made. Article 53 (a new addition introduced by the 2014 revision) now provides that:

> When citizens, legal persons or other organisations believe that a normative document, which is enacted by the State Council authorities or local governments and departments and which forms the basis for an administrative act, is unlawful, they can request the court to review the normative document when taking legal action against the administrative act.

Article 53, however, specifically stipulates that 'normative documents' do not include *guizhang*.[26] The new Art. 53 thus expands the jurisdiction of the court to review a limited type of abstract administrative act (i.e. normative documents). The scope of the ALL is thus expanded, but only to a very limited extent. For practical purposes, this limited expansion is strengthened by technical improvements made to ensure wider participation in administrative litigation – such as new definitions of 'administrative act' and 'third party', measures to address delays through internal review, and improvement for joint lawsuits. In relation to legal processes, several distinct features of the 1989 ALL that provide stronger protection for plaintiffs have been further strengthened in the 2014 revision.

First, the burden of proof falls wholly on the respondent, that is, the administrative decision-making organ. Once a lawsuit is instigated it is up to the decision makers to prove the legality of the decision and to establish a legal basis for such a decision (Art. 34 of the 2014 ALL (Art. 32 of the 1989 ALL)). The 2014 revision further provides that the court will deem it lack of evidence if the respondent refuses to provide evidence or is unable to provide the evidence within the set time limit without proper reasons (see para 2 of Art. 34 of the 2014 ALL). Further, the respondent is prohibited from collecting evidence from the applicant or the witnesses on its own authority (Art. 35 of the 2014 ALL (Art. 33 of the 1989 ALL)); such authority lies with the courts (Art. 39 of 2014 ALL (Art. 34 of the 1989 ALL)). The court is not allowed to collect evidence that would support the legality of an administrative decision if such evidence was not collected when the administrative decision was made (Art. 40 of the 2014 ALL (which amended para 2 of Art. 34 of the 1989 ALL)). In a country like China, where freedom of information is still a relatively novel idea, this evidence rule,[27] if properly implemented, has the potential to overcome some deficiencies in the Chinese administrative law system.

Second, unlike civil procedures, mediation is not applicable in administrative litigation (Art. 60 of the 2014 ALL (Art. 50 of the 1989 ALL)), and withdrawal of a case – even if the respondent has agreed to amend the original decision(s) – requires court approval (Art. 62 of the 2014 ALL (Art. 51 of the 1989 ALL)). The exclusion of mediation reflects two things: a concern of law-makers about parties' power imbalances, and a conception that public administration is not of the same nature as private rights. The approval requirement for withdrawal is essentially included to prevent complainants from being coerced by government authorities (Luo 1996: 400–1). The non-applicability of mediation does not, however, mean that the parties cannot reconcile differences between themselves (Xiao 1991: 22–6). Reconciliation is actively encouraged by the courts (Luo 1996: 401), and mediation – in a disguised form called 'coordination' – is encouraged to achieve 'voluntary' withdrawal of complaints against administrative authorities when the latter are persuaded to partially amend their decisions or compensate complainants (Zhu 2012: 136). In light of actual practice, many have argued that the revised law should incorporate mediation as a mechanism for settling disputes (see Jiang 2011; Mo 2011; Ying and Yang 2011). The 2014 revised ALL, however, continues the stipulation on the non-applicability of mediation in adjudicating administrative cases. But it does allow exceptions, mediation being allowed in cases concerning 'administration compensation or the exercise by administrative authorities of statutory discretionary powers' (see Art. 60 of the 2014 ALL).

A number of issues have been identified by scholars as causing the so-called 'three kinds of difficulties' associated with the process. First, to address the difficulties in filing a case in, and accepting a case by, courts,[28] a new article is added, which provides that

> [P]eople's courts shall protect the right of citizens, legal persons and organisations to sue and shall accept cases that should be accepted in accordance with the Law. Neither the administrative authority nor its personnel shall interfere with or prevent the court from accepting cases. The person in charge of the defendant administrative authority shall appear before the court to respond to law suits, or entrust a relevant official to appear before the court if he or she is unable to appear personally.
>
> (See Art. 3 of the 2014 ALL, being a new addition introduced by the 2014 revision)

These obligations, imposed on courts and administrative authorities, are further implemented in the revised legal processes. Thus, to reinforce the right to sue, when a complaint is made to a court it must be registered and filed on the spot as long as the complaint meets legal requirements for filing a suit. If it is not possible to determine whether the complaint meets the legal requirements, a dated receipt must be issued and a ruling as to whether to accept the case must be made by the court seven days after the complaint is filed. If the case is rejected, the ruling must provide the reasons for rejection. A plaintiff then has a right to appeal to a higher-level court. If there are corrections or supplementation required, guidance and explanations for required actions must be made to the plaintiff. Indeed, a complaint must not be dismissed without explanation or guidance having been given to the plaintiff. If a court fails to accept the case and fails to issue a ruling on the refusal, the complainant may lodge his/her suit at a higher-level court. This higher-level court may try the case itself or instruct a lower-level court to do so. Finally, a plaintiff may complain to a higher court against the trial court (or its personnel) if the court (or its personnel) fails to meet the above requirements. Disciplinary sanctions against persons directly in charge of the complaints at the lower court and against persons directly involved in the handling of the complaints may then ensue (see Art. 51 of the 2014 ALL, being a new addition introduced by the 2014 revision). These provisions mean that failure to fulfil obligations imposed by the new Art. 3 attract legal consequences or remedies.

A major difficulty surrounding the filing of cases is a lack of judicial independence. Chinese courts are funded and judges appointed by local authorities. Under the administrative jurisdiction, administrative complaints are all filed locally. It is no secret that local administrative authorities often pressure courts not to accept certain cases. In response, some local courts have taken the initiative of allowing cross-regional jurisdiction of administrative litigation. This practice has increased litigation costs and caused some problems in terms of resources; however, such initiative appears to have increased the rate of cases being accepted by courts.[29] In January 2013, the Supreme People's Court issued its Notice on Gradual Expansion of Trial Work on Relatively Centralised Jurisdiction of Administrative Cases. Under this Notice, selected intermediate courts are to centrally allocate jurisdiction to basic courts and, by doing so, avoid administrative interference in administrative litigation. This Notice thus effectively endorses local trial experiments.

The 2014 revision now incorporates these locally initiated practices. First, while the basic courts are still the first instance courts for administrative litigation (Art. 14 of the 2014 ALL (Art. 13 of the 1989 ALL)), a High Court, with the approval of the Supreme People's Court, may now designate some courts to accept cross-regional cases (see Art. 18 of the 2014 ALL (being the amended Art. 17 of the 1989 ALL)). Second, jurisdiction over administrative action against government at county level and State Council departments will be exercised by intermediate courts rather than basic courts (which are funded by county-level government) (see Art. 15 of the 2014 ALL (being the amended Art. 14 of the 1989 ALL)).

Another notable improvement is the establishment of a summary procedure scheme for small amount claims (under 2,000 yuan), or complaints against decisions that were made on the spot in accordance with law, or cases concerning the disclosure of government information, or in which parties agree to the application of summary proceedings (see Arts 82, 83 and 84 of the 2014 ALL (being new additions introduced by the 2014 revision)). Additionally, major improvements have been made to evidence rules (the reform of which had been led by the Supreme People's Court[30]), types of judicial orders and improved court powers to compel government agencies to comply with the ALL.

Conclusion

Several conclusions can be made regarding the development of procedural justice in China. First, although procedural laws were enacted in the early days of post-Mao China, the conception of procedural law then was very different from today. Procedural laws were initially conceived as working procedures for implementing substantive laws; notions of protection and safeguard were absent. Second, the development of procedural justice has taken a gradual and incremental pathway with much of the effort led by the judiciary and academics. However, an overall trend has become clearer in that the pathway has been towards the protection of parties involved in litigation. Third, while the incremental and gradual approach towards improving procedural laws has now changed the fundamental nature of these laws, many reforms are still technical in nature. Significant questions also remain around judicial independence. For some, this is perhaps the 'most glaring deficiency in the PRC's trial process' (Lawyers Committee for Human Rights 1993: 52). This remains not properly addressed and is unlikely to be resolved any time soon. The lack of judicial independence, coupled with stresses on the Party leadership, has led to a situation wherein the Party is working with, not above nor below, the law. However, in the CPC's own rhetoric, 'the Party shall supervise itself' instead of relying on the CPL. Thus, the Party continues to rely on its own extra-legal mechanism – '*Shuanggui*'[31] – in its fight against corruption. Finally, as with substantive law, the actual functioning of procedural law is obviously far from perfect. But the problems outlined in this chapter are best viewed in their historical context. The notion of procedural justice is a very recent introduction to China. By definition it needs time to be developed and adapted.

Notes

1 There is also a special civil procedure law, the *Maritime Litigation Law*. Also see Isaac Kardon's chapter in this volume.
2 Procedural justice in relation to administrative decision making is not addressed in this chapter. For detail on administrative law, see Chen Jianfu (2008: ch. 6). Also see Weitseng Chen's chapter in this volume.
3 In particular it was based on a draft prepared in 1963. See Peng (1992: 157).

4 The other six laws include a substantial criminal code, an organic law and an election law for local people's congresses and local governments, two organic laws for the people's courts and people's procuratorates respectively, and a law on Sino-foreign equity joint ventures.

5 By minimum requirements I mean those provisions embodied in the Universal Declaration of Human Rights (1948) and the International Covenant on Civil and Political Rights (ICCPR) (1966). Many of the principles in these two documents are elaborated in other UN Conventions, e.g. UN Convention against Torture and Other Cruel, Inhuman or Degrading Treatment or Punishment, and principles adopted by various UN agencies and endorsed by the UN General Assembly, e.g. General Comments made by the UN Human Rights Committee under the ICCPR, the UN Body of Principles for the Protection of All Persons under Any Form of Detention or Imprisonment (GA Resolution 43/173, 1988), Basic Principles on the Role of Lawyers, endorsed by UN Resolution 45/121 (1990), Basic Principles on the Independence of the Judiciary, endorsed by UN GA Resolution 40/146 (1985), and many more. Of course these are ideal and desired practices that are not necessarily satisfied in many countries.

6 This provision remains unchanged in the 2012 reform.

7 Article 133, a new article added to the *Civil Procedure Law* in its 2012 revision, requires that parties shall, before the court opens its formal session, undertake a process of exchange of evidence so as to clarify the focal points of disputes.

8 These Opinions were issued as *Fafa* (No. 22, 1992) on 14 July 1992. On 18 December 2008, the Supreme People's Court issued a Notice abolishing some pre-2007 interpretations, which included the abolition of Arts 136, 205, 206, 240–53 and 299 of the Opinions.

9 Issued on 6 July 1998 by the Supreme People's Court in response to pressure for reforming China's civil and economic trial methods following the revision of China's CPL in 1996.

10 Now replaced by the Interpretation of the Supreme People's Court on the Application of the Civil Procedure Law, issued on 30 January 2015, and effective on 4 February 2015.

11 A potentially important revision is the granting of a new power to the procuratorates to exercise legal supervision over court execution works. See Art. 235 (being a new addition) of the 1991 *Civil Procedure Law*.

12 Some of the rules have now been incorporated into the above-mentioned 552-article Interpretation of the Supreme People's Court on the Application of the Civil Procedure Law (2015), but the legal validity of those that have not been so incorporated is now in doubt.

13 Perhaps the other piece of comparably controversial legislation is the *State Enterprise Bankruptcy Law 1988*.

14 The initial drafting task was entrusted to the Administrative Law Research Group – an expert group established within the Legal Affairs Committee of the NPC's Standing Committee – under the direction of Professors Jiang Ping, Luo Haocai and Ying Songnian. See Potter (1994: 274).

15 The term 'legal reform constituency' is used by Potter to refer to groups of legal specialists who share common interests in pushing forward legal reforms. See Potter (1994: 273).

16 Interpretation on Certain Issues Concerning the Implementation of the 'Law of the PRC on Administrative Litigation' (issued on 8 March 2000, replacing the Opinions of the Supreme People's Court on Some Issues Relating to the Implementation of the Administrative Litigation Law issued on 11 June 1991); Provisions on Certain Issues Relating to Evidence in Administrative Litigation (issued on 4 June 2002); Provisions on Issues Concerning Adjudication of Administrative Cases Involving International Trade (issued on 27 August 2002); and Notice of the Supreme People's Court of the

PRC on Developing Pilot Work of Summary Procedure in Administrative Litigation (issued on 17 November 2010). Other judicial 'interpretations' include the Supreme People's Court's Provisions on Certain Issues in Relation to Application of Law in Adjudicate Administrative Antidumping Cases (issued on 21 November 2002) and the Supreme People's Court's Provisions on Certain Issues in Relation to Application of Law in Adjudicate Administrative Anti-subsidy Cases (issued on 21 November 2002).

17 For instance, the 2000 Supreme People's Court Interpretation significantly expands the scope of the 1989 ALL, clearly inconsistent with the ALL provisions.

18 It was first reported that the revision of the ALL was on the 2003 legislative plan of the SCNPC, but it did not proceed and no explanation was given by the SCNPC. Nevertheless, various drafting groups were established by academics, the SCNPC and the Supreme People's Court, resulting in many unofficial drafts circulating among academics. See Zhang Jiansheng (2013) and Zhen (2013).

19 In the end, the revision has been substantive, almost amounting to rewriting. The original 75-article law has now been expanded to include 103 articles, with most original articles having been revised. The revised ALL became effective on 1 May 2015.

20 That is, administrative activities that are aimed at specified events or individuals, and can only be carried out once. See Xiao (1991: 5, translated into English in FBIS-CHI-91-056, at 22–6).

21 In fact, many Chinese scholars have long advocated that this distinction should be abolished in law and that legal scholars should stop using this distinction in their writing. See Mo (2011), Li (2013c) and Lang and Lang (2014).

22 There were calls to abolish such a list altogether and, instead, provide a list of non-reviewable acts (called a negative list) so that all administrative acts would be reviewable unless provided otherwise by law. See Zhen (2013) and *People's Daily* (2014a).

23 See Art. 12 of the 2014 ALL, which revises the original Art. 11 and expands the original eight reviewable acts to 12.

24 However, this revision could also limit the scope of the Law, as the grounds are now extremely specific.

25 See Art. 60 of the Decision to Revise the ALL (adopted 1 November 2014). It is worth noting that the initial Revision Bill (December 2013) dropped the phrase 'concrete administrative acts' in the revised Art. 11, but continued the use of this phrase in Art. 2 of the ALL (which provided the right to initiate a lawsuit for infringement of rights by 'concrete administrative acts') and Art. 5 (which empowered the court to review the legality of 'concrete administrative acts' in adjudication). The phrase 'concrete administrative acts' was only completely dropped in the Second Deliberation Bill (August 2014). See the comparative table available at: www.npc.gov.cn/npc/lfzt/2014/2014-08/31/content_1876865.htm (accessed 4 December 2014).

26 For discussions on the use of such terms as regulation, rules, *guizhang*, normative documents etc. in Chinese law, see Chen Jianfu (2008: ch. 5).

27 Evidence rules are further clarified by the 2000 Interpretation and the Provisions on Certain Issues Relating to Evidence in Administrative Litigation and revised by the 2014 revision.

28 These difficulties are described as courts refusing to accept case materials, refusing to issue legal documents and refusing to file cases. As a result, a local survey indicates that between 2010 and 2012, only 38 per cent, 39 per cent and 35 per cent of complaints were accepted by courts (see *People's Daily* 2014a). Another source claims that between 1990 and 2012, Chinese courts accepted just over 1.91 million administrative cases, amounting to 83,168 cases a year and 2 per cent of the total caseload of the Chinese courts. Among those filed for suit, only 27 per cent obtained a court decision on substantive issues, with an approximate success rate of 10 per cent for complainants (see *People's Daily* 2014b).

29 In a local survey it was found that the trial implementation of cross-regional jurisdiction increased the acceptance rate from 13 to 63 per cent (see *Jinghua Time* 2013; NPC 2013).

30 See the Interpretation on Certain Issues Concerning the Implementation of the 'Law of the PRC on Administrative Litigation' and the Provisions on Certain Issues Relating to Evidence in Administrative Litigation (2002).

31 '*Shuanggui*' is a Party mechanism under which a Party cadre is ordered to appear at a 'specific time and specific place' to be investigated for, principally, corruption allegations. Despite relatively mild language, '*Shuanggui*' is, in fact, an extra-legal and secret detention mechanism operated by the Party Disciplinary Commissions without any legal regulation nor judicial oversight (although there have been internal Party regulations since 1994). Strictly, it can clearly be regarded as unconstitutional, and thus unlawful as Art. 8 of the *Chinese Law on Law-Making* holds that only the NPC and its Standing Committee have the power to enact laws on such matters as the restriction of personal freedoms or the imposition of coercive measures. For a detailed analysis of '*Shuanggui*', see Sapio (2008) and Liu Zhong (2014).

7 Addressing corruption and the trial of Bo Xilai

Historical continuities, rule of law implications

Norman P. Ho

In June 2009, at the time the organized crime crackdown in Chongqing began, then-Chongqing party chief Bo Xilai was at the height of his powers. Bo had even been regarded as a strong contender for elevation to the Chinese Politburo. By March 2012 Bo had fallen from power and was arrested on bribery, corruption and abuse of power charges. In September 2013 the court found him guilty of all counts and sentenced him to life imprisonment. The widely publicized trial of Bo generated intense media attention in both the Chinese and international media. Indeed, at or around the time of Bo's trial, Chinese and Western commentators remarked that Bo's trial represented a step forward for the rule of law in China (e.g., see Li 2013a; Liao 2013).

This chapter situates Bo's downfall and trial in its historical context as well as in the context of President Xi Jinping's 'tiger and flies' anti-corruption campaign. It argues that the Communist Party of China (CPC) – in Bo's downfall, prosecution and trial, and Xi's anti-corruption campaign more generally – has employed anti-corruption approaches that are similar to past CPC anti-corruption approaches. Ironically, some of the methods were well-utilized by Bo himself in the Chongqing organized crime crackdown (Ho 2012: 202, 210–12). In this sense, there is a continuity in approaches to anti-corruption. Techniques do not appear to have changed much, notwithstanding many revisions and improvements to China's procedural laws (see Chen in Chapter 6). When it comes to eradicating corruption, the CPC favors party-led crackdowns, campaigns and publicized trials, buttressed by Maoist rhetoric. There are, however, far-reaching implications of this continuity for China's rule of law progress, and this chapter asserts that Bo's trial may not have been the significant rule of law step that some commentators previously touted. In fact, this continuity produces notable concerns. While most applaud attempts to eradicate corruption, the use of old-style campaigns to crack down on corrupt officials and shadowy business people can also catch those deemed to be hostile to, or even opposing, elements of CPC power.

This chapter proceeds as follows: first is a brief analysis of Bo's downfall and trial, as well as the fall-out from the Chongqing organized crime crackdown of 2009–11. Second is a summary of events and criminal actions by Bo and his immediate family members (notably his wife, Gu Kailai). Third, Bo's trial is evaluated in its historical context including past CPC anti-corruption measures, from the notorious 'Gang of Four Trial' that brought an end to the Cultural Revolution to Xi's contemporary anti-corruption campaign. Continuities and similarities in post-Mao China's anti-corruption efforts are discussed with the chapter concluding with tentative predictions about the foreseeable future of anti-corruption efforts.

The fall-out and effects of the Chongqing organized crime crackdown (2009–11)

As a result of Bo's crackdown on organized crime and corruption in Chongqing (assisted by Bo's police chief, Wang Lijun) – which lasted approximately ten months – it was reported that 4,781 individuals were arrested, including wealthy businessmen, corrupt officials (such as police officers, judges and legislators) and others suspected of directly participating in, or indirectly aiding, organized crime groups in the city (LaFraniere and Ansfield 2012).[1] Immediately after the crackdown, Bo was lauded as a socialist hero for his anti-crime and anti-corruption efforts by both officials and the ordinary populace. Indeed, as Cheng Li of the Brookings Institution has pointed out (cited in LaFraniere and Ansfield 2012), the organized crime crackdown helped Bo cultivate a reputation as 'a guy who gets things done'. The biggest compliment arguably came from Xi Jinping himself, who flew to Chongqing in late 2010 and conveyed to Bo that Bo's Maoist-inspired policies in Chongqing – notably his 'singing red' campaigns – were successful and had 'touched the hearts of many people' (Garnaut 2012: 64).[2]

However, many commentators now consider Bo's crackdown on organized crime to have had very little respect for the rule of law. Some individuals were clearly framed, extorted and even tortured. Prominent Chinese law professor He Weifang (2013) argued that Bo's crackdown on organized crime actually trampled on the rule of law, deprived people of their wealth and extracted forced confessions on a large scale. Furthermore, He (2013) added that Bo himself was the 'guiding force' and 'chiefly responsible' for unjust prosecutions in Chongqing. Chinese lawyer Chen Youxi (cited in Garnaut 2013), who represented Li Zhuang (a lawyer who had become one of Bo's targets), also remarked in 2011 that 'Bo – just like the main executors of the Cultural Revolution – had disregard for the law'. The publisher of China's *Caijing* magazine, Wang Boming (in Garnaut 2013), also pointed out that Bo was essentially funding his so-called 'Chongqing Model' through the crackdown on Chongqing's entrepreneurs, pointing out in his interview with Garnaut that 'basically, [as for] the twenty richest guys in Chongqing, he [Bo] sent them all to jail and confiscated all their assets'.

Specific allegations of torture and political persecution in the organized crime crackdown also emerged. For example, Fan Qihang, a businessman in the construction industry who was charged in the crackdown, maintained his innocence and claimed that he suffered torture while in secret confinement in a military reserve camp; specifically, Fan described how he was shackled to an iron bar and that his handcuffs cut into his wrists so deeply that police guards on one occasion required one hour to remove them (LaFraniere and Ansfield 2012). Despite these torture allegations, Fan was executed in July 2010. Indeed, certain Chongqing police officers were tried in Chongqing in April 2014 due to allegations of torturing interrogation suspects during Bo's crackdown; these trials marked the first publicly reported prosecution of illicit methods used by police during the crackdown (Zuo 2014).

Furthermore, one of the biggest human rights violations of Bo's organized crime crackdown was the arrest and prosecution of Li Zhuang, a lawyer who defended Gong Gangmo, a businessman who was arrested in the crackdown and had alleged torture at the hands of the authorities. In court, however, Gong recanted his confession, claiming it was extracted by torture (his medical records documented wrist scars, believed to be from police stringing him up multiple times over a week). Later, Gong suddenly accused Li of telling him to lie about being tortured (LaFraniere and Ansfield 2012). As a consequence of this dramatic turn of events, Li was arrested in December 2009. It was later reported (Garnaut 2012: 68) that Bo and Wang had traced Li Zhuang's movements and location by his phone signal, eventually having him arrested at Chongqing's airport, where he was met personally by Wang and dozens of police cars. Li was put on trial for subornation of perjury and, in January 2010, found guilty and sentenced to two-and-a-half years' imprisonment (Huang 2012). Many believe Li was targeted by Bo on trumped-up charges given irregularities during his trial. For example, in late November 2008, the Chongqing police had sent a telegram to Beijing's judicial bureau, saying that audio-visual records from Chongqing Detention Center showed Li persuading Gong to commit perjury. But during the trial, the prosecutor did not present this evidence despite Li's request that the records be shown. He argued they would prove his innocence, but the Chongqing Jiangbei Court which heard the case declined his request. Instead, it presented a written statement from the Chongqing Detention Center claiming it had no audio-visual equipment (Huang 2012). Li appealed his conviction and the court of second instance upheld the guilty verdict, but reduced his sentence to 18 months. Li continued to claim his innocence and, in a further bizarre development in April 2011, he – while serving his jail sentence – was again brought to court, charged with enticing a witness to give false testimony in Shanghai's Xuhui Court in July 2008 during an embezzlement trial. A few days later, prosecutors dropped this charge, saying they had 'insufficient evidence' (Huang 2012). Li was released from prison in July 2011.

Garnaut (2012: 77) reported that the Li Zhuang case had caused friction between then-President Hu Jintao and Bo. Furthermore, in April 2011, it was reported by party princelings that President Hu believed, at the time, that Li Zhuang should be released (Garnaut 2012). Other commentators, such as He Weifang (in Huang 2012), have also pointed out that the Li Zhuang case was important in China's legal reform in that the case serves as an example of the rule of law violations that accompanied Bo's organized crime crackdown in Chongqing. Thus, while Bo's crackdown received much initial praise, it is now largely criticized for its reckless approach and use of force, illegal detentions, torture and targeting of well-intentioned individuals who were simply perceived to be a threat to the crackdown.

Bo's downfall: corruption in Chongqing and summary of events

Bo's downfall from the CPC was triggered when Wang Lijun dramatically attempted to escape to the US consulate in Chongqing on February 6, 2012. Wang had apparently revealed sordid details about corruption and murder in Bo's Chongqing, allegations that exploded into one of modern China's most notorious political scandals. Bo's downfall was signaled publicly during then-Premier Wen Jiabao's press conference of March 14, 2012, at the yearly meeting of the National People's Congress. In that conference, Wen outlined his program for political reform and mentioned that the mistakes of the Cultural Revolution had not been completely eliminated. This comment had the effect of directly connecting Bo's actions to the excesses of the Cultural Revolution (Garnaut 2012: 119–20). On March 15, 2012, Bo was removed from his post in Chongqing and placed in detention. On April 10, 2012 he was suspended from his Politburo and Central Committee positions for violations of CPC party discipline (Garnaut 2012: 123–4) and stripped of all his CPC posts (BBC 2013a). Bo was formally expelled from the CPC on September 28, 2012 and expelled from China's parliament on October 26, 2012, thereby removing his immunity from prosecution (BBC 2013a). On July 25, 2013, he was formally charged with corruption, bribery and abuse of power. His criminal trial began at the Intermediate People's Court in Jinan (Shandong Province) on August 22, 2013. The trial lasted five days and Bo was found guilty of all charges and sentenced to life imprisonment on September 22, 2013. An appellate court rejected Bo's appeal on October 25, 2013, upholding the original verdict and sentence (BBC 2013a).

On the charge of bribery, Bo was indicted for receiving the equivalent of US$3.56 million from two businessmen in Dalian – Xu Ming (a businessman who had first entered Bo's inner circle and patronage during Bo's tenure as Dalian mayor)[3] and Tang Xiaolin, taken directly or through Bo's wife (Gu Kailai) and son (Bo Guagua) – as well as diverting a payment to Dalian city of US$800,000 into his personal funds (with Gu's help). Abuse of power charges focused on his covering up his wife's murder of Neil Heywood, a British businessman and former friend of Gu and the Bo family, while corruption charges focused on Bo's embezzlement of five million RMB of public funds from the Dalian government in 2002 (BBC 2013b).

Given the importance of the Wang Lijun incident (i.e., his escape to the US consulate in February 2012) to Bo's downfall, it is helpful to overview events preceding and surrounding Wang's escape. Wang was appointed police chief of Chongqing by Bo and played a major role in carrying out the organized crime crackdown under Bo's direction. Wang became very close with the Bo family as well, and he himself engaged in corrupt activities. Garnaut (2012: 60) reported that Wang took billions of RMB from businessmen arrested in the Chongqing crackdown and siphoned the money into his Chongqing Public Security Bureau. The money was, apparently, used to build restaurant canteens, as well as a police museum honoring the organized crime crackdown and designed to impress central government officials visiting from Beijing. In 2010, Wang also received bribes from Xu Ming (via two apartments signed over to one of Wang's relatives living in Beijing) to release three people from jail (Garnaut 2012: 85). Wang and Bo also engaged in other corrupt activities together (BBC 2013a; Garnaut 2012: 123), with Bo and Wang running an extrajudicial wire-tapping network across Chongqing, illegally listening to phone calls that even involved top leaders such as then-President Hu Jintao.

The other major character in the events surrounding Wang's escape was Gu Kailai. While Bo was of at Dalian, Gu ran her own law firm (the Horus L. Kai law firm) and also had a consultancy business (Garnaut 2012: 41). Gu was later able to cultivate business relationships with certain foreign contacts who helped her procure and manage her family interests abroad. One of her first contacts was Patrick Devillers, a French architect, who helped Gu in Bournemouth where she had enrolled Bo Guagua in a language school (Garnaut 2012: 43). Devillers also helped Gu purchase a villa in Nice – during the second day of Bo's trial. Devillers testified that he had set up a property company to purchase the villa with Gu, with each of them initially holding 50 percent of the shares in the property company in order to avoid French property taxes and to keep the property hidden from the Chinese authorities (BBC 2013c). Gu later transferred her share to Neil Heywood due to fear of investigation (BBC 2013c).

Heywood was the other foreigner who entered the Bo family circle. Heywood, a British businessman who studied international relations at the University of Warwick, learned Chinese in Beijing (Garnaut 2012: 89). He entered the Bo family circle largely through self-introduction as, after learning Chinese, he had traveled to Dalian where he met Bo after sending out multiple introduction letters to individuals in the city (Garnaut 2012: 89). Heywood may have helped Bo Guagua in procuring admission to Harrow School in the UK, although Gu testified that she and Heywood did not meet until after Bo Guagua had already matriculated in Harrow (Garnaut 2012: 90).

Despite the initial cordial relationship, Heywood eventually had a falling-out with Gu around 2010. The falling-out was apparently ignited because Gu reportedly retracted Heywood's share interest in the property company originally set up by Devillers (BBC 2013b). Heywood's friends reported that at this point he feared for his safety – as Gu came to believe she was being betrayed by someone in her inner circle, doubting Heywood's loyalty, 'perhaps fearing that he knew too much information about her family' (Garnaut 2012: 92). The next development in the Heywood–Gu relationship was an alleged extortion email sent by Heywood to Gu on November 10, 2011. According to Gu's testimony, Heywood demanded millions of dollars from the French property business and, in the email, warned Bo Guagua that he 'would be destroyed' unless he paid the money (Garnaut 2012: 94). Gu further testified that she feared for the safety of her son, as Heywood detained Bo Guagua in a room in the United Kingdom in his quest for money. She believed that she had to 'fight to my death to stop the craziness of Neil Heywood' (Garnaut 2012: 94).[4] A few days after the email exchange, Heywood was invited to Chongqing and driven to the Lucky Holiday Hotel (Garnaut 2012: 94). Gu and Zhang Xiaojun, a family aide, went into Heywood's room with Chinese tea and a bottle of whiskey; Heywood could not hold down the alcohol and began vomiting (Garnaut 2012: 95). Later, Heywood asked for water, and Zhang gave Gu a glass bottle containing rat poison (Garnaut 2012: 95). Gu poured the poison into the water and proceeded to drop the poison-laced water into Heywood's mouth (Garnaut 2012: 96), leading to Heywood's death on November 14, 2011. Gu had also informed Wang of her murder plans on November 13, 2010 just a couple of hours before carrying out the act; she also called Wang after the murder to update him and relate all the facts about her crime as well (Garnaut 2012: 98). However, unbeknown to Gu, Wang had surreptitiously recorded the entire post-murder conversation (Garnaut 2012: 98). Wang and Gu eventually also fell out and, on January 28, 2012, Wang informed Bo that Gu had murdered Heywood (Garnaut 2012: 101, 103). At a subsequent meeting, Bo slapped Wang in the face (ibid.), and on February 2, 2012, Wang was fired as police chief by Bo (without Bo seeking the necessary central government approval). Wang's close associates were also detained by Bo (Garnaut 2012: 104). All these events culminated in Wang's dramatic escape to the US consulate in Chongqing on February 6, 2012, where he was reported (Garnaut 2012: 107) to have handed over the cellphone number of someone in Chongqing who could provide the evidence to support his claims of Gu's murder of Heywood. Wang exited the consulate the next day, but under the strict condition that he was to be handed over directly to the Ministry of State Security and not returned to Chongqing, fearing for his life (Garnaut 2012: 110).

Bo was obviously affected by these events and removed from his post as Chongqing party chief on March 15, 2012. Officials confirmed that the catalyzing reason for his removal was the Wang Lijun incident (BBC 2013a). Gu later went on trial for murder in Hefei on August 9, 2012. The trial was controversial in that there were gaps in evidence, and netizens held deep suspicions of a 'body-double being used for the real Gu' (Garnaut 2012: 125). On August 20, 2012, Gu was sentenced to a suspended death sentence. Wang was charged on September 5, 2012 with defection, abuse of power and bribery; his trial commenced on September 17, 2012 and concluded the next day, being sentenced on September 24, 2012 to 15 years' imprisonment (BBC 2013a). Bo was tried on August 22–26, 2013.

A critical appraisal of Bo's trial: implications

Bo's trial began on August 22, 2013, attended by 110 individuals, consisting of five of his family members, two companions, 19 journalists and 84 members of the general public (BBC 2013b). Bo actively participated in his own defense and maintained his innocence. He cross-examined witnesses and alleged that his admission to bribery charges was made against his will (BBC 2013b). As for the embezzlement charges, Bo blamed his wife for stealing the money, again maintaining his innocence and expressing remorse that he 'did not control his wife' (BBC 2013c). On the abuse of power charge, Wang testified that Bo had intimidated police officers into saying that his wife had not in fact murdered Heywood. Bo claimed, however, that he did not try to cover up Gu's crime (BBC 2013d).

Various commentators have had differing assessments of the Bo Xilai trial. Some pointed out positive characteristics of the Bo trial – for example, the relative openness and publicity of the trial proceedings. Stanley Lubman (2013) pointed out that the trial's openness was noteworthy in that proceedings were broadcast online via the court's official feed on Sina Weibo (China's equivalent to Twitter). Transcripts of the trial proceedings were also published on the court's Weibo page. He Weifang (2013) also pointed out that the use of Weibo by the court was surprising and that the Jinan Intermediate People's Court displayed neutrality in adjudicating the case. Prominent Peking University law professor Zhang Qianfan (in Wong 2013) remarked that the trial 'was open, and the defendant's rights well protected'. Tong Zhiwei (in Wong 2013), a law professor at East China University of Politics and Law, said that 'the Bo Trial was more open than any other corruption trial of high-ranking officials in China'. Furthermore, several important witnesses, such as Wang, actually appeared physically in court, allowing Bo to confront and cross-examine them. It has been reported (Wong 2013) that senior officials even disseminated internal orders within the Chinese security and justice apparatuses noting that the process in the Bo trial should be studied closely as it could serve as a model for proper procedure.

There were, however, also deficiencies in the trial. First, as pointed out by He (2013), the scope of the prosecution and the trial itself were not dictated by Chinese criminal law, but rather by the CPC's own disciplinary organ, the Central Commission for Discipline Inspection (CCDI) – as a result, several leads or issues were not properly pursued by prosecutors. For example, as He (2013) notes, the prosecution did not pursue Bo's crackdown on organized crime in Chongqing and the unlawful actions he took while executing the crackdown. Furthermore, not all witnesses actually appeared in court, and those who did appear were all witnesses for the prosecution; there were no witnesses for the defense, nor was there written evidence in favor of Bo (He 2013). On the witness issue, Gu Kailai was notably absent, delivering her testimony instead via video – Bo had applied twice for Gu to testify in person in court, but this was denied (He 2013). Jerome Cohen (2013a) further pointed out that China's *Criminal Procedure Law* gives one spouse the right not to have to testify against the other spouse in court – although Bo applied to cross-examine Gu, the court claimed that Gu refused but did not make not clear whether this was Gu's choice or whether she may have been coerced. There are also concerns over the use of evidence by the prosecution in Bo's trial. As pointed out by Clarke (2013), the Weibo transcripts reveal that the prosecution in court was directly using Bo's confession made in *shuanggui*, an extrajudicial interrogation and detention used by the CCDI of suspected corrupt party members. Lan (2013) points out that the proper routine practice is not for the prosecution to directly use *shuanggui* confessions in court. Rather, after the CCDI hands over the evidence derived from *shuanggui* to the prosecution, the prosecution usually re-conducts the interrogation legalizing the *shuanggui* confessions. Finally, Wee (2013) reported that Bo was not able to choose his own lawyer, namely Gu Yushu, who had originally been appointed by Bo's sister; Gu Yushu had also remarked that it was 'not convenient' to talk about why his own representation was not allowed.

Bo's life sentence – the maximum punishment – surprised some commentators, suggesting that Bo was targeted not only for his corrupt and criminal behavior, but also for his ideological leanings and his status as a possible political competitor at the highest levels. Yuhua Wang (in Steven Jiang 2013) remarked that it was a very strong verdict compared to previous cases. Wang Yukai (in BBC 2013e), a professor at Beijing's National Academy of Governance, had estimated that Bo would be sentenced to 20 years' imprisonment. Some have also suggested Bo was a victim of a political purge (Zhang Lifan, in BBC 2013f). Zhang Lifan argued that the heaviest sentence was used to punish Bo because the then top leadership power was not yet consolidated. Some have even speculated that Xi Jinping brought down Bo because he saw him as a political competitor (Garnaut 2013: 118).

It is plausible that Bo was sentenced so heavily because of the ideological underpinnings of his Chongqing policies. As I have described elsewhere (Ho 2012), Bo launched Maoist policies during his administration in Chongqing aimed at promoting a 'red GDP'. Bo mobilized the Chongqing populace in populist, Maoist campaigns, urging them to sing red songs and become familiar with Mao's maxims. His tenure as Chongqing party chief went so far as banning commercial advertising on the city's television station, filling it instead with 24-hour red and revolutionary programs. He even ordered the jailing and torture of Li Xiaofeng, at the time head of Chongqing's broadcasting corporation; Li had merely expressed concerns that Bo's red and revolutionary programs had caused a decline in revenue (Garnaut 2012: 49, 56). Bo's strong Maoist leanings attracted the ire of many contemporary civil leaders in China (especially after his arrest of Li Zhuang in 2009) and eventually also of the national leadership, most notably reflected in Wen Jiabao's March 14, 2012 press conference (Garnaut 2012). Wen (in Garnaut 2013) then described China's future as essentially 'a choice between political and economic reform, or a return to such historical tragedies as the Cultural Revolution' – a veiled, but direct, criticism of Bo, who was sacked the next day. The trial and the subsequent verdict has subsequently been interpreted as a way for Xi Jinping to consolidate his power (Zhang Lifan, in Page 2013). Zhang, a party historian and political analyst, remarked that 'by dealing with Bo Xilai in this way, [Xi is] sending a clear message … that he will strike hard at any opponents' (Zhang Lifan, in Page 2013). This has proved to be so.

With respect to rule of law developments, there are positive and negative aspects to Bo's trial. It is important to remember that the Bo trial was not just about punishing an official for crimes and corruption. It also served to remove an ideological and political threat to other powerful figures. Questions remain. Was the conduct of Bo Xilai's trial 'new' for China? If we use a historical perspective, with respect to the Bo trial and subsequent 'tigers and flies' (老虎苍蝇一起打) anti-corruption crackdown, we can see a number of similarities in how the CPC dealt with Bo and how it has dealt with corrupt officials both in the past and present.

The Bo Xilai trial and recent anti-corruption contexts: a historical perspective

This section will situate the Bo trial in both its historical context and within the more current context of Xi Jinping's anti-corruption campaign launched shortly after Xi's ascension to power. It argues that definite similarities exist in the anti-corruption measures and approaches taken by the CPC against corrupt officials, continuing from the past to the present day.

The Bo Xilai trial can be compared with the Gang of Four Trial of 1981, where a total of ten major defendants (which notably included Mao's widow, Jiang Qing) were publicly tried for offences committed in the Cultural Revolution, including illegal searches and seizures, lawless detentions, torturing suspects to extract confessions, and wounding and killing individuals without legal procedures (Cohen 2013b). Televised to hundreds of thousands of people and attended by more than 800 people and 300 journalists, the Gang of Four Trial was also, at the time, notable for its openness (Hatton 2013). Hsiung (1981) has pointed out several characteristics and reasons why the Gang of Four Trial was important to Chinese legal development then: first, the outside world gained new insights into the nature and workings of the CPC, including how the trial was conducted. Second, the Gang of Four Trial was 'staged to redirect China's official ideology by expunging the discredited ideology identified with former ultra-Maoist radicals' (Hsiung 1981: 1). In other words, the trial sought not only to discredit, dishonor and criminally punish the ten major defendants, but also to discredit the ideologies and policies to which they were wedded. Third, the Gang of Four Trial was essentially 'engineered at the top' (Hsiung 1981: 2). Fourth, the Gang of Four Trial was not meant 'to involve the public in working out a solution or policy through debating the issues [surrounding the trial and ideological splits] ... but rather to drum up mass support to stamp out all residue of the Reign of the Radicals' (Hsiung 1981: 2). Fifth, the political significance of the trial (i.e., educating the country on the correct ideological course and policy line) was more important than the legal significance of the trial (Hsiung 1981: 2). Finally, Hsiung (1981) predicted that although the Gang of Four Trial had ended, the campaign to discredit the defendants' style of communism and their supporters would continue.

Although the Bo Xilai trial occurred more than 30 years after the Gang of Four Trial, Hsiung's points remain pertinent. There are numerous similarities between the Bo trial and the Gang of Four Trial. First, Bo's trial also allowed the 'outside world' to gain new insights into how the trial was conducted. The only thing new was the technology: Bo's trial was publicized on Weibo; the Gang of Four Trial was televised. Second, the Bo trial did not seek simply to discredit, dishonor and criminally punish Bo for his crimes. It was arguably also used to discredit Bo's ideological Maoist and populist bent (which Wen Jiabao had linked to the failed Maoism of the Cultural Revolution). Third, Bo's trial was also essentially 'engineered at the top' in that the CCDI role can be viewed as a top-down approach to punishing him. Fourth, Bo's trial was not meant to involve the public in working out a solution or policy through debating the issues. For example, his policies and most likely illicit actions taken against certain members of the Chongqing public during the organized crime crackdown in Chongqing (e.g., torture of suspects) were not really pursued by the prosecution in the trial and therefore not made a public issue in the trial. The Bo trial was more about punishing, discrediting and removing Bo from public view. Fifth, the political significance of the Bo trial (e.g., removing Bo as a political competitor thereby helping to consolidate Xi's power) was also a factor. The final characteristic of the Gang of Four Trial on Hsiung's list also chimes with Bo's trial. That is, after the trial, authorities continued to go after individuals in Bo's network. Most notably, it was announced on December 6, 2014 that Zhou Yongkang – former head of China's domestic security apparatus, a Bo supporter identified by veteran CPC members as part of a movement to revive Mao (BBC 2013a) – was expelled from the CPC. He too faced prosecution for corruption charges. In all the above senses, the Bo trial, when analyzed in a historical context, had striking similarities to the 1981 Gang of Four Trial.

Situating the Bo trial in the context of the broader anti-corruption crackdown unleashed by Xi Jinping after his ascension to power in November 2012, we can also see a continuity from the Gang of Four Trial, Bo's trial and the anti-corruption campaign launched by Xi. Is it a coincidence that Xi had a history of family rivalry with Bo? Bo Yibo, Bo Xilai's father, had previously led the 1987 conservative attack on Hu Yaobang. Xi Zhongxun, father of Xi Jinping, however, had supported Hu (Garnaut 2012: 6). Xi had praised Bo's Chongqing reforms in a visit in 2010 and seemed to be on good terms and in 'factional solidarity', at least until the National People's Congress press conference of March 2012 (Garnaut 2012: 117–18). After Xi's ascent to power, his anti-corruption campaign quickly emerged. In his press speech while at the Politburo Standing Committee Members' meeting on November 15, 2012 (the first day he assumed office as the new CPC general secretary), Xi remarked that the CPC faced 'many severe challenges, and there are many pressing problems with the party that need to be resolved, especially problems such as corruption and bribe-taking by some party members and cadres [urging the CPC] … to be vigilant' (BBC 2012). More impetus was provided in a Politburo meeting chaired on December 31, 2012 in order to map out anti-corruption efforts for 2013. The Politburo ordered party disciplinary organs to investigate corruption cases and punish corrupt officials. At the same meeting, it was noted that party members should reject extravagance, conduct shorter meetings and travel with a smaller entourage; disciplinary institutions were ordered to draft detailed guidelines and rules for inspections and penalties for rule violations (Zhang 2013). The clearest verbal articulation of Xi's anti-corruption campaign was revealed in a speech he delivered to the plenary meeting of the CCDI in January 2013. Xi commented on the immense severity of the corruption problem, remarking that 'the CPC must have the resolution to fight every corrupt phenomenon, punish every corrupt official and constantly eradicate the soil which breeds corruption, so as to earn people's trust with actual results' (Xinhua News Agency 2013). Xi remarked that it was important to 'uphold the fighting of tigers and flies at the same time, resolutely investigating law-breaking cases of leading officials and also earnestly resolving the unhealthy tendencies and corruption problems which happen all around people' – in other words, to go after both powerful, high-level leaders and lower-ranked party bureaucrats (quoted in Branigan 2013). Xi was specific that 'no leniency should be shown, [that] power should be restricted by the cage of regulations' (in Branigan 2013).

Since launching the anti-corruption campaign, Xi has also pushed forward various specific anti-corruption measures such as cracking down on excessive consumption (such as lavish banquets) and ordering the seizure of homes illegally occupied by officials and improperly used public vehicles. He has also ordered that funerals for party members be simple (Roberts 2014a). The number of officials punished for disciplinary violations has increased – in 2013, the CCDI punished 182,000 officials for disciplinary violations, an increase of more than 20,000 over 2012 and of nearly 40,000 over 2011 (*The Economist* 2014). Anthony Saich (in Oster 2014) noted that the current campaign 'is the most ambitious anti-corruption campaign since at least Mao's days'. Extending into overseas jurisdictions, Chinese state media in 2015 identifies Xi's 'Operation Fox Hunt' and 'Sky Net' campaigns as pursuing allegedly corrupt former officials who have 'fled overseas'. Roberts (2014b) reported that even Jiang Zemin has cautioned Xi to take a more measured pace to the anti-corruption campaign and not to be too harsh in meting out punishment.

Xi's anti-corruption campaign, while differing from previous anti-corruption campaigns in modern Chinese history – due to its scope, duration and the high number of officials targeted – still shares similarities with previous anti-corruption measures, including Bo's own organized crime crackdown in Chongqing. Like the Gang of Four Trial and Bo trial, Xi's anti-corruption campaign is certainly 'engineered at the top'. In other words, it is a top-to-bottom approach led and dictated by the CPC, not by China's criminal law or judicial organs. Xi's campaign is also regarded by analysts as a way to deal with political rivalries and consolidate power, just as such campaigns were used previously by Chinese leaders to eliminate enemies – for example, Mao used his three-anti and five-anti campaigns in 1951 to root out corruption but also to eliminate opposition to the CPC. The Gang of Four Trial was certainly used to humiliate, discredit and punish Jiang Qing and other party members for their radical brand of Maoism. Jiang Zemin's Three Stresses Party Rectification in 1998 deposed several senior officials. Hu Jintao in 2008 deposed then-Shanghai party chief Chen Liangyu, a member of political rival Jiang Zemin's Shanghai clique who had opposed Hu's reform agenda, on corruption charges (Moses 2014; Zhan 2014). Bo's own organized crime crackdown aimed at destroying corrupt elements in Chongqing but also extorted businessmen and targeted individuals Bo considered as political enemies. If we take this historical and macroscopic view, trials and anti-corruption measures can be conflated, as illustrated in mid-2015 by the arrest, prosecution and life sentence given to retired senior leader of the CPC, Zhou Yongkang, who had been a member of the Seventeenth Politburo Standing Committee and chief of China's powerful domestic security service.[5] The reliance on public campaigns and public trials led and dictated by the CPC, rather than judicial organs, courts or criminal procedures, continues.

Continuity also exists in the use of Maoist rhetoric. Bo's organized crime crackdown received much of its ideological justification from Bo's populist, Maoist narrative. Although such policies and rhetoric were later criticized, Xi too has attempted to revitalize Maoist rhetoric to legitimize his anti-corruption campaign. In his 2011 speech for the ninetieth anniversary of the foundation of the CPC, Xi argued that 30 years of Maoism and 30 years of reforms were of equal importance (Veg 2014). More recently, Xi has organized self-criticism sessions, harkening back to the Mao era. He has urged cadres to 'look at themselves in a mirror', 'adjust their clothes', 'wash up' and 'cure their illness' – all expressions taken from Mao's rhetoric (Veg 2014). Minnie Chan (2014) reported that CPC documents show Xi has urged party members to 'embrace the spirit of Mao' and that 'China would fall into chaos if it totally repudiates Mao thought'. Jean-Phillipe Beja (quoted in Minnie Chan 2014) points out that 'all of Xi's slogans, including "catching big tigers" … originate from Mao'. Indeed, the most important slogans of Xi's anti-corruption campaign – catching tigers, as well as small flies – are in fact derived from Maoist rhetoric. It has been pointed out (Keck 2013) that the use of Maoist rhetoric by Bo and Xi is slightly different, as Xi has utilized Maoism to mobilize primarily the CPC and its members, while Bo, on the other hand, had been focused on mobilizing the Chongqing masses. Nevertheless, the general use of Maoist rhetoric in strengthening and justifying anti-corruption measures remains a constant thread.

Conclusion

There are clear similarities and continuities in the anti-corruption measures employed by the CPC – from the Gang of Four Trial, Bo's downfall, Xi's anti-corruption campaign and other anti-corruption campaigns cited. The CPC remains the main actor and director of such measures including the use of publicized campaigns and trials, the use of non-judicial anti-corruption measures to eliminate political enemies, and reliance on Maoist rhetoric for legitimization. Some far-reaching implications emanate from these similarities and continuities. First, the Bo trial was not as significant, nor as 'new' a step for China's rule of law progress, as some commentators have suggested. Second, there do not appear to have been any meaningful changes in how the CPC tackles corruption despite substantial progress in developing a competent judiciary and substantial revisions to China's procedural law. This continuity is concerning. Anti-corruption campaigns appear to remove not only corrupt officials but other individuals who may be arbitrarily perceived to be hostile to the leader(s) directing the anti-corruption campaign. This is strikingly similar to how Bo himself used the organized crime crackdown in Chongqing to extort businessmen and remove individuals he perceived as threats to his authority – such as Li Zhuang. Under Xi's leadership, there has also been a crackdown on dissidents under the cover of a broader (and generally popular) anti-corruption campaign. For instance, 15 anti-corruption activists were detained in Beijing in the spring of 2013 after publicly pushing for no more than transparency on CPC officials' assets (Roberts 2014a). As Bo was criticized for his oppressive and heavy-handed organized crime crackdown, Xi's anti-corruption campaign has been described as creating 'a climate of fear, [with] Xi himself appearing to be frighteningly ruthless' (Kor 2014, citing Kerry Brown). The short- to medium-term outlook for substantial anti-corruption reform whereby rule of law, procedural fairness, consistent and transparent use of courts can be utilized, thus seems quite bleak. For the longer term, however, it is noted that improvements to procedural law and improved legal and judicial capability across China have been made and have the potential to help.

Notes

1 For a more detailed analysis of the organized crime crackdown and apprehended criminals, see Ho (2012: 202–14).
2 Xi Jinping's trip to Chongqing and these positive assessments of Bo's leadership were widely reported at the time by the *Chongqing Daily*. NB after Bo's downfall, this news and positive assessments have largely been removed from the Chinese Internet (see Garnaut 2012: 129).
3 During his tenure as mayor of Dalian, Bo developed close relationships with entrepreneurs in the city, including Xu Ming. It is reported that Bo helped Xu Ming by awarding him key construction contracts in the city. Many believe Bo also helped Xu Ming by cutting through various administrative approvals to procure a 10 percent stake in China Pacific Insurance. In return, Xu Ming invested in Gu Kailai's consultancy firm (see Garnaut 2012: 36, 38–9).
4 Gu's accounts have been contested by Bo Guagua (see Garnaut 2012: 94).
5 In addition to bribery and corruption charges against Zhou, Wen (2015) cites a Supreme People's Court report on judicial work that suggested that 'Zhou and Bo had worked in "cliques" to engage in political conspiracy against the party; [they] trampled on rule of law, sabotaged party unity and engaged in nonorganisation political activities.'

8 China's land use and urbanization

Challenges for comprehensive reform

Richard Hu

Introduction

This chapter investigates China's new land use and urbanization reforms, the issues that have led to the reforms and the challenges for the foreseeable future. Set against the backdrop of a new generation of leadership, the central government has undertaken a series of new and significantly different reforms from previous generations. They constitute a package of measures toward building 'the China Dream' first propagated by President Xi Jinping. This package is formalized as the *Four Comprehensives* – to comprehensively build a moderately prosperous society, deepen reform, advance the rule of law and strictly govern the Party. The Four Comprehensives' deepening of reform is directly relevant to land use and urbanization and this analysis dissects two key, interrelated, policy documents: (1) Section Six of the Decision of the Central Committee of the CPC on Some Major Issues Concerning Comprehensively Deepening the Reform,[1] and (2) the National New-type Urbanization Plan.[2]

The Third Plenum's *Decision* outlined comprehensive reforms concerning a wide range of legal, economic, social and political issues. It set an ambitious roadmap toward 2020 and beyond. The tasks set in the *Decision* are for a systemic, scientific and effective institutional system to be established. The *Decision* ushers in the third stage of all-encompassing reforms, following reforms in 1978 and 1992. Land use and urban development occupy an important position in the Decision with *land market reform* the most radical (Aglietta and Bai 2014). The National New-type Urbanization Plan, a follow-up policy document to the *Decision*, is China's first national urbanization plan. It represents a significant commitment toward achieving 'genuine urbanization' (K.W. Chan 2014: 1).

With the 2015 announcement of the Four Comprehensives, it is an opportune time to review the new land use and urbanization reforms. The government has now been operating under new leadership for more than two years. The key reformist documents have been released. This enables an assessment about the extent to which the deepening reforms address problematic issues, and how future development is likely to be impacted. This chapter thus synthesizes land use and urbanization issues with a content analysis of the new reform documents. The synthesis covers issues that have been debated in the literature since 2012,[3] and includes suggestions about possible future reform directions. Cross-tabulating the issues with reform measures helps identify the challenges the reforms are expected to confront. The analysis has four thematic lenses: (1) the 'general system', examining the overall structure and development of land use and urbanization, (2) urban area, (3) rural area, and (4) the government's role. The lenses of urban and rural differentiate the dual urban–rural track of Chinese society. Given the government's crucial role in China's development, this lens is included to look ahead at China's comprehensive land use and urbanization reforms.

Land use

The general land use system in China has been governed by a dual-track system that differentiates urban and rural land in terms of ownership *and* market rights. This dual-track system is the largest barrier to further land reforms (Hu 2011). It has contributed to numerous social problems, urban land scarcity, inefficiency of land resource allocation and 'exacerbated social injustice' (Zou *et al.* 2014: 9114). Further, land policies have been piecemeal, failing to provide a holistic approach to deep-rooted structural problems. The existing system lacks a framework incorporating all the policies that target specific problems while being implemented in parallel (Liu *et al.* 2014a). The problem lies in both policy making *and* implementation. Consequently, the interests of legitimate stakeholders are often encroached upon during contestation over construction land involving multiple interest parties (Tang *et al.* 2012).

The urban area and the rural area have both common and different land use problems. In cities, the transfer of land use rights is gradually responding to institutional reforms that have led to a 'steady improvement in terms of transparency, efficiency and access to information' (Koroso *et al.* 2013: 417). Nevertheless, the market has significant weaknesses in equity, stakeholder engagement, corruption and expropriation (Koroso *et al.* 2013: 417). This brings about problems beyond the construction land and presents social, economic and political challenges. They are reflected in the numerous massive protests and corruptions associated with land development every year. With regard to urban land use itself, major problems include construction land vacancy and inefficient use (Liu *et al.* 2014a), and illegal residential buildings constructed in peri-urban areas (Paik and Lee 2012). The former refers to the urban space of low-density and decentralization in the form of urban sprawl; the latter refers to so-called 'Minor Property Housing' (MPH). MPH is constructed on rural collective land in suburban areas by a joint land development comprising township and village governments, land developers and peasants – without proper legal development approval.

In the rural area, unclear property rights, including unclear *land* property rights, is the root cause for most land-related problems. They take the forms of 'unclear rural land property rights (subject), incomplete rural land property rights (object), uneven urban-rural land development rights, and an imperfect land property rights management system' (Chen and Yang 2014: 75). These problems have also led to inefficient use of rural land, demonstrating a different set of inefficiency-attributes from urban land. The inefficient use of rural land takes various forms related to 'facilities land' and 'unused land', and uncoordinated farmland and rural housing land (Liu *et al.* 2014a: 111). A lack of transfer rights of collectively owned land is regarded as a major reason for the inefficient land use in rural areas (Li 2012), including inefficiently utilized rural residential properties under the existing land use regulations (Wang *et al.* 2012). Another major problem confronting rural land use is related to urban development. It is the loss of arable land due to non-agricultural use conversion that has been aggravated along with the accelerated urbanization process (Liu *et al.* 2014a).

The government's role is at the core of criticism of China's land system. There are two aspects of the criticism: the government's monopoly over land, and the government's incentive from 'land finance' – revenues from selling land. The local government is the de facto owner of development rights, and the only winner in the recent land use policy that links urban and rural construction land changes (Deng 2013). The government's monopoly enables it to expropriate land below market prices (Bertaud 2012). The government's monopoly also enables it to seek extra revenues from selling land. China's fiscal decentralization and rural tax reform have further pushed the local governments to exploit land finance. The local governments have embraced and manipulated market forces for their political agenda from land commodification for municipal finance (Lin 2014). In cities, entrepreneurial local governments have changed from protectionist market actors to investment promoters with monopoly power over land markets and controlling land supply (Wang Lei 2014). In addition, the government officials turn to land finance to win inter-city competitions to promote economic growth (Wu *et al.* 2015). In rural areas, township governments have changed from predatory taxation in the 1990s to 'land trade' in order to address the fiscal crises brought about by rural tax reforms (Takeuchi 2013: 755). Local government land-hoarding and speculation have been found to be positively and significantly correlated with land price increases (Du and Peiser 2014).

Three broad suggestions have been made to address the above problematic issues, including a strategic policy system, property rights reform and a free rural land and residential property market. First, a strategic land use policy system is crucial to guiding sustainable land use in the future to address the current policies that lack reciprocities and multi-layer connections (Liu *et al.* 2014b). An organic strategic land use policy system is proposed, consisting of a strategic layer to provide a land use support strategy to ecological and food security, a layer to focus on policy making according to the strategic objective and a layer to supply necessary protective mechanisms or supplementary measures to land consolidation (Liu *et al.* 2014b). While the components and configurations of the policy system are open to debate, a systemic approach is necessary to consolidate and streamline the existing policies. Second, property rights reform should unify land use in both urban and rural areas. For urban land use, reform should legitimize construction landownership, better define public interest, establish channels for expression of the public interest and clarify governments' functions in land interest adjustment (Tang *et al.* 2012). For rural land use, reform should clarify the rural land property right subject, propel the real right of the rural land contractual management, unify the urban–rural market of land for construction and confirm the rural land property right and issue property right certificates (Chen and Yang 2014). In essence, the reform should change the primary role of rural land from welfare to property to achieve urban–rural harmony and land use efficiency (Li 2012). Third, on the basis of the property right reform, a free market should be in place for rural land and residential property. Liberalization of the rural land market has been experimented in Shenzhen, which is a landmark step in reforming the current dual-track land system and indicates a potential new round of land policy revolution (Zou *et al.* 2014). A further free trade of rural residential properties is expected. Coupled with a household registration system, free trade of rural residential properties will facilitate permanent migration out of the countryside (Wang *et al.* 2012). Numerous rural migrants live and work in cities but maintain their rural properties, leading to inefficient rural land use. One impediment is that the rural residential property is not transferable due to a lack of legally defined property rights and a free market.

The new round of land use reforms are outlined in Item 11 of the Third Plenum's Decision 'Establishing Unified Urban–Rural Construction Land Market' and Chapter 24 of the National New-type Urbanization Plan, 'Deepening Reforms on Land Management Systems'. The new land use reforms address all the issues and suggestions discussed above, and go even further in breadth and depth. The exception is the role of government, which is beyond the scope of land use reforms. The new reforms are situated under one umbrella objective of establishing a unified urban–rural construction land market, which governs all reformist regulations. To address the conflicts over land-related benefits, the new reforms propose to establish a mechanism for the distribution of incremental benefits from land that takes into account the interests of the state, the collective and the individual. Raising individual income from such benefits would be one important result of reform. To address inefficient land use in cities, the new reforms propose to broaden the scope of compensated use of state-owned land, to reduce land appropriation for non-public welfare projects and to establish regulative mechanisms for land use scale and structure in cities and towns. To address land expropriation and conversion in rural areas, the new reforms propose to narrow the scope of land expropriation, regulate land appropriation procedures and improve mechanisms by which rural land is requisitioned so that such mechanisms contain multiple layers of security. The new reforms aim to strengthen the arable land protection system.

The most important development in the new reforms concerns the rural land market. One prominent measure is to grant equal market rights and prices for collectively owned land in rural areas and state-owned land in urban areas. The implication is profound. The rural collectively owned and profit-oriented construction land can then be sold, leased and appraised as shares, and would enter the market with the same rights and at the same prices as state-owned land, on the premise that it would conform to planning and land use control. Peasants' market rights for land and residential property would be clarified. The new reforms propose to endow peasants with the right to occupy, use, profit from and transfer contracted land and to mortgage and guarantee contraction rights, as well as to promote peasants' house property to be mortgaged, guaranteed and transferred. To facilitate the transfer of rural land and property, the new reforms propose to establish a rural property circulation and transaction market, to promote open, fair and regulated operation of rural property circulation, and to improve the secondary market for land leasing, transfer and mortgage.

Urbanization

China's society has been marked by a sharply defined urban–rural dichotomy (Ye *et al.* 2013). This dichotomy has called for the need for urbanization; it has also been a major impediment to urbanization. It has been the core issue in the previous urban reforms as well as the current round of so-called 'new-type urbanization'. The general system of China's urbanization has been closely linked with its economic growth. One critique is that China's urbanization is incomplete urbanization or under-urbanization. That is, China's urbanization lags behind its industrialization and development status (Lu and Wan 2014). This has been attributed to the dual urban–rural social structure. In particular, the Hukou and land systems exert institutional constraints on labor mobility, which have led to segregation, efficiency loss, distortion in the urban system and adverse impacts on equity (Lu and Wan 2014). However, one counter-argument is that China's urbanization process has progressed faster than its economic growth since 2004, and it is the right time to rethink under-urbanization and its counter-measure in development strategy (Chen *et al.* 2013). The faster urbanization process calls for a shift in emphasis from *quantity* to *quality* in the new stage of urbanization.

Different urbanization issues have affected both urban and rural areas. Understanding China's urban development needs to be situated in the broad economic restructuring and the gradual, experiential national reform. All have been transitional. China's urban policies to date have been state-directed, growth-oriented and centered on land development and spatial restructuring (Wei 2012). An overemphasis on economic growth and the physical dimension of urban development has posed unprecedented challenges for sustainability and liveability. Rapid urban growth has been accompanied by increasing environmental pollution and social problems. These negatively impact upon the economic competitiveness and environmental sustainability of many Chinese cities (see Xu's macroeconomic analysis in Chapter 4). Largely due to the partiality of urban policies, China's urbanization has been described as 'landed urbanization', or criticized as 'pseudo-urbanization'. By landed urbanization, it means that the growth of Chinese cities has been based on fast urban land expansion and under-urbanization of the population (Ye *et al.* 2013; Wu *et al.* 2015). Land commodification, rather than human capital or advanced technology, has played an instrumental role in the growth and transformation of Chinese cities (Lin 2014). Pseudo-urbanization refers to the urban sprawl inflating the urban population without necessarily urbanizing the overall landscape or economy (Yew 2012). As a result of the landed or pseudo-urbanization, a large number of rural migrant workers, estimated at 245 million in 2014, live in cities without urban residency and access to social services (K.W. Chan 2014). They are the major subjects of the new urbanization reforms.

China's rural area is confronting problems arising from both the urbanization process and rural policies. The foremost problem is depopulation. Liu *et al.* (2014a) refer to this as a rural 'hollowing phenomenon' from rural out-migration. The phenomenon takes various forms. The rural population, the rural laborer population in particular, is quickly decreasing. Those who stay in the countryside are either the aged or children; they will move to cities as family migrants in due course. Some rural lands and residential properties are vacant, ruined or abandoned, aggravating land use inefficiency. The second problem is landless peasants due to land expropriation (Liu *et al.* 2014b). The peasants are not financially rewarded at a market price from converting the collective ownership of rural land for non-agricultural purposes. The landless peasants lack the necessary vocational skills and social security to survive after losing the land, which presents a challenge to their livelihood and causes socio-economic problems. The third problem is the environmental cost and the loss of local cultural flavor. China's urbanization strategies that aimed at shifting current land use and moving the local population have contributed to increasing economic efficiency. However, the process has also been associated with an increase in fossil energy consumption and environmental pressure, as well as reduction of the local characteristics of the areas impacted (Siciliano 2012).

The central government launched the 'New Socialist Countryside' campaign to guide the rural development almost one decade ago. In essence, the 'New Socialist Countryside' campaign authorizes local state expropriation of rural land from farmers, and then incorporates evicted farmers into township residency and urban citizenship. The campaign has alleviated rural land politics. The incorporation of rural residents into urban residency enables the de-politicization of resistance to land expropriation by changing the residency-based grounds on which legitimate claims to land can be made (Chuang 2014). But land consolidation is not a panacea for rural development issues including regional discrepancies, rural poverty and rural land use issues. The key problem is how to re-employ surplus rural laborers and resettle land-loss farmers (Long *et al.* 2010).

The government's role in urbanization is similar to that in the land use system. The central question concerns the government's intervention into and incentive from the urbanization process. Since the turn of the century, Chinese cities have experienced a shift from industrialism to urbanism in political legitimacy and policy discourse (Qian 2012). This shift signifies a transformative interest of the government from growing the economy only to also growing the cities. China's urbanization is called 'administrative urbanization' to reflect the government's strong involvement. The government has dual incentives from administrative urbanization. Financially, the local government can generate revenue from land finance as discussed above. Land finance has significantly contributed to the land-based urbanization that is characteristic of urban sprawl and expansion (Yew 2012). Politically, local government has approached urban restructuring to realize gains from the property market boom, restructure urban space and strengthen urban governing capacity (Qian 2012). The urban governing capacity here embodies financial resources to support urban development and infrastructure, as well as political favors for local officials to be promoted.

A wide range of suggestions have been made to improve China's urbanization strategy and policies to address the above issues. China's urbanization is outpacing its industrialization and economic growth. It is time to rethink 'under-urbanization' to improve the quality of urbanization rather than emphasizing urbanization quantity (Chen *et al.* 2013). At the strategic level, two major suggestions stand out. One is to shift urban planning from an emphasis on economic growth; the other is to coordinate urban and rural development. To diversify from an emphasis on economic growth, China's urban planning needs to include a stronger regulatory function, greater emphasis on environmental quality and stronger analytical, communicative and advocacy roles, and to revive and strengthen property rights and reformulate urban communities (Abramson 2006). Coordinated urban–rural development planning has been experimented in Chengdu. The transferable experiences from Chengdu include grass-roots citizen participation; clarity in property ownership and use rights; transparency in land transactions; a modern market in land rights; agricultural modernization; consolidation and rationalization of industry, land and housing; public services equalization; human-scale development sensitive to local culture; and diversified economic development capitalizing on local comparative advantage (Ye *et al.* 2013). These experimental experiences seem to have been instrumental to the new reforms.

The Hukou system occupies a central position in the policy suggestions. It has been criticized as a key impediment to a 'genuine urbanization', and should be thoroughly reformed or altogether abolished (K.W. Chan 2012). Achieving a genuine urbanization will fix an alarming three-decade-long trend of a rising proportion of the disenfranchised, second-class population of rural migrant workers in cities (K.W. Chan 2014). A more specific suggestion is to link land reform with Hukou reform to coordinate urban–rural development. The practice has been experimented in Chengdu and Chongqing to enable long-term migrants to convert their rural residential land into construction-use land quotas that are then transferred to the city of their employment for urban expansion (Lu and Wan 2014). This approach offers a way to address land-based urbanization and coordinate it with population-based urbanization. For rural areas, attention should be paid to caring for farmers' future livelihoods in the process of implementing the 'New Socialist Countryside' campaign (Long *et al.* 2010). The local character of rural areas should be taken into account by policy makers and planners if rural development targets are to be viable (Siciliano 2012).

Taken together, Section Six, 'Improving Integrated Urban–Rural Development System and Mechanism', in the *Decision*, and the National New-type Urbanization Plan, outline a blueprint for China's future urbanization. Together they address the dual urban–rural social structure to achieve an integrated urban–rural development. In principle, they offer the most comprehensive reforms on China's urbanization strategy yet as they address the widest range of issues that have been raised or criticized for decades. Under the rhetoric of 'new-type urbanization with Chinese characteristics', they are underpinned by four principles: (1) human-centric urbanization, (2) coordinated development of cities of various sizes, (3) coordinated development of industry and cities, and (4) coordinated urbanization and new countryside. The 'human-centric' concept goes beyond the usual physical and construction dimensions typical of most urban plans in China. It vows to grant equal rights and services to both rural and urban residents.

The most important part of the new reforms deals with the urbanization of rural residents. This involves Hukou system reform and equal citizenship for rural migrants in cities. The National New-type Urbanization Plan specifies steps to transfer rural residents to cities through loosening the Hukou system. Hukou restrictions will be gradually relaxed for small to medium cities, but will continue to be controlled for large cities. The new reforms take a giant stride in the 'citizenization' of rural migrants in cities by extending urban public services to cover all permanent residents, including housing, social security, life and health insurance. The new reforms take into account the problem of land-based urbanization, and tries to propel population-based urbanization by linking fiscal transfer payments with a more urbanized rural population – to tighten urban construction land provision.

The new reforms adopt three major measures for integrated urban–rural development. They are a unified urban–rural market for equal exchanges of factors of production, including land; balanced allocation of public resources between urban and rural areas; and integrated urban–rural planning, infrastructure and public services. These measures enable equal market rights, equal resources and equal development for urban and rural areas to bridge the divide in the existing dual urban–rural track structure. The new reforms also provide guidelines for urban development and rural development respectively. For the urban area, the new reforms suggest financing innovation including allowing social capital to finance infrastructure investment and operation. This measure is meant to alleviate the local government's reliance on land finance for infrastructure investment. The new reforms are indicative of the need to decentralize governance – to empower prefectures and towns with larger populations and stronger economies – and a need to better coordinate inter-regional development. For the rural area, the new reforms aim to promote a new form of agricultural operation system. This would function on the basis of family operation and land contraction, marketization, scale economy and modern business operations. The new reforms seek to endow peasants with more property rights, including rights to collectively owned property, market rights to housing property for capital gain and a rural property rights market.

Challenges and tensions

Modifiers such as 'deepened' and 'comprehensive' are used to describe the new round of reforms. Apart from being propaganda rhetoric, they reflect the depth and scope of the new reforms compared to the previous ones. However, they do not go without criticism. One criticism is that they are 'mainly old wine in old bottles', setting forth broad principles or political slogans that have been mostly discussed or debated for many years with no major theoretical or ideological breakthrough (Peerenboom 2014a: 7). Concerns have been raised about the extent to which they provide appropriate policy interventions into the structural issues in contemporary China, including land use and urbanization (Aglietta and Bai 2014). Most certainly, the reforms will proceed with challenges and tensions.

A foremost challenge for the deepening reform strategy is implementation. As this round of reforms set ambitious objectives and a stringent achievement deadline of 2020, implementation is particularly contingent. It is not clear whether the deadline is a result of a political aspiration for a decimal year, or a more sophisticated set of calculations. For example, the National New-type Urbanization Plan specifies a target of granting 100 million new urban Hukou until 2020, including commensurate public services such as education, health and housing. According to a preliminary estimate, what this means is an average of about 17 million new urban residents per year, 50 percent higher than the average achieved in the decade 2000–10 (K.W. Chan 2014). Pursuing this goal will incur massive political, economic and social resources if there is to be a smooth transition. Notably, this has not been achieved before. The pace of implementation is clearly important to the government. However, the political feasibility of the reforms depends on the sequencing of implementation; early stage benefits may serve to legitimize more contentious future policy decisions (Aglietta and Bai 2014). The central government has not yet unveiled its strategic roadmap with clear milestones toward 2020, although a few institutional arrangements have been made. These include the establishment of the Central Leadership Group of Deepened Reforms to streamline and coordinate the implementation process.

The long, deeply rooted tensions embedded in the dual urban–rural social structures will continue to impact upon the efficiency and effectiveness of the new reforms on land use and urbanization. There are three broad groups of categories at the heart of the tensions: (1) ongoing social inequality, (2) the urban–rural divide, and (3) an interventionist, centralist government. Social inequality has been accelerating in China, involving income inequality and regional equality (Knight 2013). In cities, unaffordable housing presents a stringent issue for the poor urban class, due to the Hukou system, privatization and house ownership, and resettlement (Chen 2012). Chen argues the urban poor tend to be path-dependent, privatization-oriented and development-driven; a mechanism to ensure the poor's basic right to housing is still lacking. The new urbanization plan acknowledges the issue and suggests the need to address it in principle, but it does not specify how and when. The housing crisis is even more acute in the high-end cities like Beijing, Shanghai and Guangzhou that aspire to global city status (Timberlake *et al.* 2014). Negative social consequences are often covered by the global glamour in these cities. In the rural area, addressing the social exclusion resulting from land acquisition and land loss has long been debated without reaching a consensus on policy intervention. One prevailing suggestion is that the central government should support land-lost peasants to settle in cities (Hui *et al.* 2013). This suggestion has been echoed in the new reforms that grant rural migrants equal citizenship and public services in cities. At the same time there are warnings against privatizing rural land and property. The argument is that privatization runs against the nature of collective ownership and will exacerbate class inequality and social tension (Lian and Lejano 2014). This ideological terrain is where the new reforms do have ambiguities in that rural property transferability lacks a clearly defined property right.

Will the new reforms effectively address China's urban–rural relationship? Only time will tell. The dual urban–rural track of social structure has been deeply institutionalized and operationalized for several decades. The systemic and structural complexities generate multiple challenges for any policy intervention. The urban–rural conflict involves property, resources and development (Yu *et al.* 2014). These dimensions of conflict seem to be captured in the new reforms in that they target a unified urban–rural land market and coordinated urban–rural development planning. Uncertainty remains as to how the urban–rural divide is to be structurally untangled. There are two contributory factors central to the uncertainty: (1) urban bias in the development strategy and a resulting lack of social provision of public goods in rural areas; and (2) severe and multi-dimensional constraints on the peasantry (Wang *et al.* 2013). From a policy perspective, these factors appear to be caught by the new reforms, at least on the surface, with appropriate measures. What prevents any easy policy intervention are non-institutional factors – social, demographic, historic, cultural, locational and behavioral factors – that contribute to path-dependency in the urban–rural divide. Understanding China's urbanization requires an integrative framework of a dichotomy of institutional and non-institutional factors (Hu 2013a). It follows that interventions should deploy a similar dichotomy. It is therefore noteworthy that 'non-institutional interventions' are outside the scope of the new reforms.

The government's role in China's land use and urbanization is complex. The government has been *the* key driver of historical land use and urban reforms, as well as a key impediment to further reforms (see Hu 2012). This schizoid role of government as reformer/reform impediment explains much of the paradox in these reforms (Hu 2013b). This paradox continues in the new reforms. Compared to other countries, factors like state, institution and cultural background have a stronger explanatory power with regard to China's social–spatial divides (Madrazo and Kempen 2012). It follows that government policy is often strongly contested. A most contentious point is how reform can see the government wean itself off the benefits of 'land finance' and land-based urbanization. Local governments especially have been deeply entangled with the financial benefits of land-grabbing from peasants. This is often at the core of social tensions and instability, and has eroded political trust from local communities (Cui *et al.* 2014). In contrast, the community's trust in the central government to solve the problems remains (Cui *et al.* 2014). This gives the central government an opportunity to drive reforms, taking a 'top-down' approach. The biggest challenge confronting local government is loss of land finance. For instance, Xue and Wu (2015) assert that the development approach by an entrepreneurial government has reached its limits. The International Monetary Fund, however, reports that while local government finance is weak, it is within a sustainable threshold, with room for policy intervention (Zhang and Barnett 2014). The new reforms call for financing innovation and attracting social capital into infrastructure investment and operations. The policy directions are imposed by the central government, but the shift is supposed to be effected by local government. This shift from a reliance on 'land finance' to 'innovative and social financing' will not be simple.

Conclusion

Historically, China's planning around urbanization has been 'land-based' rather than 'population-based'. Urban expansion has been accompanied by burgeoning numbers of rural migrants moving to live in cities without urban citizenship and thus access to public services. Associated with the urbanization process are depopulation and land-loss peasantry in rural areas. China's land use and urbanization are both subject to government monopoly and control. Local government political and financial incentives have, under previous administrations, come from selling land and promoting urban growth. This has contributed to many problems, including corruption, risky financing, exploitation of peasants and so on. This chapter has synthesized various suggestions for improvement, with a focus on reforming rural property rights, liberalizing the land market and loosening Hukou restrictions. The chapter contributes to the newest understanding of China's land use and urbanization by documenting the deepening reforms and analyzing the central issues, tensions and challenges ahead. The dual urban–rural social structure is at the root of many of the tensions. Previous reforms and policies have lacked an integrative framework and thus failed to effectively address the significant problems.

Land use inefficiencies have been identified in both urban and rural areas. Unclear land property rights and loss of arable land present particularly serious rural area land use challenges. The new land use and urbanization reforms are part of a package of comprehensive strategic reforms, governed by the strategic objective of a unified urban–rural land market and integrated urban–rural development. These reform measures seek to address the key issues with some suggestions for improvement going further in scope and depth than before. The ambitious rhetoric is, however, confronted by a reality of challenges and tensions deeply rooted in structural and political complexity: China's social inequality, the urban–rural divide and a central government that sets the rules, but largely relies on local governments to implement them.

Notes

1 Adopted in November 2013 at the Third Plenum of the Eighteenth Central Committee of the CPC (hereafter, the Third Plenum's *Decision*); Section Six is entitled 'Improving Integrated Urban–Rural Development System and Mechanism'.

2 Released in March 2014.

3 For details see Hu (2011: ch. 10) on property law reforms, and (2012: ch. 5) on 'understanding Chinese real estate'.

9 Individual rights protection or social management?

Equal employment laws and policies in China

Su Lin Han

Introduction

The principle of equality and non-discrimination has long been embraced by the Chinese Constitution and prescribed by many of the country's equal employment laws and policies. Despite such commitment, China has not implemented key equal employment laws and policies aimed at protecting specific disadvantaged groups such as women and people with disabilities. Chinese courts routinely refuse to handle employment discrimination lawsuits. Government regulators rarely take enforcement actions against employers for discriminatory employment practices. Much of the enforcement difficulties can be attributed to a lack of clear judicial and legislative guidance for courts to handle discrimination claims. The lax enforcement by government regulators also reflects the issue's low policy priority. However, even more inherent obstacles stem from the government's distrust of the use of private enforcement in individual rights protection cases. The government's overarching goal of maintaining social control and stability is often at odds with the decentralized nature of privately initiated litigation of individual rights claims. This distrust is not new and emanates from the PRC's history of preferring collective, non-adversarial approaches to dispute resolution. But it has blunted the government's resolve to overcoming significant legal deficiencies that prevent a proper functioning of its existing judicial mechanism for resolving individual discrimination claims. Instead, the government continues to rely on traditional 'top-down' social management tools to marshal the resources of a centralized political and bureaucratic machinery outside the legal framework to tackle the country's employment discrimination problem.

As China's leadership turns to its brand of 'rule of law' as a new strategy to improve governance and bolster the Party's political legitimacy, a central concern is how to improve the delivery and benefits of rule of law to an increasingly 'rights conscious' populace through stronger enforcement of individual rights protection promised by existing laws. The challenge is how this can be accomplished given the unmistakable signal from the CPC's Fourth Plenum of the Party-state's determination to maintain a firm grip on issues containing the potential to impact on social stability. This chapter argues that alternative enforcement models that enhance the role of the government in delivering its promise of individual rights protection may be a workable compromise between the government's strong desire to manage employment discrimination as a collective social issue on the one hand, and the ability of private citizens to benefit from legalized individual rights protection on the other hand. Accomplishing such paradoxical goals, however, will be a difficult balancing act.

China's challenges in enforcing employment discrimination laws and policies

Historically, implementation of China's long-standing principle of equality and non-discrimination was carried out as part of the state's central planning function – outside the legal framework. Under China's centrally planned economy, the state owned, managed and regulated all businesses called *danwei*. It was able to enforce equal employment policies, most notably gender equality and protection measures, through a centralized worker allocation system, uniform hiring and firing rules, and informal dispute resolution mechanisms within each *danwei* directly supervised by government regulators.[1]

As Yueh shows in Chapter 5, the introduction of market-based reforms in the late 1970s ushered in rapid growth of a vibrant private sector and a burgeoning labor market in China, along with a diminished central planning role of government in regulating employment relations. Employers, including government and state-owned companies, now have more autonomy in hiring and firing decisions. At the same time, employment discrimination has proliferated. This has resulted in increased labor tension and rising demand from a more rights conscious workforce to have grievances heard and claims resolved.

Such pressure has led to the adoption of several important national legislations to protect the equal employment rights of special disadvantaged groups such as women and people with disabilities. Most notable is the 2008 *Equal Employment Promotion Law* (EPL).[2] In addition to providing administrative penalties-based public enforcement, the EPL opened the door for private rights of action against employment discrimination by allowing workers to sue their employers in court.[3] Private enforcement of statutes through court litigation has a long tradition in many legal cultures and has played a major role, for example, in the enforcement of US federal civil rights statutes and the development of US equal employment discrimination laws.[4] The introduction of private rights of action by the EPL and other Chinese laws such as recent anti-trust laws, reflects the influence of international legal development and the progression of rule of law in China over the past decade and evidenced in more tolerance for non-state actors to play a bigger role in enforcing legal protections. At the same time, this new 'tolerance' carries major challenges to the state's long-standing practices of top-down control and management of rights protection issues with broader social stability implications.

Limited private enforcement

Since the adoption of the EPL, there has been an uptick in employment discrimination lawsuits, often brought by younger, more educated plaintiffs with the support of public interest lawyers. According to one study, approximately 70 anti-discrimination cases were brought or accepted by courts between 2008 and 2011, compared to 20 or so such cases between 2000 and 2007.[5] However, major legal and political hurdles have prevented court litigation from gaining sufficient traction in China to become an effective private enforcement tool of employment discrimination laws.

For example, notwithstanding the EPL's express authorization for individuals to file employment discrimination claims with China's Basic People's Courts, many courts refuse to accept even the filing of such claims. A common explanation for such rejection is that employment discrimination is not included in the list of 'permitted civil causes of action' issued by China's Supreme People Court.[6] Among the successful filings, a substantial number involved plaintiffs who were carriers of Hepatitis B (HBV carriers),[7] but their underlying causes of action were often violations of privacy rights, not employment discrimination.[8] Gender and disability cases are rare, and they too tend to be accepted where causes of action are 'violation of personal rights' rather than employment discrimination.[9] Chinese courts also struggle with a lack of legal and judicial guidance on substantive legal issues such as what constitutes 'employment discrimination' and who bears the burden of proof. Neither the EPL nor any other laws defines 'employment discrimination'. Questions also remain as to whether the burden of proof, which generally rests on plaintiffs in civil lawsuits, can be shifted to defendant employers in employment discrimination cases.[10]

Even more daunting for private enforcement are political challenges. The decentralized nature of privately initiated litigation that is essential to a 'bottom-up' approach to enforcing individual rights claims is inherently at odds with the government's long-standing 'command-and-control' approach to managing systemic social problems which places a premium on the state's ability to maintain social control and order. The alliance between discrimination victims and non-governmental rights advocacy in bringing the so-called 'impact litigation' in employment discrimination appears to have heightened political sensitivity about private litigation. This is due, in part, to the perceived threat of private litigation to state control of the direction and outcome of social changes that are an inevitable consequence of such litigation.

Chinese courts, which have thus far enjoyed limited independence in the adjudication of individual cases and whose decisions are directly influenced by the state's political agenda and policy priorities, are unable and unwilling to take the lead in resolving individual employment discrimination claims as it is an area fraught with political sensitivity. Instead, the general attitude of courts toward discrimination cases has been characterized as 'restraint' and 'judicial non-activism'.[11] Since 2008, the Supreme People's Court has twice amended its list of permitted civil causes of actions. Yet 'employment discrimination' has not been listed. Nor has the High Court issued any judicial interpretation or guiding cases to clarify the outstanding legal issues for lower courts.

Victims of employment discrimination currently have few non-judicial alternatives for bringing their claims. Despite improvements to China's labor arbitration, proceedings are generally closed to employment discrimination claims as the scope tends to be limited to disputes arising out of *existing labor contracts* and labor relations.[12] This precludes claims against discriminatory *hiring* practices. The prospect of bringing a separate employment discrimination action for labor arbitration, as opposed to an auxiliary claim to labor contract dispute, is also dim as neither the EPL nor the labor arbitration law expressly authorizes such claims to be handled through labor arbitration.[13]

Weak administrative enforcement

Under the EPL, China's Ministry of Human Resource and Social Security (MOHRSS), often referred to as the 'relevant labor administration department in charge', is responsible for overseeing compliance. This includes establishing a complaints handling system to accept and verify complaints and to take action against violations.[14] However, the prevailing view among Chinese academics (e.g., Liu Minghui 2014: 46) and likely also held by MOHRSS, is that the EPL has failed to grant specific labor supervisory authority necessary for MOHRSS to take administrative enforcement action against employment discrimination.[15] The available evidence suggests that in practice, MOHRSS rarely accepts or investigates employment discrimination complaints. For example, in 2012, female college students from eight Chinese cities filed complaints with the local MOHRSS offices alleging gender discrimination by 267 employers for posting 'male only' hiring ads online. Only 30 percent of their complaints received a response from MOHRSS and only one employer was issued a fine. The students alleged that most MOHRSS offices were unwilling to handle their complaints.[16]

Two recent high-profile court decisions, hailed by domestic media as China's first 'gender and residency discrimination' cases, underscore the challenges and uncertainty faced by private litigants. The first is a 2013 gender discrimination lawsuit that ended in a court settlement. It involved a female college graduate accusing a private employer, whose job advertisement specifically excluded 'female applicants', of gender discrimination. The plaintiff's initial complaint to the local MOHRSS office was rejected and her subsequent administrative appeal of the agency's decision was also denied.[17] Her civil lawsuit against the employer for gender discrimination in violation of the EPL was 'in limbo' for over a year before a Beijing local court accepted her case.[18] The reasons given for the court's delay was the need to seek higher-level approval, ostensibly on the ground that employment discrimination was 'not a permitted cause of action'. The 'sensitive' nature of the lawsuit was not mentioned, but is a more likely explanation. When the case was finally settled, the plaintiff received an apology from the employer who also paid RMB30,000 (US$5,000) into a gender equality fund. In the second case, in 2014, another female college graduate brought an employment discrimination claim against a MOHRSS office in Nanjing for excluding job applicants who did not have 'local residency status'.[19] The plaintiff failed to convince three local courts and a labor arbitration tribunal to accept her case. When the case was finally accepted by the order of an appeals court, the plaintiff was required to amend her cause of action from 'employment discrimination' to 'violation of personal rights' because local judges were unable to find legal precedents or existing rules regarding her discrimination claim. The case was settled in favor of the plaintiff who received RMB11,000 (US$1,800) in compensation.

Ineffective policy response

Although employment discrimination is well-entrenched, it has not commanded the same policy priority as other social stability 'hotspots' in China. For example, in labor relations, MOHRSS has been preoccupied with volatile and higher-profile issues such as low employment rates for new college graduates and back-pay for rural migrant workers.[20] It has not been until recently that employment discrimination began to catch the attention of top-level policy makers as a contributing factor to high unemployment among recent college graduates. Yet the government's policy response remains characterized by top-down mobilizing of political and bureaucratic machinery, as opposed to promoting individual assertion of rights claims through existing judicial and administrative enforcement channels.

Since the mid-2000s, the perennial difficulty faced by millions of Chinese college graduates in finding suitable employment captures national attention each graduation season. According to MOHRSS, during the first half of 2014, only 7 percent (560,000) of that year's 7.27 million graduates received job offers before graduation, making it 'the worst hiring season in history'.[21] A recent Peking University study analyzing the employment data of 350,000 new college graduates born in the 1990s found their employment rate to be as low as 14.3 percent.[22] In addition to these dismal statistics is strong employer preference for hiring male graduates. For example, female graduates accounted for 48 percent of graduates in 2013.[23] Yet the All China's Women's Federation reports that more than 90 percent female graduates in 2013 experienced gender discrimination in their job searches; over 70 percent reported not being offered a job because of gender.[24]

The employment status and discrimination issues impacting such a large, educated youth population that is active on China's social media raises 'social stability' concerns for the state. This concern was most recently illustrated in the arrest of five young women's right's activists around International Women's Day on March 8, 2015 for drawing public attention to the prevalence of sexual harassment.[25] Yet for years, the official response by MOHRSS and other central government ministries has been limited to promotion of employment of college graduates by sponsoring job fairs, job training programs and hiring incentives for employers.[26] Recently, however, a few high-level Party and government documents have singled out employment discrimination as a root cause of the unemployment problem and a possible solution. For instance, the Party's Third Plenum *Decision* (2013) included 'elimination of employment discrimination' as part of the overall strategy for promoting employment of college graduates.[27] In 2014, China's State Council issued a notice for improving college graduate employment, calling all regions and all relevant government departments to 'proactively adopt measures to promote equal employment [and to] prohibit employers from setting discriminatory [hiring] requirements on the basis of ethnicity, race, gender, religious beliefs and residency status'.[28] Numerous lower-level government policy documents echoed such calls, including a 2013 directive from the Ministry of Education prohibiting employers from imposing gender and residency status requirements at college job fairs.[29]

These documents do not specifically refer to the role of public and private enforcement tools provided by existing employment discrimination laws even though these are essential for reaching the government's policy goals of 'correcting discriminatory practices'. This 'absence' reflects official ambivalence toward using rule of law, especially through private court litigation, to address individual grievances against employment discrimination. These documents also show that despite repeated official rhetoric about reining in employment discrimination, the government's social management options have not been sufficiently adaptive to China's changing labor market conditions under which many employment decisions are no longer subject to state control. The Chinese public, especially female college graduates bearing the brunt of discrimination in the workplace, has little confidence that the new government rhetoric is enough to stem China's tide of employment discrimination.[30]

China's affirmative action plan on the employment of workers with disabilities is another example of ineffective government anti-discrimination policy. Official statistics reveal that the current level of unemployment among China's disabled urban residents (who account for 35 percent of the country's 85 million disabled population) exceeds 10 percent. This compares to a 5 percent unemployment rate in the general population.[31] For those with a mental disability, the employment rate is less than 10 percent. By law (which codifies a government affirmative action policy adopted since the early 2000s), all employers in China are required to staff no less than 1.5 percent of their workforce with disabled workers. Failure to comply may result in administrative fines to employers to be paid to various locally managed disabled worker employment-guarantee funds.[32] Recent studies by the China Disabled Persons Union and others reveal extensive non-compliance among employers. For instance, more than 90 percent of employers opted to pay the fine and only 4.7 percent of Beijing's 445,000 employers reported hiring disabled workers.[33] The extent of non-compliance has sparked a public outcry against both the apparent failure of the affirmative action policy and the suspected misuse by officials of the funds intended to improve employment prospects for disabled workers.[34] Such a policy response that relies primarily on administrative fines for enforcement, even when the fines are substantial and uniformly levied, has failed to have either punitive or deterrent effects on discriminatory employment practices against people with a disability. It merely puts a price tag on the 'business cost' of discrimination by employers.

Improving public enforcement: a workable compromise for rights protection in China?

Many challenges faced by China in enforcing employment discrimination laws and policies reflect its internal political constraints on individual rights advocacy, and the failure of the authoritarian state's 'command-and-control' social management strategies to solve contemporary social problems. In particular, the difficulties for private court litigation to take root as an important enforcement tool is a direct result of the Party-state's unwillingness to cede any real control of the management of a systemic social problem to non-governmental actors. In comparison, private litigation has been effectively used to enforce equal employment rights laws and advance social changes elsewhere. In countries such as the United States and those in Europe, its success is predicated upon two basic premises: a willingness of the state to 'deputize private litigants and their attorneys to enforce the law' and the ability of an independent judiciary to shape laws and public policies through court decisions.[35] Both are currently substantively missing in China's political landscape.

Despite China's 2015 launch of judicial reforms to reduce Party and government officials' interference in courts' adjudication of individual cases (see Qianfan Zhang in Chapter 1), their primary focus appears to be mainly for improving courts' capability and efficiency in resolving legal disputes, and not to boost independence of the judiciary, which is to remain loyal to the Party's political prerogatives.[36] The Party leadership makes it clear that under its brand of 'rule of law', which must serve as the 'ballast for social order and stability', rights claims of the masses can only be asserted through 'legally sanctioned channels' and 'stirring up trouble' as a way of resolving conflicts is not to be tolerated.[37] Amidst the recent rise in government crackdowns on the activities of non-government rights advocacy groups and public interest lawyers, which specifically target those involved in 'workers' rights, legal advocacy, and discrimination',[38] whether legal advocacy of equality and non-discrimination rights will remain 'legally sanctioned' is far from politically settled. This uncertainty will likely affect the viability of court litigation as a private enforcement option in China, at least in the near term. Yet as the state faces mounting pressure to develop better governance tools to replace its outdated social management regime, a central question must be answered: whether, in the absence of a robust private enforcement alternative, China's administrative enforcement system can be reformed to fit the leadership's current rule of law narrative while still offering improved individual rights protection?

Experience from a range of jurisdictions with longer histories of laws protecting equal employment rights suggests that private enforcement litigation, although well-established since the advent of civil and human rights legislation in recent decades, is a relatively new phenomenon.[39] Public enforcement administered by government agencies has also been widely used as an alternative, or complementary, mechanism to achieve the twin policy objectives of protecting individual rights and combating employment discrimination. In the United States, for example, Title VII of the *Civil Rights Act* was adopted in 1964 to prohibit workplace discrimination. While the law relies on private court litigation as a major enforcement mechanism,[40] it also authorizes the establishment of a special government administrative agency, the Equal Employment Opportunity Commission (the EEOC), to lead public enforcement and implementation of federal equal employment protection laws and policies. Today, the EEOC reviews nearly 100,000 private discrimination claims annually through its administrative claims handling process.[41] Its investigative and prosecutorial powers focus on a smaller number of employment discrimination cases involving more egregious and systemic violations. Similar administrative enforcement models have been adopted in a number of other jurisdictions, including the United Kingdom, Australia, Hong Kong and Taiwan, to complement private court enforcement, reflecting the different statutory and policy priorities based on local conditions.

Several key features of the EEOC and similar administrative enforcement models elsewhere may be of particular relevance in exploring public enforcement alternatives for China's employment discrimination laws:

- *Government as first responder to privately initiated claims.* In the United States, the EEOC is the entry point for filing all federal employment discrimination claims, which must filed and reviewed by the EEOC before they are permitted to proceed to private litigation in court. The EEOC's administrative claims handling and resolution process allows the government to identify, investigate and prioritize discrimination complaints based on neutral findings of merits. It also allows the government to facilitate speedy resolution of claims through an informal mediation process at an early stage without finding fault. When EEOC investigations find violations, the agency will seek voluntary conciliation between employers and employees. The threat of government prosecution if conciliation is unsuccessful can, of course, 'incentivize' employers to settle. EEOC-monitored settlements can include remedies such as back-pay and reinstatement, as well as injunctive relief to force employers to correct discriminatory conduct and prevent future violations. The EEOC's administrative claims proceedings are privately initiated and the government is bound by a statutory obligation to receive, investigate and conciliate charges of employment discrimination.[42] From the perspective of an individual claimant, the EEOC not only provides an easily accessible and low-cost forum for impartial determination of their discrimination claims, but the government can also become a powerful ally in advocating their rights once employer violations are found.
- *Government as public advocate for equal rights protection.* As the chief public advocate and enforcer of federal employment discrimination laws and policies, the EEOC has the authority to bring public interest lawsuits

against employer violations on behalf of and for the benefit of individual claimants. In recent years, the EEOC has focused this aspect of its enforcement efforts on selectively litigating cases that involve systemic discrimination affecting classes of workers, a strategy that has enabled the agency to achieve broader societal impact by targeting patterns of employment practices in specific industries or sectors.

- *Government as leader in promoting social change through collaborative governance and voluntary compliance.* The EEOC also implements the government's equal employment protection and anti-discrimination laws and policies through non-adversarial education and outreach initiatives. The agency partners with non-governmental rights advocacy groups and employers to improve compliance by proactively identifying problem areas and providing best practice guidelines. This collaborative governance approach focuses on problem-solving by promoting non-governmental stakeholder participation and voluntary compliance. The US jargon is that this helps create a 'win–win solution' for the government, employers and workers.

Administrative enforcement practices in Hong Kong and Taiwan similar to the EEOC have been used in two recent local experiments in China. In 2012, Shenzhen adopted China's first gender equality legislation, which provided for the establishment of an administrative enforcement agency specialized in implementing the new law, including handling individual gender-based employment discrimination claims.[43] In Hebei Province, an EEOC-like multi-agency equal employment promotion commission was established in 2012 by a local municipal government to handle employment discrimination claims and to promote non-discriminatory employment practices through public education and outreach to workers and employers.[44] These experiments appeared to be driven by strong local interests to explore public enforcement alternatives for improving equal employment rights protection for women. Their experience draws attention to the benefits and challenges of adopting an effective public enforcement model in China.

Administrative claims process as an attractive public enforcement option

Having an administrative claims process dedicated to handling employment discrimination complaints can be an attractive public enforcement alternative for both workers and local governments in China. By placing an affirmative duty on a government agency to receive, investigate and resolve individual complaints, the process takes away the uncertainty faced by victims of discrimination in China who have few options for filing their equal employment rights claims. At the same time, the process allows local governments to channel and prioritize potentially numerous and volatile individual complaints through orderly disposition and provides them with an early opportunity to mediate and resolve the disputes, which can often escalate if left unresolved. Experience of the EEOC and other similar agencies shows that just by having a government investigator listen to such complaints helps to alleviate much of the workers' frustration even before their claims are resolved. This possible 'social stability' function of the administrative claims resolution process can be attractive to local Chinese government officials as their performance evaluations often hinge on their ability to resolve and reduce local disputes.

Public interest litigation as a potent enforcement tool

The enhancement of the public enforcement system also has the potential to pave the way for the government to expand its enforcement power through public interest litigation. Although China remains strongly averse to class action lawsuits initiated by private litigants, recent law and policy changes, including the newly revised *Civil Procedures Law*, the Party's Fourth Plenum documents and the Supreme People's Court newly released interpretation of the *Civil Procedures Law*, indicate the government's increasing interest in using public interest lawsuits – initiated by government or quasi-government entities – to tackle issues that have broad societal impact and which will likely involve state actors as defendants. At this stage, such legal and policy shift appears to be limited to environmental protection and food safety cases but may open the door for discrimination issues in the future. An EEOC-like enforcement agency tasked with the specific mandate to combat employment discrimination could be an ideal vehicle for such public interest lawsuits. It would not only allow the state to selectively target 'vested interests' represented by government and state-owned employers and the most egregious discriminatory employment practices affecting large classes of workers, but give the state better control over the direction and outcome of social changes brought by such litigation.

Collaborative governance as an effective regulatory tool for voluntary compliance and discrimination prevention

Market-based economic reforms have changed the dynamics of labor regulation in China, challenging the traditional state command-and-control regulatory model for implementing and enforcing non-discrimination policies in the workplace. The need for adopting more innovative regulatory tools is more urgent for Chinese local governments, which are simultaneously tasked with implementing competing central policy mandates to promote economic and job growth on the one hand, and maintain social stability on the other. There is a growing recognition of the more complex and interdependent relationship between local governments and private-sector actors, and a need to incentivize rather than penalize employers to induce compliance. A more collaborative governance process would allow local governments to recalibrate conventional state-centric, penalty-driven regulatory approaches by transforming their role from *enforcer* to *leader of problem-solving* processes. This change would rely more on employer and non-governmental stakeholders' participation and voluntary compliance for achieving the policy goal of discrimination prevention.

Public–private collaboration as an alternative avenue for non-governmental rights advocacy

Experience in Hebei and Shenzhen suggests that a more participatory model of public enforcement can provide an alternative but limited platform for non-governmental rights advocacy in a challenging political environment.[45] Under such a model, non-government actors were shown to be able to contribute to the design and institutional capacity-building of the new employment discrimination agency. They could lend legal expertise to facilitate claims filing and settlement negotiation, partner with the government to help identify discriminatory practices and propose solutions to ensure better voluntary compliance. In addition they were able to assist the government in public outreach and awareness-raising among grass-roots constituents. Future public interest litigation may be a new opportunity for non-government rights advocacy to work in conjunction with the government to identify and address common concerns.

Notwithstanding the potential benefits of an improved public enforcement mechanism, the Shenzhen and Hebei experience spotlights obstacles for developing such a system under China's restrictive political environment and complex government bureaucracy. First, local reform initiatives can suffer if there is a lack of high-level government endorsement to help remove government bureaucratic barriers against the creation of a new agency. Political cover is often a prerequisite to ensure policy consistency and priority for longer-term structural reforms to be institutionalized. Under China's government *bianzhi* system, which controls budgetary and personnel allocations for government agencies, the creation of a new government agency is subject to separate central government *bianzhi* approval in addition to legislative authorization. Such *bianzhi* approval can be particularly difficult to obtain where local reforms lack high-level, central endorsement. Local governments can sidestep the *bianzhi* issue by creating new agencies pursuant to local government executive orders. The problem is, of course, that such entities lack their own budgets and personnel, and must rely on the political backing of incumbent local leaders. Such an arrangement is difficult to sustain due to cyclical changes in local government leadership and subsequent policy re-prioritizing.

Second, local experiments are often subject to limitations imposed by existing national laws. This can make implementation difficult. For example, under the EPL, administrative enforcement powers are vested solely in labor supervision authorities. Without statutory authorization, an EEOC-like new agency would lack the enforcement power to investigate claims or to force settlements by employers when violations are found. In Hebei, the new equal employment promotion commission was successful in stopping overt gender discrimination hiring practices at local job fairs by issuing legal opinions advising employers of their violations.[46] However, the commission must leverage the local MOHRSS office's labor supervision authority to compel employers to respond to specific charges or to launch investigations of alleged employment discrimination practices.

At the time of writing, shifting political winds in China and increasing government animosity toward non-government advocacy of non-discrimination rights is casting long shadows over local commitments to experiment. In an area that requires local governments to execute the politically delicate task of enforcing individual rights protection, without being perceived as jeopardizing its ultimate goal of maintaining social control and stability, the political balancing act is particularly daunting. In such an uncertain political climate, it is much safer for local officials, as with court officials, to steer clear of taking affirmative action to respond to right claims and to stay within the more familiar territory of promoting equality and non-discrimination policies through job training and general outreach programs.

Conclusion

Combating workplace discrimination is a continuing challenge worldwide. China is no exception. While significant progress has been made in China by adopting laws and policies against employment discrimination, enforcement has been stymied by political constraints. The individual exercise of equality and non-discrimination rights through private rights of action and non-governmental rights advocacy face historical and ideological opposition. Yet the state's existing regulatory tools are clearly outdated, unable to respond effectively to discriminatory employment practices under changing market conditions.

If China's current rule of law initiative is to be taken seriously, alternative enforcement models, at the very minimum, must be considered. Advancing individual rights protection through an administrative enforcement process that puts the government at the helm of resolving individual discrimination claims and steering changes in employment practices through a more participatory regulatory regime may be one workable alternative. Experience internationally has demonstrated the efficacy of such a public enforcement model. Experiments in Hebei and Shenzhen also show promises of such a model to complement or be used as an alternative to private court enforcement in China.

Whether an enhanced public enforcement mechanism can achieve its intended goals within China's complex political and social context will depend on many factors. This is especially so with respect to ensuring meaningful *individual* rights protection. These factors include: (1) high-level political commitment and priority for the government to entertain privately initiated employment discrimination claims – through a dedicated administrative claims process; (2) sufficient official tolerance of non-governmental assertion and advocacy of individual rights within defined channels, such as the administrative claims process described above, to allow citizens to benefit from rights protection as promised by law; (3) statutory enforcement powers necessary for a new equal employment agency to investigate and resolve individual complaints and to prosecute egregious employment practices impacting classes of workers; (4) well-defined legal principles and standards governing the procedural and substantive parameters of the administrative claims process – to ensure government accountability and fairness; and (5) willingness of the new agency to embrace collaborative governance as a new regulatory tool to engage non-governmental stakeholder participation and increase voluntary compliance.

Notes

1 See Yan Tian (2012), 'Rethinking the Modern Origins of China's Anti-Discrimination Legislation', *Peking University Law Journal*, 24(3): 560–77, at: http://journal.pkulaw.cn/ContentPDFType.aspx?isDL=rd&id=159373.
2 Other laws include the 1995 *Labor Law*, the 2005 *Law on the Protection of Women's Rights* and the 2008 *Law on the Protection of Disabled Persons*.
3 See Art. 62 of the EPL.
4 See S. Burkank, S. Farhan and H. Kritzer (2011), 'Private Enforcement of Statutory and Administrative Law in the United States (and Other Common Law Countries', U of Penn Law School, Public Law Research Paper No. 11-08, at: http://papers.ssrn.com/sol3/papers.cfm?abstract_id=1781047.
5 See Zhou Wei (2012), 'The Development of China's Anti-discrimination Law', *Tsinghua Law Journal*, 6 (2), at: http://166.111.104.103/homepage/uploads/files/zhouwei%281%29.pdf.
6 See Supreme People's Court of the PRC (2008), 'Stipulations on Causes of Actions in Civil Cases' (amended in 2011), at: www.npc.gov.cn/npc/xinwen/fztd/sfjs/2008-03/03/content_1425565.htm and www.lawinfochina.com/display.aspx?lib=law&id=8607. See also Liu Minghui (2014), 'Lack of Legislation Reflected in the First Legal Case of Gender-Based Discrimination', *Collection of Women's Studies*, 2: 44.
7 The inclusion of 'carriers of infectious disease viruses' as a protected class under the EPL is the result of successful public pressure mounted by activists representing China's approximately 100 million HBV carriers. Employers are now prohibited from imposing illegal health screening requirements on job applicants who are HBV carriers. More recently, this protection has been invoked by carriers of the AIDS virus against discriminatory hiring decisions based on their HIV status (see www.legaldaily.com.cn/index/content/2014-10/09/content_5791355.htm?node=20908).
8 See Zhou Wei, ibid.
9 See Zhejiang News, November 14, 2014, http://zjnews.zjol.com.cn/system/2014/11/14/020357961.shtml, reporting cause of action as 'violation of personality rights' in a recent court decision on gender-based employment discrimination.
10 See Liu Chunling (2012), 'Difficult Burden of Proof Issues in Gender-Based Employment Discrimination Cases and Solutions', *China Women's News*, September 19, at: http://acwf.people.com.cn/n/2012/0919/c99013-19044852.html.
11 See Zhou Wei, ibid. at p. 25.
12 See *Law on the Mediation and Arbitration of Legal Disputes 2007*, Art. 2.
13 See Yan Tian, ibid.
14 See Art. 60 of the EPL.
15 Liu Minghui, ibid. at p. 46, calls for amending Art. 11 of the State Council Regulations on Labor Security Supervision to include employment discrimination within MOHRSS' labor supervisory authority. MOHRSS can, however, issue minor fines against illegal employer health screening of HBV carriers pursuant to its own EPL implementing regulations (see MOHRSS 2007, 'Provisions on Employment Service and Employment Management', Art. 68, at: www.mohrss.gov.cn/SYrlzyhshbzb/ldbk/jiuye/JYzonghe/201412/t20141229_147451.htm).
16 See http://news.xinhuanet.com/legal/2013-01/26/c_114510501.htm.
17 See Liu Minghui, ibid. at p. 46.
18 See *China News Weekly*, August 2, 2013, at: http://news.sina.com.cn/c/sd/2013-08-02/164227846264.shtml.

19 See *Xinan Evening News*, August 8, 2014, http://news.qq.com/a/20140806/064939.htm.

20 See Finance.china.com.cn, March 9, 2012, http://finance.china.com.cn/roll/20120308/575863.shtml.

21 For details see *Huaxia Times*, August 2, 2014, at: http://finance.ifeng.com/a/20140802/12846723_0.shtml.

22 See China News Network, July 30, 2014, http://finance.chinanews.com/it/2014/07-30/6441526.shtml.

23 See People's Daily Online, May 15, 2013, www.chinapeace.gov.cn/2013-05/15/content_7642910.htm.

24 See People's Daily Online, ibid. and *Guangming Daily*, May 5, 2014, http://news.xinhuanet.com/edu/2014-05/05/c_126460827.htm.

25 See S. Lubman (2015), 'Detained Female Activists Illustrate Contradiction in Chinese Law Reforms', *Wall Street Journal*, April 9, at: http://blogs.wsj.com/chinarealtime/2015/04/09/detained-female-activists-illustrate-contradiction-in-chinese-law-reforms.

26 See *Huaxia Times*, ibid.

27 See Chinese Communist Party Central Committee Decision Concerning Several Major Issues in Comprehensively Deepening Reform (2013), para 43, http://news.xinhuanet.com/politics/2013-11/15/c_118164235.htm.

28 See General Office of the State Council (2014), 'Notice Regarding Employment and Job Creation for 2014 Graduates from Regular Institutions of Higher Learning', May 13, at: www.gov.cn/zhengce/content/2014-05/13/content_8802.htm. A similar notice was issued in May 2013. See www.gov.cn/zwgk/2013-05/16/content_2404378.htm.

29 See www.chinanews.com/edu/2013/05-22/4841996.shtml.

30 See *Guangming Daily*, ibid., quoting a recent study by the Communications University of China indicating that more than 80 percent of female graduates question the effective implementation of these policies.

31 See Caixin Online (2014a), 'Unemployment among Disabled Exceeds 10%', October 1, at: http://china.caixin.com/2014-10-01/100735095.html, and *Legal Daily* (2013), 'Country's Disabled Population Exceeds 85 Million: Experts Call for Changing Law on Protection of Disabled Persons in Due Time', December 3, at: http://gongyi.ifeng.com/news/detail_2013_12/03/31748755_0.shtml.

32 See Art. 33 of the *Law on Protection of Disabled Persons* and the State Council Regulation on Employment of Disabled Persons (amended in 2008).

33 See Caixin Online (2014b), 'The Predicament of Disability Guarantee Funds', June 5, at: http://china.caixin.com/2014-06-05/100686574.html, and *New Beijing Daily* (2011), '90% Employer Would Rather Pay Disability Guaranty Fund for the Long Term Rather than Hire Disabled Workers', August 25, at: http://gongyi.163.com/11/0825/11/7CA3HSAD00933KC8.html.

34 It is estimated that in 2010, Beijing collected RMB500 million (US$82 million) and Shenzhen collected RMB5 billion (US$820 million) since 2005. See http://china.caixin.com/2014-06-05/100686574.html.

35 See S. Farhang (2010), 'An Introduction to Private Enforcement Regimes', in *The Litigation State: Public Regulation and Private Lawsuits in the United States* (Princeton, NJ: Princeton University Press), p. 4, at: http://press.princeton.edu/chapters/s9350.pdf.

36 See Meng Jianzhu, Secretary of the CPC Central Political and Legal Committee (2014), 'Improving the System of Judicial Management System and Operation of Judicial Powers', *People's Daily*, November 7, at: http://legal.people.com.cn/n/2014/1107/c42510-25990066.html, distinguishing the 'independent exercise of adjudicative power by Chinese courts' under the leadership of the Party from 'Western-style judicial independence'.

37 See Wang Yongqing, Secretary-General of the CPC Central Political and Legal Committee (2014), 'Better Use of Rule of Law Thought and Rule of Law Methods to Implement Legal Political Work: Deepening Study of the Spirit of a Series of Xin Jinping's Important Speeches', *People's Daily*, July 28, at: http://theory.people.com.cn/n/2014/0728/c40531-25351145.html.

38 See *New York Times* (2015), 'In China, Civic Group's Freedom, and Followers, Are Vanishing', February 26, at: www.nytimes.com/2015/02/27/world/asia/in-china-civic-groups-freedom-and-followers-are-vanishing.html.

39 See Farhang, ibid. at p. 4.

40 Ibid.

41 See EEOC charge and litigation statistics, http://eeoc.gov/eeoc/statistics/enforcement/charges.cfm and www.eeoc.gov/eeoc/statistics/enforcement/litigation.cfm.

42 It is important to note that whether the EEOC finds discrimination or not, an individual claimant retains the right to litigate his or her discrimination claim in court.

43 See *Nanfang Daily* (2012), 'Shenzhen to Establish Gender Equality Promotion Agency', June 29, at: http://news.ifeng.com/gundong/detail_2012_06/29/15651201_0.shtml.

44 See reports of the Hebei experiments by *Worker's Daily* (2012), 'First Equal Employment Promotion Commission Established: Combating Employment Discrimination as Measure of Government Performance', October 28, at: http://politics.people.com.cn/n/2012/1028/c70731-19412192.html, and *China Women's Journal* (2014), 'Replicate Xinle's Experience to Promote Equal Employment', March 20, at: http://acwf.people.com.cn/n/2014/0320/c99013-24685120.html.

45 See *Hebei Legal Daily* (2013), 'Xinle Says No to Employment Discrimination', June 13, at: http://szbz.hbfzb.com/html/2013-06/13/content_25913.htm?div=-1, describing collaborative efforts among the local municipal government, the All China Women's Federation (the Party's official women's organization) and non-government public interest lawyers in the Hebei experiment.

46 See *Hebei Workers Daily* (2013), 'Xinle's Experiment to Promote Equal Employment', June 29, at: www.hbgrb.net/epaper/images/2013-06/29/7B/WQZX7bWQZX7BC629_0001.PDF.

Part III

China's socialist rule of law and international legal re-ordering

10 Sovereignty vs rights

China's reasons for rejecting the Rome Statute of the International Criminal Court

Jing Tao

Introduction

The Rome Statute of the International Criminal Court (ICC) is the most legalized human rights treaty at the global level. The Statute creates a permanent and independent Court to prosecute individuals for genocide, aggression, war crimes and crimes against humanity. The adoption and entry into force of the treaty indicates that the international legal environment has changed over the past two decades with increasing importance attached to human rights vis-à-vis state sovereignty. With China's emphasis on deepening its socialist rule of law, the People's Republic has become an active participant and enthusiastic member in many international economic and political institutions at both the global and regional levels. This engagement has been developing since the mid-1990s and it is more integrated with the international legal framework than at any time in its history. This chapter will argue, however, that China's rejection of the Rome Statute reflects the fact that some conservative and sovereignty-centered perspectives still prevail.

In the human rights arena, numerous studies have shown that China has made progress with regard to international common practices and standards (see Kent 1999; Foot 2000; Peerenboom 2012: 167), and that China's approach toward state sovereignty has also softened over time (Carlson 2005). In contrast to its original critical view of the United Nations (UN) peacekeeping operations in the 1980s, for instance, China has gradually changed its attitude, becoming an active supporter and participant (J. Chen 2009). It has also signed almost all major multilateral human rights treaties, including the International Covenant on Economic, Social and Cultural Rights (ICESCR) and the International Covenant on Civil and Political Rights (ICCPR) (D. Chen 2009). Such cooperation and participation provides some evidence of China's gradual integration with the international human rights regime. In the same year China signed the ICCPR, however, it voted against the Rome Statute – the only legalized international human rights treaty with a *mandatory jurisdiction mechanism*.

The treaty was adopted with 120 states in favor, 21 abstentions and seven nations against – consisting of China, Iraq, Israel, Libya, Qatar, the United States and Yemen. Given that China and the United States usually hold different views on human rights issues, their common rejection of this treaty is intriguing. There are similarities and differences in the reasons for the United States' rejection of the treaty and these are considered briefly later in this chapter. In China's case, voting behavior in the United Nations Security Council (UNSC) has usually been 'restrained, measured and largely acquiescent' (Wuthnow 2011: 32). In terms of negotiating and signing international treaties, China rarely takes a direct confrontational stance in rejecting an international agreement that is widely supported by a range of developed and developing countries. Indeed, China's Deputy Head of the Delegation to the Rome Conference, Liu Daqun (2006: 1) pointed out that the Rome Statute was the *only* multilateral treaty that China voted against.

This chapter examines this anomaly in China's approach to international institutions: Why did China take a negative stance on the Rome Statute when it had been strengthening its ties with all other types of multilateral institutions from the late 1990s? The chapter addresses two main reasons for China's non-cooperative stance on the Rome Statute. First, Chinese decision makers prioritize state sovereignty over human rights and are unwilling to accept binding legal obligations that may contain high sovereignty costs. Second, the legalized Rome Statute sets up an independent court with mandatory jurisdiction and does not allow states to make reservations. Such treaty provisions may constrain China's autonomy in handling extreme situations concerning its regime security and territorial integrity, deterring China from participation. Indeed, Von Stein (2008: 243) argues that 'harder commitments make shirking more difficult, but these institutional features may deter from joining the very states whose practices are least consistent with the treaty's requirements'.

The findings of this chapter add to the literature on China's integration with the international legal world in that prior literature has, in general, tended to view China as being gradually socialized by international norms. But this does not adequately address the nature and quality of the socialization of the People's Republic of China (PRC) or the degree to which rising China may seek to influence global legal infrastructure. Indeed, most studies have focused on China's policy changes in relatively 'soft' institutions. This study, however, uses a high-cost 'hard law' to examine the depth of China's integration into the international legal framework. It indicates that China is still in a weak stage of socialization and will sign international treaties *only* when its core sovereignty of territorial control rights and regime security is not, in any way, impeded. Given that China's leaders have, historically, often perceived the spread of human rights norms as threatening to its core sovereignty, Chinese socialization in the human rights regime has not followed a linear process.

Beginning with a discussion of the hard law features of the Rome Statute, the chapter provides an overview of China's official positions on major treaty provisions and briefly discusses the process of negotiating the Rome Statute between 1993 and 1998. It then analyzes the discourses on human rights of former President Jiang Zemin from 1989 to 2000. Concerns about China's territorial integrity and regime legitimacy revealed in Jiang's (2006) work have shaped Chinese leaders' attitudes to rights, and restrained them from fully embracing international human rights norms to this day. The chapter concludes by considering the impact of major treaty provisions on China's core sovereignty and the prospects of PRC policy development with respect to human rights.

The Rome Statute and the significance of its 'hard law' provisions

The Rome Statute is a hard law treaty in that it creates a permanent, independent international criminal court with inherent and compulsory jurisdiction over four types of crime: genocide, crimes against humanity, war crimes and the crime of aggression. It also grants prosecutors the *ex officio* right to investigate a crime based on referrals by states or the UNSC, or in response to information provided by individuals and non-governmental organizations (NGOs).

The mandatory jurisdiction mechanism of the Rome Statute and independent ICC reflects a trend toward legalization in world politics. Highly legalized treaties provide hard laws when they attempt to define rules unambiguously, bind states, scrutinize behavior through international and domestic legal mechanisms, and delegate broad authority to independent legal entities to implement the rules they contain (Goldstein *et al.* 2000: 385–99).[1] When states ratify a treaty with automatic jurisdiction, they formally commit to accepting independent legal institutions as the highest authority in adjudicating disputes. When private actors, such as individuals, firms and NGOs, can bring a case directly to international courts or arbitration panels, states' decision-making autonomy and sovereign rights may be limited (see Keohane *et al.* 2000). This point is examined in detail in the sections that follow.

As sovereignty can be viewed as a set of control rights over territory, population and all types of political, economic and social affairs within a state's own boundaries (Carlson 2005: 11; Cooley and Spruyt 2009: 4), delegating decision-making authority and acceptance of the mandatory jurisdiction of an international institution requires a state to give up some portion of its control rights and bear costs of sovereignty loss. 'Sovereignty costs' are defined here as 'the costs for a state to cede sovereign control rights and policy autonomy to other parties' (Elkins *et al.* 2006: 842; also see Abbott and Snidal 2000: 436). Simply put, hard laws with precise provisions, binding obligations and delegation mechanisms impose higher sovereignty costs than soft laws do.

The ICC created by the Rome Statute is an institutional innovation in the areas of international human rights and criminal law. There are four major features stipulated in the Rome Statute that make it 'hard law'. First, the ICC has inherent and compulsory jurisdiction over four types of core crimes if *either* the territorial state (within whose borders the alleged crime has been committed) *or* the suspect state (nationality of the suspect) is a state party to the Statute (ICC 2001: 10). This means the Court will have jurisdiction over crimes if *one* of the above two states ratifies the treaty – even if the other state is not a party. Moreover, even if neither of the above states ratifies the treaty, the ICC can still exercise jurisdiction when the crime is referred to it by the UNSC. Thus, not only will states' parties be required to accept the Court's jurisdiction upon ratification or accession, but non-party states may also be subject to the Court's rule – in certain circumstances.[2]

Second, in terms of the relations between the ICC and national courts, although the Rome Statute designates the ICC as a complement to national courts in adjudicating crimes, it can step in to conduct an investigation and open a trial if the Court decides that a state or national court is 'unwilling or unable' to prosecute matters on its own (ICC 2001: 13). Third, the triggering mechanism of crime investigation grants the ICC Prosecutor the right, *ex officio*, to commence an investigation. The Prosecutor can investigate a crime when a situation is referred to him/her by states' parties or by the UNSC, when he/she has consent from the Pre-Trial Chamber of the Court on the basis of information received from *other sources*, such as individuals or NGOs (ICC 2001: 11). Fourth, the Rome Statute does not allow any substantive reservations for states to opt out of their obligations (ICC 2001: 72). States must accept the treaty *as a whole* and cannot selectively accept treaty provisions when ratifying or acceding to the Rome Statute.

The Rome Statute of the ICC as a legalized international treaty is important for studying the relations between China and the international community, because hard laws with high sovereignty costs are better settings than soft ones to evaluate the *depth* of China's integration as well as the *relative weight* of traditional Westphalian sovereignty and rising human rights and humanitarian norms in shaping China's foreign policies. China's integration with the world has been analyzed in a range of prior literature (see Kim 1994; Economy and Oksenberg 1999; Johnston, 2003, 2008, 2013). Its interests, behavior and policies have changed notably over the past few decades in almost every legal area.[3] But such changes have often been gauged using China's behavior at the beginning of its economic reform as a benchmark for measurement. This benchmark alone is insufficient. As soft institutions and laws do not require strong binding obligations, participation may not impose high sovereignty costs and states are usually more willing to cooperate. Evaluating China's responses may be more fruitful when the State is required to cede significant control of the adjudication process to an independent legal authority. Hard law, with high sovereignty costs, will provide more testing grounds for assessment than soft law.

What China's negotiations in the Rome Statute reveal

In general, China supported the establishment of a permanent international criminal court. What it opposed in the 1998 Rome Statute was the format and jurisdiction of the Court. China preferred a soft treaty and a conservative model for the ICC, with limited jurisdiction over more limited types of crimes. This section will show by a detailed analysis of Chinese delegates' public statements in the UN's Sixth Committee meetings from 1993 to 1998, and at the Rome Conference in 1998, that China's positions on the ICC reflected an overarching normative frame of state sovereignty. It was even reluctant to view the establishment of the ICC as a human rights issue, perceiving it as 'war-related' security politics. As a result, China's positions diverged from the Rome Statute on four major issues regarding the power and status of the Court: (1) the relations between the ICC and national courts; (2) the Court's inherent and mandatory jurisdiction; (3) the Prosecutor's *ex officio* right to investigate crimes (i.e., the triggering mechanism); and (4) the scope of crimes under the Court's jurisdiction.

First, Chinese negotiators insisted that the relations between the ICC and national court should be defined by the most important guiding principle of 'complementarity'. This means the ICC 'could function only as an adjunct to national courts' (and should not exercise its jurisdiction) 'when a case was already being investigated, prosecuted or tried by a given country' (UN 1998a: 75, 1996: 20). Delegate Chen Shiqiu elaborated the principle on behalf of the PRC, that

> [It was meant to apply] when it was impossible for national courts to formally try someone accused of a serious international crime.... The international criminal court should not supplant national courts, nor should it become a supra-national court or act as an appeal court for national court judgments.
>
> (UN 1998a: 13)[4]

Although the Rome Statute recognizes the 'complementarity' principle in its Preamble, and Art. 17 stipulates that the Court could intervene only when national courts were 'unwilling or unable genuinely to carry out the investigation or prosecution' (ICC 2001: 13), Chinese delegates still believed Art. 17 and other substantive treaty provisions violated the principle, overriding a state's judicial sovereignty. They suggested the ICC should only apply its jurisdiction when national courts were *unable* to try a case – i.e., 'in the event that a State's judicial system collapsed' (UN 1998b: 6) – but have no rights to judge whether a national court is *unwilling* to take an action, or whether an investigation or prosecution by a national court is fair.

Article 17 does, however, stipulate that the Court can judge ongoing legal proceedings of any state, including a non-party; and if it decides that intention exists to shield a crime, or the trial is not fair, it can exercise its jurisdiction and retry a case (see ICC 2001: 13). Chinese negotiators strongly opposed this article, arguing that allowing the ICC to judge a state's judicial system and legal proceedings, and to negate the decision of a national court, actually makes the Court 'an appeals court sitting above the national court ... [and further] it was highly possible that such a provision would be abused for political purposes' (UN 1998b: 6).

Second, Chinese delegates had serious reservations concerning the inherent and mandatory jurisdiction of the Court on the basis that it 'directly infringed on the judicial sovereignty of States', arguing that the acceptance of the Court's jurisdiction must be in accordance with the principle of state sovereignty and 'based on the voluntary consent of States' Parties' (UN 1998b: 5, 1996: 20, 1995: 14). As delegate Duan Jielong said:

> The inherent jurisdiction of the court, when extended to cover all core crimes, would accord precedence to the court over national courts; that was clearly at variance with the principle of complementarity and could adversely affect the cooperation between States and the court and the effective functioning of the court.
>
> (UN 1997: 12)

During the negotiations, Chinese delegates promoted an 'opt-in' mechanism which would have allowed states the freedom to choose whether, and for which crimes, they would accept the Court's jurisdiction (UN 1993: 5). Under such a mechanism, the ICC could exercise its jurisdiction over only states' parties that had given pre-consents upon ratification.

Article 12 of the Rome Statute, however, requires all states' parties to automatically accept the ICC's jurisdiction. Moreover, even if a state is not a party to the Statute, it cannot completely avoid the Court's jurisdiction (ICC 2001: 10). Such a provision was beyond the positions of the Chinese government. As one Chinese delegate maintained, it not only grants the ICC mandatory jurisdiction over states' parties, but imposes an obligation upon non-parties, 'constituting an interference in the judicial independence or sovereignty of States' (UN 1998a: 123–4).

Third, Chinese delegates intended to narrow the definitions of core crimes and limit the scopes of crimes that fall into the Court's jurisdiction. They especially opposed the inclusion of 'domestic armed conflicts' and 'violation of human rights in peaceful time' within the definitions of war crimes and crimes against humanity respectively, asserting that

> the criteria determining jurisdiction [should be] the universality of the consequences of the crime and the seriousness of the crime, [and] what the international community needed … *was not a human rights court but a criminal court that punished international crimes of exceptional gravity.*
>
> (UN 1996: 14; UN 1998b: 6; italics added)

Chinese delegates perceived the establishment of the ICC from a 'security' rather than a 'human rights' perspective, suggesting that only *armed conflicts in international settings* could be serious and extensive enough to justify the concern of the international community, while human rights violations in domestic contexts, or in peaceful times, would not. Delegate Qu Wensheng put it this way:

> The Rome Statute failed to link those crimes to armed conflicts and thereby changed the major attributes of the crimes. In listing specific acts constituting crimes against humanity, the Statute added a heavy dose of human rights law.... The injection of human rights elements would lead to a proliferation

> of human rights cases, weaken the mandate of the Court to punish the most serious crimes and thus defeat the purpose of establishing such a court.
>
> (UN 1998b: 6)

Fourth, Chinese negotiators did not agree that the Prosecutor should have the *ex officio* right to initiate an investigation based on information received from any sources such as NGOs and individuals. They insisted that only states' parties and the UNSC could refer cases to the Court. The Chinese government's major concern regarding the triggering mechanism was that an independent Prosecutor and broader access to the Court by all types of state and non-state actors may lead to the abuse of the Court and encroachment of state sovereignty (UN 1998a: 5, 1998b: 6).

As Chinese decision makers perceived states as *the* major actors of the international society, they did not think that non-state NGOs and individuals should enjoy the same legal status. Head of the Chinese delegation to Rome, Wang Guangya, maintained that 'a cautious approach should be adopted when addressing such questions as trigger mechanisms and means of investigation, in order to avoid irresponsible prosecutions that might impair a country's legitimate interests' (UN 1998a: 75).

Although clear gaps existed between major provisions of the Rome Statute and China's stances, China was not always in the minority. Many of its positions were shared by the United States. Being great powers, neither the United States nor China wanted to delegate sovereignty to a higher international authority. But relative power was not the only important factor determining preferences. Underlying reasons for the great powers' rejection of the treaty differ. For example, although the United States shared similar positions to China on major treaty provisions, unlike China, US human rights domestic protection is highly institutionalized; the chances of US leaders being prosecuted for domestic human rights violations or humanitarian disasters are very low. What concerned the United States was that its leaders and military personnel should be exempt from the ICC's jurisdiction when its troops carry out military operations outside US territory. The lead US negotiator, Ambassador David Scheffer (1998), indicated that the treaty purports to establish an arrangement whereby US armed forces operating overseas could be conceivably prosecuted by the international court, which could inhibit the ability of the United States to use its military to meet alliance obligations and participate in multinational operations, including humanitarian interventions to save civilian lives.[5]

In contrast, any Chinese human rights violations are more likely to occur domestically. Accepting the legalized Rome Statute would have increased the chances of China's domestic affairs being overviewed by an independent international legal authority. In certain extreme situations, the mandatory jurisdiction of the ICC is what was viewed as threatening to China's territorial integrity and regime legitimacy. Therefore, the political reasons China opposed the ICC may be regarded as more defensive and inward-looking compared to US reasons for rejecting the treaty.

China's core sovereignty issues vs 'Western style' human rights (*renquan*)

The ICC negotiations reveal that Chinese leaders prioritize state sovereignty over human rights and humanitarian issues. China's leaders' acceptance of human rights norms has been limited and restrained. This is because they perceive those norms as intertwining with issues affecting China's core sovereignty – the most important and indivisible sovereign control right constituting core national interests (see Wang 2000, 2006). Although China has actively participated in the international human rights regime, and has softened its stance on sovereignty since the late 1970s, Chinese leaders have consistently attached most importance to China's regime security and territorial unification,[6] especially regarding jurisdiction over Tibet, Xinjiang and Taiwan. Their stances on those core sovereignty issues have rarely softened since the establishment of the PRC in 1949 (Carlson 2005: 677–98; see also Fravel 2008; Johnston 2013).

The superiority of state sovereignty and the limited degree to which Chinese leaders internalize human rights norms are most evident in former President Jiang Zemin's discourses on human rights, in the *Selected Works of Jiang Zemin*. It is important to note that Jiang's works were edited and completed under the personal guidance of his successor, Hu Jintao, and the Political Bureau of the CCP Central Committee. It thus represents not only the beliefs of Jiang, but the consensus and collective efforts of the CCP's ideological machine. Collectively they therefore have some continuous influence on future leadership. Jiang's works thus remain an authoritative and reliable *ideological source* for tracing norms and ideas advocated by the CCP center, and the degree to which Chinese leaders believe in different international norms. For instance, more than 80 percent of Jiang's articles that reference the concept of human rights (*renquan*)[7] explicitly or implicitly associate 'human rights' and 'humanitarianism' with 'Western/international hostile forces' and treat these ideas as tools to 'Westernize and divide [*xihua fenhua*] China' or to 'interfere in China's domestic affairs [*ganshe neizheng*]'.[8] Of the seven articles that do not attribute instrumentalist meanings to human rights (or that recognize positive values in those norms), six have qualifications emphasizing either the superiority of state sovereignty or the relativity of the terms.[9] Viewing human rights as a potential threat brought by 'Western hostile forces' to China's regime security and unification shows that Chinese leaders still possess serious doubts and insecurity about what may come with these concepts.

Because of regime and ideological differences between Chinese and Western counterparts, Chinese leaders have, for some time, nurtured distrust of the West. Jiang (2006, Vol. 3: 8), for example, clearly held that some hostile Western/international forces view China as 'a thorn in their side', 'not wanting to see a socialist China becoming unified and stronger' (2006, Vol. 3: 139), 'and will not stop attacking China and interfering in China's internal affairs' (2006, Vol. 3: 235). These perceptions have, without doubt, shaped political understandings of the relationship between human rights, regime security and state sovereignty. Further, as Jiang said in a CCP Central Committee meeting in 2000:

> Nowadays, China is the biggest socialist state in the world and has continuously developed and become increasingly wealthier and stronger. Western hostile forces have intensified all types of means and measures to implement the political strategy of Westernizing and dividing our country, and sought to sabotage CCP's leadership and China's socialist regime.... In recent years, they have ceaselessly made use of the so-called 'human rights', 'democracy', 'freedom', 'ethnic' and 'religious' issues as well as Dalai Lama and the Taiwan issue to launch attacks on us. They have also colluded with those so-called overseas 'pro-democracy activists' and our domestic hostiles and attempted to take joint actions with those people.
>
> (Jiang 2006, Vol. 2: 83)[10]

Jiang's statements reveal that Chinese leaders not only perceive that 'hostile forces' mainly come from the West, but also that domestic and overseas dissidents and 'secessionists/separatists' such as ethnic minorities from Tibet and Xinjiang as well as Taiwan-independence forces (*taidu shili*) are internal and external enemies. The 'Jiang view' holds that these people are most likely to attract international attention and are empowered by international human rights agencies. It follows that, to some Chinese leaders, human rights and humanitarianism, as well as other values of democracy and liberty, have never been about the rights and freedom of individual Chinese people. Rather, these concepts are intertwined with other more dangerous and explosive ethnic, religious and territorial tensions, such as Tibet and Taiwan, and pro-democracy advocates in Hong Kong who can be used by both international and domestic 'enemies' to challenge China's national unification and regime security. Because of the potential threats that democracy, freedom and human rights norms may impose on China's core sovereignty, territorial unity and regime legitimacy, Chinese leaders' recognition of the universality of those ideals has been restrained.

In Jiang Zemin's discourses on human rights, five of the seven articles that do not attribute instrumentalist meanings to human rights are speeches given in *international contexts*. Whereas 16 of the 19 articles that associate the concept with Western or international hostile forces exclusively target *domestic audiences*. The differences in content delivered to international audiences indicate some weak socialization effects of international human rights norms on China: although Chinese leaders themselves have doubts about human rights, they are simultaneously aware of the popularity and legitimacy of the norm at the global level, and recognize positive meanings of the norm to satisfy international expectations.

Yet even when facing international audiences, Chinese leaders still prioritize state sovereignty over human rights, insisting that 'human rights cannot be discussed without sovereignty'.[11] Moreover, Jiang emphasized the relative meanings of 'human rights' and their 'realization' as contingent on the socio-economic status of each state and that 'sustainability and development' (*shengcun quan he fazhan quan*) were the most important rights of the Chinese people.[12]

What is the potential impact of the Rome Statute on China's core sovereignty?

Although Chinese leaders always prioritize state sovereignty over human rights, those sovereignty concerns do not prevent China from being an active participator in the international human rights regime. Given that China has signed most international human rights and humanitarian treaties, its leaders' restrained acceptance of the rights norms is clearly not the sole determinant of China's rejection of the Rome Statute. The treaty does reflect a more liberal human rights view compared to those held by a socialist rule of law, and sovereignty costs are significantly higher than those of soft human rights treaties. The possibility that the treaty may, in certain extreme situations, have negative implications for China's core sovereignty makes it worth examining sovereignty cost details. Indeed, what are the specific treaty provisions that 'deter' China's participation and why?

Definitions of core crimes: implications for China

Because the dominant concern for Chinese leaders regarding human rights issues is the potential danger that those norms will be used by 'hostile forces' to interfere in China's domestic affairs, the Chinese delegation during the negotiation focused on minimizing this possibility by seeking to limit the jurisdiction and authority of the court vis-à-vis sovereign states. In terms of the definition of 'core crimes', if the scope of those crimes could not be restrained to 'war-related humanitarian issues in international contexts', some Chinese government internal actions such as suppressing dissidents and separatists and, at an extreme level, taking Taiwan by force could fall under the ICC's jurisdiction. Article 7, 'Crimes against Humanity', specifies 11 types of crimes committed as part of a widespread or systematic attack directed against any civilian population. These include many human rights violations: torture, enforced disappearance, sexual violence, and imprisonment and deprivation of physical liberty as infringing fundamental rules of international law. But Art. 7 does not limit the definition of crimes to 'in wartime' (ICC 2001: 3–5). Had China become a state party to the Statute, Art. 7 might have limited its ability to suppress political dissidents or deal with threats to territorial unification, especially in ethnic minority regions such as Tibet and Xinjiang.

As Jiang (2006: Vol. 1, 394–5) emphasized:

> [we must] forcefully strike secessionist movements and crimes in Tibet; handle emergencies firmly, resolutely, and promptly; and nip potential riots in the bud. Be highly alert to the infiltration and sabotage activities of international hostile forces and the Dalai Group and crack them down once they are detected.

In terms of Xinjiang, 'we must unite together, strongly oppose and forcefully clamp down activities that destroy ethnic and national unification.... We must not hesitate or compromise even slightly on such critical issues' (Jiang 2006:

Vol. 2, 158). Xi Jinping steadfastly holds to these stances, emphasizing that 'any foreign countries should not expect that we will trade our core interests, nor should they expect that we will swallow the bitter pill of our sovereignty, security and developmental interests being harmed'.[13] An official interpretation of Xi's emphasis on China's 'core interests' recently published in *A Reader of General Secretary Xi Jinping's Important Speeches* (hereafter *A Reader*; 2014) points out: 'We must resolutely contain disruptive activities of separatist forces – Taiwan-independence, Tibetan-independence, East-Turkistan forces and so on – at the international level, prevent international terrorists from infiltrating into our country, and safeguard national sovereignty and security.' Had China become a member state of the Rome Statute, overseas ethnic minorities as well as other state and non-state actors would have been able to resort to the ICC to sue Chinese leaders and challenge the legitimacy of repressive or heavy-handed government actions. As Tan Shigui (2003: 68), a leading mainland Chinese scholar on criminal law, maintains:

> Although human rights acts concerning China have constantly been defeated at the UN Commission on Human Rights, [Western anti-China forces] do not submit to defeat. The establishment of the International Criminal Court undoubtedly allows [them] to see new hope, and crimes against humanity within the ICC's jurisdiction may also become judicial weapons [*sifa wuqi*] to interfere China's internal politics.

In addition to Art. 7, the inclusion of 'domestic armed conflicts' within the broader category of 'war crimes' could also have implications for the Taiwan issue. The possibility that the ICC may exercise jurisdiction in the event of China resorting to force to achieve national reunification would be viewed politically as a weakening of China's deterrence strategy and an empowering of Taiwanese pro-independence forces. In order to deter Taiwan from pursuing *de jure* independence, the Chinese government had long ago declared its position that it would not give up the possibility of using military force to solve the Taiwan issue. Deng Xiaoping in 1979 put it this way:

> We try to use peaceful means to bring Taiwan back to the motherland and achieve national unification. The problem is that if we promise that we will not use military forces, it will tie our hands and make the Taiwan authorities refuse to negotiate with us for peaceful reunification. This will in turn lead to the use of military force to solve the problem.
>
> (Quoted in State Council of the PRC 1994: 154)

This deterrence strategy was further strengthened and legalized in China's *Anti-Secession Law* (2005). Article 8 of that law says:

> In the event that the Taiwan independence secessionist forces should act under any name or by any means to cause the fact of Taiwan's secession

> from China, or that major incidents entailing Taiwan's secession from China should occur, or that possibilities for a peaceful reunification should be completely exhausted, the state shall employ non-peaceful means and other necessary measures to protect China's sovereignty and territorial integrity.
>
> (*Xinhua Net* 2005)

As the Rome Statute definition of war crimes does not exclude domestic armed conflicts, any use of military force by the Chinese government to reunite with Taiwan could, theoretically, fall within the Court's jurisdiction. A Chinese ICC expert states:

> If the Taiwan authority pursues independence, the Chinese government must resort to military force to solve the Taiwan issue, and armed conflicts will be inevitable. Such conflicts are similar to non-international armed conflicts under the definition of war crimes of the Statute; once conflicts begin, international anti-China forces may make use of the ICC in the name of war crime to intervene, investigate, and even sue China's military actions of resuming Taiwan, and interfere China's internal politics.... This is one of the major reasons that the Chinese government rejects the Statute and does not participate in the ICC.
>
> (Zhang 2009: 256–7)

The ICC has already been perceived by some pro-independence Taiwanese as, potentially, an effective tool to counter China's deterrence strategy. On the same day the ICC was established at The Hague (July 7, 2002), several human rights and pro-independence NGOs in Taiwan formed the Taiwan Coalition for the International Criminal Court. The Convener of the Coalition, Li Shengxiong, Secretary-General of the pro-independence organization World United Formosans for Independence, argued in 2003 that 'because China ... threatens Taiwan with more than 400 missiles and its military force, it does not dare to sign the Rome Statute and participate in the ICC'. Li added that Taiwan should become a member of the ICC as soon as possible, to not only safeguard international human rights, but also save itself from external invasion and war (Li Shengxiong 2003).

Implications for China of the Prosecutor's **'ex officio** ***right'***

In addition to concerns about the definition of core crimes, the Chinese government also worries that the Prosecutor's *ex officio* right is too broad and that free access of non-state actors to the ICC might weaken the government's control over cases referred to the Prosecutor. The view is that such powers would inevitably lead to legally binding rulings unfavorable to the Chinese government. These concerns are not unfounded. In fact, the international NGO coalition – the CICC – had played an indispensable role in advocating for an independent court and legalized Rome Statute throughout the negotiations. CICC members took part in the Rome Conference and, with nearly 500 participants, represented the largest delegation. The group currently includes 2,500 civil society organizations in 150 different countries, and it continuously works to strengthen international cooperation with the ICC (Coalition for the ICC 2015).

Several CICC members are perceived by the Chinese government as potential 'hostile forces' aiming to 'Westernize and divide China'. In addition to the aforementioned Taiwan Coalition for the ICC, Human Rights Watch and Amnesty International are two other influential NGOs that might provide information to the Court concerning China. Both organizations are founding members of the CICC and currently among its 16-member steering Committee. Since the Tiananmen Incident in 1989, both organizations have strengthened scrutiny of China. Their annual reports on world human rights conditions have specific China sections, in which the Chinese government's treatment of ethnic minorities in Tibet and Xinjiang attracts special attention. For example, Human Rights Watch's *World Report* has consistently criticized the government's activities and policies in Tibet since 1989 and in Xinjiang since 1990; it has also started commenting upon political development and human rights conditions in Hong Kong since 1992 (Human Rights Watch 1989–2013).

Moreover, the Prosecutor's right to initiate investigation *proprio motu* based on information provided by non-state actors increases the chance that the ICC could interfere in China's internal affairs by issuing legally binding rulings unacceptable to the Chinese government. In order to reduce the Prosecutor's power and ensure that he/she would not simply represent 'the West', or be used by 'hostile forces', Chinese delegates proposed during the negotiations that the composition of judges in the Pre-Trial Chamber represent all major legal systems and regions of the world. Without consensus of the Chamber, the Prosecutor could not start an investigation. The Rome Statute did not, however, incorporate China's suggestion.

Why does the compulsory jurisdiction of the ICC impose the highest sovereignty costs?

Even though the definitions of 'core crimes' and the Prosecutor's '*ex officio* right' have strong boundary-transgressing features and Chinese leaders do not internalize human rights norms, China might still have been able to sign the Rome Statute had the treaty adopted a flexible 'opt-in' mechanism. This would allow states to choose whether, and for which crimes, they would accept the ICC's jurisdiction. Such a mechanism would significantly lower the sovereignty costs of the Statute and change the nature of the treaty from hard to soft law. In fact, before the Rome Statute, China had already signed 18 human rights treaties and, in the same year after China voted against the Statue, it also signed the ICCPR in October 1998. All those treaties are soft law in nature, incorporating flexible arrangements for states to lower sovereignty costs when compared to the Rome Statute.

The 1984 Convention against Torture (CAT), for example, defines the crime of 'torture' and stipulates a series of obligations for states. Yet the treaty's 'opt-in' reservation clause allows states to voluntarily choose whether to accept the authority of the Committee against Torture, a monitoring institute established by the CAT. Although CAT grants the Committee the right to investigate reports of torture – submitted by either state or non-state actors – on its own initiative, through confidential inquiries and fact-checking missions within a state's territory, this right is conditional on the *pre-consent* of states. As Art. 28 of the Convention states, 'Each State may, at the time of signature or ratification of this Convention or accession thereto, declare that it does not recognize the competence of the Committee provided for in article 20' (UN 1984a).

Without such an 'opt-in' mechanism, the right to self-initiate an investigation by the Committee (based on information provided by states, individuals and/or NGOs) would have resembled the *ex officio* right of the ICC Prosecutor. The CAT, in that scenario, would have imposed higher sovereignty costs on states than the current one does. The soft law nature of CAT is a reason China signed that treaty as early as in 1986 and ratified it immediately in 1987. Upon signing, however, China declared its formal reservation as follows: 'the Chinese government does not recognize the competence of the Committee against Torture as provided in Article 20 of the Convention' (UN 1984b). This simple comparison between the Rome Statute and the CAT shows that the mandatory jurisdiction clause of the ICC imposes highest sovereignty costs among all treaty provisions, and China, without an opt-in mechanism, was unwilling to sign the harder law treaty.

Conclusion

China's rejection of the Rome Statute reveals an amalgam of conservative and sovereignty-centered views as prevailing over broader conceptions of rights. China is still at a relatively weak stage of integration with the international human rights regime, and reserves the right to seek to influence international legal frameworks to better reflect its own interests. This study has shown that the senior leadership continues to perceive the spread of human rights norms as containing sovereignty threats that could affect regime security. In this light, China's integration in the human rights regime cannot be expected to be a linear process. Moreover, binding legal obligations and the mandatory jurisdiction of such a 'hard law' treaty could have negative implications for China's core sovereignty including the domestic management of tensions in Tibet and Xinjiang, and other sensitive political areas such as Taiwan and Hong Kong. As the treaty does not allow flexible arrangements for China to exempt itself from the Court's jurisdiction, the sovereignty costs are seen as too high.

To this day, China's leaders clearly perceive 'Western-style' human rights and related enforcement issues as not conducive to China's political and legal reforms. On these issues, they essentially conform to Jiang's meta-narrative. As Xi Jinping recently put it, 'we need to borrow beneficial fruits of political civilization of mankind, but we must not copy Western political institutions and models, and must not accept any condescending preaches of foreign countries' (in the official *Reader* 2014). The *Reader* further elaborates Xi's words: 'On important issues, such as human rights, election system, and the rule of law, we must be self-confident because we are in the right [*lizhiqizhuang*] and must not adopt Western political institutions and models as our standards' (*Reader* 2014).[14]

In the context of China's deepening socialist rule of law, steady advances and integration in softer international treaties are noted; and China will continuously improve human rights domestically, as long as those rights are not perceived as incompatible with its core sovereignty. However, expectations that the PRC might accept the 'harder' provisions of an international treaty such as the Rome Statute any time soon may be very disappointed.

Notes

1 For additional discussion of definitions of 'legalization and hard law', see Abbott *et al.* (2000), Abbott and Snidal (2000).

2 A good example is the Libyan case. Libya voted against the Rome Statute at the Rome Conference and thus is not a state party of the treaty. Yet the ICC issued an arrest warrant for Libya's former leader Colonel Gaddafi, his son Saif al-Islam, and Abdullah al-Senussi, head of Libya's state security services, based on UNSC Resolution 1970 which referred Libya's situation to the ICC.

3 For example, see Garrick (2011, 2012), Peerenboom (2012), Peerenboom and Ginsburg (2014).

4 All direct citations of UN documents use the past tense because UN meeting records are summaries rather than direct quotations of delegates' speeches.

5 For the full text, see Hearing before the Subcommittee on International Operations of the Committee on Foreign Relations, US Senate, 105th Congress (July 23, 1998).

6 In the July 2009 US–China Strategic and Economic Dialogue, the then Chinese State Councilor Dai Bingguo listed and ranked China's core interests: 'for China, our concern is we must uphold our basic systems, our national security; secondly, sovereignty and territorial integrity; and thirdly, economic and socially sustained development.' US Department of State, July 28, 2009 at: http://m.state.gov/md126599.htm.

7 There are 26 articles written between 1989 and 2000 referencing the concept of 'human rights', 19 of which attach strong negative meanings to the concept. As 1989–2000 covers the Rome Statute negotiating period, Jiang's human rights discourses shed light on China's treaty rejection.

8 For Jiang, 'Westernizing China' refers to threats to China's one-party regime and the CPC's leadership, and 'dividing China' refers to threats to China's territorial and national unification.

9 The only article that does not impose any conditions on the legitimacy of the concept of human rights specifically discusses the rights of people with a disability.

10 Jiang made similar comments on various occasions, for example, Jiang (2006, Vol. 2: 521–2, Vol. 3: 235).

11 For instance, in a speech at the UN Millennium Summit (2000) Jiang maintained:

> The dialogues regarding human rights issues must be carried out on the basis of respecting state sovereignty; this is the most fundamental and effective way to protect and promote human rights causes. As long as there exist state borders in the world and people live in their own countries, protecting national independence and sovereignty is the highest interest of every national government and its people.
>
> (Jiang 2006, Vol. 3: 110)

12 See Jiang (2006, Vol. 1: 334, 338, Vol. 2: 52–6). Further, as Jiang said in a revealing speech when he visited the United States in 1997:

> China is a developing country with more than 1.2 billion population; this national situation determines that the rights of sustainability and development are the most fundamental and important human rights in China. If the problem of how to feed the people and keep them warm cannot be solved, it is impossible to pursue other types of rights.
>
> (Vol. 2: 53)

13 Propaganda Department of Chinese Communist Party Central Committee (2014). Although the book does not include the full-text articles of Xi Jinping, it provides official and authoritative interpretation of Xi's important speeches. Major chapters of the book can be found at: People's Net, http://theory.people.com.cn/GB/68294/386509.

14 *Lǐ zhí qì zhuàng* (理直氣壯) meaning 'bold and confident with justice on one's side'.

11 The impact of Chinese legal reform on WTO dispute resolution

Ji Li

Introduction

The WTO Dispute Settlement Mechanism (DSM), with compulsory jurisdiction over World Trade Organization member states and the authority to issue binding decisions, has been widely regarded as a milestone in the path of establishing a global legal order. Dispute resolution under the mechanism typically proceeds as follows. After a trade dispute occurs, the complaining member state may file a formal request for consultation at the WTO DSM to force a negotiation with the responding state. If the following consultation fails to resolve the dispute, the complaining state may request adjudication by an independent panel of experts. The panel issues an official report, which may be appealed by either party to the Appellate Body (AB) on issues of law. The AB then makes a final binding decision, non-compliance with which may trigger WTO-authorized trade retaliations. By June 2015, member states had filed 496 formal requests for consultation. The vast majority of the disputes channeled to the WTO DSM have been fully resolved through either settlement or litigation. Only 13 disputes resulted in compliance proceedings, and non-compliance was found in merely six of them.

Given the new regime's significant practical and theoretical implications, a vast literature has emerged to explore various factors that either contribute to its success or continue to flaw this unprecedented trade dispute resolution system. In the prior endeavors, however, scholars have largely neglected the intersubjective nature of trade disputes and the linkage between a country's domestic social norms and its choice of dispute resolution method. Failing to consider this normative aspect, extant theories cannot explain why countries with domestic social norms against litigation, having become more 'legally aggressive' in resolving trade disputes under the WTO DSM, continue to refrain from suing each other. The intersubjective theory elaborated below illuminates the dual orders of trade dispute resolution that coexist despite the success of the WTO DSM, and China's role in preserving the system for informal settlement of trade disputes. The ongoing legal reform in China will not substantially alter its domestic norms against litigation, but China's growing power will amplify the norms' global implications.

This chapter proceeds with a brief summary of the literature on the WTO DSM, followed by an elaboration on the intersubjective (normative) theory, its application and its contribution to the literature. Applying the normative theory, the chapter then discusses how China's ongoing legal reform and its growing power will impact international trade dispute resolution.

Literature review and a new norm-based theory

The vast literature on the WTO DSM has generated many insights about the judicialization of international trade dispute resolution. But most extant studies have so far focused on objective and structural factors. For instance, to understand what determines the escalation of a trade dispute to a case in the WTO DSM, many explore variables at the state level such as state capacity, political power, volume of trade and the size and dependence of the disputant's economy.[1] Some look beneath the state level and contend that characteristics of domestic stakeholders also play a critical role in shaping trade dispute resolution.[2] Still others find certain attributes of the trade barriers and the disputes to be important determinants of a state's selection of dispute resolution mechanisms.[3] While shedding light on how certain objective political, economic, procedural or structural factors determine a member state's choice of dispute resolution method, the fast-growing literature has neglected the role of domestic norms. Given that the dispute resolution process is inherently an intersubjective one engaged by norm-bound human actors, the neglect leaves a huge theoretical gap.

Some recent work on dispute resolution in the WTO begins to fill the gap by taking norms seriously. A few scholars stress the normative tensions between certain national or regional culture on the one hand and the adversarial and legalistic nature of the WTO DSM.[4] Others take a step further by reconceiving dispute resolution under the WTO framework as normative intercourses among the member states.[5] A few recent studies are also beginning to empirically investigate trade dispute resolution as an intersubjective process.[6] These normative works, by focusing either on normative conflicts per se or learning and socialization in the WTO, have paid scant attention to the impact of domestic norms on trade dispute resolution. Given that domestic norms play a dominant role in shaping the views and behavior of trade officials interacting at the WTO, neglecting the factor leaves a hole in the normative theories.[7] Moreover, the sociological approach to international law and politics has long been criticized for lacking explanatory power. For instance, one can hardly predict trade dispute resolution and state behavior merely by conceptualizing the WTO as a learning process.

To fill the gaps, this section presents an intersubjective model for analyzing international trade dispute resolution. One distinct feature of the model is the unit of analysis. Instead of states, governments or firms, the theory examines individuals and groups of human actors whose behavior is guided by values and cognitive systems formed in domestic settings. After all, it is human agents, not abstract collective entities such as sovereign governments, that raise, negotiate, litigate and resolve trade disputes. When such terms are used in this chapter, they refer to the group of officials and other stakeholders acting on behalf of the state in trade dispute resolution. Another feature distinguishing this intersubjective model from other constructivist studies of the WTO is that it allows normative changes to occur in a rational and predictable way. Built on Chong's prior work, the model stresses that past investment 'in acquiring knowledge and skills and forming social ties and group identifications affect the individual's assessment of the relative merits of current choices', and 'someone who has developed the dispositions necessary to succeed in one normative environment tends to be reluctant to major changes of the norm and will oppose any such initiatives'.[8] In other words, how individuals adapt to a new set of norms and values depends on (1) the investment in their prior existing norms, and (2) the balance between the diverging incentives.[9] One can infer from the theory that individuals having invested heavily in existing norms will adapt slowly or resist such adaptation.

This rational choice model of normative change offers a useful analytic tool to explore the normative conflicts in international trade dispute resolution after the establishment of the WTO DSM. As noted above, the new institutional platform provides the member states a wider range of options to resolve trade disputes, from negotiating a settlement, mediation, settlement during the mandatory consultation, to requesting a panel review, the report of which may be further appealed to the AB on issues of law. The decision at any phase in the dispute resolution process should reflect the decision makers' perceptions regarding the proper way to resolve disputes and how they interpret other parties' decisions. When human agents from varying normative environments are involved in trade dispute resolution under the WTO DSM, complex conflicts of norms are inevitable.

The intersubjective theory helps make sense of the conflicts and their implications. Based on their social propensity to legally resolve disputes, WTO member states can be categorized into litigious states and non-litigious states. In litigious countries, legal dispute resolution is generally viewed as a common method for clarifying legal and contractual ambiguities and misunderstandings. Settlement out of court is preferred only for cost-saving purposes, not any moral principle of preserving harmony. Thus, settlement offers are not intended or interpreted as an expression of goodwill. In contrast, a country features a non-litigious domestic social norm if its citizens exhibit a strong preference for non-judicial dispute resolution for its perceived appropriateness, not low cost. In such societies litigation is typically intended and interpreted as a strong signal of hostility. A lawsuit is initiated only to send such a message to the other party, to terminate long-term cooperative relationships, or in extreme situations where substantial interests are at stake yet no alternative solutions are available. Excessive concessions for settling disputes are viewed as a gesture of goodwill, and preserving harmony is valued more than sporadically clarifying or protecting individual rights through lawsuits.[10] Of course, in reality most societies contain elements of both litigious and non-litigious norms, so what the label conveys is variance in degree. Relatively speaking, the United States is a highly litigious country, whereas Japan is widely regarded as a prototypical non-litigious society.

Built on the US court model, the WTO DSM is a dispute resolution platform familiar to actors from litigious societies. Having invested heavily in litigious norms, officials and other stakeholders from these countries encounter few conflicting incentives in the WTO DSM. On the contrary, they may even benefit from a reputation of litigiousness.[11] These litigious states would litigate disputes in the WTO DSM as long as simple cost–benefit analysis justifies the move, being unaware, ignoring or discounting the disputing parties' normative predispositions. To US trade officials, for instance, suing the United Kingdom is more or less the same as suing China, though such an action is interpreted differently in the two societies.

In contrast, for parties from non-litigious countries, adjudicating trade disputes at the WTO DSM deviates from their past experiences. Having invested heavily in non-litigious norms, these actors are naturally inclined to settle. Thus, in spite of the formal procedures available under the WTO DSM, non-litigious parties will try to avoid using them. As in their domestic settings, lawsuits will be filed only to signal hostility, terminate cooperative relationships or resolve disputes of great importance when alternative solutions are unavailable. To a certain extent such settlement preference may reflect systemic lack of capacity to litigate complicated cases, but more importantly it echoes their long-formed predispositions against formal dispute resolution.

But social norms may change if exposed to conflicting information and incentives.[12] At the early stage of participation in the WTO, parties from non-litigious countries were inclined to treat other member states as trade partners and to settle all disputes. Therefore, very few non-litigious states would initiate lawsuits soon after the inception of the WTO DSM. Yet free from such normative restraints, actors from litigious countries filed lawsuits frequently. When a litigious state sues a non-litigious state, trade officials and other stakeholders in the latter tend to interpret the action as signaling hostility, lack of commitment to cooperation, or interests of great importance at stake. They would retaliate to the former and make concessions for the latter, or take a mixed response.[13] Such reactions, however, would be ineffectual if targeted at litigious states that are immune to retaliation, as their agents interpret excessive concessions not as a gesture of goodwill, but a sign of weakness in legal position or capacity to exploit. Such interpretation, instead of facilitating settlement, may even lead to more lawsuits.

The 'unexpected' frequent filings by powerful litigious states conflict with the pre-existing non-litigious norms and cause the non-litigious parties to adapt. But the adaptation will be partial if the investment in original norms is substantial and the cost of changes high. Instead of adopting litigious norms wholesale and completely rejecting their traditional non-litigious norms, the agents will engage in social differentiation, treating the 'litigious type' differently from the familiar non-litigious states. As a result, in subsequent dealings with litigious states, agents from non-litigious states are no longer constrained by the norm against formal dispute resolution. They will mimic their counterparts from litigious states, i.e., choosing dispute resolution methods based on fact-specific cost-benefit analysis. The 'legally aggressive', however, reflects the partial adaptation in the form of differentiation, so shared norms against litigation will continue to govern trade dispute resolution among non-litigious states.

The two-by-two matrix illustrates the causal relationship between domestic social norms governing dispute resolution and a member state's behavior in the WTO DSM (see Figure 11.1).[14] Everything else equal, two litigious states are more likely to litigate trade disputes against each other. In contrast, two non-litigious states tend to avoid the WTO DSM because they share the norm against formal dispute resolution (Quadrant I of Figure 11.1). As the filing of a lawsuit is interpreted as a signal of hostility, lack of commitment to long-term cooperation, or substantial interests at stake, a non-litigious state not intending to send such signals will refrain from litigation in the WTO DSM. Moreover, under the shared norm deviation from the pattern of behavior will be punished, resulting in a static mode of trade dispute resolution characterized by low frequency of litigation.[15]

The same non-litigious state, however, may sue a litigious state after learning and differentiation. Based on past experience as respondents and observation as third parties, trade officials and other stakeholders from non-litigious states can learn to appreciate that litigious states do not interpret litigation as signals of hostility or concessions as gestures of goodwill. Having made the differentiation, non-litigious states will be more inclined to sue litigious states, and the decision will turn on fact-heavy cost–benefit analysis, not the sense of appropriateness, which leads to medium or even high frequency of dispute escalation (Quadrant III of Figure 11.1).[16]

The intersubjective model supplements existing theories by explicating the bifurcated normative and behavioral adaptations of non-litigious states. For instance, the model is more capable than other theories in explaining the resolution of trade disputes between Korea, China and the United States. Among these three, Korea and China are usually viewed as non-litigious societies and the United States is generally considered as one of the most litigious countries in the world. Both Korea and China experienced a steep learning curve in resolving trade disputes under the WTO DSM. Governed by a non-litigious norm, China was initially on the responding side of several cases, including those filed in

		Complaining state's domestic social norms	
		Non-litigious	Litigious
Responding state's domestic social norms	Non-litigious	I Low	II Medium
	Litigious	III Medium to high	IV High

Figure 11.1 Frequency of litigation as a function of disputing state's domestic social norms (source: Ji Li 2015).

2007 by the US government that took senior Chinese officials by surprise. While US officials had considered the filing as a routine exercise of its rights under the WTO DSM, Chinese officials, embedded in a non-litigious state, interpreted the move as a personal insult and a clear sign of hostility.[17] Puzzled by the interpretation, ranking US officials tried to convince the Chinese counterparts that the filing was not a sign of hostility, but rather a common practice in resolving international trade disputes.[18] Their Chinese leaders were reported to have 'understood that the United States was more accustomed to litigating disputes'.[19] The Chinese government immediately responded by filing a complaint against the United States at the WTO DSM, which a non-litigious social norm would allow once a cooperative relationship had been terminated by a lawsuit. Chinese officials also responded to litigation threats by making excessive concessions.[20] Because of its size and power, the United States was largely immune to retaliations from China. Moreover, its reactions to excessive concessions were typically more aggressive legal actions. In response to such conflicts with the non-litigious norms, Chinese parties adapted by differentiating the United States as a litigious state and began to treat it in a legalistic manner. By June 2015, China had filed nine suits against the United States at the WTO DSM.

Korea went through a similar learning process after being sued by litigious states in the WTO DSM. Not long after the formal dispute resolution mechanism took effect, both the United States and the European Union filed cases against Korea. Repeated conflicts with Korea's non-litigious norms led to a normative adaptation. In 1997, the Korean government filed a case against the United States in the WTO DSM and prevailed. The US government neither perceived the lawsuit as 'demise of diplomatic relations' nor retaliated.[21] Korean officials, having learned to differentiate the United States from other non-litigious states, now base their decisions about trade disputes with the United States solely on mechanical cost–benefit analysis in which the legal merits of the cases play a central part.[22] In the 17 cases Korea had filed at the WTO DSM by June 2015, as many as 11 were targeted at the United States.

Though non-litigious states such as Korea and China have become more 'legally aggressive' against litigious states like the United States, their shared non-litigious norms continue to govern how they resolve disputes with each other. Given the generally benign diplomatic relations, China and Korea have resolved all their trade quarrels through bilateral negotiations. In other words, for the shared social norm against litigation the Korean government would not resolve disputes with China in the same manner as with the United States.[23]

It is worth emphasizing that the intersubjective theory does *not* rule out litigation between non-litigious states. When lawsuits are filed, the shared non-litigious norm guides the interpretation of such moves as a signal of hostility or of the fact that the complainant's substantial interests are at stake yet less confrontational solutions are unavailable. And, fully aware of and anticipating such interpretation, parties from the non-litigious state will make such a move only if the benefit justifies the subsequent retaliation cost. As long as these conditions are met, we may observe lawsuits between non-litigious states. In certain circumstances, i.e., deteriorating diplomatic relations, non-litigious states may even sue each other quite frequently. For instance, Korea sued Japan at the WTO DSM during a downturn in their diplomatic relations, and the move was interpreted by the Japanese as meant for something other than resolving the underlying trade dispute.[24] Likewise, while in usual circumstances the shared non-litigious norm would restrain Japan from suing China, even at the invitation of the US government, the norm did not stop Japan from filing lawsuits against China when Sino-Japanese relations reached a nadir.[25] It also merits mentioning that the intersubjective model allows varying normative adaptation by different parties. As noted, how individuals adapt to a new set of norms and values depends on their investment in prior existing norms and the balance between the diverging incentives. While most actors from a non-litigious society are heavily invested in norms against formal dispute resolution and therefore adapt slowly by differentiation, their lawyer colleagues may welcome the use of the WTO DSM.

To recapitulate, this section elaborates on the intersubjective theory for trade dispute resolution. Given its compulsory jurisdiction, the WTO DSM enables litigious states to drag non-litigious states into the formal procedures to resolve trade disputes. In response to the conflicts with their domestic norms against formal dispute resolution, the non-litigious states adapt by differentiation (e.g., *United States v. Korea or China*). The non-litigious states subsequently become legally aggressive against litigious states (e.g., *Korea or China v. United States*). But they litigate selectively. Sharing the same social norms against formal dispute resolution, the newly aggressive non-litigious states continue to refrain from suing each other unless they intend to send strong extra-legal signals (e.g., *Korea v. Japan* and *Japan v. China*). Put differently, trade disputes between non-litigious states normally do not escalate to lawsuits, unless hostility is intended or substantial interests are at stake yet alternative resolutions are unavailable.

Rather counterintuitively, the existence of the formal dispute resolution mechanism and its active use by non-litigious states may actually facilitate settlement of disputes among non-litigious states. With clearly demonstrated legal capacity to litigate, a state can more effectively signal goodwill to a non-litigious state by refraining from litigation. Take Korea for an example. Having sued the United States numerous times, Korea has demonstrated ample capacity to play the legal game in the WTO DSM. Thus, its efforts to settle trade disputes with China will not be misinterpreted as lacking capacity, but respect and commitment to a long-term cooperative relationship. And the more frequently Korea sues and prevails over the United States, the more the Chinese officials and other stakeholders will appreciate its restraint from litigating against China.[26] Such appreciation may well facilitate trade dispute resolution in the long run.

Impact of the ongoing Chinese legal reform and China's rising power on international trade dispute resolution

Powerful non-litigious states are crucial to preserving the non-litigious norm as a shared normative institution to govern trade dispute resolution now that the formal WTO DSM exists. Thus, substantial changes in either China's domestic social norm against litigation or its power will have significant global impact. This section begins by discussing how the ongoing Chinese legal reform will likely alter the non-litigious norm. The Third Plenary Session of the Eighteenth Communist Party Congress announced an ambitious formal plan to deepening systematic reforms, including reform of the Chinese legal system.[27] Unlike previous proposals, the current plan intends to tackle some of the most serious structural problems with Chinese courts. First of all, in contrast to the populist turn against law under the previous party leadership, the reform now emphasizes the court's proper role in resolving disputes. To facilitate litigation, the Supreme People's Court (SPC) systematically lowered the barriers to sue. It promulgated a case filing registration rule in 2015 to replace the filing review rule that had been in operation for decades and had prevented many disputes from entering the judicial procedure. Prior to the reform the courts encouraged or pressed disputants to settle; now litigation is allowed to proceed as long as a few basic legal requirements are met. After the new case registration rule took effect, the SPC reported a monthly increase of 29 percent in filed lawsuits nationwide. In Henan Province, the number of case filings in May 2015 grew by as much as 71.3 percent. Moreover, the national rate of successful case filing surpassed 90 percent.[28]

The legal reform also aims at professionalizing the judiciary. Judges will be managed in a system separate from other government bureaucrats. Adjudicating judges will be empowered relative to other collective decision-making bodies and be held individually responsible for their decisions. Extrajudicial influence over the handling of cases will be documented and strictly prohibited. To insulate lower courts from the pressure of local power-holders, the control over their personnel and financial matters will be elevated to the provincial level. Additionally, the SPC has begun to set up circuit courts to adjudicate cases implicating provincial governments and has encouraged lower courts to follow by establishing cross-jurisdictional tribunals. To enhance judicial legitimacy and appeal to the populace, the reform also includes plans to make courts more transparent.

The systematic legal reform, if effectively implemented, will certainly move China a major step closer to the rule by law. But it is unlikely to change the Chinese norm against litigation in any significant manner. While previous legal reforms could be analogized to a pendulum swinging between indiscriminate institutional transplantation from the West and blind embrace of domestic norms and institutions, the ongoing reform is best described as judicial professionalization rooted in Chinese values. The current administration under Xi has repeatedly stressed that the 'three self-confidences', in China's political system, in the party line and in party theory, should guide the systematic reforms.[29] Xi later added that self-confidence in Chinese values was just as important.[30] There is yet no convincing evidence that Xi is 'signalling left while turning right'. So it is safe to infer that the Centre harbors no intent to move China toward an adversarial system of dispute resolution. Despite the surge in case filings triggered by the case registration reform, senior SPC officials downplayed its long-term impact on dispute resolution behavior by emphasizing the Chinese social context and the norm against litigation.[31] Not long ago the Chinese government consciously restrained the judiciary from functioning as an active dispute resolution body. Though the current administration appears to have taken a step back, it still puts an emphasis on alternative dispute resolution to maintain social stability. On the other hand, social norms are sticky. So even if the systematic legal reform after the Eighteenth Party Congress led to more lawsuits, a bottom-up transformation of the norm against litigation will unlikely occur in the near future. Professional courts and non-litigious social norms may coexist, as illustrated by China's East Asian neighbors, i.e., Korea and Japan.

While the non-litigious norm remains static, China's growing power will amplify the norm's impact on the international regime of trade dispute resolution. Start with China's rising hard power, defined by Joseph Nye as the ability to use economic and military might to make others follow the power-holder's will. Under the non-litigious norm, disputes should be settled through negotiation, and litigation would be interpreted as a sign of hostility and the demise of diplomatic relations, to which retaliation would normally follow. Credible retaliation is necessarily based on hard power. When the United States first sued China in the WTO DSM, angered Chinese leaders took retaliatory measures such as terminating cooperation in intellectual property rights protection. However, the US government was largely immune to retaliations given its superior power status. Repeated litigation against China by the retaliation-proof state posed direct conflicts with China's non-litigious norms, causing Chinese officials and other stakeholders to learn and adapt by differentiating the United States from other non-litigious countries and selectively apply the same litigation techniques as perfected by the United States to resolving trade disputes at the WTO DSM with powerful litigious states.

Though the United States and the European Union are by and large immune to China's retaliatory measures against litigation, few other member states are in the same league. As China's hard power continues to grow, its retaliation, or threat of it, in response to litigation attempts in the WTO DSM will become more costly to the targeted states. For litigious states less powerful than the United States, Chinese retaliatory measures will create conflicts with their domestic norms that routinize and rationalize legal resolution of disputes. It will force them to do what China initially did in response to US filings in the WTO DSM, i.e., learning to differentiate China as a non-litigious state and refrain from litigating trade disputes with the Chinese government. The same logic applies to non-litigious countries that are, thanks to the incentives created by the litigation dynamic in the WTO DSM, moving toward the litigious end in terms of resolving trade disputes. In other words, while powerful litigious states such as the United States are pulling countries toward more frequent use of the WTO DSM, China with its growing economic might is dragging them back to negotiated dispute resolution with credible retaliation. To that end, officials and other stakeholders from China should reinforce their non-litigious reputation and make clear the consequences of suing the Chinese government.

In addition, the growth of China's soft power, defined as the ability to attract and co-opt, will have subtle but more profound implications on the legal regime for international trade dispute resolution.[32] A huge chasm currently exists between the two sets of dispute resolution norms. The non-litigious norms that interpret litigation as a signal of hostility that justifies retaliation is considered by those having invested in and internalized the litigious norms as 'immature'. The formal legal regime under the WTO DSM, modeled on the US adversarial system, is held by many in high esteem partially because it was modeled on the *US* system. If China's soft power continues to rise, litigious societies may one day begin to question the superiority or efficacy of the US model for trade dispute resolution. That attitudinal shift, though unlikely in the near future given the relatively slow accumulation of China's soft power, will herald major institutional reforms of the WTO DSM.

Though litigation under the WTO DSM contradicts domestic norms of China and other non-litigious countries, it is not in their long-term interest to oppose the existing system. As the normative theory implies, the WTO DSM enables non-litigious states to resolve trade disputes between each other when their diplomatic relations break down, foreclosing informal resolution channels. Japan's recent lawsuits against China are good illustrative examples. The WTO DSM functions as a safety valve that keeps the downward spiral of trade relations in check during a deterioration of diplomatic relations. In addition, the WTO DSM is useful for non-litigious states as it provides an effective signaling platform. As noted earlier, non-litigious states with the capacity to sue will be able to effectively signal goodwill by refraining from filing formal complaints under the WTO DSM, which should facilitate informal resolution of the trade disputes in the long run.

Despite the stakes in the WTO DSM, non-litigious states will certainly benefit from a less litigious regime for trade dispute resolution free of 'legal trickeries'. Rational pursuit of the litigious states and subsequent reactions from the non-litigious states create a prisoner's dilemma problem resulting in a suboptimal collective outcome, i.e., over-litigation of trade disputes at the WTO DSM. China has officially proposed to reform the WTO DSM to limit the number of lawsuits developed countries could file each year against a developing country.[33] The proposal did not garner much support as it failed to recognize that many litigious states were developing countries benefiting from the formal dispute resolution regime. China should instead focus on more concrete and targeted reforms. For instance, the remedies awarded to victims of any violation of the WTO rules should include monetary compensation for past damages, which will allocate some costs for the delay to the defending party, forcing it to reconsider the benefits from engaging in time-consuming 'legal trickeries'.[34] China should also support reforms of the WTO DSM that will strengthen negotiated settlement of trade disputes rather than litigation. Even if these proposed institutional reforms are not adopted, China, with its non-litigious norms and growing power, should be able to unilaterally slow down the lawyering 'race to the bottom' in trade dispute resolution under the WTO DSM and channel more disputes away from the formal resolution mechanism.

Conclusion

The intersubjective theory identifies two clusters of states with diverging inclinations for judicial resolution of trade disputes. Non-litigious states such as China prefer negotiated settlement and adjudicate trade disputes only in extreme situations, whereas litigious states such as the United States are inclined to litigate and push the boundary of the law. Though the WTO DSM contains a variety of dispute resolution procedures, the aggressive use of litigation by the United States and other litigious members have triggered a lawyering race and are pulling more states into the dynamic of formal resolution of trade disputes.

China as a powerful non-litigious state plays a crucial role in resisting the trend and maintaining the parallel systems of international trade dispute resolution. The ongoing legal reform in China will not substantially alter its non-litigious social norm, yet China's growing power will likely amplify the norm's international implications. In other words, the stakes involved in the conflicts between the two sets of norms grow in tandem with China's rising power. Responding to the normative conflicts, litigious countries that are not immune to retribution from China will be incentivized to differentiate China from litigious countries and will hesitate before suing it. That will slow down the trend of 'over-lawyering' in resolving trade disputes at the WTO DSM, if not the broader movement of judicializing international trade conflict resolution. That said, the WTO DSM serves major interests of China and other non-litigious member states. Properly reformed in response to the diversity of domestic norms, the WTO DSM will better function as the ultimate international regime for trade dispute resolution and gain more support and trust from the emerging power.

Notes

1 Andrew Guzman and Beth Simmons, 'Power plays and capacity constraints: the selection of defendants in WTO Disputes' (2005) 34 *Journal of Legal Studies* 557; Marc L. Busch, Eric Reinhardt and Gregory Shaffer, 'Does legal capacity matter? A survey of WTO members' (2009) 8 *World Trade Review* 559, 576; Chad P. Bown, 'Participation in WTO Dispute Settlement: complainants, interested parties, and free riders' (2005) 19 *World Bank Economic Review* 287; Pilar Zejan and Frank Bartels, 'Be nice and get your money: an empirical analysis of World Trade Organization on trade disputes and aid' (2006) 40 *Journal of World Trade* 1021.

2 Christina L. Davis and Yuki Shirato, 'Firms, governments, and WTO Adjudication: Japan's selection of WTO Disputes' (2007) 59 *World Politics* 274.

3 Andrew Guzman and Beth Simmons, 'To settle or empanel: an empirical analysis of litigation and settlement at the World Trade Organization' (2002) 31 *Journal of Legal Studies* 205.

4 Shin-yi Peng, 'The WTO legalistic approach and East Asia: from the legal culture perspective' (2000) 1 *Asian-Pacific Law and Policy Journal* 78, 89.

5 Sungjoon Cho, 'Beyond rationality: a sociological construction of the World Trade Organization' (2012) 52 *Virginia Journal of International Law* 321, 344.

6 Joseph A. Conti, 'Learning to dispute: repeat participation, expertise, and reputation at the World Trade Organization' (2010) 35 *Law & Social Inquiry* 625.

7 Liesbet Hooghe, 'Several roads lead to international norms, but few via international socialization: a case study of the European Commission' (2005), 59 *International Organization* 861.
8 Dennis Chong, *Rational Lives Norms and Values in Politics and Society* (University of Chicago Press, 2000) 47.
9 Ibid.
10 A thorough discussion of the cause of low litigiousness is beyond the scope of this chapter. For representative works in this literature, see, for instance, Takeyoshi Kawashima, 'Dispute resolution in contemporary Japan' in Arthur Von Mehren (ed.), *Law in Japan: the Legal Order in a Changing Society* (Harvard University Press, 1963) 41; Frank K. Upham, *Law and Social Change in Postwar Japan* (Harvard University Press, 1987); John Owen Haley, 'The myth of the reluctant litigant' 4 *Journal of Japanese Studies*; Robert C. Ellickson, *Order Without Law: How Neighbors Settle Disputes* (Harvard University Press, 1991); Eric A. Posner, *Law and Social Norms* (Harvard University Press, 2000).
11 Conti, op. cit. at 633.
12 Chong, op. cit.
13 Ji Li, 'Interactions between domestic social norms and international law over trade dispute resolution' in M. Kanetake and A. Nollkaemperand (ed.), *The Rule of Law at the National and International Levels: Contestations and Deference* (Hart Publishing, 2015).
14 Ibid.
15 Ibid.
16 Ibid.
17 Steven R. Weisman, 'Little headway with China on finance' *New York Times* (December 13, 2007).
18 Thomas J. Christensen, Deputy Assistant Secretary for East Asian and Pacific Affairs, Remarks Before the U.S. China Economic and Security Review Commission (delivered by John Norris, Director of the Office of Chinese and Mongolian Affairs on Mr. Christensen's behalf), Washington, DC, February 2, 2007.
19 Weisman, op. cit.
20 Ji Li (2007).
21 Dukgeun Ahn, 'Korea in the GATT/WTO Dispute Settlement System: legal battle for economic development' (2003) 6 *Journal of International Economic Law* 597.
22 Ji Li (2015), op. cit.
23 Ibid.
24 Ibid.
25 Ibid.
26 Ibid.
27 Paragraph 32, *CCP Central Committee Resolution re Major Issues in the Systematical Deepening of the Reform [中共中央关于全面深化改革若干重大问题的决定]* (November 12, 2013), available at http://news.xinhuanet.com/politics/2013-11/15/c_118164235.htm.
28 Jing Li, *Shishi Lian Dengjizhi Gaige Shouyue Quanguo Fayuan Dengji Li'an Chao Baiwanjian*, June 4, 2015, at: http://legal.people.com.cn/n/2015/0604/c42510-27104481.html.
29 *The Economist* (2013).
30 For a summary of Xi's comments on self-confidence in Chinese culture and value, see 'Shenro Bawo he Jianchi Wenhua Zixin' (2015) 5 *Hongqi Wengao*, at: www.qstheory.cn/dukan/hqwg/2015-03/10/c_1114583418.htm.
31 Luo Sha and Chen Fei, 'Li'an Dengjizhi, Ni Yinggai Zhidao de Liujianshi' *Xinhuanet* (April 15, 2015), at: www.hn.xinhuanet.com/2015-04/15/c_1114977186.htm.
32 Joseph S. Nye, 'Soft power' (1990) 80 *Foreign Policy* 153.
33 Georgiev and van der Borght (2006).
34 Ji Li (2015), op. cit.

12 China's maritime interests and the law of the sea

Domesticating public international law

Isaac B. Kardon

Introduction

China's efforts to build and 'perfect' its maritime legal system are the focus of this chapter. It critically analyzes the political and strategic environment in which China's domestic law reforms interact with the international legal system with respect to the law of the sea. Specifically, how do People's Republic of China (PRC) domestic law reforms relate to China's international legal obligations under the 1982 UN Convention on the Law of the Sea (UNCLOS)? The UNCLOS treaty codifies much of the international law of the sea.[1] But does the PRC maritime legal system promote compliance with it? What specific legal, political and strategic factors underlie efforts of the Chinese leadership to define, protect and expand the PRC's legal rights in the maritime domain? How do domestic definitions, applied under the 1998 *Law of the People's Republic of China on the Exclusive Economic Zone and the Continental Shelf* (EEZ) and originally adopted at the Ninth National People's Congress, interact with UNCLOS? Given China's several active maritime disputes, this chapter seeks to clarify ways international maritime law is being developed and codified in the domestic context, then put into practice on the international stage.[2]

A principal concern of the chapter is how international legal obligations to maritime law and policy influence (if at all) Chinese practices. In turn, it probes how Chinese practices influence the development of the law of the sea. Central arguments are that: (1) a high degree of 'political discretion' colors China's approach to its law of the sea obligations; (2) the high degree of state authority being exercised over the maritime space promotes a political and legal goal of *closure*. 'Closure' in this context means the use of legal measures as instruments of political efforts to prosecute China's claims in several international maritime disputes, including sovereignty over disputed islands and associated maritime jurisdiction. Finally, (3) the legal instruments of closure are used as part of a full-spectrum political effort to prosecute China's claims in disputes with its oceanic neighbors over island sovereignty and maritime jurisdiction (i.e., 'maritime disputes').[3] The chapter concludes by evaluating how China's legal preferences and deepening maritime policies may influence the development of the law of the sea. Through state practice, China seeks to shape international interpretations of UNCLOS by encouraging states to acquiesce to Chinese authority over contested space (i.e., closure) and thereby contribute to the formation of new norms specific to China's littoral areas. In this way, international law becomes 'domesticated', with Chinese rules becoming the norm for other regional users of maritime space. This domestication entails specific limitations on traditional freedoms of the seas and favors the creation of de facto rights for China through the exercise of power, rather than acceptance of rights bestowed by international treaties or judicial settlement of contested rights through international arbitration.

The international law of the sea regime: the Chinese context

China's engagement with the law of the sea regime places significant demands on Beijing. Among them, three stand out: (1) the rules and norms codified in UNCLOS oblige China to develop and implement domestic maritime legal reforms at a time of acute struggles with its neighbors over sovereignty and maritime jurisdiction. Meanwhile, (2) significant organizational challenges impede PRC efforts to develop laws to govern the administration and economic exploitation of a large and contested maritime area. Finally, (3) these efforts occur in the context of a wider geopolitical struggle, with China seeking to consolidate its authority in the region and shape the development of international rules and norms. Thus, the drive to build and 'perfect' the PRC maritime legal system should be viewed in the broader domestic context of deepening socialist reform.

State-led efforts to govern maritime space within and beyond the limits of PRC jurisdiction give rise to familiar domestic issues that face China's overall law reform efforts to promulgate and implement thousands of new laws, regulations and rules. Maritime law presents distinctive challenges for reform, however, due in large part to maritime disputes. Under these circumstances, Chinese leaders face legal-design challenges, not only to manage the complex functional tasks of its massive 'blue' maritime economy and degraded marine ecosystems, but also to achieve effective control of disputed areas. As Jing Tao shows in Chapter 10, China considers protection of sovereignty and territorial integrity to be a paramount interest. The strategic function of maritime law reform is to safeguard China's claimed sovereignty, as well as its 'maritime rights and interests'.[4]

The first section summarizes the formal process by which UNCLOS is internalized in the PRC domestic legal system, then identifies political influences on implementation. The second section details specific ways in which UNCLOS-derived rights and duties have been adopted (and sometimes ignored) domestically. Centrally directed maritime legal reforms essentially use the law as an *instrument* of both domestic governance and international statecraft. Pathways through which China's domestic maritime law reforms may affect the international law of the sea regime are then briefly examined. One venue in which this influence is felt is the ongoing UNCLOS Annex VII arbitration, launched by the Philippines in January 2013. While refusing to acknowledge or participate in the suit, China seeks to enforce its domestic laws in maritime areas for which the Philippines is seeking a remedy from the arbitrators. This 'externalization' of Chinese domestic rules into the international political arena is one consequence of China's domestication of the law of the sea.

Bringing UNCLOS into China's domestic code

The formal and informal *processes* by which international law affects the PRC legal system are vague and sometimes contradictory, but can be analyzed in terms of: (1) the legal scheme whereby treaty and customary obligations take domestic effect; (2) the formal relationship between domestic law and law derived from international legal sources; and (3) the practical, political relationship of legal rules to other sources of authority in the Chinese Party-state beyond domestic law. Chinese political leaders exercise enormous discretion over the promulgation and implementation of rules derived from international legal obligations. Indeed, they can develop and use international law as an instrument of multifarious ends, some consistent with international legal obligations, and others unrelated or even contrary to them.

International law applies, sometimes

When China ratifies an international treaty, there is a variety of formal, procedural steps delegating authority to various state actors. Yet there is no clear guidance as to how norms or laws are to take domestic effect. Hanqin Xue, China's sitting judge on the International Court of Justice (and a leading Chinese scholar of international law), and Qian Jin, indicate that:

> [U]nder Chinese law, there is no statute that explicitly regulates the forms or modalities for implementing treaty provisions at the domestic level or in national courts [and] ... as is obvious, treaties vary in terms of their status and legal effect on the domestic legal system; not all treaties constitute part of domestic law.
>
> (Xue and Jin 2009: 300)

There is no Constitutional provision concerning international law, and only scattered references to international law in national legislation. These are drafted ambiguously and some appear to contradict one another; still others only address narrow facets of the effects of international law on domestic law.

With no systematic procedure for incorporating treaties, and no necessity for treaties to take domestic legal effect, PRC law is unclear when China ratifies an instrument like UNCLOS. There are, however, a few things we can say with certainty based on existing legislation, especially the 1990 PRC *Law on the Procedure of the Conclusion of Treaties* (*Treaty Law*). First, the legislature – specifically the National People's Congress (NPC) and its Standing Committee – *is empowered* to decide whether to ratify or denounce 'treaties and important agreements' (NB these terms are not defined); the President is to execute that decision on ratification or abrogation (1990 *Treaty Law*, Art. 3). Second, the State Council, with its mixed executive and legislative powers, *is authorized* to manage most other parts of the process – from negotiating and drafting, to formally concluding the treaty – via its diplomatic organ, the Ministry of Foreign Affairs. The State Council is also empowered to 'administer specific affairs concerning the conclusion of treaties and agreements with foreign states' (1990 *Treaty Law*, Art. 3). Indeed, China's international treaties often give rise to large volumes of new national legislation, administrative regulation and departmental and local rules. In practice, however, the State Council (presumably acting on superior political orders from the Party Central Committee) appears to exercise the only real authority in determining when, where and how such laws are promulgated.

Are there formal sources of law in the PRC with respect to treaties?

The *Treaty Law* does refer, at Art. 10, to 'domestic legal procedures for [a treaty's] entry into force'. This implies a prescribed set of rules governing the process, but there are no statutes to this effect. Xue and Jin (2009: 305 fn 12) note that the NPC considered regulating the different pathways during the drafting of the 2000 *Legislation Law*, but the proposal was tabled due to the complicated nature of implementing treaties. It might be argued that the complicated nature of implementing treaties is, in fact, a main reason why the NPC *should* have codified the procedure. But this speaks to an important aspect of the Chinese legal system: that legal reforms may be deferred or distorted due to political prerogatives of other senior actors in the Chinese state and the Communist Party of China (CPC). Lacking a clear statutory basis, and given the formal and informal weakness of the PRC judiciary (see Qianfan Zhang in Chapter 1), the underlying source of law that obliges China to respect treaty and customary law obligations is the *jus cogens* customary norm of *pacta sunt servanda*,[5] reinforced by frequent pronouncements by political authorities that 'China respects and upholds international law, especially the UN system'.[6] This is a basic norm in international society, but appears insufficient to ensure compliance when a state's self-defined 'national interests' are at stake.

The uncertain status of international law in the domestic legal hierarchy

There are many ways the PRC accommodates its treaty obligations, though institutionalized domestic provisions are lacking. Xue and Jin (2009: 305) identify three forms, or modalities, to implement treaty obligations:

- execution by administrative measures;
- transformation of treaty obligations; and
- direct application of treaties under specific national legislation.

From a comparative law perspective, such diversity is not unusual. It reflects a basic theoretical issue in international legal law as to whether a system is monist or dualist (or neither). This can play out in various ways when states determine the circumstances under which international law can trump domestic law, or vice versa (see Franck and Thiruvengadam 2003). Some consensus exists among Chinese legal scholars that China has a 'mixed system' in which ad hoc judgments determine which pathway will be followed (see Jiang Hong 2014). In short, some international laws trump some PRC domestic laws some of the time! Yet it is generally understood that China will not ratify any treaty that it perceives to be in conflict with its domestic law. One explanation for the lack of any statutory basis for dealing with this problem is what Wang Tieya (1998: 209) calls a 'presumption of harmony'.[7] This presumption is a common feature of the Chinese politico-legal system and reflects the 'ultimate leadership of the party' to resolve conflicts, as opposed to an independent judicial system or other institutionalized mechanism for adjudicating among competing legal rights.

Certain legislative provisions do, however, support *the expectation* that treaties can trump domestic law where 'rules of conflict' apply. These are found in some articles of legislation indicating where treaty provisions prevail over conflicting domestic law – unless China has made a specific reservation to the treaty on the issue in conflict.[8] These rules only appear, however, in clauses relating to dealings with 'foreign elements'. They therefore fail to provide a general rule for how China's international legal obligations are to interact with domestic laws and regulations where there is a tension. To address gaps in Chinese law, certain domestic laws refer to the role of international law or 'international practice' – an undefined term generally thought to stand in for 'customary international law'. But as Xue and Jin (2009) explain:

> Despite the widespread use of these types of provisions in Chinese law, it cannot be concluded in sweeping terms that international law prevails over domestic law under the Chinese legal system, because the prevailing force of treaties in domestic law is not derived from any legal provision of the Constitution or a national law of general application, but is confined to those international obligations explicitly undertaken by China.

What do Chinese political leaders intend when they ratify an international treaty? The following sections examine varied reasons why Beijing ratifies international treaties.

International law in the political continuum

The relationship between the Chinese Party-state and the PRC legal system has been examined in the earlier chapters of this volume. Maritime law is an excellent example of that relationship, illustrating how international law can be 'law' yet retain such an indeterminate status in the domestic code. This indeterminacy is an important feature of China's relationship to the law of the sea regime and explains how legal reforms in this sector can serve various ends. From this study three observations about politico-legal processes surrounding maritime law in China can be made: (1) the Party retains a virtually unchallengeable authority to interpret and implement law on an ad hoc basis; (2) the intense politicization of maritime law and policy inclines Chinese leaders to take liberties with the function, scope and content of its international legal obligations under the law of the sea; and (3) the rights and duties generated by the treaty may also be attractive as an instrument of domestic governance.

Ruling the country through law (依法治国)

The *Decision* of the Fourth Plenum of the Eighteenth CPC Central Committee (October 2014) offers a recent and authoritative account of how the Party understands its relationship to law. The 'absolute leadership of the Chinese Communist Party' in the context of various aspects of Chinese law is mentioned 14 times, a clear articulation of how the concept 依法治国 is intended. Namely, that the law does not exist independent of the political regime.[9] The *Decision* is not an innovation, but rather the crystallization of authoritative Party doctrine and the principle that the law serves the Party and it is through the Party that the state and its citizens are served.[10] The *Decision* asserts any legislation that bears on 'important' policy decisions should be reported to the central Party leadership, as opposed to being negotiated in the legislature. Yet, what is 'important' has no precise definition and deliberately invites political judgment on an ad hoc basis, and activates various informal power relations among the various legal and para-legal actors in the Party-state.

China, like several other parties to UNCLOS, made declarations upon ratification that may not be consistent with the treaty. For example, China asserts a 'security' interest such that foreign warships need Beijing's express permission to exercise their right of innocent passage, contrary to UNCLOS rules on this subject (see UNCLOS Arts 17 and 21 enumerating the relevant rights and duties). PRC treaty interpretations can therefore, sometimes, accord to a logic that is not strictly legal.[11] Indeed, several Chinese statutes and regulations explicitly allow room for 'political discretion'. Xiao and Luo (2002) argue there has been a pattern in PRC efforts to invoke an 'ordre public' doctrine, meaning a state may override international legal obligations on the basis of its own judgment about what constitutes a disruption to its domestic social and political order. Recent reform efforts explicitly allow political organs to suspend or dismiss 'inconvenient elements' of domestic laws and, by implication, obligations to any international law.[12]

Helping the head speak to the hands and feet

Political dominance over the domestication of international law does not, however, imply that those laws are meaningless. The decision to ratify and implement all or part of a treaty often has consequences across, for example, in the economic domain, or with respect to human rights. In the case of the law of the sea, however, motives tend to be more specialized. For instance, UNCLOS is not a treaty that generates rights for individuals against state coercion. Rather, it is an agreement to coordinate state practices across many functional areas such as fisheries, resource exploitation, navigation, boundary delimitation and environmental protection, and to avoid 'market failures' by efficiently allocating rights (see Posner and Sykes 2009). It thereby attempts to mitigate conflicts over use of the world's oceans. Standardizing efforts to comply with the treaty carries enormous legislative and administrative challenges for Convention signatories.

China has gradually adopted its domestic maritime code, responding to some but not all demands of the Convention. It has used the language of the treaty to guide the legislative process. Since China's ratification of UNCLOS, the NPC and State Council have engaged in a range of legislative and regulatory activity concerning maritime laws.[13] At the heart of these efforts has been a determination to claim and administer the new maritime rights created by the Convention, especially those concerning the vast new exclusive economic zone (EEZ) that extends 188 nautical miles beyond any area over which China had ever previously claimed jurisdiction. This introduced a new and powerful set of economic, administrative and bureaucratic demands, with law the only practical remedy. While China has invested heavily in naval and maritime law enforcement capacity to seize or defend this space if necessary, it plainly prefers gradual, nominally 'legal' means to realize the various economic, political and strategic goals associated with control over such valuable maritime space. From a management standpoint, legal reform provides *a technocratic way* to communicate from the Center (i.e., 'the head') to the various ministries, state organs, local agencies and actors (i.e., 'the hands and feet')[14] toward realizing China's maritime rights and interests.

Defining, protecting and expanding China's maritime rights and interests

UNCLOS is much more than a 'prompt' for administrative activity and source of rules that may serve pre-existing Chinese interests. Its close association with the intensely politicized and strategic set of conflicts along China's maritime periphery make it a tool of domestic administration and international statecraft. Rights derived from the Convention can confer legitimacy to Chinese claims and practices. Though political discretion tends to dominate PRC legislative and regulatory processes, the law can be used as a subtle instrument to promote China's control over contested maritime space. 'China's maritime rights and interests' (中国的海洋权益) are a constant trope in PRC law and public policy discourse, signifying the gamut of national and local concerns with the maritime domain. The depth of the concerns indicate that China prefers to move toward *closure* on its maritime disputes. That is to say, this analysis identifies a distinct thread running through China's relationship with the law of the sea regime that tends toward the fullest possible expression of PRC legal authority over all of the UNCLOS zones – and additional, undefined zones.

Closing ranks around China's maritime rights and interests

The lack of rigorous, homegrown requirements for China's UNCLOS compliance means that its maritime rules may be best analyzed as signals of Chinese intent rather than mandatory restraints on action. Meanwhile, the domestic rules themselves are related to, but not entirely consonant with, the international legal framework laid out in UNCLOS. Since the landmark 1992 PRC *Law on the Territorial Sea and the Contiguous Zone* ('Territorial Sea Law'), the concept of 'maritime rights and interests' has come to denote the whole raft of political, economic and strategic goals associated with the maritime domain.[15] Indeed, the 'rights and interests' narrative provides a reasonably comprehensive vehicle for analyzing China's maritime reform goals.

But what precisely are these goals? How are they pursued through legal reform? Much of the accompanying legislative and administrative effort has been organized around the idea of developing 'comprehensive management' (综合管理) of the maritime sector.[16] Significant official energy and resources are being employed to address three basic political goals: (1) coordinate and 'de-conflict' the maritime bureaucratic and regulatory apparatus; (2) promote efficient, orderly and productive use of maritime resources and development of the 'blue' economy; and (3) define, protect and expand China's maritime rights and interests. The former two goals account for the bulk of practical PRC activity with much of the domestic maritime legislation, regulation and rules promulgated to manage and promote China's growing maritime economy.

In 2014, a first-ever Five-Year Plan (FYP) specifically for National Maritime Development was drafted by leading maritime agencies under the authority of the State Council. It is in this economic arena that an effective, relatively transparent maritime legal system is most useful to Chinese leaders. Such a system is intended to efficiently allocate proper *usage rights* and prevent abuses that hinder development. The growing maritime sector already accounts for 10 percent of China's gross domestic product and up to 16 percent in the rich coastal provinces (see Takeda 2014). Promoting the development of the 'blue economy' is obviously a primary goal of the leadership. Critically, efforts to coordinate the bureaucracy and develop maritime resources are also consistent with the pursuit of *closure*, which effectively displaces international legal rules and norms with China's domestic maritime code.

Domestically, the Chinese leadership has used UNCLOS as an instrument to protect and expand China's maritime rights and interests. But how these uses take effect *internationally* is another matter. The following subsections therefore examine the domestic and international ends served by the promulgation of laws, regulations and rules that promote this expansion. The EEZ commands special focus, as this zone encompasses the vast majority of waters under Chinese jurisdiction and comprises the principal contested space in China's maritime disputes.[17]

Augmented jurisdictional content of state authority

The PRC's political drive toward closure is evident in the way the EEZ is interpreted in domestic law. A class of 'surplus/residual rights' (剩余权利) or 'vested interests' (既得利益) is often read into the EEZ regime by Chinese legal experts, who do not specify what they are but insist that they exist.[18] As UNCLOS scholar Zhou Zhonghai (2006: 119) suggests:

> The Convention has left ample room and space for an adjustment process of enlarging jurisdiction of the coastal states and reducing the freedom of high sea, largely due to residual rights contained in maritime law. Especially in the new area of the EEZ, the allotment of coastal countries' sovereign rights, exclusive jurisdiction, the freedom of high seas, and other states' user rights is not very clear.

China's maritime laws aim to use this 'adjustment process' to augment certain substantive rights in maritime zones. It appears that residual rights and vested interests are a subset of China's maritime rights and interests, but these are not specified and remain ambiguous in Chinese oceans law and policy.

The PRC's 1998 *EEZ Law* provided landmark legislation with respect to 'extra' PRC rights in its maritime zones. For the most part it established sovereign rights and specific jurisdiction as created and standardized in UNCLOS. It also stands as a high-level example of the process of building out the content of Chinese maritime rights. Specifically, the law stipulates unspecified 'historical rights' in Art. 14 and thus makes undefined claims to jurisdictional competence not expressly conferred in the Convention itself.[19] The 1998 *EEZ Law* makes no distinction between commercial and government vessels, implicitly extending Chinese authority over the activities of military ships that are not subject to coastal state jurisdiction under UNCLOS.[20] This domestic adaptation of an international treaty has the effect of arrogating certain security-related rights to China not found in the Convention. The resulting internal effect is that officials at lower levels are required to regulate and administer new 'security-related' jurisdiction.

Another aspect of China's EEZ legal regime that expands the content of Chinese maritime rights is found in PRC insistence that all disputed islands claimed by China are entitled to an EEZ (and continental shelf).[21] The Convention itself only grants these broad entitlements to continental coastlines and full-fledged, juridical 'islands'. Again, there are indeterminate definitions of such islands in UNCLOS Art. 121. Chinese law and practice exploits UNCLOS's vagueness, for example by declaring (but not delimiting the baselines or boundaries of) an EEZ from the Spratly Islands in the South China Sea. It could be argued that a 'common sense reading' of the Convention would reject China's interpretation, given that there is no indigenous human habitation on the aggregate two square kilometers of surface area of the entire Spratly group, which comprises several hundred rocks, reefs and low-tide elevations. Few, if any, meet the UNCLOS standard sustaining 'human habitation or economic life of their own' required of an 'island'. Itu Aba, on Taiwan, is the only feature that seems to clearly fit this indeterminate definition. The notion that China is, at present, entitled to a 200-nm EEZ from disputed features of this nature is plainly invalid in terms of the law of the sea, especially given that many claimed Spratly features are submerged and are in close proximity to opposing neighboring South China Sea states' coastlines.[22]

In effect, China seeks to create additional rights for itself – some derived from the EEZ, some derived from creative interpretations of the EEZ, and some wholly independent (e.g., 'residual rights'). This 'creeping jurisdiction' is not unfamiliar in state practice of the law of the sea. Scholars and practitioners have for some time pointed out the costs associated with UNCLOS's indeterminate language.[23] However, it does provide procedural and substantive guidelines for managing that indeterminacy. For example, the Convention obliges states bordering 'semi-enclosed seas' – a geographic characteristic of both of China's maritime flanks, the South and East China Seas (SCS and ECS) – to 'cooperate with each other in the exercise of their rights and in the performance of their duties under this Convention' (UNCLOS III, Part IX, Art. 123) by coordinating their practices over a number of different functional areas (such as managing resources, protecting the environment and conducting scientific research). Yet China appears to reject this provision on the basis that disputes should be dealt with according to domestic rules and regulations. The PRC does not acknowledge that other claimants have legitimate rights or duties in the disputed areas.[24] Consequently, China does not view the UNCLOS injunction to cooperate as bearing upon it. Of concern to SCS neighbors is that the PRC maritime project proceeds to fill out the content of its domestic maritime code with what may be *exclusive* rights to fish, exploit oil and gas, regulate military navigation, conduct marine scientific research and build military installations on disputed features (shoals, reefs, rocks and islands) in the SCS. Despite the clear existence of disputes and the corresponding obligation to undertake provisional measures to manage disputed areas, China sets its maritime rights and interests as above those of other states in disputed zones.

Enlarged geographic scope of state authority

PRC maritime rules also tend to expand the geographic *scope* in which the state exercises the augmented jurisdiction described above. This amounts to what Kraska (2010: 35) calls '[t]he exercise of Chinese jurisdiction in its neighbors' EEZs'. China claimed the various exclusive rights and specific jurisdiction associated with EEZs in its 1998 *EEZ Law*, but has not demarcated nor formally delimited its EEZ boundaries. Essentially, all of China's maritime boundaries are under dispute and require a negotiated solution or adoption of formal dispute resolution mechanisms as laid out in UNCLOS Part XV. Again, the U-shaped-line map looms large as an extra-legal factor informing China's efforts to realize its maritime rights and interests. In this case, it involves asserting unspecified 'historical' rights to waters circumscribed within the line.

In geographic terms, the practice of expanding the scope of Chinese jurisdiction begins 'at the waters' edge': China's policy of straight baselines.[25] The black letters of UNCLOS are unambiguous in limiting straight baselines to special circumstances (see UNCLOS Art. 7). As China's geography does not often satisfy UNCLOS requirements, the PRC baselines are an unlawful expansion of its jurisdiction – what law of the sea experts refer to as 'excessive claims'.[26] The Convention prescribes 'normal baselines' – from the low-water line – except where 'the coastline is deeply indented ... or if there is a fringe of islands along the coast in its immediate vicinity' (UNCLOS III, Part II, s. 2, Art. 7, 'Straight Baselines'). Chinese domestic law makes straight baselines the *only* mode of delimiting the 12-nm territorial sea and draws straight baselines across bays and around island groups.[27] This allows China to claim maritime zone entitlements significantly further out to sea than it would otherwise be able to do. The practical effect is to extend the limits of China's jurisdiction further out to sea than lawfully entitled; it creates larger areas of sovereign internal waters and territorial seas, and pushes out EEZ and continental shelf entitlements further from the Chinese coast. Thus the straight baseline policy promotes closure.

China's domestic legal position on 'archipelagic baselines' is similarly geared toward expansion, enclosing a larger volume of ocean space than UNCLOS provides. UNCLOS provisions on archipelagic baselines are unambiguous in that they apply *only* to states 'constituted wholly by one or more archipelagos' (UNCLOS III, Part IV, Art. 46, 'Use of Terms'). China refers to all of its disputed island groups as 'archipelagos' (群岛) that, by extension, warrant status as 'archipelagic states'; it has officially drawn straight (archipelagic) baselines to enclose the Paracel and Diaoyu/Senkaku island groups.[28] This creates large zones of 'archipelagic waters' – equivalent to internal waters in most respects. PRC law therefore assigns itself a greater geographic scope for exercising its maritime rights, which, as discussed above, are also augmented by ambitious domestic legal efforts to build out their content. Any reasonable interpretation of UNCLOS would see this as unlawful.

Another example of the practice of broadening the scope of Chinese maritime rights is in the 'standard list of zones' ascribed to Chinese jurisdiction in virtually all of its maritime rules. For example, the 2002 *Marine Environmental Protection Law* says: '[t]his law shall apply to the internal waters, territorial seas and contiguous zones, exclusive economic zones and continental shelves of the PRC and *all other sea areas under the jurisdiction of the PRC*' (italics added).

The 'all other sea areas' construction is standardized all the way down to the level of local regulations. This language does not identify which geographic areas are subject to the PRC jurisdiction, nor describe the content of that jurisdiction. This vagueness appears to be deliberate. The imprecision even extends to a Supreme Court interpretation of the 1999 *Special Maritime Procedure Law*. The Court held that

> The phrase 'the sea areas under jurisdiction' as prescribed in Item 3 of Article 7 of the Special Maritime Procedure Law, refers to the contiguous

> zones, exclusive economic zones, continental shelves, *and other sea areas that are under the jurisdiction of the People's Republic of China.*[29]

In short, the Court answers a politically sensitive question with a tautology.

The Court's reasoning is best understood as a vivid illustration that political demands outweigh legal clarity. Indeed, the judiciary (and other Chinese legal actors) must be flexible when interpreting the scope of Chinese maritime entitlements. This flexibility extends to State Oceanic Administration (SOA) departmental rules on 'National Maritime Functional Zones'. This is an exhaustive and highly specialized inventory of all the different layers of state authority in maritime space. But it, too, declines to define 'other sea areas'. For example, among eight marine functional zones, there are 'reserve zones' that 'have not been developed and utilized for the time being due to social and economic factors, or whose basic functions *should not be clearly defined*'.[30] Persistent maritime disputes in many zones complicate the exercise of Chinese jurisdiction and probably constitute the 'social and economic factors' cited in this document. Specification, at this stage, could jeopardize favorable settlement of complex usage issues in future maritime delimitation.[31]

A further example of how this imprecision is practiced is found in 2013 Hainan fisheries measures (办法),[32] in which the provincial legislature specifies rules for implementing the 2004 *PRC Fisheries Law*. It includes the provision that local rules apply within the *two million square kilometers* of maritime space under Hainan's jurisdiction. Yet this staggering figure does not delimit the geographic scope of the zone over which Hainan claims authority. The volume of water space is substantially greater than any EEZ-based estimation of the extent of China's lawful fisheries jurisdiction.[33] Because national-level laws and regulations make such ambiguous claims to 'jurisdiction', it is likely that provincial agencies feel authorized to interpret and enforce these indeterminate PRC fishery laws as expansively as possible – especially because 'protecting maritime rights and interests' is a known political priority in Beijing.

The various roles of the state in maritime zones

China's domestic legal reforms attempt to articulate new functional roles for various state actors. These roles cover an array of jurisdictional functions, including fisheries management, port safety, laying submarine cables and so on. This section focuses only on functional developments that bear on China's efforts to prosecute disputed claims in the SCS and ECS. Domestic maritime rules are best understood in the broader strategic context in which the PRC seeks to protect its maritime rights and interests, a key facet of maintaining PRC 'territorial integrity'. In this context, effective administration of China's maritime economy also means: (1) securing physical control necessary to operate in strategically valuable space; (2) limiting access for other potential users of that space; and (3) conveying to others the increasing strategic and political costs for failing to acquiesce to China's expanding posture.

Although it is debatable whether control over uninhabited islands and maritime zones rightly bears on China's 'territorial integrity', the conflation of the two has made 'maritime rights-protection' an overwhelming priority, a function typically performed by China's growing maritime law enforcement (MLE) agencies. Deployment of the growing Chinese MLE fleet nominally serves to promote and regulate PRC economic activity, but also functions as a routinized display of 'effective control', and may deter foreign users of Chinese-claimed maritime space. These now-regular shows of paramilitary force indicate that the laws and rules to legitimize these efforts are, in part, strategic. Law reforms in this sense can be understood as tools that help realize political and operational goals. Indeed, the instrumental use of law to consolidate effective control is visible and strategically salient in the PRC's ongoing efforts to regulate military activities in its EEZs.[34]

The Chinese government, military and maritime legal community argue that international and domestic law forbid foreign warships from operating in EEZs without prior coastal state permission. The PRC has taken various operational and diplomatic steps to restrict such access. As yet, however, there is no clear, specific legal prohibition, nor any attempt to stringently enforce this rule; there has been much posturing and a number of operational run-ins, including the fatal EP-3 incident in 2001, and the *Impeccable* incident in 2009, both episodes in which Chinese military or civilian vessels and aircraft aggressively intercepted US Navy vessels or aircraft (see Ji Guoxing 2009; Mastro 2011). One reason for the lack of clarity in the domestic rules may be that PRC authorities believe international law already grants coastal states a license to regulate such military activities on the basis of the potential threat they pose to the security of the coastal state, the innately 'non-peaceful purposes' of such activities, the status of certain military activities as 'marine scientific research' (MSR) (which are expressly regulated in the Convention), and their potentially harmful effects to marine environment and mammal life. Chinese interlocutors also sometimes invoke the UN Charter provisions regarding the threat or use of force as the source of norms that prohibit any military activities in China's EEZ.[35] Regardless of the legal justification, no clear statement in PRC law or policy lays out exactly which military activities China believes are unlawful, nor has China practiced in such a way as to make the underlying rule clear.

The above arguments are commonly rehearsed in public forums by Chinese officials and experts. Curiously they were not the subject of a Chinese statement upon ratifying the Convention,[36] nor are they developed in any identifiable domestic rules. These omissions may reflect a PRC belief that UNCLOS already sufficiently supports Chinese interests in restricting access (i.e., promoting closure) in its EEZs.[37] Meanwhile, the lack of a strictly defined legal regime in this functional area allows the PLA Navy to conduct comparable activities in foreign EEZs (see 2014 Office of the Secretary of Defense Annual Report).

A restriction on military activities in EEZs generally is consistent with China's consistent aim to create non-specific 'security'-related jurisdiction in maritime zones. This undefined security jurisdiction is a domestic innovation on what is intended as an exhaustive rendering of coastal state jurisdiction in UNCLOS. The PRC's 1992 *Territorial Sea Law* assigns authority to the PRC to 'exercise powers within its contiguous zone for the purpose of preventing or punishing infringement of its security, customs, fiscal, sanitary laws and regulations or entry–exit control within its land territories, internal waters or territorial sea' (Art. 13). UNCLOS does not include 'security' as a jurisdictional competency in the contiguous zone. Its inclusion in domestic legislation (including many subsidiary regulations and rules) is a calculated move to acquire additional rights. Not only is this an augmentation of the normal content of coastal state jurisdiction, it is a signal that China's subjective judgment of its security will influence the degree of control it seeks to exercise in maritime zones.[38]

Conclusion

This critical appraisal of China's maritime interests and the law of the sea surfaces three sets of issues worthy of further comment. The first concerns the relationship between the international law of the sea, as expressed in the UNCLOS treaty, and China's incorporation of its obligations under UNCLOS in domestic law, especially with respect to the EEZ. In China's domestication of UNCLOS, the PRC claims exclusive, substantive rights beyond those justified by the international treaty. Ambiguity in UNCLOS is interpreted domestically in ways that expand China's rights in substantive and geographic terms. The government's drive to build its 'blue economy' is one driver for this expansion, but so too is the desire for *closure* – that is, to enforce an interpretation of UNCLOS that gives China greater authority to regulate activity in its claimed maritime zones. These considerable liberties taken in the incorporation of UNCLOS reflect the political dominance of the CPC over government efforts to 'perfect' China's maritime legal system. These law of the sea reforms are congruent with the ends of the Fourth Plenum and its corresponding goal to improve governance at local levels; perhaps more significantly, however, the reforms serve the broader political goals of a regime with designs on expansive, extra-legal authority over maritime space.

A second set of issues relates to China's maritime disputes. Specifically, the extension of China's maritime legal code through an expanding constellation of legislation, regulation, and rules, including at provincial and local levels, is part of a full-spectrum effort to legitimize and enforce China's disputed claims over islands and maritime space in the SCS and ECS. The resulting practices of authorized Chinese actors in disputed maritime space have not resolved China's maritime disputes with Japan over the Senkaku/Diaoyu islands, or with Malaysia, Brunei, Indonesia, Taiwan, Vietnam and the Philippines over maritime claims in the South China Sea. Rather, they have led to increasing friction on the surface of the water and in the diplomatic arena, as more Chinese military, paramilitary and civilian vessels saturate disputed space. This numbers game does not require skillful diplomacy nor international arbitration under UNCLOS dispute resolution mechanisms; rather, through sheer scale and willful practice, China hopes to effect a desired outcome of near-total authority over contested waters and islands.

The third set of issues relates to the international implications of the above two. First, it should be expected that China, as an emerging superpower, will seek to influence international law in ways that reflect its own interests. This study shows that it is doing this in the law of the sea domain by domesticating its treaty obligations, then reinterpreting certain provisions in the treaty to suit its preferences. Such 'auto-interpretation' may well be the norm in international politics – especially among great powers – but the crudeness of China's efforts in this vein, and the significant political strife associated with them in China's maritime disputes, indicate that the practice is destabilizing. This confrontational approach hinders the effectiveness of the law of the sea regime and undermines legal dispute resolution mechanisms. Given that the disputing nations are unlikely to simply acquiesce to China's efforts to expand its jurisdiction and control over disputed space, limited armed conflict with either the Philippines or Vietnam cannot be ruled out categorically; indeed, China has already escalated disputes over SCS islands in 1974 and 1988, seizing islands previously occupied by Vietnam in two fatal naval clashes. Despite these risks, the Xi administration is acting strategically in pushing through its ambitious 'blue economy' agenda, supported by deepening socialist law reforms. China's conduct in and after the pending UNCLOS arbitration with the Philippines will be important for the integrity of the law of the sea regime and as an indication of how (or whether) China's maritime rights and interests can be reconciled with the existing regional political order.

Notes

1 The Third United Nations Convention on the Law of the Sea (negotiated 1973–82, effective 1994) is generally understood to be the 'Constitution for the Oceans', a comprehensive legal framework governing the use and protection of the world's oceans. It codifies long-established customary rules and norms concerning coastal state authorities in maritime space and flag state rights and duties. China is one of 167 state parties to the convention, making it of the world's most comprehensive international legal instrument after the UN Charter.

2 The United Nations General Assembly Resolution A/RES/174(II) November 21, 1947 sets domestic codification as the standard normative goal underlying continuing efforts to improve and expand the international legal system.

3 For an overview of disputes and their legal and political setting, see Dutton (2014).

4 This 'rights and interests' construction is found in innumerable leadership statements, policy documents, departmental rules and, increasingly, domestic laws and regulations. President Xi Jinping has referred to them, as well as China's 'maritime sovereignty' on numerous occasions, including issuing a call for China to 'be prepared to cope with complicated issues, and improve our capabilities to resolutely maintain the nation's maritime rights and interests' (quoted in Xiamen University South China Sea Institute, *South China Sea Bulletin* No. 8, August 2013).

5 There is an argument that China's generic obligations to treaties are codified with its 1997 accession to the 1969 Vienna Convention on the Law of Treaties (VCT). But if

not mirrored in domestic law, the source of obligation to honor the VCT remains the *pacta sunt servanda* norm.

6 This is a long-standing rhetorical position, seen recently when President Xi announced that all countries should 'jointly promote the rule of law in international relations [and] … that this requires all parties to abide by international law and well-recognized basic principles' (Xi Jinping 2014d).

7 For details see Wang Tieya (1994, 1998).

8 For example, see the 1982 *Civil Procedure Law* of the PRC, Art. 189 and the 1991 *Civil Procedure Law*, Art. 238. Similar provisions are found in the 1985 *Law of Succession*, 1987 *Postal Law*, 1989 *Environmental Protection Law* and 1984 *Patent Law*.

9 See Peerenboom (2014b) for detailed discussion of the *Decision*. Also see Feng Chongyi in Chapter 3.

10 Lubman (2000: 297) claims that in both Chinese tradition *and* Communist practice, law was regarded as 'an ensemble of rules for administering a society, rather than as an arrangement of norms that create rights in the persons and entities in that society'.

11 China's official statement on ratification is at: www.un.org/depts/los/convention_agreements/convention_declarations.htm, June 7, 1996. Here China arrogates to itself certain additional rights over 'innocent passage' in its territorial seas, and further claims over 'archipelagos' as being under its jurisdiction. This is not permitted under the Convention, for example, see UNCLOS Part XVII, Art. 309, which prohibits any reservations or declarations that are not 'expressly permitted by other articles'.

12 For example, see the new Art. 13 of the PRC *Law on Legislation* adopted in the 2015 amendment: '全国人民代表大会及其常务委员会可以根据改革发展的需要，决定就行政管理等领域的特定事项授权在一定期限内在部分地方暂时调整或者暂时停止适用法律的部分规定' [The NPC and its Standing Committee can decide to authorize some local governments to suspend or adjust the application of parts of laws concerning specific matters of administrative management for a certain period, according to the needs of reform and development], at: http://npc.people.com.cn/n/2015/0327/c14576-26759529.html.

13 At least 300 pieces of national-level legislation and administrative regulation use important language from the convention. For more extended discussions on the various UNCLOS demands presented to the PRC, see Nguyễn Thị Lan Anh (1988, 2012), J.C.F. Wang (1992), Wang Tieya (1994) and Klein (2005).

14 This metaphor is drawn from Jacques deLisle (2012), unpublished presentation at Cornell Law School, October 18.

15 Article 1 of the *Territorial Sea Law* states:

> This law is formulated in order to enable the People's Republic of China (PRC) to exercise its sovereignty over its territorial sea and its rights to exercise control over its contiguous zone, and to safeguard State security as well as its maritime rights and interests.

16 For what this means, see the official document 'Ocean Discovery Net Plan', 2014, issued by the State Oceanic Administration, China's lead maritime agency, at: www.soa.gov.cn/zwgk/gjhyjwj/ybjz_254/201412/t20141218_34581.html.

17 Although outside the scope of this chapter to examine the full range of legal activity and documentation on this matter, the author notes a very high level of repetition in language in the many iterations of the various rules at every level of the legal and administrative hierarchy.

18 For details see Jianwen (2003). Also see Wei Dan (2014).

19 Some experts engage with this problem, others ignore it. See discussions in Wu and Nong (2014). Also see Schofield and Storey (2009) on factors contributing to rising tensions.

20 See UNCLOS III, Art. 236.

21 Specifically, the April 2011 'Note Verbale' to the UNCLOS Commission on the Limits of the Continental Shelf; also see Sheng-ti Gau (2011).
22 Beckman and Schofield (2014) estimate that 13 features might reasonably be called 'islands', and could therefore generate EEZs. In this event, they would still need to be delimited with respect to the coastlines of neighboring states and would be given only partial effect.
23 This international compromise reflects the diversity of interests and stakeholders and is vague and remains problematic. For background, see Oxman (1984), Beckman (2013) and Roach and Smith (2012: 242) on UNCLOS commentary.
24 These areas prominently include those circumscribed by the infamous 'U-shaped line' in the SCS, published by the former Nationalist government of China, recently submitted to a UNCLOS body without explanation of its intended legal significance. The U-shaped line does not appear anywhere in Chinese domestic law or regulation.
25 Announced in the 1992 *Territorial Sea Law* and delimited in 1996 and 2012 State Council declarations on PRC baselines. They were, however, first developed in the September 4, 1958 Declaration on the Territorial Sea as the first official claim to straight baselines (see: http://news.xinhuanet.com/ziliao/2003-01/24/content_705061.htm). The 1992 *Law of the PRC on the Territorial Sea and Contiguous Zone* codified it as legislation (see: www.npc.gov.cn/wxzl/wxzl/2000-12/05/content_4562.htm). The 1996 Declaration on the Baselines of the Territorial Sea (at: www.fmprc.gov.cn/mfa_chn/ziliao_611306/tytj_611312/tyfg_611314/t556673.shtml) and the 2012 Statement of the Government on the Baselines of the Territorial Sea of Diaoyu Dao and Its Affiliated Islands (at: http://news.xinhuanet.com/politics/2012-09/10/c_113025365.htm) provide the actual basepoints from which the straight baselines are generated.
26 See Roach and Smith (2012).
27 An official map displayed by an SOA official at an October 2014 workshop showing a straight baseline across the mouth of the Bohai Bay, representing another (unpublished) instance of this practice.
28 The 1996 and 2012 declarations of baselines enclose the entire island groups, rather than individual features.
29 The Supreme People's Court Interpretations on the Application of the Special Maritime Procedure Law of the People's Republic of China, effective February 1, 2003 (adopted at the 1259th meeting of the Adjudication Committee of the Supreme People's Court on December 3, 2002, No. 3 Interpretation [2003] of the Supreme People's Court).
30 2012 SOA Division of National Maritime Functional Zones 2011–2020, Chapter 3 (Section 8), at: www.soa.gov.cn/zwgk/fwjgwywj/gwyfgwj/201211/t20121105_5255.html.
31 For discussion see Beckman (2013) and Zheng (2013).
32 See the Twelfth Five-Year Plan of the Hainan Maritime Safety Administration (MSA) (Hainan Maritime Safety Administration, July 7, 2012) at: www.hnmsa.gov.cn/news_2489.aspx.
33 The PRC has not specified its EEZ claims, which in any case would be provisional due to the existence of maritime boundary delimitation disputes in the East and South China Seas. Nonetheless, even hypothetically extending EEZs from all Chinese-claimed features, the zone created would be substantially less than two million square kilometers (see Beckman and Schofield 2014).
34 See O'Rourke (2014).
35 For background detail, see Dutton (2010), Zhang Haiwen (2010), Pedrozo (2010, 2011).
36 The PRC did, however, make such a statement claiming that 'military exercise of innocent passage through the territorial sea requires coastal state authorization'; see: 'Declarations and Statements', at: www.un.org/depts/los/convention_agreements/convention_declarations.htm.

37 Although this interpretation of the convention is not widely shared, some 27 coastal states have law or policy that infringes on the rights of warships in EEZs (see Kraska and Pedrozo 2013). The issue of military activities was a source of disagreement during the negotiation of the convention and resulted in deliberate silence in the treaty text on the subject; most UNCLOS scholars agree that this silence reflects the fact that China and others supporting this view did not prevail. Indeed, the US position is that the lack of a positive prohibition and its consistent practice are sufficient to make military activities in foreign EEZs lawful.

38 Some Chinese legal scholars see a pattern of PRC efforts to invoke an 'ordre public' doctrine, which means a state may override international legal obligations on the basis of its own judgment about what constitutes a disruption to its domestic social and political order (see Xiao and Luo 2002).

13 Screening the 'dragon's gift'?

National security review of China's foreign direct investment

Weitseng Chen

Introduction

On July 15, 2014, the US Court of Appeals surprised many pundits in both the United States and China by striking down the decision made by the Committee on Foreign Investment in the United States (CFIUS) that had blocked a Chinese foreign investment project for national security reasons. Right after the news came out, major Chinese media outlets circulated the line borrowed from the CEO of Ralls Corporation, the winning party: '*Unprecedented and historical victory in suing the Obama Administration!*'[1] Ralls' project is one of the only two transactions that the CFIUS has blocked since it was established in 1975.[2] A nationalistic mark was left on the minds of the Chinese people in that both projects involved Chinese companies. Nevertheless, this decision added a new dimension to increasing tensions between the United States' long-lasting open policy on foreign investment and soaring Chinese outbound investment around the world, including into the United States.

This tension can be traced back to the passage of the *Foreign Investment and National Security Act of 2007* (FINSA). The FINSA is seen as an institutional response to several controversial acquisitions proposed by foreign companies in the mid-2000s; in particular, one by the state-owned Dubai Ports World of P&Q, which controlled several American ports, and another by the China National Offshore Oil Corporation (CNOOC) that aimed to acquire Unocal, an American oil company.

The FINSA expanded the power delegated to the existing CFIUS and the Obama administration has increased the scrutiny of foreign investment ever since. Soon after the passage of the FINSA, however, the global financial crisis hit the US economy badly and increased the domestic demand for foreign capital, including capital from China. These contrasting objectives led to a series of disputes regarding Chinese investments, including Ralls' project. As a consequence, public anger at Americans on this matter remains prominent in China. In 2012, Wang Quishan, then-PRC vice-premier, openly chastised US cabinet members for performing 'political background checks', adding that Americans were not asked about politics when investing in China.[3]

This chapter reviews recent developments in the Ralls case, which concerns the mandate and jurisdiction of the CFIUS. The chapter also analyzes China's official response to the CFIUS practices, a recently proposed national security review mechanism in the draft of the *PRC Foreign Investment Act*, released in January 2015. The chapter proceeds as follows: the next section introduces the current practices of the CFIUS, followed by a review of the Court of Appeals' decision on the Ralls case. The fourth section discusses the proposed Chinese national security review mechanism, followed by an analysis of the notions underlying the review criteria in both the United States and China and forecasts future development. The final section concludes.

Mandate and jurisdiction of the CFIUS

The CFIUS examines the national security implications of proposed acquisitions of US companies by foreign purchasers, which are called 'covered transactions' under the FINSA. A covered transaction is one that involves a 'merger, acquisition, or takeover' that can result in foreign control of any person engaged in interstate commerce in the United States.[4]

Similar to national security reviews in other jurisdictions, the nature of the review conducted by the CFIUS is political, albeit in the form of a regulatory review.[5] This political nature can be illustrated by the fact that the CFIUS did not block the investment project of a Danish firm installing similar windfarms in the same area where Ralls Corporation planned to install and operate. Denmark poses no threat to US interests whatsoever, commercially or geopolitically, but China does.[6]

As a matter of fact, the creation of the current national security review was driven at varying stages by the United States' three major economic and political rivals over the past decades. Japanese corporate power grew significantly in the 1980s, followed by the threat of terrorism from the Middle East since the September 11 attacks. Now Chinese outbound foreign investment is seen as having the potential to upset US hegemony.

To begin with, Japanese firms posed great challenges to American firms in the 1980s, which faced takeover offers from Japanese conglomerates. The close relationship between the Japanese government and the firms clashed with the regulatory regime in place at that time, including anti-trust law and corporate governance. US reactions were colored by US–Japan trade frictions, exchange rate controversies and cultural misconceptions; all stemmed from concerns about national security.[7] Fujitsu's attempted acquisition of Fairchild Semiconductors in 1986 turned out to be the major impetus behind the passage of the Exon–Florio provision in 1988, which gave rise to the national security review mechanism exercised by the CFIUS to date.[8] By the early 1990s, however, Japan's experience in the United States was readily explainable by existing FDI theories.[9] The subsequent recession in Japan, together with the economic recovery in the United States, never gave the CFIUS a chance to block any Japanese investment.

As the commercial threats by Japanese firms faded away, the wealth of the Middle East raised concerns in the wake of the 9/11 terrorist attacks. The direct motivation for the FINSA was the 2006 acquisition of P&Q, a port operator that operates major US port facilities, by Dubai Ports World, one of the largest marine terminal operators owned by the sovereign wealth fund of the government of Dubai. This transaction initially went through under the radar until the media uncovered the complicated lobbying networks and political economy involved. The salience of national security triggered a heated debate and led to the enactment of the FINSA, codifying the existing practices of the CFIUS while increasing its regulatory power and congressional supervision. The FINSA expanded the list of factors concerning national security that the CFIUS should consider, including: (1) the potential effects of a transaction on critical infrastructure, such as major energy assets and critical technologies; (2) for transactions that could result in foreign government control of a US company, the subject country's record of compliance with regulatory regimes of non-proliferation, export control and other US counter-terrorism efforts; and (3) long-term projections of US needs for critical resources and material.[10]

Considering that the term 'control' is widely defined by the FINSA, it is easier than not to establish 'foreign control' in cases of Chinese investments, especially those by Chinese national champion firms to date. The FINSA defines 'control' as:

> The power, direct or indirect, whether or not exercised, through the ownership of a majority or a dominant minority of the total outstanding voting interest in an entity, board representation, proxy voting, a special share, contractual arrangements, formal or informal arrangements to act in concert, or other means, to determine, direct, or decide important matters affecting an entity; in particular, but without limitation, to determine, direct, take, reach, or cause decisions regarding the matters listed in §800.204(a), or any other similarly important matters affecting an entity.[11]

In brief, it focuses on the possibility of substantive influence exerted through shareholding, regardless of a majority or minority holding.

Given the FINSA's broad mandate, what remains to be clarified is the jurisdiction of the CFIUS; for instance, to what extent the CFIUS' decisions are subject to judicial review, which may offer constitutional protection for foreign entities viewed by the President as national security threats. This is not only an issue of constitutionalism, but also one of pragmatic considerations. Foreign investors could be scared away by any legal uncertainty, let alone the risk of being blocked entirely by the US government. A recent case in point is Huawei, the biggest IT manufacturer from China, which announced its decision to withdraw from the American market in 2013 in the face of public scrutiny of its alleged connection with the People's Liberation Army. Since then, Huawei has switched its focus and invested in European markets.[12] In short, the challenge for any national security review is how to strike a balance between eliminating national security threats on the one hand, and maintaining the countries' business competitiveness on the other.

Post-Ralls national security review in the United States

In their decision on *Ralls Corporation v. CFIUS*, the federal judges stated: '[Although] matters intimately related to foreign policy and national security are rarely proper subjects for judicial intervention … it is error to suppose that every case or controversy which touches foreign relations lies beyond judicial cognizance.'[13] This view underlies the general position manifested in the Court's decision, in which the judges went on to search for the proper boundary of judicial review of the decisions made by the CFIUS. To begin with, the text of the FINSA explicitly restricts judicial review of all actions taken by the President under the statute.[14] As far as the Ralls case is concerned, the scope, as the CFIUS argued, includes:

> The President's choice not to provide Ralls with more notice than it had already received, his decision not to confide in Ralls his national security concerns, and his judgment about the appropriate level of detail with which to publicly articulate his reasoning.[15]

However, the Court disagreed.

The US Supreme Court has long held that a statutory bar to judicial review precludes review of constitutional claims only if there is 'clear and convincing' evidence that the Congress so intended.[16] As such, a broadly worded statutory bar does not preclude a judicial review, at the very least, based on a *procedural* due process claim.[17] In applying this standard, the Court determined that neither the text of the statutory bar stipulated by the FINSA nor its legislative history provides 'clear and convincing evidence' that Congress intended to preclude judicial review of Ralls' procedural challenge to the Presidential Order based on the due process principle.[18] Courts are barred from reviewing final actions the President takes 'to suspend or prohibit' any covered transaction that threatens to impair national security; however, this restriction does not extend to the reviewability of a constitutional claim challenging the *process* preceding the presidential action.

The other potential obstacle for the judicial review is whether the Presidential Order based on the CFIUS's decision is a non-judiciable political question. The political question doctrine excludes from judicial review those controversies involving policy choices and determinations of vital values that are constitutionally committed for the resolutions of legislative or the executive branches.[19] In this regard, the Court of Appeals is of the opinion that courts do not automatically decline to adjudicate legal questions if they may implicate foreign policy or national security. Instead, courts 'must conduct 'a discriminating analysis of the particular question posed' in the specific case before the court to determine whether the political question doctrine prevents a claim from going forward'.[20] The Court went on to conclude that the political question doctrine does not bar judicial review of CFIUS decisions.

Having clarified the Court's jurisdiction over disputes regarding CFIUS decisions based on procedural claims, the Court ruled on the merit of the 'due process' claim. It was confirmed that Ralls did not challenge the President's determinations that the acquisition in question threatens national security and that the prohibition of the acquisition is necessary to mitigate the national security threat. Instead, by referring to the Due Process Clause, Ralls argued that they were at least entitled to have notice of, and access to, the evidence on which the President relied and an opportunity to rebut that evidence before such non-justiciable determinations were made.[21] The Court sided with Ralls, albeit with qualifications.

The Court decided that, given the fact that Ralls' property interests were deprived by the President's determination, Ralls should have been given access to the evidence and information supporting the determination as well as the opportunity to rebut such evidence at a meaningful time and in a meaningful manner. That said, the Court qualified its opinion on two grounds. First, the due process doctrine does not require disclosure of classified information.[22] In other words, the CFIUS still can deny access to classified information on which the President relies. Although the procedure that had been followed in issuing the Presidential Order blocking Ralls violated due process, this does not mean that the President must, in the future, disclose his thinking on sensitive questions and classified evidence related to national security in reviewing a covered transaction.[23]

Second, the Court of Appeals did not opine as to whether the 'executive privilege claim' can support the CFIUS' decision and justify withholding not only classified, but also unclassified, information on which the CFIUS and President rely to reach their determinations. Executive privilege is the power claimed by the executive branch to resist subpoenas and other interventions by the legislative and judicial branches to access certain information and personnel. The CFIUS did not raise the executive privilege argument until the final stage of proceedings, and therefore the Court of Appeals left it to the district court to decide whether executive privilege may shield the ordered disclosure of unclassified information. Given that executive privilege is an extraordinary assertion of power, not to be lightly invoked,[24] it will be interesting to see if the CFIUS will raise the executive privilege claim, the last resort, to defend its decision on the Presidential Order.

In short, the Court of Appeals has provided a straightforward framework for the CFIUS review procedure, thereby clarifying the mandate and jurisdiction of the CFIUS. The mandate of the national security review mechanism is to strike a balance between national security threats and a friendly foreign investment regime. Some commentators also argue that the current statutory mechanisms are institutionally sufficient to cope with national security threats as a result of foreign investment, including those from sovereign wealth funds, state-owned enterprises, or any other government-linked entities.[25] Enforcement, as well as any new initiative to deal with similar concerns, needs to be prudent so as to not create excess uncertainty and impose undue burden on potential foreign investors. As in the Ralls case, the Court may review whether the CFIUS has provided procedural protections for parties involved in the covered transactions, even though the final determinations for official actions are non-judiciable and non-reviewable.

National security review in China

As the world's top recipient of FDI, unlike the United States, China has not created a comprehensive national security review. In 2008, China's new *Anti-Monopoly Law* (AML) created an embryonic review mechanism. Article 31 of the AML briefly states that foreign acquisitions of domestic firms concerning national safety are subject to national security review according to relevant regulations. Article 31 appeared as more of an announcement than providing a functional review structure.

However, a controversial merger in 2010 between Huawei and 3Leaf served as a trigger to facilitate the process of creating a comprehensive review procedure.[26] In 2010, Huawei planned to acquire intellectual property rights from 3Leaf Systems, a California-based company that specialized in building high-end computer servers. After the initial investigation, however, the CFIUS suggested that Huawei 'voluntarily' divest of the investment or risk an adverse recommendation to the President to undo the deal. Huawei eventually withdrew from the deal, and Chinese regulators were upset by the CFIUS's decision. In a public statement, China's Ministry of Commerce (MOFCOM) criticized US regulators, suggesting the United States should 'abandon prejudice, avoid adopting protectionist measures and treat investments from China and other countries properly'.[27]

In 2011, shortly after this controversy, MOFCOM issued the Regulation on Implementing of the Security Review System for Mergers and Acquisitions of Domestic Enterprises by Foreign Investors.[28] A couple of months later, various local commerce bureaus posted a table on their websites broadly listing 57 industries that fall within the scope of industries subject to the national security review, such as those involving major agricultural products, major energy sources and resources, major infrastructure facilities, major transportation services, key technologies, or the manufacture of major equipment.[29] To preserve flexibility, however, MOFCOM kept the list 'low profile' by, in the beginning, neither confirming nor denying its existence.[30] Nonetheless, China has thereafter begun creating the Chinese counterpart to the CFIUS.

The CFIUS' decision to block Ralls' investment served as another key driver of China's construction of a national security review. In response to this decision, China did not express frustration in a written statement, but then-Vice Premier Wang Qishan delivered one orally and publicly, before US officials at a dinner in Washington.[31] In January 2015, MOFCOM finally announced in detail how the national review mechanism would be conducted.

The procedure for the national security review and the organization in charge of this review were revealed in the draft of the *PRC Foreign Investment Act* (FIA). Chapter 4 of the FIA lays out the details of the organization and procedure that, in many regards, are very similar to their US counterparts. To begin with, the State Council was planning to establish the National Security Review Committee (NSRC), an inter-agency committee similar to the CFIUS. The NSRC makes its recommendation to the State Council about cases that may constitute threats to national security. It is *the State Council that makes the final decision* as to whether to block an investment project.

With respect to factors that the NSRC needs to scrutinize, the FIA provides a very broad list that, like the vaguely defined 'national security' in the FINSA, delegates enormous discretion to the reviewers. In addition to factors such as 'key technology', 'critical infrastructure', 'foreign control' or 'Internet security', the FIA also provides a catch-all provision – 'any other factor the NSRC deems necessary'. Other similarities exist between the NSRC and CFIUS, such as pre-filing communication, negotiation procedure, conditional approval and re-investigation due to omitted disclosure. The FIA also encourages any public agency, market participant or competitor in the industry in question to submit a request to the NSRC in order to initiate an investigation.

Notwithstanding these similarities, the NSRC enjoys greater power than the CFIUS. First, given Ralls' initial victory in its suit against the CFIUS, the MOFCOM makes it clear in the FIA that the NSRC's decisions are *immune from any judicial review* via administrative reconsideration and litigation. As such, the NSRC will not face the potential of an embarrassing outcome as the CFIUS faced in Ralls' case.

Furthermore, the NSRC is granted more time to investigate and contemplate cases. Unlike the CFIUS review procedure, the FIA designed a two-stage procedure consisting of a 'normal' and a 'special' review. The difference between two stages, albeit unclear in the draft FIA, seems to involve the level of scrutiny and scope of other agencies involved. Once the normal review procedure begins, the NSRC has to reach a decision within 30 days as to whether the case needs to be submitted for the special review. An additional 60 days is allowed for the special review to recommend whether the case should be blocked by the State Council. Compared to the 45 days granted to the CFIUS, this total 90-day procedure provides the NSRC with more leeway and bargaining time for negotiating with the foreign firms in question.

It is notable that the draft FIA currently excludes foreign investment in the financial and banking industry. This may reflect the involvement of foreign financial institutions in Chinese banks' various restructuring efforts, including domestic and overseas IPOs and privatization. Here the aim is to inject fresh capital into China's banking and financial systems that have been attempting to curb the issues of non-performing loans and accrual of large debts owed by local governments.

Comparative regulatory frameworks

In general, there are two models of regulatory framework for dealing with China's outbound investment, commonly termed 'state capitalism' nowadays. One examines whether a critical level of 'state ownership' is present in the entity in question. The other focuses on the existence of 'state control'. The difference lies in whether 'state control' over a given firm depends on 'state ownership' (or not). A privately owned firm may still be subject to strong influence exerted by the government through other channels such as CPC networks.

With respect to the screening approach based on state ownership, Milhaupt and Zheng have pointed out the problems of 'ownership bias' are commonly manifested in the anti-trust, anti-corruption and anti-subsidy regulation frameworks, among others.[32] These regulations apply the 'ownership-oriented' test to decide, for example, whether employees of SOEs receiving bribes should be deemed to be 'foreign officials' for purposes of the *Foreign Corruption Practice Act*, or whether or not SOEs should be viewed as 'public bodies' that are subject to anti-subsidy law.[33] In the context of reviewing compliance with regulations of the Office of Foreign Asset Control, which implements the United States' economic and trade sanctions, the Securities and Exchange Commission (SEC) also faced similar difficulties in deciding the scope of disclosure that Chinese companies listed in the United States must include in their annual reports.[34] For instance, it is unclear whether the SEC can ask for information pertaining to not just the complying companies but also their beneficial shareholders, subsidiaries and affiliates, through which some may have (prohibited) direct or indirect arrangements with firms in Iran, Syria and Sudan.[35] The underlying problem is that 'state ownership' does not serve as a sufficient criterion for the purpose of the regulations in question. Hence, regulators often conflate government ownership with government control. The latter, which is of concern to the regulators, may exist not only in SOEs but also in privately owned companies that have close, if not closer, relationships with the government.

In contrast to the ownership-based approach, CFIUS review does not seem to present the problem of ownership bias when dealing with similar challenges posed by the Chinese state capitalism institutions. For instance, the case of the privately owned Ralls Corporation demonstrates how the CFIUS takes a holistic approach rather than sticking to the ownership-based test for scrutinizing the sources of national security threats. As 'control' is vaguely defined in the FINSA, this government control-based approach leads to a different problem than that of ownership bias. That is, the standards the CFIUS applies are *so* broad that the Court of Appeals has been required to adjudicate on a balance between national security concerns and foreign investment policy.

Considering the developments of state-centered institutional ecology, together with increasingly sophisticated financial engineering, the more flexible control-centered approach is arguably better suited for the purpose of national security review. Contrary to a common impression in the West of the rise of Chinese state capitalism, Nicholas Lardy, in his most recent empirical studies, has shown that the level of privatization of Chinese state-owned enterprises (SOEs) has hit a record high.[36] Nevertheless, Milhaupt and Zheng argue that in the Chinese context the dichotomy between SOEs and privately owned enterprises (POEs) is false, and that there is less state control over SOEs, and greater state control over POEs.[37] A similar observation is offered by Musacchio and Lazzarini in their cross-country study of state capitalism. Empirical evidence shows that Chinese state capitalism institutions have developed a hybrid of majority and minority shareholding in various forms of business entities, which is a variant of earlier version of state capitalism in Asia.[38] As a result, the ownership-based approach may improperly constrain, even distract, regulators from their original purpose.

In the event that it is implemented without objective standards and procedural accountability, this broad approach based on governmental control is doomed to give rise to an increase in political accusations and confrontation. China specialist Susan Shirk described the initial confidence of CNOOC's CEO, who had been advised by Goldman Sachs, that CFIUS would approve the company's proposed acquisition of UNOCAL: '[We] were following a system that was set up by leading Western companies.' The CEO, however, was subsequently crushed by the CFIUS decision and said '[we] discovered that what Westerners taught us is not the way the West wants to go'. 'People's hopes in the United States were dashed.... They think the United States will try to contain us regardless of whether or not we behave responsibly.'[39]

Nowadays, Chinese regulators are not shy about expressing public anger at the CFIUS. China's creation of its own national security review that mimics much of the CFIUS but possesses more power, can be viewed as an institutional response to that revelation. The long-term impact of the Chinese national security review remains to be observed. On the one hand, the national review mechanisms in both the United States and China offer regulators and firms under investigation time and space for commercial and political negotiations. Negotiations can be conducted during the pre-filing consultation and further 'incentivized' by the possibility of revisions, conditional approvals or withdrawals of filing.[40] The hope is that in the long term the threat of national security review exerted by both sides may lead to equilibrium – similar to the balance struck from nuclear terror.

On the other hand, such a potential equilibrium may become fragile or destabilized if the parties use excessive practices. In contrast to the post-Ralls review regime, China makes its national security review immune from judicial review. It is possible that Chinese regulators may use the broadly delegated power for matters other than mitigating national security concerns, such as providing protective treatment for strategic industries or domestic firms. Recently, for example, the National People's Congress published the draft legislation of China's first anti-terror law. According to the bill, Chinese regulators are entitled, in the name of national security, to require technology firms selling computer equipment in China to hand over encryption keys and install security 'backdoors'.[41] This legislation would have serious implications for market competition, as it raises the market-entry threshold for foreign firms and facilitates the increase of local firms' market share.[42]

Conclusion

This chapter reviews the most recent developments in national security review of foreign direct investment in the United States and China. It can be argued they seem to be going in different directions. The US Court of Appeals overruled the CFIUS decision that blocked Ralls' project and confirmed that the national security review is not immune from judicial review of claims based on the 'due process' principle. Consequently the precedent is set for foreign firms being investigated by the CFIUS to receive increased judicial protection. China will allow no judicial review process. In part, this goes back to the frustration and anger in China about the CFIUS' previous decisions blocking Chinese investment projects in the United States. China subsequently released its own blueprint for national security review. The review to be conducted by the NSRC generally mimics the procedure and institutional setting of the CFIUS model, with the notable exception that the NSRC has greater power and is immune from any form of judicial review. Although the Court of Appeals' decision on the Ralls case can be viewed as a triumph of an independent and impartial justice system and was welcomed by the Chinese people and Chinese regulators, it is definitely not a model Chinese regulators are allowed to emulate as the State Council has final say.

It remains to be seen as to whether the creation of the NSRC and the judicial correction of CFIUS practices will further institutionalize political concerns regarding foreign capital, prevent retribution between the United States and China and lead to a balanced approach. Such equilibrium could be enhanced through negotiations between regulators and firms in question. Indeed, the procedures for such negotiations are provided by the FINSA in the United States and the draft FIA in China. However, this equilibrium could be easily destabilized by excessive review practices, especially those based on considerations beyond national security concerns, such as erecting market-entry barriers for foreign competitors under the cover of 'national security'. Considering the wide delegation of power and immunity of judicial review, the current draft of China's FIA raises more concerns than the CFIUS review practices, which have been corrected by being placed under judicial review.

As with many international trade disputes, the nature of national security review is political. While lawyers try to devise legal frameworks to institutionalize and regulate such disputes, the heat of controversy often makes it difficult to contain tensions to a legal proceeding alone. Looking ahead, we will see how China's rise impacts on international legal regimes. As this study has shown, there is some irony, as China asserts itself, in that similar legal mechanisms are borrowed from the West but implemented with Chinese characteristics.

Notes

1 See, e.g., ChinaNews, http://finance.chinanews.com/cj/2014/07-16/6391792.shtml; CCTV, http://jingji.cntv.cn/2014/07/16/ARTI1405498954676698.shtml.

2 The US President Gerald Ford established the CFIUS as an inter-agency committee in 1975 for monitoring the impact of foreign investment and for coordinating the implementation of policies on such investment.

3 McGregor (2012).

4 Section 721 of the *Defense Production Act of 1950*, codified as amended at 50 U.S.C. app. §2170.

5 Chen (2014), at 39–40.

6 Rosen and Hanemann (2012).
7 Graham and Marchick (2006) at 23; Milhaupt (2008), at 2.
8 For a further discussion, see Foreman (1989), at 186.
9 Milhaupt, *supra* note 7, at 3.
10 50 U.S.C. app. §2170(f).
11 Department of the Treasury, Regulations Pertaining to Mergers, Acquisitions and Takeovers by Foreign Persons, 31 CFR Part 800, RIN 1505-AB88 (2008).
12 Thomas (2013).
13 *Ralls Corp. v. Committee on Foreign Investment in the United States, et al.*, No. 13-5315 (D.C. Cir. July 15, 2014), at 24.
14 Section 6 of the FINSA.
15 *Supra* note 13, at 19; 50 U.S.C. app. §2170(e).
16 See, e.g., *Bowen v. Mich. Acad. of Family Physicians*, 476 U.S. 667, 681 (1986); *Califano v. Sanders*, 430 U.S. 99, 109 (1977); *Weinberger v. Salfi*, 422 U.S. 749, 762 (1975).
17 *Supra* note 13, at 16.
18 Ibid., at 20.
19 See, e.g., *El-Shifa Pharm. Indus. Co. v. U.S.*, 607 F.3d 836, 840 (D.C. Cir. 2010).
20 *Supra* note 13, at 25.
21 Ibid., at 27.
22 Ibid., at 35.
23 Ibid., at 38.
24 *Cheney v. U.S. District Court for District of Columbia*, 542 U.S. 367, 389 (2004).
25 Epstein and Rose (2009).
26 Saha (2012), at 216.
27 Raice and Dowell (2011).
28 *Supra* note 25.
29 MOFCOM Circular 6 (2011).
30 Baker & McKenzie (2011).
31 Wingfield (2012).
32 Milhaupt and Zheng (2015).
33 Milhaupt and Zheng also examine the ownership-based test in the context of anti-trust law and predict that Chinese SOEs will post a challenge sooner or later to the 'single-entity defense' that usually bars anti-trust claims involving horizontal agreements among members of a single corporate family. Chinese SOEs accused of conspiracy in violation of s. 1 of the *Sherman Act* may raise the single entity defense that immunes units of a single unity from s. 1 liability. Ibid.
34 Chen Weitseng (2013).
35 Ibid., at 364.
36 Lardy (2014).
37 *Supra* note 32, at 57.
38 Musacchio and Lazzarini (2012), at 4–5.
39 Shirk (2008: 250–1), reporting on what Chinese officials had told her privately.
40 Section 5 of the FINSA; Arts 52, 54, 55 and 58, Draft of *PRC Foreign Investment Act.*
41 Mozur (2015), Martina and Hughes (2015).
42 According to market analyses, more than 90 percent of high-end servers and mainframes in China were still produced by foreign firms, but Chinese companies are catching up very quickly. Ibid. Also, Lohr (2014).

14 Conclusion

China's socialist rule of law reforms under Xi Jinping

John Garrick and Yan Chang Bennett

Introduction

The significance of what the contributors have said in this book about China's law reforms under Xi Jinping is by no means confined to the legal domain. Nor is it confined to the domestic sphere, as significant law reforms in the People's Republic can have global implications. What happens in China now has ramifications for us all. Nation-states remain central to international legal ordering. As Halliday and Shaffer (2015: 5) aptly put it, 'we do not live in a post-national world'. But alone they do not define the territorial boundaries of legal ordering.

The chapters chronicle a social and economic system striving to find a balance between regulation and freedom, with state planning held as an antidote to potential domestic unrest in a changing world order with China rising to the top. The deepening socialist rule of law is emblematic of the CPC. Under Xi Jinping, the Party's governing ideology is to extend market reforms beyond 'opening up' (开放) and encouraging Chinese enterprises to 'go out' (走出去) while retaining power within the one-Party system. This creates an intriguing legal system in which laws support market economics (and WTO requirements), and ensure incentives for production, distribution, satisfaction of growing consumer demands and the appearance of fairness. Yet, the political orthodoxy continues to follow a Marxist–Leninist ideology, with Chinese characteristics, that echoes the language of Mao Zedong and Deng Xiaoping. This orthodoxy is now expressed as 'four comprehensives' (四个全面; '*si ge quan mian*'): to build a moderately prosperous society, deepen reform, govern the nation according to law and to tighten Party discipline (*People's Daily* 2015).

What happens behind closed doors in Beijing may never be known. However, this book offers a portrait of the nexus of power, economy and law based on extensive research and knowledge of the country. Not everything can be explained adequately. Some apparent contradictions include systematic efforts to improve procedural fairness in the People's Republic (Chen, Chapter 6) while at the same time there is the use of non-judicial anti-corruption measures to eliminate political enemies, accompanied by Maoist rhetoric for legitimization (Ho, Chapter 7).

An aim of the book, however, is to explain how decisions made in Beijing may affect the everyday experiences of ordinary people who simply seek a fair deal in protecting their interests through a just legal system. Much of the law and legal system deals with the administration of relatively non-controversial business matters and it is worth remembering that China is the world's second largest economy with the vast majority of its trade carried out through mutually accepted legal structures.[1] Indeed, Yueh (Chapter 5) shows that solid macroeconomic policies and the quality of the business environment are more important to China's economic growth and investors than judicial enforcement. Clarke (2003b) reached a similar conclusion, but he emphasized that property rights protection (i.e., protection from random expropriations) is a crucial factor.

Xu (Chapter 4) argues China is staring at the 'middle-income trap'; the tendency for countries to stop growing as quickly once they reach a certain level of annual per capita income. Although optimists suggest China has a way to go before it falls into the trap, others are not convinced. From Xu's macroeconomic perspective, new sources of growth are urgently needed and he backs his assertion with persuasive evidence. Yet contradictions do emerge between judicial reform (Zhang, Chapter 1), constitutional reform (Hand, Chapter 2) and the enforcement of rights (Feng, Chapter 3; Han, Chapter 9; and Tao, Chapter 10). The first part of the book explains how and why such contradictions exist. The second part examines how ideological incoherence can, paradoxically, be both constructive (in pragmatic ways) and also have distorting effects on specific areas of law and development.

Xi's leadership sees the establishment of 'socialist rule of law with Chinese characteristics' as the foundation for *all legal reforms* and the 2014 Plenum laid out five general principles to guide this process: (1) the leadership of the Party; (2) the dominant position of the people; (3) equality before the law; (4) the combining of rule of law with rule of virtue; and (5) the need for China to chart its own path. Feng (in Chapter 3; Clarke 2014, among others) argue these principles deliver little other than meaningless 'feel-good' language. By way of contrast, Peerenboom (2014b: 8) says it is 'not surprising to see this type of pragmatic, measured, ameliorative language at this stage of development … [and] that as a middle-income country, China faces a long, hard slog in establishing rule of law'. He adds that progress is slow and incremental without miracle solutions, and that:

> Reforms in one area give rise to new problems, often times in other areas. There is no choice but to grind it out, tackling issues as they arise. The Party is under no illusions that it will be easy: 'Comprehensively promoting ruling the country according to law is a systemic project; it is a broad and profound revolution in the area of state governance, and requires long-term, arduous efforts'.
>
> (Peerenboom 2014b)

The third part shows China's grand plans for deepening economic reform and socialist rule of law have far-reaching implications for global governance and international legal ordering. With growing economic and military power, China will seek to influence international legal and financial systems. As Xu notes, China's deepening socialist rule of law is also associated with a set of macro-economic policies promoting structural reform in the economy and internationalization of the renminbi. There may be obstacles to expansion of the RMB's role in international trade and finance, including China's domestic financial system in which interest rates are tightly controlled and state-owned banks dominate financial intermediation. Kennedy and Cheng (2012: 21) argue that this is because the system is 'meant to serve the government's industrial policy priorities'. Hence, Chinese leadership in reforming global financial architecture is 'unlikely until China's own development strategy changes more fundamentally' (Kennedy and Cheng 2012: 21).

This Conclusion reflects on the main themes and points raised by the expert contributors. Conclusions reached by the authors depend, to a degree, on their perspectives and methodologies. Consensus was never sought, nor expected. But there are main recurring themes that are all, in some way, related to the nexus of party power, law and growth.

Socialist ideological developments under the Xi leadership

Qianfan Zhang (Chapter 1) examines China's judicial reforms from the end of the Cultural Revolution in 1976 to the present, and directions for the next five years are considered. In particular, he draws our attention to two areas: (1) a limited deregulation of the courtroom to reduce judicial bureaucracy with the intention to enable individual judges to assume more responsibility in deciding cases; and (2) the centralization of judicial administration to reduce local protectionism (*difang baohu zhuyi*). Some procedural problems are identified, but primarily the new judicial reforms are more substantively limited by politics and by a political regime in which the ruling party alone has final say on how far-reaching reforms can be. Zhang points out that a high degree of skepticism exists as to whether judicial reform can truly take place. Indeed, at the time of writing, civil rights activist Xu Zhiyong is in prison; rights lawyer Pu Zhiqiang is still awaiting trial after he was arrested over 18 months ago; and several women's rights activists, who had simply been handing out leaflets to draw attention to the prevalence of sexual harassment on public transport, were held in custody – the day before the 2015 International Women's Day. They were charged with the crime of 'picking quarrels and causing trouble'.[2] There seems little the judiciary can do to prevent or remedy such overt political action. Zhang further shows how the *Decision* is progressive in promoting rule of law on the one hand, but on the other hand, the expression 'leadership of the party' is repeated multiple times to reinforce the Party's leading function in judicial reform. It remains unclear how the Party leadership can be reconciled with 'rule of law'. As Zhang puts it in Chapter 1, rule of law should rest upon 'the principle that all private individuals, as well as public institutions, submit themselves to the impartial application of the law'.

Keith Hand's (Chapter 2) assessment of constitutional supervision brings China's socialist rule of law reforms into sharp relief. Over the past two decades, citizens have used constitutional argument and legal mechanisms to pressure the Party and promote constitutional interpretations that incorporate some meaningful constraints on Party power. Hand explains how the Fourth Plenum *Decision* can be viewed as a constitutional interpretation intended to stifle such citizen efforts with 'Party leadership' being the core of the socialist rule of law state. While the legal system may be a useful tool to discipline lower levels of the bureaucracy, ensure the implementation of economic policy and protect rights within limits, it is *the Party*, not the National People's Congress or its sub-units, that is final arbiter of the fundamental political questions implicit in many constitutional claims. Hand suggests the Party may fear that even the modest step of establishing a weak constitutional supervision committee 'could generate ideological confusion'. He notes that one of the principal arguments advanced by proponents of a constitutional supervision committee in the early 1980s 'was that China needed a specialized organ to prevent a repeat of the constitutional violations of the late Mao era'. It is clear enough that this history resonates in the current political-legal environment with the Party emphasizing its supremacy in China's constitutional order and Xi Jinping asserting his dominance over the Party. Indeed, Hand notes that Xi has emerged as China's most powerful leader since Deng Xiaoping and possibly Mao himself. As Feng Chongyi (in Chapter 3) suggests, current ideological campaigns are raising uncomfortable memories of the Mao era. Hand adds that a Party decision to create a constitutional supervision committee:

> would be a symbolic step that could reassure observers both inside and outside China about Xi's governance intentions. [The Party's] continued reticence will reinforce anxiety about those intentions. More than three decades after the adoption of the 1982 Constitution, the fate of constitutional supervision in China still appears to be tied to political system reform.

Feng Chongyi (Chapter 3) focuses on the CPC's main reasons to deepen law reform. His research examines three primary sources: the *Decision*, *Document No. 9* and Xi Jinping's speeches since becoming CPC General Secretary. Feng notes that the overarching principle of the *Decision* is to enhance the Party's authority and control over legal procedure and outcomes of 'politically sensitive' cases. Feng also identifies the CPC theory of law reform as being a necessary tool to help the economic growth agenda, which is to instill more public faith in the legal system and facilitate better legal protections of economic interests. Feng further claims that moves to curb local protectionism, reduce grass-roots corruption in the court system and uphold justice in ordinary legal proceedings (i.e., those without political significance) are politically motivated to improve the Party's image.

Feng also claims the CPC leadership is driven by the 'political imperative of pursuing regime survival at the expense of any other concern, including rule of law'. Even though new sources of wealth and power are being tapped, reform remains bound to Leninist historical frameworks that are dressed up by more contemporary narratives. A principal concern of Feng's chapter is the conflation of anti-corruption measures and the elimination of dissent and political opposition (both real and imagined). Feng argues this conflation draws on 'extra-legal' methods and can be interpreted as part of an *endgame* for the CPC to retain power. Without adequate checks on the authority of the Party, Feng says political and legal development is heavily circumscribed by the overarching authority of the Party-state with Chapter 2 providing a specific example of this major limitation. In this context, Feng claims 'the fruits of world civilization will remain in higher branches, perhaps out of reach of this socialist construction of "rule of law" '.

Detailing China's transition from a command economy toward a socialist market economy, Qiyuan Xu (Chapter 4) points out China now faces multiple challenges in transitioning from a position of strong economic growth to one of sustainable development. Xu argues that structural reforms must address both demand- and supply-side issues. With regard to the *demand side*, he points to China's need to reduce reliance on the two old engines of growth – investment and export – by stimulating domestic consumption. Key reforms include implementing export rebates as a neutral policy, constructing a mature social credit system and reducing transaction costs in the domestic market. Xu also points to anti-corruption measures as being associated with the need to boost domestic consumption and, in turn, this is linked to cleaning up local government fiscal responsibility and breaking down local protectionism. In boosting consumption, improvements to the social welfare system, household registration (Hukou) reforms, reductions in income disparity and industry structuring, such as further deregulation of the services sector, are anticipated over the next five to ten years.

With regard to the *supply side*, Xu points out the government is pursuing sustainable development in light of decelerating economic growth. The 'new normal' should see reforms to the following production factors: (1) labor: reduce reliance on the 'population dividend' and release the human capital bonus by shifting from manufacturing and export-driven growth to services sector-driven growth; (2) capital: implement staged financial deregulation to liberalize the 'real' economy; and (3) technical progress: implement laws and policies to transform China from an 'imitative' economy to an 'innovative' economy, such as amendments to improve the *Patent Law of the PRC 2009*.[3] From a macroeconomic perspective, Xu indicates that the dividends of deepening economic reforms require much more than this, including a fairer distribution of rural and urban services, better social welfare redistribution and concerted improvements to public goods and services such as environmental protection, less corruption and a fair and just legal system more generally.

Major challenges for China's socialist rule of law

The law/growth nexus in China

The challenges of managing China's remarkable economic growth are well documented. Yueh (Chapter 5), however, points out that while China gradually integrated itself into the global economy during the 1990s, the world economy, too, has undergone a transformation. A growing body of international economic laws and rules has emerged with China and international legal frameworks each influencing the development of the other. Yueh notes that the relationship between law and markets also appears asynchronous for China, with a pattern showing that law may have created a market in the case of IPRs and enabled corporations, but that substantive regulations generally were passed *after* there was an evident economic necessity. Examples of such necessity include the abuse of monopoly power or financial sector scandals. Although a law or administrative dictate, or absence of strict prohibition, may create a market, this factor alone is not sufficient to argue the sequence must be for laws to precede markets. Yueh argues that laws both precede *and* follow markets. She describes different facets of an evolving picture, with China being difficult to fit into any one paradigm given its history and context.

At the heart of this 'history and context' is a Chinese paradox whereby a socialist market economy has developed within a property system controlled by the state. Even at the earliest stages of reform, the lack of laws establishing clearly defined property rights appear to have not been as pertinent as in other countries. For instance, early on, China had made clear that it would not expropriate the assets of foreign investors and that they would be allowed to repatriate their profits (see the 1979 *Joint Venture Law*). China's economic transition has been driven by a series of experiments and trials or, as Deng famously put it, 'crossing the river by feeling for stones' ('*mozhe shitou guo he*'). Yueh indicates that although the influence of the global rules-based system is gradually growing, there are numerous limitations and China and its firms are expected to seek a framework that will better advantage themselves. Indeed, China's successes, and the prospect of strengthening its laws alongside robust economic growth, has the possibility of being a model for emulation among some developing countries.

Procedural justice in post-Mao China and addressing corruption

Jianfu Chen in Chapter 6 makes several conclusions about the development of procedural justice in China. Procedural laws, as enacted in the early days of post-Mao China, were a very different conception compared to those today. They were initially conceived as 'working procedures' for implementing substantive laws, with notions of 'protection and safeguard' absent. Chen points out that the development of procedural justice has taken a gradual, incremental pathway toward the protection of parties involved in litigation. However, many reforms are technical rather than fundamental in nature. As with Zhang's findings in Chapter 1, significant questions remain around judicial independence with the Party continuing to rely on political-legal committees and its own extra-legal mechanism, '*Shuanggui*', in its fight against corruption (see Chapters 6 and 7 for details). Nevertheless, the notion of procedural justice is a recent introduction to China and therefore needs time to be developed and adapted to local conditions.

Some contrasts exist, however, between efforts toward procedural justice and some anti-corruption measures. Ho (Chapter 7), for instance, shows similarities and continuities in CPC anti-corruption measures, from the Gang of Four Trial to Bo's downfall and Xi Jinping's 'tigers and flies' (老虎苍蝇一起打) campaign. In these, the CPC is *the* main actor and director, using publicized campaigns and trials, non-judicial anti-corruption measures to eliminate political enemies and a reliance on Maoist rhetoric for legitimization. Anti-corruption campaigns appear to remove not only corrupt officials, but others perceived to be politically unreliable, perhaps even 'bad elements' bent on destroying the Party. Ironically, this is similar to how Bo had used the organized crime crackdown in Chongqing to extort businessmen and remove individuals he perceived as threats to his authority.

Under Xi's leadership, there has been a crackdown on dissidents under the cover of the broader anti-corruption campaign, which has also extended to and stressed 'the party's absolute leadership over the People's Liberation Army (PLA)'.[4] Military corruption, although seldom spoken of in public, is now being targeted by Xi's campaign.[5] Furthermore, there may yet be international implications of the domestic anti-corruption campaign, as China tenaciously pursues corrupt 'fugitives' who have fled overseas to escape charges at home.[6] As Fu Hualing (2014) argues, corruption closely correlates with legitimacy, and political leaders in China have found it expedient to use anti-corruption campaigns to remove their political foes and rein in the bureaucracy to enhance their legitimacy in the eyes of the general public. Fu's argument (2014) is that the Party's anti-corruption campaign is a tool for the concentration of political power. Against this backdrop, Ho views the short- to medium-term outlook for consistent procedural fairness and transparent use of the courts as not so encouraging. For the longer term, however, there is significant potential to build upon improvements to judicial capability, procedural fairness and the legal system across China more generally.

Land and urbanization reforms

Hu's Chapter 8 reveals how China's planning around urbanization has, historically, been 'land-based' rather than 'population-based'. Urban expansion, accompanied by rural migrants moving to cities without urban citizenship, has lacked some public services. Urbanization has been associated with depopulation and land-loss among rural peasants. Hu shows how China's land use and urbanization are both subject to government monopoly and control, with local government political and financial incentives having substantially come from selling land and promoting urban growth. Many problems including corruption, risky financing and exploitation of peasants are attributed to this nexus of political power, monopoly practices and corrupt financial 'incentivization'.

This chapter refers to specific new reforms in rural property rights, liberalizing the land market and loosening Hukou restrictions. The dual urban–rural social structure is highlighted as being at the root of many reform challenges, with previous reforms and policies having lacked an integrative framework and thus failing to address significant problems. The new land use and urbanization reforms are part of a package of comprehensive strategic reforms, governed by the strategic objective of a unified urban–rural land market and integrated urban–rural development. The reforms are also driven by the imperative of stability maintenance. Land disputes and related corruption are a major source of protest and instability and these measures seek to address underlying key issues. Indeed, the ambitious rhetoric is confronted by a reality of deeply rooted structural and political complexities. China's social inequalities (see Sun and Guo 2012; Han, Chapter 9; Zang 2016), the urban–rural divide, deeply vested interests at local levels, and a central government that sets the rules but largely relies on local governments to implement them, will remain major challenges.

Equal employment opportunity and rights protection

Since the establishment of the PRC in 1949, there have been enormous changes in the lives of women. Despite extraordinary progress, the country's political apparatus has far fewer female members than male, with numbers dropping dramatically further up the political hierarchy. In 2015, only two women, Sun Chunlan and Liu Yandong, are in China's 25-strong, all-powerful Politburo. In Chapter 9, Su Lin Han refers to China's progress in law and policy reform against employment discrimination. Despite progress, enforcement has been stymied by political constraints against the individual exercise of equality and non-discrimination rights through private rights of action and rights advocacy, for example, in the detention of anti-discrimination activists mentioned earlier.

Han's arguments center on the state's outdated regulatory tools that have, thus far, failed to respond effectively to discriminatory employment practices under changing market conditions. She points to some ideological incoherence between the socialist ideals of law reform on the one hand, and expanded market conditions on the other. To help deal with this conundrum, Han offers an alternative enforcement model to advance individual rights protection. This model involves an administrative enforcement process that 'puts the government at the helm of resolving individual discrimination claims and steering changes in employment practices through a more participatory regulatory regime' (Chapter 9). Han asserts that such a public enforcement model is proven in other jurisdictions.

In China, such an approach could complement, or be used as an alternative to, private court enforcement. This would sit well with Fan Yu's vision (2012: 200) for alternative dispute resolution (ADR) procedures to be more effectively utilized in Chinese employment disputes with, inter alia, the *People's Mediation Law 2010* becoming more 'integral to ADR and the legal system more generally'.

Han refers to possible political and contextual obstacles to an enhanced 'public enforcement mechanism', especially when it comes to ensuring individual rights protection. Key factors include getting high-level political 'buy-in' to privately initiated employment discrimination claims through a dedicated administrative claims process. Achieving sufficient official tolerance of non-governmental advocacy of individual rights may not be easy. Historically, PRC leaders have often criticized such rights as being Western ideas that do not help China (see, for instance, Jiang Zemin's and Xi Jinping's comments quoted in Tao's Chapter 10). Progress on rights will require statutory enforcement powers for any new equal employment agency to investigate and resolve individual complaints. This, too, is likely to be problematic. However, if a new agency were willing to embrace 'collaborative governance' as a new regulatory tool, and engage non-governmental stakeholders to participate, Han predicts there would be increased 'voluntary compliance'.

International implications of China's socialist rule of law

At least three distinct categories of international implications are identified in China's socialist rule of law development, affecting: (1) bilateral relations; (2) regional relations; and (3) those with global ramifications. Jing Tao (Chapter 10) addresses the global in arguing that China's rejection of the Rome Statute reveals an amalgam of conservative and sovereignty-centered views prevailing over broader conceptions of rights. Tao claims that China is still at a relatively weak stage of integration with the international human rights regime, not surprisingly reserving the right to influence the international legal framework to better reflect its own interests. Tao's study shows that key elements of the PRC leadership perceive the spread of human rights norms as a threat to Chinese sovereignty. As such, China's integration in the international human rights regime cannot be expected to be linear. Attempts to legally bind China to the mandatory jurisdiction of the International Criminal Court (ICC) have been viewed as having negative implications for China's core sovereignty. This goes to concerns about the domestic management of tensions in Tibet and Xinjiang, and other sensitive political areas such as Taiwan and Hong Kong.[7] As Tao points out, the Rome Statute does not allow flexibility for China to exempt itself from the Court's jurisdiction, and thus was rejected because sovereignty costs were perceived to be too high.

Tao meticulously documents Jiang Zemin's essentially anti-Western narrative in explaining why China rejected the Rome Statute and this narrative continues under the Xi regime. As Xi recently put it:

> We need to borrow beneficial fruits of political civilization of mankind, but we must not copy Western political institutions and models, and must not accept any condescending preaches of foreign countries.... On important issues, such as human rights, [the] election system, and rule of law, we must be self-confident because we are in the right [*lizhiqizhuang*][8] and must not adopt Western political institutions and models as our standards.
>
> (*Official Reader* 2014)

At the same time, Tao notes steady domestic advances and integration in soft international treaties, suggesting these developments provide evidence that China continues to improve human rights conditions, as long as those rights are not perceived as incompatible with its core sovereignty and political system.[9]

Ji Li (Chapter 11) provides a norm-based theory to analyze how China's domestic social norms governing dispute resolution can affect discourses over international trade dispute resolution. Against the backdrop of the WTO Dispute Settlement Mechanism (DSM), he argues that even where non-litigious states substantially strengthen their legal capacity, they may continue to refrain from suing each other because of shared norms against litigation. He argues that even with enhanced legal capacity to litigate under the WTO DSM, China may facilitate the settling of disputes between non-litigious states as a positive signaling function of 'litigation avoidance'. Although Li points out that most trade officials recognize the WTO regime as legitimate, such professionals are not the only actors in the process. Important decision makers and stakeholders in international trade disputes are heavily invested in domestic norms and may be reluctant to adapt.

The WTO DSM enables non-litigious states to resolve trade disputes between each other when their diplomatic relations break down, foreclosing informal resolution channels. However, litigation is not the best solution for all trade disputes. Litigious states have exploited the formal system by 'over-lawyering', rendering the system more complex, costly and time-consuming. Non-litigious states have made efforts to curb the use of the system by litigious states and China has officially proposed reforms to the WTO DSM – to limit the number of lawsuits developed countries can file each year against a developing country. As there has been a trend that China is making more aggressive use of the formal WTO disputes resolution procedures, however, there remains a question as to whether this is because China is 'non-litigious' or because China may be disadvantaged and/or the target of many claims.

Li's study has broad international implications in that without effective independent tribunals, international rule of law, widely or narrowly defined, will remain an illusion that can vanish with a change of heart by powerful participating states. As one of the most frequently used international adjudicatory institutions, the WTO DSM showcases how internationally agreed rules are implemented. Li finds two clusters of states with diverging normative inclinations for judicial dispute resolution. Non-litigious states (including China) prefer mediation in the shadow of the law (leaving judicial resolution of disputes to extreme situations), whereas litigious states (including the United States) are inclined to litigate and push the boundaries of the law. The former risks disuse of international tribunals, hence lack of opportunities to establish sufficient jurisprudence and strengthened institutional authority. The latter raises the concern of 'over-lawyering', which can result in unnecessarily complex adjudicatory procedures. Both outcomes harm the institution's legitimacy and development of international rule of law.

Viewed via a framework of the interface between national and international rule of law, broadly defined, the avoidance of non-litigious states in using formal international adjudication constitutes de facto contestation to a legal order modeled on the norms and institutions of litigious states. Lack of positive responses to this contestation will inevitably damage long-term prospects of international rule of law. Looking ahead, China is expected to actively influence substantive and procedural rule design for international adjudicatory tribunals – to better reflect its domestic social norms governing dispute resolution.

In Kardon's critical appraisal of the law of the sea and China's maritime interests, three central sets of issues are outlined. The first concerns the relationship between the international law of the sea, as expressed in UNCLOS, and China's incorporation of its obligations under UNCLOS in domestic law. In China's domestication of UNCLOS, the PRC is claiming exclusive, substantive rights beyond those justified by the international treaty. Kardon shows how ambiguity in UNCLOS is interpreted domestically to expand China's rights and interests. He refers to the government's drive to build its 'blue economy' as underpinning this expansion along with the CPC desire for *closure* – that is, to enforce an interpretation of UNCLOS that gives China greater authority to regulate activity in its claimed maritime zones.

His second set of issues relates to the extension of China's exclusive economic zone through expanding regulations and rules at national, provincial and local levels. Together these seek to legitimize and enforce China's claims over the South and East China Seas. However, the resulting practices of authorized Chinese actors in disputed maritime space have not resolved China's maritime disputes with Japan over the Senkaku/Diaoyu islands, or with Malaysia, Brunei, Indonesia, Taiwan, Vietnam and the Philippines over maritime claims in the South China Sea. As Kardon explains, there has been increasing friction, both on the surface of the water and in the diplomatic arena, as more Chinese military, paramilitary and civilian vessels saturate disputed space. This tactic does not require skillful diplomacy nor international arbitration under UNCLOS dispute resolution mechanisms. The numerous foreign and security policy actors within China clearly favor Beijing taking a forceful foreign policy stance in maritime matters.

This gives rise to a third set of issues related to the international implications of Beijing's forceful maritime stance. The *People's Daily* (see Zhong Sheng 2012) routinely warns that China cannot stand idly by and 'tolerate encroachment on China's rights by other countries'. A consequence has been that governments across the region have taken steps to align themselves more closely with Washington. However, they do not want to be placed in a situation in which they have to choose between China and the United States. Kardon argues China will seek to influence the international regime to better reflect its own interests. Although it is unlikely that a limited armed conflict with either the Philippines or Vietnam would occur over the maritime disputes, it cannot be categorically ruled out. As Kardon points out, China has already escalated disputes over South China Sea islands in 1974 and 1988, seizing islands previously occupied by Vietnam in two fatal naval clashes. Despite the risks, the Xi administration is acting strategically in pushing through its ambitious 'blue economy' agenda. With respect to deepening domestic reforms to the law of the sea, the political analogy that Xi appears, in this specific context, to be 'more Putin than Gorbachev' might not be unreasonable.

Chen Weitseng (Chapter 13) analyzes bilateral issues in developments in the national security review of foreign direct investment regimes in the United States and China. He argues that each has taken a different direction. In the United States, for instance, the Court of Appeals recently overruled the US regulator's (CFIUS) decision that had blocked a Chinese company project (Ralls) from investing in the United States on national security grounds. The Court of Appeals' decision shows that in the United States, a national security review is not immune from judicial review of claims, based on the principle of 'due process'. A precedent is thus set for foreign firms being investigated by the CFIUS to receive increased judicial protection. By way of contrast, China will not allow *any* form of judicial review process related to national security. Chen argues that this categorical position partly stems from frustration and anger in China, related to the earlier CFIUS decision on Ralls. China's blueprint for its own national security review (to be conducted by the NSRC) generally mimics the CFIUS model. The notable exceptions, however, are that the NSRC has greater power and is immune from judicial review. Chen views the Court of Appeals' decision in Ralls' case as 'a triumph of an independent and impartial justice system', but it is not a model Chinese regulators are allowed to follow. In the PRC, it is the State Council that has final say.

The institutionalization of political concerns regarding foreign capital has the potential to help prevent retribution between the United States and China and lead to some equilibrium between these two economic powers. Any balance struck could be easily destabilized, however, by excessive review practices, under the guise of 'national security', that may actually be 'de facto' market-entry barriers for foreign competitors. As Chen points out, 'the nature of national security review is political'. Legal frameworks may be devised to institutionalize and regulate disputes, but the heat of controversy can make it difficult to contain tensions to a legal proceeding alone. China's rise is impacting on international legal and financial regimes. It would be paradoxical if the implemented socialist 'rule of law' reforms, as enforced by China in practice, lead to more clashes between China and the rest of world, at least in the short term. National security review is one example where this is possible.

Looking ahead: the thrust of the CPC's new grand narratives

The 'four comprehensives' narrative attempts to tie together the need for economic and legal reforms, Party discipline and the 'Chinese dream' of national rejuvenation.[10] The nexus of law reform and growth examined in this book reveals that China does not easily fit into any one paradigm for development. China's slowing growth rate has also triggered a new government phrase, 'the new normal', signifying the importance of deepening economic reforms as China presses hard to rebalance its economy – away from investment-led growth to a more consumption-driven economy. But this recalibration is not easy to achieve. Corruption remains problematic and crucial reforms in the state-owned sector are very difficult for the government, despite its determination to 'build the Chinese dream' and promulgate the four comprehensives (Hu, Chapter 8). The 'new normal' has significant implications for the progress of law reform. The 10 percent increase in the number of cases accepted by the People's Courts in 2014 over the previous year alone has serious resource implications; any prolonged economic slowdown will have direct ramifications for legal development generally.

This volume has highlighted the need to understand and disaggregate institutional contexts in which law reform takes place. We are reminded of the ongoing importance of skilled international diplomacy. Heightened tension that has characterized the South China Sea maritime disputes is a prime example. These disputes are best resolved through skillful negotiation and independent and impartial legal means, rather than the arbitrary imposition of any one country's domestic rules, or by force. For smaller countries, concerns about natural justice are being weighed against the imperatives of cooperating with an economic superpower under the leadership of a powerful and, as portrayed domestically in state-controlled media, popular corruption-fighter. In the trade context, Scott and Wilkinson (2012: 27–8) show how China's experiences within the WTO have led the PRC toward particular 'behavioral patterns', best understood in their historical context. When China acceded in 2001, the WTO, though only six years old, 'had more than 50 years of institutional history structuring how its diplomacy takes place. China's ability to influence these practices and procedures was, and is, highly circumscribed' (Scott and Wilkinson 2012: 27–8). Against this background, it is hardly surprising that China might pursue its goals more assertively at the international level.

Under the 'four comprehensives', governing by rule of law seems like a major step forward. It implies the CPC is itself subject to an impartial and independent authority. The chapters herein suggest, however, that this is not necessarily what the leaders intend. Although no organization can overstep China's constitution, the law is viewed more as *an instrument* to help advance China's interests and clean up the system, rather than as a way of placing checks on Party power. As Peerenboom (2014b: 20) says:

> Rule of law is a contested concept … and has served a wide variety of political agendas.… The CPC is entitled to put forth its own conception of rule of law, however, it cannot simply put an end to debates about the meaning of rule of law by championing its own particular conception, no matter how loudly it beats the drums or how high it raises the banner of socialist rule of law with Chinese characteristics.

Enforcing party discipline, including the use of various anti-corruption measures, shows the Party still polices itself. Some advances in judicial reform and procedural fairness are noted. It is also highly unlikely that Chinese leaders would want to unleash self-destructive nationalist forces. At the same time, there are signs in the domestication of international laws that do not bode well for international governance and legal ordering. Yet hope remains. In the long term, the current political campaign may be a surface storm that, once it passes, will have had little effect on deeper currents. China's fast-growing, computer-savvy, urban middle classes are becoming more aware of their rights. They will not be easily satisfied if the promise of a virtuous rule of law is not redeemed.

Notes

1 The Supreme Court President, Zhou Qiang, reporting to the NPC in 2015 shows the number of cases accepted by Chinese courts in 2014 (15,651,000) was up about 10 percent from the previous year. Over 63 percent of cases heard were civil (including commercial, family law and intellectual property cases). Criminal cases (including parole-related) accounted for just over 10 percent of cases (with many minor offences handled as administrative, rather than criminal). The dimensions of these figures reveal the sheer scale of the challenge to court and judicial reform. For comprehensive figures see: *Supreme People's Court Monitor* (March 15, 2015) at: http://supremepeoplescourtmonitor.com.

2 *The Economist* (March 21, 2015b: 24).

3 The *Patent Law of the PRC* was promulgated in 1984. In 1985, China acceded to the Paris Convention for the Protection of Industrial Property, followed by the Patent Cooperation Treaty in 1994. When China joined the WTO in 2001, it became a member of the TRIPS agreement. To comply with its international obligations, as well as to facilitate its own innovative development, China has subsequently amended its *Patent Law* three times: in 1992, 2000 and 2009.

4 *The Economist* (2015a: 25).

5 Ibid., at p. 25 claims

> corruption is worst in departments dealing with logistics, weapons procurement and political matters (the latter is in charge of maintaining party loyalty and appointments). Paying bribes for promotion is widespread and 9 of the 16 senior officers (15 being generals) recently disgraced were from the PLA's political wing.

6 Wen and Garnaut (2015) claim that the high priority Xi Jinping has given to the international operations of the domestic anti-corruption campaign, 'Fox Hunt' and 'Sky Net', 'has raised incentives and pressures for police officials at all tiers of Chinese government to bring fugitives back home and uncover hidden assets'.

7 Indeed, for many in Taiwan, the connection between Hong Kong's 2014–15 pro-democracy 'umbrella protests' and Taiwan's future is clearer. Beijing's refusal to grant any democratic voting concessions to Hong Kong has given Taiwanese activists insight into what they perceive to be the true nature of the 'one country, two systems' policy, which Beijing has proffered as a path to unification with the mainland.

8 *Lǐ zhí qì zhuàng* (理直氣壯) meaning 'bold and confident, with justice on one's side'.

9 At the time of writing, the International Bar Association's Human Rights Institute (IBAHRI) wrote to President Xi Jinping expressing concern at the number of lawyers, human rights activists and support staff who have faced arrest, questioning and detention in China since July 9, 2015. The IBAHRI letter indicates that 132 human rights lawyers had been summoned, arrested, questioned and/or detained by Government authorities across 24 provinces of China with some detained incommunicado; without access to legal counsel; unable to notify family members; and/or detained under residential surveillance and not in an officially recognized place of detention; see the letter at: tinyurl.com/oehn3wg.

10 See *BBC News China* (February 25, 2015) at: www.bbc.com/news/world-asia-china-31622571.

Bibliography

Abbott, K. and Snidal, D. (2000) 'Hard and Soft Law in International Governance', *International Organization*, 54 (3): 421–56.

Abbott, K., Keohane, R., Moravcsik, A., Slaughter, A. and Snidal, D. (2000) 'The Concept of Legalization', *International Organization*, 54 (3): 401–19.

Abramson, D.B. (2006) 'Urban Planning in China', *Journal of the American Planning Association*, 72 (2): 197–215.

Acemoglu, D. and Johnson, S. (2005) 'Unbundling Institutions', *Journal of Political Economy*, 113 (5): 949–95.

Acemoglu, D., Johnson, S. and Robinson, J. (2005) 'Institutions as the Fundamental Cause of Long-run Economic Growth', in P. Aghion and S. Durlauf (eds.), *Handbook of Economic Growth*, Amsterdam: Elsevier, pp. 385–472.

Aglietta, M. and Bai, Guo (2014) 'China's Roadmap to Harmonious Society: Third Plenum Decisions on Major Issues Concerning Comprehensively Deepening Reforms', *CEPII Policy Brief*, (3): 1–12.

Ahn, D. (2003) 'Korea in the GATT/WTO Dispute Settlement System: Legal Battle for Economic Development', *Journal of International Economic Law*, 6 (3): 597–633.

Ai, W. (2015) 'Shenru Bawo he Jianchi Wenhua Zixin', at: www.qstheory.cn/dukan/hqwg/2015-03/10/c_1114583418.htm [July 20].

Alford, W. (2000) 'The More Law, the More…? Measuring Legal Reform in the People's Republic of China', *Stanford Center for International Development*, Working Paper No. 59, Stanford University.

Allen, F., Qian, J. and Qian, M. (2005) 'Law, Finance and Economic Growth in China', *Journal of Financial Economics*, 77 (1): 57–116.

Amnesty International (1991) *China – Punishment without Crime: Administrative Detention*, ASA 17/27/91.

Amnesty International (1992) *Torture in China*, ASA 17/55/92.

Amnesty International (1996) *China: No One Is Safe*, ASA 17/01/96.

Anderson, J. (2011) 'Market Reform: Reflections on China's Economic System', in J. Garrick (ed.), *Law, Wealth and Power in China: Commercial Law Reforms in Context*, London: Routledge.

Baker & McKenzie (2011) 'Update on China's National Security Review Regime: List of Sensitive Industries Revealed', Client Alert, at: www.bakermckenzie.com/files/Uploads/Documents/China%20Update%202012/al_china_nationalsecurityreview_oct11.pdf.

Bayle, M.D. (1990) *Procedural Justice: Allocating to Individuals*, Dordrecht/Boston/London: Kluwer Academic Publishers.

BBC News (2012) 'Full Text of Speech by New Communist Party General Secretary Xi Jinping at the Politburo Standing Committee Members' Meeting with the Press, Great Hall of the People, Beijing', November 15, at: www.bbc.co.uk/news/world-asia-china-20338586.

BBC News (2013a) 'Bo Xilai Scandal: Timeline', November 11, at www.bbc.com/news/world-asia-china-17673505.

BBC News (2013b) 'Bo Xilai Trial as Blogged by the Court, Day 1', August 23, at www.bbc.com/news/world-asia-china-23777038.

BBC News (2013c) 'Bo Xilai Trial as Blogged by the Court, Day 2', August 23, at www.bbc.com/news/world-asia-china-23803063.

BBC News (2013d) 'Bo Xilai Trial as Blogged by the Court, Day 3', August 24, at www.bbc.co.uk/news/world-asia-china-23826587.

BBC News (2013e) 'China Media: Bo Xilai Verdict', September 19, at www.bbc.com/news/world-asia-china-24156578.

BBC News (2013f) 'China Media Discuss Bo Xilai's Sentence', September 23, at www.bbc.com/news/world-asia-china-24200752.

BBC News China (2015) 'China's Xi Jinping Unveils New "Four Comprehensives" Slogans', February 25, at: www.bbc.com/news/world-asia-china-31622571.

Beckman, R. (2013) 'The UN Convention on the Law of the Sea and the Maritime Disputes in the South China Sea', *American Journal of International Law*, 107 (1): 142–63.

Beckman, R. and Schofield, C. (2014) 'Defining EEZ Claims from Islands: A Potential South China Sea Change', *University of Wollongong Research Online*, at: http://ro.uow.edu.au/cgi/viewcontent.cgi?article=2414&context=lhapapers.

Beijing News (2014) 'Yifa Zhiguo ShouxianYao Yixian Zhiguo' [To Rule the County in Accordance with Law, We Must Rule in Accordance with the Constitution], *Xinjing Bao Wang*, October 17, at: www.bjnews.com.cn/news/2014/10/17/337633.html.

Beijing Youth Daily (2014) Zuigao Renmin Fayuan Yuan Yuanzhang Jianyi Zai Quanguo Renda Zengshe Xianfa Weiyuanhui [Former SPC President Recommends Adding a Constitutional Supervision Committee under the NPC], *Beijing Qingnian Bao*, November 8, at: http://politics.people.com.cn/n/2014/1108/c70731-25993887.html.

Bennett, Y.C. (2012) 'Chinese Contract Law after the UN Convention on Contracts for the International Sale of Goods', in J. Garrick (ed.), *Law and Policy for China's Market Socialism*, London: Routledge.

Berkowitz, D., Pistor, K. and Richard, J. (2003) 'Economic Development, Legality, and the Transplant Effect', *European Economic Review*, 47 (1): 165–95.

Bertaud, A. (2012) 'Government Intervention and Urban Land Markets: The Case of China', *Journal of Architectural and Planning Research*, 29 (4): 335–46.

Blankenagel, A. (1992) 'Toward Constitutionalism in Russia', *East European Constitutional Review*, 1: 25–8.

Bo, Peng (2014) 'Judicial Reform Strengthens Judges' Responsibility', July 23, *People's Daily*.

Bowen v. Mich. Acad. of Family Physicians, 476 U.S. 667 (1986).

Branigan, T. (2013) 'Xi Jinping Vows to Fight "Tigers and Flies" in Anti-Corruption Drive', *Guardian*, January 22, at: www.theguardian.com/world/2013/jan/22/xi-jinping-tigers-flies-corruption.

Brown, C.P. (2005) 'Participation in WTO Dispute Settlement: Complainants, Interested Parties, and Free Riders', *World Bank Economic Review*, 19 (2): 287–310.

Brzezinski, M.F. (1993) 'The Emergence of Judicial Review in Eastern Europe: The Case of Poland', *American Journal of Comparative Law*, 41: 153–200.

Buckley, C. (2013) 'Vows of Change in China Belie Private Warning', *New York Times*, February 14.

Bui Ngoc Son (2014) 'The Discourse of Constitutional Review in Vietnam', *Journal of Comparative Law*, 9: 191–221.

Burkank, S., Farhang, S. and Kritzer H. (2011) 'Private Enforcement of Statutory and Administrative Law in the United States and Other Common Law Countries', November 16, *SSRN*, at: http://papers.ssrn.com/sol3/papers.cfm?abstract_id=1781047.

Busch, M.L., Reinhardt, E. and Shaffer, G. (2009) 'Does Legal Capacity Matter? A Survey of WTO Members', *World Trade Review*, 8 (4): 559–77.

Butler, W.E. (1988) *Soviet Law*, London: Butterworths.

Butler, W.E. (1991) *Basic Documents of the Soviet Legal System*, New York: Oceana Publications.

Cai, Dingjian (1995) 'Constitutional Supervision and Interpretation in the People's Republic of China', *Journal of Chinese Law*, 9: 219–45.

Cai, Dingjian (1999) 'Preliminary Comments on the Reform of the Court System', *Strategies and Management* [*Zhanlü yu Guanli*], 1: 97–102.

Cai, Dingjian (2007) 'Fagui Bei'an Shencha Bu Shi Weixian Shencha' [Filing and Review of Regulations Is Not Constitutional Review], *Zhongguo Mingshang Falü Wang*, June 16.

Cai, Fang (2009) 'China's Future Demographic Dividend: Digging New Source of Economic Growth', *Chinese Journal of Population Science* [*Zhongguo Renkou Kexue*], 23: 1.

Cai, Fang and Lu, Yang (2013) 'Population Change and Resulting Slowdown in Potential GDP Growth in China', *China and World Economy*, 21: 2.

Caixin Online (2014a) 'Unemployment among Disabled Exceeds 10%', October 1, at: http://china.caixin.com/2014-10-01/100735095.html.

Caixin Online (2014b) 'The Predicament of Disability Guarantee Funds', June 5, at: http://china.caixin.com/2014-06-05/100686574.html.

Califano v. Sanders, 430 U.S. 99 (1977)

Cao, Siyuan (2005) 'Shijie xianzheng chaoliu: geguo xianfa bijiao' [The World Trend of Constitutionalism: A Comparison of Constitutions in Countries of the World], May 4, at: www.chinesepen.org/Article/sxsy/201112/Article_20111213050822.shtml.

Carlson, A. (2005) *Unifying China, Integrating with the World: Securing Chinese Sovereignty in the Reform Era*, Stanford, CA: Stanford University Press.

CCP (2010) 'A Proposal about the 12th Five Year Plan for National Economic Development', Beijing: People's Publishing House.

CCP Central Organisation Department, CCP Central Propaganda Department and Ministry of Education (2013) 'Guanyu jiaqiang he gaijin gaoxiao qingnian jiaoshi sixiang zhengzhi gongzuo de ruogan yijian' [Some Suggestions to Strengthen and Improve the Ideological and Political Work Regarding Young Academics in Universities], May, at: www.moe.edu.cn/publicfiles/business/htmlfiles/moe/s7060/201305/152333.html.

CCP Centre and State Council (1996) 'Regulations on Strengthening Public Security Work in the Great Proletarian Cultural Revolution', in M. Schoenhals (ed.). *The Cultural Revolution, 1966–1969: Not a Dinner Party*, Armonk, NY: M.E. Sharpe, pp. 49–51.

CCTV (2014) 'Ralls Won the Case against Obama: An Unprecedented Victory', at: http://jingji.cntv.cn/2014/07/16/ARTI1405498954676698.shtml.

Chan, Kam Wing (2012) 'Crossing the 50 Percent Population Rubicon: Can China Urbanize to Prosperity?' *Eurasian Geography and Economics*, 53 (1): 63–86.

Chan, Kam Wing (2014) 'China's Urbanization 2020: A New Blueprint and Direction', *Eurasian Geography and Economics*, 55 (1): 1–9.

Chan, M. (2014) 'Xi Says Party Must Embrace Mao Spirit to Survive, Xi Jinping Quoted as Saying', *South China Morning Post*, September 28, at: www.scmp.com/news/china/article/1602828/party-must-embrace-mao-spirit-survive-xi-jinping-quoted-saying?page=all.

Chang, Wen-Chen, Thio, Li-ann, Tan, Kevin and Yeh, Jiunn-rong (2014) *Constitutionalism in Asia: Cases and Materials*, Oxford: Hart Publishing.

Chen, Binkai, Lu Min and Zhong, Ninhua (2010) 'Household Consumption Constrained by Hukou System', *Economic Research Journal* (Jingji Yanjiu), 56: S1.

Chen, D. (2009) 'China's Participation in the International Human Rights Regime: A State Identity Perspective', *The Chinese Journal of International Politics*, 2 (3): 399–419.

Chen, Guangzhong (1989) 'Forty Years of the Chinese Criminal Procedure Science', *Journal of the China University of Political Science and Law* [*Zhengfa Luntan*], Pt I in no. 4, at 5–14; Pt. II in no. 5, at 1–8.

Chen, Guangzhong (ed.) (2005) *The Procedure on Criminal Re-trial and the Protection of Human Rights* [*Xingshi Zaishen Chengxu yu Renquan Baozhang*], Beijing: Beijing University Press.

Chen, Guo (2012) 'Housing the Urban Poor in Post-reform China: Some Empirical Evidence from the City of Nanjing', *Cities*, 29: 252–63.

Chen, Jianfu (1997) 'A Moderate Step in a Right Direction: The Revision of the Criminal Procedure Law in the PRC', *Journal of Chinese and Comparative Law*, 3 (1): 120.

Chen, Jianfu (2008) *Chinese Law: Context and Transformation*, Leiden/Boston: Martinus Nijhoff Publishers.

Chen, Jianfu (2013) *Criminal Law and Criminal Procedure Law in the People's Republic of China: Commentary and Legislation*, Leiden/Boston: Martinus Nijhoff Publishers.

Chen, Jing (2009) 'Explaining the Change in China's Attitude toward UN Peacekeeping: A Norm Change Perspective', *The Journal of Contemporary China*, 18 (58): 157–73.

Chen, Juan and Yang, Shaolei (2014) 'Rural Land Property Right System of China: Defects and Solutions', *Canadian Social Science*, 10 (2): 75–83.

Chen, Mingxing, Liu, Weidong and Tao, Xiaoli (2013) 'Evolution and Assessment on China's Urbanization 1960–2010: Under-urbanization or over-urbanization?', *Habitat International*, 38: 25–33.

Chen, Weitseng (2013) 'Institutional Arbitrage: China's Economic Power Projection and International Capital Markets', *Columbia Journal of Asian Law*, 26 (2): 347.

Chen, Weitseng (2014) 'From the Middle East to the Far West: What Can Chinese Overseas Investments Tell Us about Law and Development and Global Regulatory Regimes?' in N. Lenze and C. Schriwer (eds.), *Converging Regions: Global Perspectives on Asia and the Middle East*, London: Ashgate.

Chen, Z. (2003) 'Capital Markets and Legal Development: The China Case', *China Economic Review*, 14 (4): 451–72.

Cheney v. U.S. District Court for District of Columbia, 542 U.S. 367 (2004).

China Law and Governance Review (2004) 'Luoyang City "Seed" Case Highlights Chinese Courts' Lack of Authority to Declare Laws Invalid', June, No. 2, at: www.chinareview.info/issue2/pages/case.htm.

China News (2014) 'Ralls Won the Case against Obama in the US Court of Appeals', at: http://finance.chinanews.com/cj/2014/07-16/6391792.shtml.

China News Weekly (2013) 'First Gender Discrimination Lawsuit Not Accepted [by Court] for One Year: Judge Awaits Approval from Superiors', August 2, at: http://news.sina.com.cn/c/sd/2013-08-02/164227846264.shtml.

China Women's Journal (2014) 'Replicate Xinle's Experience to Promote Equal Employment', March 20, at: http://acwf.people.com.cn/n/2014/0320/c99013-24685120.html.

China Xinhua News Network (2013) 'Graduates Repeatedly Encounter Employment Discrimination Chinese Style: Experts Call for Legislation for Breakthrough' [citing a notice issued in April 2013 by the Ministry of Education prohibiting employment discrimination at college job fairs], May 22, at: www.chinanews.com/edu/2013/05-22/4841996.shtml.

China Xinhua News Network (2014) 'Graduating Class Fully Encompassing the Post-90s Generation: More Realistic about Jobs' [citing a joint study in 2014 by Ganji.com and Peking University entitled 'Ganji.com Report on Post-90s Generation Employment'], July 30, at: http://finance.chinanews.com/it/2014/07-30/6441526.shtml.

Chinese Human Rights Defenders (2015) 'Silencing the Messenger: 2014 Annual Report on the Situation of Human Rights Defenders in China', March, at: www.chrdnet.com/wp-content/uploads/2015/03/Silencing-the-Messenger_2014-Annual-Report-on-the-Situation-of-Human-Rights-Defenders-in-China 1.pdf.

Cho, S. (2012) 'Beyond Rationality: A Sociological Construction of the World Trade Organization', *Virginia Journal of International Law*, 52 (2): 321–54.

Chong, D. (2000) *Rational Lives: Norms and Values in Politics and Society*, Chicago; London: University of Chicago Press.

Choo, C. and Yin, X. (2000) 'Contract Management Responsibility System and Profit Incentives in China's State-owned Enterprises', *China Economic Review*, 11 (1): 98–112.

Christensen, T.J. (2007) The Deputy Assistant Secretary for East Asian and Pacific Affairs Remarks Before the U.S. China Economic and Security Review Commission (delivered by John Norris, Director of the Office of Chinese and Mongolian Affairs), *The State Department*, Washington, DC, February 2, at: http://2001-2009.state.gov/p/eap/rls/rm/2007/79866.htm.

Chuang, J. (2014) 'China's Rural Land Politics: Bureaucratic Absorption and the Muting of Rightful Resistance', *The China Quarterly*, 219: 649–69.

Clarke, D.C. (2003a) 'Corporate Governance in China: An Overview', *China Economic Review*, 14 (4): 494–507.

Clarke, D.C. (2003b) 'Economic Development and the Rights Hypothesis: The China Problem', *American Journal of Comparative Law*, 51: 89–111.

Clarke, D.C. (2013) Email to *CHINALAW*@hermes.gwu.edu, August 22.

Clarke, D.C. (2014) 'The Fourth Plenum's "Decision": My Take', October 29, at: http://lawprofessors.typepad.com/china_law_prof_blog/2014/10/the-fourth-plenums-decision-my-take.html.

Coalition for the International Criminal Court (2015) 'Our History', at: www.iccnow.org/?mod=cicchistory (accessed January 23, 2015).

Coase, R. (1937) 'The Nature of the Firm', *Economica*, 4 (16): 386–405.

Coffee, Jr., J.C. (2001) 'The Rise of Dispersed Ownership: The Roles of Law and the States in the Separation of Ownership and Control', *Yale Law Journal*, 111 (1): 1–82.

Cohen, J. (2013a) 'Bo Xilai's Trial Underlines Need for Cross-Examination in Court', *South China Morning Post*, August 27, at: www.scmp.com/comment/insight-opinion/article/1299512/bo-xilais-trial-underlines-need-cross-examination-court.

Cohen, J. (2013b) 'Criminal Justice in China: From the Gang of Four to Bo Xilai', *Human Rights Watch*, July 25, at: www.hrw.org/news/2013/07/25/criminal-justice-china-gang-four-bo-xilai.

Cohen, J. (2014a) 'Struggling for Justice: China's Courts and the Challenge of Reform', *World Politics Review*, January 14, at: www.worldpoliticsreview.com/articles/13495/struggling-for-justice-chinas-courts-and-the-challenge-of-reform.

Cohen, J. (2014b) 'China's Socialist Rule of Law Still Offers Real Hope of Improvements to Legal System', *South China Morning Post*, at: www.scmp.com/comment/insight-opinion/article/1631895/chinas-socialist-rule-law-still-offers-real-hope.

Commentator of *Qiushi Magazine* (2013) 'Yike ye buneng fangcong he xueruo yishi xingtai gongzuo: renzhen xuexi shixing quanguo xuanchuan sixiang gongzuo huiyi jingshen' [We Cannot Slacken or Weaken in Ideological Work Even for One Moment: Earnestly Study and Implement the Spirit of the National Propaganda and Ideology Work Conference], September 1, at: https://chinacopyrightandmedia.wordpress.com/2013/09/01.

Congressional-Executive Commission on China (CECC) (2012) *Prospects for Reforming China's Reeducation through Labor System*, May 9.

Conti, J.A. (2010) 'Learning to Dispute: Repeat Participation, Expertise, and Reputation at the World Trade Organization', *Law and Social Inquiry*, 35 (3): 625–62.

Cooley, A. and Spruyt, H. (2009) *Contracting States: Sovereign Transfers in International Relations*, Princeton, NJ: Princeton University Press.

Council of Supply Chain Management Professionals (2012) 'Research Survey Results', at: https://cscmp.org/member-benefits/survey-results.

CPC Central Committee (2013) 'Decision Concerning Several Major Issues in Comprehensively Deepening Reform', November 15, at: http://news.xinhuanet.com/politics/2013-11/15/c_118164235.htm.

CPC Central Committee (2014) 'CCP Central Committee Decision Concerning Some Major Questions Comprehensively Moving Governing the Country According to Law Forward', at: https://chinacopyrightandmedia.wordpress.com/2014/10/28.

Creemers, R. (2014) 'China's Constitutionalism Debate: Content, Context, and Implications', *SSRN*, at: http://papers.ssrn.com/sol3/papers.cfm?abstract_id=2511526.

Cui, E., Tao, R., Warner, T.J. and Yang, D.L. (2014) 'How Do Land Takings Affect Political Trust in Rural China?' *Political Studies*, 63: 91–109.

Cui, Min (1995) 'A Summary of the Discussions on Revising and Perfecting the Criminal Procedure Law', *Modern Law Science* [*Xiandai Faxue*], 1: 92.

Cull, R. and Xu, L.C. (2005) 'Institutions, Ownership, and Finance: The Determinants of Profit Reinvestment among Chinese Firms', *Journal of Financial Economics*, 77 (1): 117–46.

Dam, K.W. (2006) *The Law–Growth Nexus: The Rule of Law and Economic Development*, Washington, DC: The Brookings Institution.

Davis, C.L. and Shirato, Y. (2007) 'Firms, Governments, and WTO Adjudication: Japan's Selection of WTO Disputes', *World Politics*, 59 (2): 274–313.

Davis, K.C. (1972) *Administrative Law Text* (3rd edn.), St Paul, MN: West Publishing Co.

Defense Production Act (US) (1950), codified as amended at 50 U.S.C. app. §2170.

deLisle, J. (2012) 'Exceptional – and Ordinary – Powers in an Exceptional State: Patterns and Lessons from China's Use of Law to Address Threats to Security and Order', unpublished presentation at Cornell Law School, October 18.

deLisle, J. (2014) 'Law and the Economy in China', in G.C. Chow and D.H. Perkins (eds.), *Routledge Handbook of the Chinese Economy*, London: Routledge.

Deng, Feng (2013) 'Land Development Right and Collective Ownership in China', *Post-Communist Economies*, 25 (2): 190–205.

Department of the Treasury (US) (2008) 'Regulations Pertaining to Mergers, Acquisitions and Takeovers by Foreign Persons', 31 CFR Part 800, RIN 1505-AB88.

Dowdle, M. (2002) 'Of Parliaments, Pragmatism, and the Dynamics of Constitutional Development: The Curious Case of China', *New York University Journal of International Law*, 35: 1–200.

Du, J. and Xu, C. (2006) 'Regional Competition and Regulatory Decentralization: Case of China', Working Paper, Chinese University of Hong Kong, London School of Economics and Hong Kong University of Science and Technology.

Du, J. and Xu, C. (2009) 'Which Firms Went Public in China? A Study of Financial Market Regulation', *World Development* (Special Issue on Law, Finance, and Economic Growth in China), 37 (4): 812–24.

Du, Jinfeng and Peiser, R.B. (2014) 'Land Supply, Pricing and Local Governments' Land Hoarding in China', *Regional Science and Urban Economics*, 48: 180–9.

Dutton, P.A. (2010) 'Three Disputes and Three Objectives: China and the South China Sea', at: www.usnwc.edu/getattachment/feb516bf-9d93-4d5c-80dc-d5073ad84d9b/Three-Disputes-and-Three-Objectives-China-and-the (accessed April 21, 2015).

Dutton, P.A. (2014) Testimony before the House Foreign Affairs Committee Hearing on China's Maritime Disputes in the East and South China Seas, January 14, Washington, DC, at: http://unclosdebate.org/citation/1332/testimonty-peter-dutton-chinas-maritime-disputes-east-and-south-china-seas.

The Economist (2013) 'Mixed messages: Xi Jinping Signals Left While Turning Right. Or Is It the Other Way Round?' June 29, at: www.economist.com/news/china/21580195-xi-jinping-signals-left-while-turning-right-or-it-other-way-round-mixed-messages.

The Economist (2014) 'Corruption: Less Party Time', January 25, at: www.economist.com/news/china/21595029-communist-partys-anti-graft-campaign-has-had-surprising-impact-new-report-shows-how.

The Economist (2015a) 'Xi Jinping Flexes His Muscle against Army Corruption', February 14, pp. 25–6.

The Economist (2015b) 'Beijing: A Bad Day for Women', March 21, p. 24.

Economy, E. and Oksenberg, M. (eds.) (1999) *China Joins the World: Progress and Prospects*, New York: Council on Foreign Relations Press.

Editor (2003) 'Supreme Court Brings "Liu Yong Case" to Trial Today with Two Suspense', *Beijing Morning Post*, December 18.

Editor (2008) 'The Yunnan Version of "Xu Ting Case" May Change Its Sentencing', *Chutian Metropolitan Daily*, April 16.

Editor (2009) 'Deng Yujiao's Mother Suddenly "Fired" Lawyer', *Oriental Morning Post*, May 24.

Editor (2014) 'Interpreting the Shanghai Plan of Judicial Reform Requires Massive Detailed Implementation Measures', *People's Daily*, July 15.

Elkins, Z., Guzman, A.T. and Simmons, B.A. (2006) 'Competing for Capital: The Diffusion of Bilateral Investment Treaties, 1960–2000', *International Organization*, 60 (4): 811–46.

Ellickson, R.C. (1991) *Order Without Law: How Neighbors Settle Disputes*, Cambridge, MA: Harvard University Press.

El-Shifa Pharm. Indus. Co. v. U.S., 607 F.3d 836 (D.C. Cir. 2010).

Engels, F. (1990) 'The 1891 Preface to Marx's Civil War in France', in Karl Marx and Frederick Engels, *Collected Works, Vol. 26*, New York: International Publisher, pp. 357–98.

Epstein, R.A. and Rose, A.M. (2009) 'The Regulation of Sovereign Wealth Funds: The Virtues of Going Slow', *University of Chicago Law Review*, 76: 111.

Equal Employment Opportunity Commission of the United States (1997–2014) 'EEOC Charge and Litigation Statistics FY1997-FY2014', at: http://eeoc.gov/eeoc/statistics/enforcement/charges.cfm and www.eeoc.gov/eeoc/statistics/enforcement/litigation.cfm.

Equal Employment Promotion Law of the People's Republic of China (2008) at: www.gov.cn/flfg/2007-08/31/content_732597.htm.

Fan, G. (1994) 'Incremental Change and Dual-tack Transition: Understanding the Case of China', *Economic Policy*, 19(Supp.): 99–122.

Fan, G. (2003) 'China's Nonperforming Loans and National Comprehensive Liability', *Asian Economic Papers*, 2 (1): 145–52.

Fan, J.P.H., Morck, R., Xu, L.C. and Yeung, B. (2009) 'Institutions and Foreign Direct Investment: China versus the Rest of the World', *World Development*, Special Issue on Law, Finance and Economic Growth in China.

Fan, Yu (2012) 'Alternative Dispute Resolution in China', in Garrick, J. (ed.) *Law and Policy for China's Market Socialism*, London: Routledge.

Farhang, S. (2010) *The Litigation State: Public Regulation and Private Lawsuits in the United States*, Princeton University Press, at: http://press.princeton.edu/chapters/s9350.pdf.

Feldbrugge, F.J.M. (1993) *The End of the Soviet System and the Role of Law*, Dordrecht: Martinus Nijhoff.

Feldstein, M. (2011) 'On the End of China's Surplus', *Project Syndicate*, at: www.project-syndicate.org/commentary/the-end-of-china-s-surplus.

Feng, Chongyi (2008) 'Democrats within the Chinese Communist Party Since 1989', *Journal of Contemporary China*, 17 (57): 673–88.

Feng, Chongyi (2011) 'The Changing Political Identity of the "Overseas Chinese" in Australia', *Cosmopolitan Civil Societies: An Interdisciplinary Journal*, 3 (1): 121–38.

Feng, Chongyi (2013) 'Preserving Stability and Rights Protection in Contemporary China: Conflict or Coherence?' *Journal of Current Chinese Affairs*, 2 (2): 21–50.

Feng, Qi and Su, Degeng (2000) 'How to Reform the Court Institution' [Fayuan Zhidu Ruhe Gaige], *People's Court Daily*, April 28.

Finance.china.com.cn (2012) 'Yin Weimin: Most Concerned with Migrant Workers and College Graduate Employment', March 9, at: http://finance.china.com.cn/roll/2012 0308/575863.shtml.

Foot, R. (2000) *Rights beyond Borders: The Global Community and the Struggle over Human Rights in China*, New York: Oxford University Press.

Foreign Investment and National Security Act (US) (2007).

Foreman, C.J. (1989) 'Omnibus Trade and Competitiveness Act of 1988: Putting the Brakes on Foreign Investment', *Georgia Journal of International and Comparative Law*, 19: 175.

Franck, T.M. and Thiruvengadam, A.K. (2003) *International Law and Constitution-Making*, at: http://chinesejil.oxfordjournals.org/content/2/2/467.full.pdf.

Franks, J.R., Mayer, C. and Rossi, S. (2009) 'Ownership: Evolution and Control', *Review of Financial Studies*, 22 (10): 4009–56.

Fravel, M.T. (2008) *Strong Borders, Secure Nation: Cooperation and Conflict in China's Territorial Disputes*, Princeton, NJ: Princeton University Press.

Freedom House (2015) 'The Politburo's Predicament: Confronting the Limitations of Chinese Communist Party Repression', January, at: http:/freedomhouse.org/sites/default/files/12222014_FH_ChinaReport2014_FINAL.pdf.

Fu, Heping and Wei, Lei (2000) 'A Preliminary Inquiry on the Establishment of the Institution of Professional Secretaries' [Zhiye Shujiguan Zhidu Goujian Chutan], *People's Court Daily*, May 26.

Fu, Hualing (2014) 'Wielding the Sword: President Xi's New Anti-Corruption Campaign', University of Hong Kong Faculty of Law, Research Paper No. 2014/030, at: http://papers.ssrn.com/sol3/papers.cfm?abstract_id=2492407.

Garlicki, L. (1987) 'Constitutional and Administrative Courts as Custodians of the State Constitutions: The Experience in East European Countries', *Tulane Law Review*, 61: 1285–306.

Garlicki, L. (1988) 'Constitutional Developments in Poland', *St. Louis University Law Journal*, 32: 713–35.

Garnaut, J. (2012) *The Rise and Fall of the House of Bo*, Melbourne: Penguin Specials.

Garnaut, J. (2013) 'The East Is Still Red: Bo Xilai's Downfall Doesn't Mean China Is Moving Away from Mao', *Foreign Policy*, August 22, at: http://foreignpolicy.com/2013/08/22/the-east-is-still-red.

Garrick, J. (2011) *Law, Wealth and Power in China: Commercial Law Reforms in Context*, London: Routledge.

Garrick, J. (2012) *Law and Policy for China's Market Socialism*, London: Routledge.

General Office of the CPC Central Committee (2013a) 'Communiqué on the Current State of the Ideological Sphere', April, at: https://chinacopyrightandmedia.wordpress.com/2013/04/22.

General Office of the CPC Central Committee (2013b) 'Notice Regarding Employment and Job Creation for 2013 Graduates from Regular Institutions of Higher Learning', May 16, at: www.gov.cn/zwgk/2013-05/16/content_2404378.htm.

General Office of the CPC Central Committee (2014) 'Notice Regarding Employment and Job Creation for 2014 Graduates from Regular Institutions of Higher Learning', May 13, at: www.gov.cn/zhengce/content/2014-05/13/content_8802.htm.

General Office of the CPC Central Committee (2015) 'Opinions Concerning Further Strengthening and Improving Propaganda and Ideology Work in Higher Education under New Circumstances', January 19, at: https://chinacopyrightandmedia.wordpress.com/2015/01/19.

Georgiev, D. and van der Borght, K. (2006) *Reform and Development of the WTO Dispute Settlement System*, London: Cameron May.

Ginsburg, T. (2003) *Judicial Review in New Democracies: Constitutional Courts in Asian Cases*, Cambridge: Cambridge University Press.

Ginsburg, T. and Moustafa, T. (eds.) (2008) *Rule by Law: The Politics of Courts in Authoritarian Regimes*, Cambridge: Cambridge University Press.

Glaeser, E., La Porta, R., Lopez-de-Silanes, F. and Shleifer, A. (2004) 'Do Institutions Cause Growth?' *Journal of Economic Growth*, 9: 271–303.

Goldstein, J., Kahler, M., Keohane, R. and Slaughter, A. (2000) 'Introduction: Legalization and World Politics', *International Organization*, 54 (3): 385–99.

Graham, E.M. and Marchick, D.M. (2006) *U.S. National Security and Foreign Direct Investment*, Washington, DC: Peterson Institute of International Economics.

Green, S. (2014) 'Protecting Trademarks in China', *Law Society Journal*, 52 (3): 56–8.

Groves, T., Hong, Y., McMillan, J. and Naughton, B. (1995) 'China's Evolving Managerial Market', *Journal of Political Economy*, 103 (4): 873–92.

Gu, Angran (1989) *The Socialist Legal System and Legislative Work* [*Shehui Zhuyi Fazhi He Lifa Gongzuo*], Beijing: China University of Political Science and Law Press.

Guangming Daily (2014) 'Overt and Hidden Restrictions: How Female College Students Overcome Employment Discrimination' [citing surveys by the All China Women's Federation 'Guangzhou Female College Students Investigation Report' and the Media and Gender Research Center, Communication University of China], May 5, at: http://news.xinhuanet.com/edu/2014-05/05/c_126460827.htm.

Guardian (2009) 'Chinese Woman Who Killed Official Bailed after Online Outcry', May 27, at: www.theguardian.com/world/2009/may/27/china-bails-deng-yujiao.

Guo, Jinchao (2014) 'Li Keqiang: China's Huge Foreign Exchange Rate Reserve Is a Ponderous Burden', *Chinanews*, at: http://finance.ifeng.com/a/20140511/12307297_0.shtml.

Guo, Y. (2011) 'In Search of Wealth and Power: The Character of the Chinese State and Limits to Change', in J. Garrick (ed.), *Law, Wealth and Power in China: Commercial Law Reforms in Context*, London: Routledge.

Guoxing, J. (2009) 'The Legality of the "Impeccable Incident" ', *Security*, 5 (2): 16–21.

Guzman, A. and Simmons, B.A. (2002) *To Settle or Empanel? An Empirical Analysis of Litigation and Settlement at the World Trade Organization*, Chicago: University of Chicago Press.

Guzman, A. and Simmons, B.A. (2005) 'Power Plays and Capacity Constraints: The Selection of Defendants in World Trade Organization Disputes', *Journal of Legal Studies*, 34 (2): 557–98.

Haley, J.O. (1978) 'The Myth of the Reluctant Litigant', *Journal of Japanese Studies*, 4 (2): 359–90.

Halliday, T.C. and Shaffer, G. (eds.) (2015) *Transnational Legal Orders*, New York: Cambridge University Press.

Hand, K. (2007) 'Using Law for a Righteous Purpose: The Sun Zhigang Incident and Evolving Forms of Citizen Action in the People's Republic of China', *Columbia Journal of Transnational Law*, 45: 114–95.

Hand, K. (2011) 'Resolving Constitutional Disputes in Contemporary China', *University of Pennsylvania East Asia Law Review*, 7: 51–159.

Hand, K. (2013) 'Understanding China's System for Addressing Legislative Conflicts: Capacity Challenges and the Search for Legislative Harmony', *Columbia Journal of Asian Law*, 26: 139–265.

Hatton, C. (2013) 'Famous Trials of China's Communist Party', *BBC News*, August 21, at: www.bbc.co.uk/news/world-asia-china-23765803.

Hausmaninger, H. (1992) 'From the Soviet Committee on Constitutional Supervision to the Russian Constitutional Court', *Cornell International Law Journal*, 25: 305–37.

He, Baogang and Warren, M. (2011) 'Authoritarian Deliberation: The Deliberative Turn in Chinese Political Development', *Perspectives on Politics*, 9: 268–89.

He, Bing (2008) 'Is Judicial Democracy a False Proposition?' *Economic Observer Daily*, August 28.

He, Haibo (2012) 'The Perplexity of Administrative Litigation', *Journal of the East China University of Political Science and Law*, 2, at: http://article.chinalawinfo.com/Article_Detail.asp?ArticleID=68848 (accessed February 24, 2014).

He, Rikai (1999) 'The Judicial Reform: From Power to Authority' [Sifa gaige: Cong Quanli Zouxiang Quanwei], *Law Science* [*Falü Kexue*], 4: 30–8.

He, W. (2013) 'Bo Xilai Trial Was a Satire – But Advanced the Rule of Law in China', *CS Monitor*, August 29, at: www.csmonitor.com/Commentary/Global-Viewpoint/2013/0829/Bo-Xilai-trial-was-a-satire-but-still-helped-to-further-rule-of-law-in-China.

He, Weifang (2000) 'The Road toward Judicial Reform' [Sifa Gaige zhi Lu] (Part II), *Beijing University Law Information* [*Beida Falü Xinxi*], 4: 3.

Hebei Legal Daily (2013) 'Xinle Says No to Employment Discrimination', June 13, at: http://szbz.hbfzb.com/html/2013-06/13/content_25913.htm?div=-1.

Hebei Workers Daily (2013) 'Xinle's Experiment to Promote Equal Employment', June 29, at: www.hbgrb.net/epaper/images/2013-06/29/7B/WQZX7bWQZX7BC629_0001.PDF.

Heilmann, S. and Perry, E. (2013) 'Embracing Uncertainty: Guerrilla Policy Style and Adaptive Governance in China', *China Analysis*, 103: 1–29.

HLR Note (1985) 'Note: Concept of Law in the Chinese Anti-Crime Campaign', *Harvard Law Review*, 98: 1890.

Ho, N.P. (2012) 'Organized Crime in China: The Chongqing Crackdown', in J. Garrick (ed.), *Law and Policy for China's Market Socialism*, London: Routledge, pp. 202–14.

Ho, P. (2006) *Institutions in Transition: Land Ownership, Property Rights and Social Conflict in China*, Oxford: Oxford University Press.

Holmes, S. (2003) 'Lineage of the Rule of Law', in J.M. Maravall and A. Przeworski (eds.), *Democracy and the Rule of Law*, Cambridge: Cambridge University Press.

Hooghe, L. (2005) 'Several Roads Lead to International Norms, but Few via International Socialization: A Case Study of the European Commission', *International Organization* (International Institutions and Socialization in Europe), 59 (4): 861–98.

Hsiung, J. (1981) 'Introduction: The Trial of the "Gang of Four" and Its Implication in China', *Maryland Series in Contemporary Asian Studies*, 3: 1–4.

Hu, R. (2011) 'Property, Wealth and Law Reforms in China's Urban Revolution', in J. Garrick (ed.), *Law, Wealth and Power in China: Commercial Law Reforms in Context*, London and New York: Routledge, pp. 199–217.

Hu, R. (2012) 'Understanding Chinese Real Estate: The Property-boom in Perspective', in J. Garrick (ed.), *Law and Policy for China's Market Socialism*, London and New York: Routledge, pp. 87–100.

Hu, R. (2013a) 'Drivers of China's Urbanisation and Property Development', *Australasian Journal of Regional Studies*, 19 (2): 156–80.

Hu, R. (2013b) 'China's Paradoxical Reforms on Land and Real Estate Property Markets', *Global Built Environment Review*, 8 (3): 11–21.

Huang, J. and Rozelle, S. (1996) 'Technological Change: The Re-discovery of the Engine of Productivity Growth in China's Rural Economy', *Journal of Development Economics*, 49: 337–69.

Huang, Jinrong (2010) 'Gongyi Shangshu de Xingdong Luoji' [The Operational Logic of Public Interest Litigation], *Fazhi yu Shehui Fazhan* [*Development of the Legal System and Society*], 4: 135–7.

Huang, S. (2012) 'Li Zhuang: Chinese Defense Lawyer Who Was Found Guilty of Suborning Perjury', *The Wrongful Convictions Blog*, March 31, at: http://wrongfulconvictionsblog.org/2012/03/31/li-zhuang-chinese-defense-lawyer-who-was-found-guilty-of-suborning-perjury.

Huaxia Times (2014) 'MOHRSS: Only 7% Employment among 7.27 Million College Graduates', August 2, at: http://finance.ifeng.com/a/20140802/12846723_0.shtml.

Hui, Eddie Chi Man, Bao, Hai Jun and Zhang, Xiao Ling (2013) 'The Policy and Praxis of Compensation for Land Expropriations in China: An Appraisal from the Perspective of Social Exclusion', *Land Use Policy*, 32: 309–16.

Human Rights Watch (1989–2013) *World Reports*, at: www.hrw.org/node/79288.

Human Rights Watch (2008) *'Walking on Thin Ice': Control, Intimidation and Harassment of Lawyers in China*, April, at: www.hrw.org (accessed March 26, 2012).

Hurst, W.J., Kinkel, J. and Sowash, A. (2012) 'Implementing China's Labor Law Reforms: Interests and Obligations at the Firm Level', in J. Garrick (ed.), *Law and Policy for China's Market Socialism*, London: Routledge.

International Criminal Court (2001) *Rome Statute of the International Criminal Court*, The Hague: International Criminal Court.

International Monetary Fund (2012) 'People's Republic of China: 2012 Article IV Consultation', IMF Country Report No. 12/195.

Investigation Center of Chinese Social Sciences, Peking University (2014) *Report on Chinese People's Livelihood Development*, Beijing: Peking University Publishing House.

Japan Patent Office (2013) 'The Number of Applications and Registrations in 2013', at: www.jpo.go.jp/torikumi_e/hiroba_e/2013syutsugan_kensuu_e.htm.

Jefferson, G.H. and Rawski, T. (2002) 'China's Emerging Market for Property Rights', *Economics of Transition*, 10 (2): 585–617.

Ji, Weidong (2003) 'Hexianxing Shencha Zhidu de "Liangbu Zou" Silu' [The Two Step Road to a Constitutionality Review System], *Renda Yanjiu* [*People's Congress Studies*], 2003: 10–11.

Jiang, Hong (2014) 'Consideration of the Relationship between International and Domestic Law' [国际法与国内法关系的思考], *Journal of Liaoning Administration College* [辽宁行政学院学报], 16: 3.

Jiang, Ming'an (2011) 'Six Major Difficulties in Revising the ALL', originally published in *Legal Daily* [*Fazhi Ribao*], November 30, p. 7, at: http://article.chinalawinfo.com/Article_Detail.asp?ArticleId=65850 (accessed February 24, 2014).

Jiang, Shigong (2013) 'How to Explore a Chinese Path to Constitutionalism? A Response to Larry Cata Backer', *Modern China*, 40: 196–213.

Jiang, Steven (2013) 'Bo Xilai Found Guilty on All Charges, Sentenced to Life in Prison', CNN, September 23, at: http://edition.cnn.com/2013/09/21/world/asia/china-bo-xilai-verdict.

Jiang, Zemin (2006) *Jiang Zemin wenxuan* [*Selected Works of Jiang Zemin*], Vols. 1–3, Beijing: People's Press.

Jinghua Time (2013) 'First Major Revision to the ALL in 23 Years', *Jinghua Time* [*Jinghua Shibao*], December 23, at: http://news.xinhuanet.com/politics/2013-12/23/c_125898246.htm (accessed December 23, 2013).

Johnston, A. (2003) 'Is China a Status Quo Power?' *International Security*, 27 (4): 5–56.

Johnston, A. (2008) *Social States: China in International Institutions 1980–2000*, Princeton, NJ: Princeton University Press.

Johnston, A. (2013) 'How New and Assertive Is China's New Assertiveness?' *International Security*, 37 (4): 7–48.

Jones, W.C. (2003) 'Trying to Understand the Current Chinese Legal System', in C.S. Hsu (ed.), *Understanding China's Legal System: Essays in Honor of Jerome A. Cohen*, New York and London: New York University Press.

Kaufmann, D., Kraay, A. and Mastruzzi, M. (2007) 'Governance Matters VI: Governance Indicators for 1996–2006', World Bank, Policy Research Working Paper No. 4280.

Kawashima, T. (1963) 'Dispute Resolution in Contemporary Japan', in A. von Mehren (ed.), *Law in Japan: The Legal Order in a Changing Society*, Cambridge, MA: Harvard University Press, pp. 41–72.

Keck, Z. (2013) 'Let's Hope Xi Jingping's a Maoist', *The Diplomat*, August 28, at: http://thediplomat.com/2013/08/lets-hope-xi-jinpings-a-maoist.

Keith, R.C., Zhiqiu, L. and Hou, S. (2013) *China's Supreme Court*, London: Routledge.

Kennedy, S. and Cheng, S. (eds.) (2012) *From Rule Takers to Rule Makers: The Growing Role of Chinese in Global Governance*, Bloomington: Indiana University and the International Centre for Trade and Sustainable Development, Switzerland.

Kent, A. (1999) *China, the United Nations, and Human Rights: The Limits of Compliance*, Philadelphia: University of Pennsylvania Press.

Keohane, R., Moravcsik, A. and Slaughter, A. (2000) 'Legalized Dispute Resolution: Interstate and Transnational', *International Organization*, 54 (3): 457–88.

Kim, S. (ed.) (1994) *China and the World: Chinese Foreign Relations in the Post-Cold War Era*, Boulder, CO: Westview Press.

Klein, N. (2005) 'Dispute Settlement in the UN Convention on the Law of the Sea', *Cambridge Studies in International and Comparative Law*, 39.

Knight, J. (2013) 'Inequality in China: An Overview', *World Bank Research Observer*, 29: 1–19.

Koo, A.Y.C. (1990) 'The Contract Responsibility System: Transition from a Planned to a Market Economy', *Economic Development and Cultural Change*, 38 (4): 797–820.

Kor, K. (2014) 'This Graft War Is Unlike China's Past Efforts', *Straits Times*, December 27, at: www.straitstimes.com/the-big-story/asia-report/china/story/graft-war-unlike-chinas-past-efforts-20141227.

Koroso, N.H., Molen, P. van der, Tuladhar, A.M. and Zevenbergen, J.A. (2013) 'Does the Chinese Market for Urban Land Use Rights Meet Good Governance Principles?' *Land Use Policy*, 30: 417–26.

Kraska, J. (2010) 'How the United States Lost the Naval War of 2015', *SSRN*, at: http://ssrn.com/abstract=1648631.

Kraska, J. and Pedrozo, R. (2013) *International Maritime Security Law*, Dordrecht: Martinus Nijhoff.

Kuss, K.-J. (1986) 'New Institutions in Socialist Constitutional Law: The Polish Constitutional Tribunal and the Hungarian Constitutional Council', *Review of Socialist Law*, 12: 343–66.

LaFraniere, S. and Ansfield, J. (2012) 'Crime Crackdown Adds to Scandal Surrounding Former Chinese Official', *New York Times*, March 26, at: www.nytimes.com/2012/03/27/world/asia/bo-xilais-china-crime-crackdown-adds-to-scandal.html?pagewanted=all&_r=0.

Lan, R. (2013) Email to *CHINALAW*@hermes.gwu.edu, August 22.

Lang, Zijun and Lang, Kuaiyuan (2014) 'Several Proposals in Scientifically Restructuring the ALL', February 24, at: www.aisixiang.com/data/65199.html.

La Porta, R., Lopez-de-Silanes, F., Shleifer, A. and Vishny, R. (1997) 'Legal Determinants of External Finance', *Journal of Finance*, 54 (20): 1131–50.

La Porta, R., Lopez-de-Silanes, F., Shleifer, A. and Vishny, R. (1998) 'Law and Finance', *Journal of Political Economy*, 106 (6): 1113–55.

Lardy, N. (2014) *Markets over Mao: The Rise of Private Business in China*, Washington, DC: Peterson Institute of International Economics.

Lau, L.J., Qian, Y. and Roland, G. (2001) 'Reform without Losers: An Interpretation of China's Dual-track Approach to Transition', *Journal of Political Economy*, 108 (1): 120–43.

Lawyers Committee for Human Rights (1993) *Criminal Justice with Chinese Characteristics: China's Criminal Process and Violations of Human Rights*, New York.

Legal Daily (2011) 'Some Aspects of the Revised CPL Seen as Backward Steps: Experts Claim They Are the Results of Compromise', at: www.legaldaily.com.cn/index_article/content/2011-09/09/content_2942365.htm?node=5955 (accessed September 10, 2011).

Legal Daily (2013) 'Country's Disabled Population Exceeds 85 Million: Experts Call for Changing Law on Protection of Disabled Persons in Due Time', December 3, at: http://gongyi.ifeng.com/news/detail_2013_12/03/31748755_0.shtml.

Legal Daily (2014) 'Jiangsu's First AIDS Employment Discrimination Lawsuit Results in RMB40,000 Compensation for Plaintiff', October 9, at: www.legaldaily.com.cn/index/content/2014-10/09/content_5791355.htm?node=20908.

Lenin, V. (1964) 'The State', in *Collected Works*, London: Lawrence and Wishart, pp. 470–88.

Lenin, V. (1972) 'The Proletarian Revolution and Renegade Kautsky', in *Selected Works of Lenin, Vol. III* [Chinse translation], Beijing: People's Publishing House.

Li, Ji (2007) 'From See You in Court – To See You in Geneva: An Empirical Study of the Role of Social Norms in International Trade Dispute Resolution', *Yale Journal of International Law*, 32: 485.

Li, Ji (2013a) 'Does Law Matter in China? An Empirical Study of a Limiting Case', *George Washington. International Law Review*, 46: 119–70.

Li, Ji (2013b) 'Suing the Leviathan: An Empirical Analysis of the Changing Rate of Administrative Litigation in China', *Journal of Empirical Legal Studies*, 10 (4): 817.

Li, Ji (2013c) 'Thoughts on and Proposals for the Revision of ALL', June 29, at: www.aisixiang.com/data/65200.html (accessed February 24, 2014).

Li, Ji (2015) 'Interactions between Domestic Social Norms and International Law Over Trade Dispute Resolution', in M. Kanetake and A. Nollkaemper (eds.), *The Rule of Law at the National and International Levels: Contestations and Deference*, Oxford: Hart Publishing.

Li, Jing (2015) *Shishi Lian Dengjizhi Gaige Shouyue Quanguo Fayuan Dengji Li'an Chao Baiwanjian*, June 4, at: http://legal.people.com.cn/n/2015/0604/c42510-27104481.html.

Li, Jun (2003) 'A Quantitative Analysis of the Influence from Income Gap to Consumption', *Journal of Quantitative and Technical Economics* [*Shuliang Jingji Jishu Jingji Yanjiu*], 20: 9.

Li, Keqiang (2015) *Government Work Report of 2015*, Beijing: People's Publishing House.

Li, L. and Mou, X. (2013) 'Commentary: Bo's Trial Underscores China's Resolve for Rule of Law', *Xinhua*, August 27, at: http://news.xinhuanet.com/english/indepth/2013-08/27/c_132667916.htm.

Li, Lixing (2012) 'Land Titling in China: Chengdu Experiment and Its Consequences', *China Economic Journal*, 5 (1): 47–64.

Li, Shengxiong (2003) 'Guoji xingshi fayuan shiyong luoma guiyue guandian lun zhanzheng zui' [On War Crimes Based on ICC's Application of the Rome Statute], at: www.wufi.org.tw/%E5%9C%8B%E9%9A%9B%E5%88%91%E4%BA%8B%E6%B3%95%E9%99%A2%E9%81%A9%E7%94%A8%E3%80%8E%E7%BE%85%E9%A6%AC%E8%A6%8F%E7%B4%84%E3%80%8F%E8%A7%80%E9%BB%9E%E8%AB%96%E6%88%B0%E7%88%AD%E7%BD%AA (accessed January 22, 2015).

Li, Yahong (2000) 'The Law-making Law: A Solution to the Problems in the Chinese Legislative System?' *Hong Kong Law Journal*, 30: 120–40.

Li, Yanfeng (2000) 'Xiao Yang Teaches Students at the Judge Institute, Emphasizing Active and Stable Push for the Court Reform', *People's Court Daily*, June 2.

Li, Z. and McKenzie, D. (2014) 'Crackdown on Dissent ahead of Tiananmen Square 25th Anniversary', CNN, May 7, at: http://edition.cnn.com/2014/05/07/world/asia/china-pu-zhiqiang-detention.

Li, Zhaotao (2008) 'Xu Ting's Lenient Sentence Provoked Amazements on the Court, Which Explained That Special Case Should Receive Special Sentencing', *Information Times*, April 1.
Lian, Hongping and Lejano, R.P. (2014) 'Interpreting Institutional Fit: Urbanization, Development, and China's "Land-Lost" ', *World Development*, 61: 1–10.
Liang, Run (2011) 'Human Capital and Economic Growth in China', Center for Human Capital and Policy (CHCP), Peking University, Working paper, October 26, at: www.nsd.edu.cn/cn/userfiles/Other/2011-10/2011102415410256462049.pdf.
Liao, R. (2013) 'Why Bo Xilai's Trial Is a Victory for the Rule of Law in China', *The Atlantic*, August 7, at: www.theatlantic.com/china/archive/2013/08/why-bo-xilais-trial-is-a-victory-for-the-rule-of-law-in-china/278448.
Lin, Feng (2011) 'Where Are China's Economic and Legal Reforms Taking the People's Republic: Democracy with "Chinese Characteristics"?' In J. Garrick (ed.), *Law, Wealth and Power in China: Commercial Law Reforms in Context*, London: Routledge.
Lin, G.C.S. (2014) 'China's Landed Urbanization: Neoliberalizing Politics, Land Commodification, and Municipal Finance in the Growth of Metropolises', *Environment and Planning A*, 46: 1814–35.
Lin, J.Y. (1992) 'Rural Reforms and Agricultural Growth in China', *American Economic Review*, 82 (1): 34–51.
Lin, Yan and Ginsburg, T. (2014) 'Constitutional Interpretation in Law-Making: China's Invisible Constitutional Enforcement Mechanism', *American Journal of Comparative Law*, at: http://papers.ssrn.com/sol3/papers.cfm?abstract_id=2541852.
Liu, Chunling (2012) 'Difficult Burden of Proof Issues in Gender-Based Employment Discrimination Cases and Solutions', *China Women's News*, September 19, at: http://acwf.people.com.cn/n/2012/0919/c99013-19044852.html.
Liu, Daqun (2006) 'Preface', in Shiguang Li, Daqun Liu and Yan Ling (eds.), *Guoji xingshi fayuan luoma guiyue pingshi [A Study of the Rome Statute of the ICC]*, Beijing: Peking University Press.
Liu, Minghui (2014) 'Lack of Legislation Reflected in the First Legal Case of Gender-based Discrimination', *Collection of Women's Studies*, 2.
Liu, Songshan (2010) '1981 Nian: Taidong Er Weixing de Xianfa Weiyuanhui Sheji' [1981: Embryonic Plans for a Constitutional Supervision Committee That Did Not Take Shape], *Zhengfa Luntan*, 5.
Liu, Songshan (2011) 'Peng Zhen yu Xianfa Jiandu' [Peng Zhen and Constitutional Supervision], *Zhongguo Faxue*, 5.
Liu, Wenfeng (ed.) (2012) *The New Criminal Procedure Law: Interpreting the New and Revised Provisions and Their Legislative Grounds [Xin Xingshi Susongfa: Xinzeng Xingai Tiaowen Jingjie yu Lifa Liyou]*, Beijing: Press of the People's Court.
Liu, Yansui, Fang, Fang and Li, Yuheng (2014a) 'Key Issues of Land Use in China and Implications for Policy Making', *Land Use Policy*, 40: 6–12.
Liu, Yansui, Yang, Ren, Long, Hualou, Gao, Jay and Wang, Jieyong (2014b) 'Implications of Land-use Change in Rural China: A Case Study of Yucheng, Shandong Province', *Land Use Policy*, 40: 111–18.
Liu, Zhong (2014) 'On Shuanggui', *Comparative Law Journal [Zhongwai Faxue]*, 1, at: www.criminallaw.com.cn/article/default.asp?id=11708 (accessed April 14, 2014).
Lohr, S. (2014) 'In 2015, Technology Shifts Accelerate and China Rules, IDC Predicts', *New York Times*, December 2, at: http://bits.blogs.nytimes.com/2014/12/02/in-2015-technology-shifts-accelerate-and-china-rules-idc-predicts.

Long, Hualou, Liu, Yansui, Li, Xiubin and Chen, Yufu (2010) 'Building New Countryside in China: A Geographical Perspective', *Land Use Policy*, 27: 457–70.

Lu, F.S. and Yao, Y. (2009) 'The Effectiveness of the Law, Financial Development, and Economic Growth in an Economy of Financial Repression: Evidence from China', *World Development* (Special Issue on Law, Finance, and Economic Growth in China), 37 (4): 736–77.

Lu, Ming and Wan, Guanghua (2014) 'Urbanization and Urban Systems in the People's Republic of China: Research Findings and Policy Recommendations', *Journal of Economic Surveys*, 28 (4): 671–85.

Lu, Zhide (2013) 'Seeking Truth from Facts and the Mass Line Are the Two Most Fundamental Things', *Education Practice Learning and Experience Exchange Conference* (in Chinese), at: http://qzlx.people.com.cn/n/2013/0813/c364565-22543570.html (accessed May 17, 2014).

Lubman, S. (2000) *Bird in a Cage: Legal Reform in China after Mao*, Stanford, CA: Stanford University Press.

Lubman, S. (2013) 'What the Bo Xilai Trial Means for China's Legal System', *Wall Street Journal China Real Time Report*, September 26, at: http://blogs.wsj.com/chinarealtime/2013/09/26/what-the-bo-trial-means-for-chinas-legal-system.

Lubman, S. (2014) 'Power Shift: Hopeful Signs in China's Legal Reform Plan', *Wall Street Journal*, July 10.

Lubman, S. (2015) 'Detained Female Activists Illustrate Contradiction in Chinese Law Reforms', *Wall Street Journal*, April 9, at: http://blogs.wsj.com/chinarealtime/2015/04/09/detained-female-activists-illustrate-contradiction-in-chinese-law-reforms.

Ludwikowski, R. (1988) 'Judicial Review in the Socialist Legal System: Current Developments', *International and Comparative Law Review*, 37: 89–108.

Ludwikowski, R. (1991) 'Searching for a New Constitutional Model for East-Central Europe', *Syracuse Journal of International Law and Commerce*, 17: 91–170.

Luo, Chuliang (2004) 'Uncertainty During Economic Transition and Household Consumption Behavior in Urban China', *Economic Research Journal* [*Jingji Yanjiu*], 50: 4.

Luo, Haocai (1995) 'Using Administrative Litigation Functions to Promote the Implementation of the Administrative Litigation Law', *Administrative Law Review* [*Xingzhengfa Yanjiu*], 4: 2.

Luo, Haocai (ed.) (1996) *Administrative Law* [*Xingzhengfa Xue*], Beijing: Beijing University Press.

Luo, Sha and Chen, Fei (2015) 'Li'an Dengjizhi, Ni Yinggai Zhidao de Liujianshi', *Xinhuanet*, April 15, at: www.hn.xinhuanet.com/2015-04/15/c_1114977186.htm.

Ma, Hui (2013) 'ALL Revision Bill: Experts Say It Will Have Very Limited Effect', *21st Century Economic Report*, December 26, at: http://news.qq.com/a/20131226/000951.htm (accessed February 24, 2014).

Ma, Xueling (2015) 'The Second Circuit Court of the Supreme Court Will Open Today', January 31, at: www.chinanews.com/fz/2015/01-31/7022181.shtml.

McConville, M. (ed.) (2011) *Criminal Justice in China: An Empirical Enquiry*, Cheltenham: Edward Edgar.

McCoy, T. (2014) 'China Scored 99.9 Percent Conviction Rate Last Year', *Washington Post*, March 11, at: www.washingtonpost.com/news/morning-mix/wp/2014/03/11/china-scored-99-9-percent-conviction-rate-last-year.

McGregor, R. (2012) 'Beijing Attacks US Investor Checks', *Financial Times*, December 21, p. 2.

Maddison, A. (2001) *The World Economy: A Millennial Perspective*, Paris: OECD.

Madrazo, B. and Kempen, R. van (2012) 'Explaining Divided Cities in China', *Geoforum*, 43: 158–68.

Maggs, P.B. (1991) 'Enforcing the Bill of Rights in the Twilight of the Soviet Union', *University of Illinois Law Review*, 4: 1049–63.

Mao, Zedong (1938) 'Problems of War and Strategy', in *Selected Works, Vol. II*, Beijing: People's Publishing House.

Martina, M. and Hughes, K. (2015) 'China Draft Counterterror Law Strikes Fear in Foreign Tech Firms', February 27, at: www.reuters.com/article/2015/02/27/us-china-security-idUSKBN0LV19020150227.

Mastro, O.S. (2011) 'Signaling and Military Provocation in Chinese National Security Strategy : A Closer Look at the Impeccable Incident', *Journal of Strategic Studies*, 34 (2): 219–44.

Meng, Jianzhu (2014) 'Improving the System of Judicial Management System and Operation of Judicial Powers', *People's Daily*, November 7, at: http://legal.people.com.cn/n/2014/1107/c42510-25990066.html.

Middleton, J. (1998) 'The Soviet Experiment with Constitutional Control: The Predictable Failure of the USSR Constitutional Supervision Committee', in R. Mullerson, M. Fitzmaurice and M. Andenas (eds.), *Constitutional Reform and International Law in Central and Eastern Europe*, The Hague: Kluwer Law International.

Milhaupt, C.J. (2008) 'Is the U.S. Ready for FDI from China? Lessons from Japan's Experience in the 1980s', Columbia Center on Sustainable Investment, at: www.vcc.columbia.edu/pubs/documents/MilhauptFinalEnglish.pdf.

Milhaupt, C.J. and Zheng, W. (2015) 'Beyond Ownership: State Capitalism and the Chinese Firm', *Georgetown Law Review*, 103.

Ministry of Human Resources and Social Security of the PRC (MOHRSS) (2014) 'Provisions on Employment Service and Employment Management' (as amended), at: www.mohrss.gov.cn/SYrlzyhshbzb/ldbk/jiuye/JYzonghe/201412/t20141229_147451.htm.

Minzner, C. (2011) 'China's Turn against Law', *American Journal of Comparative Law*, 59: 935–83.

Mo, Yuchuan (2011) 'Several Proposals Concerning the Revision of the ALL', *Prosecution Daily* [*Jiancha Ribao*], 10: 3, at: www.aisixiang.com/data/46074.html (accessed February 24, 2014).

MOFCOM (2011) 'The Notice on Establishing a Security Review System for Mergers and Acquisitions of Domestic Enterprises by Foreign Investors', Circular 6, at: www.gov.cn/zwgk/2011-02/12/content_1802467.htm (accessed April 14, 2015).

Moore, M. (2014) 'China Kills off Discussion on Weibo after Internet Crackdown', *Telegraph*, January 30, at: www.telegraph.co.uk/news/worldnews/asia/china/10608245/China-kills-off-discussion-on-Weibo-after-internet-crackdown.html.

Moses, R. (2014) 'Power Struggles: Seeing China's Anti-graft Campaign in a Different Light', *Wall Street Journal China Real Time Report*, June 27, at: http://blogs.wsj.com/chinarealtime/2014/06/27/power-struggles-seeing-chinas-anti-graft-drive-in-a-different-light.

Mozur, P. (2015) 'New Rules in China Upset Western Tech Companies', *New York Times*, January 28, at: www.nytimes.com/2015/01/29/technology/in-china-new-cyber security-rules-perturb-western-tech-companies.html?LS=EMS1127110&_r=0.

Murray, L. (2015) 'China Records Worst Year for Human-Rights Detainees since 1990s', *Financial Review*, at: www.afr.com/news/world/china-records-worst-year-for-human rights-detainees-since-1990s-20150318-1m2803.

Musacchio, A. and Lazzarini, S.G. (2012) 'Leviathan in Business: Varieties of State Capitalism and Their Implications for Economic Performance', Working Paper, at: http://ssrn.com/abstract=2070942.

Nanfang Daily (2012) 'Shenzhen to Establish Gender Equality Promotion Agency', June 29, at: http://news.ifeng.com/gundong/detail_2012_06/29/15651201_0.shtml).

Nathan, A.J. (1997) *China's Transition*, New York: Columbia University Press.

Nathan, A.J. (2003) 'Authoritarian Resilience', *Journal of Democracy*, 14: 6–17.

Naughton, B. (1995) *Growing out of the Plan: Chinese Economic Reform, 1978–1993*, Cambridge: Cambridge University Press.

New Beijing Daily (2011) '90% Employer Would Rather Pay Disability Guaranty Fund for the Long Term Rather than Hire Disabled Workers', August 25, at: http://gongyi.163.com/11/0825/11/7CA3HSAD00933KC8.html.

New York Times (2015) 'In China, Civic Group's Freedom, and Followers, Are Vanishing', February 26, at: www.nytimes.com/2015/02/27/world/asia/in-china-civic-groups-freedom-and-followers-are-vanishing.html.

Nguyễn Thị Lan Anh (1988) 'UNCLOS and Maritime Security in the South China Sea', *Diplomatic Academy of Vietnam*, at: www.nghiencuubiendong.vn.

Nguyễn Thi Lan Anh (2012) 'UNCLOS and Maritime Security in the South China Sea', *Third International Workshop*, at: http://nghiencuubiendong.vn/en/conferences-and-seminars-/the-third-international-workshop-on-south-china-sea/655-unclos-and-maritime-security-in-the-south-china-sea-by-nguyen-thi-lan-anh.

Nong, Hong (2014) 'Beyond Oil and Gas: Alternative Fields and Models of Joint Management', in Wu Shicun and Nong Hong (eds.), *Recent Developments in the South China Sea Dispute: The Prospect of a Joint Development Regime*, London and New York: Routledge.

NPC (2013) 'Expanding the Scope for Case Acceptance and Ensuring Enforcement of Judgements', December 25, at: www.npc.gov.cn/npc/ltzt/2014/2013-12/25/content_1820671.htm (accessed December 28, 2013).

NPC Standing Committee (2013) 'Explanations on the Revision Bill of the Administrative Litigation Law of the PRC', delivered at the Sixth Session of the Twelfth NPC Standing Committee, December, at: www.npc.gov.cn/npc/lfzt/2014/2013-12/31/content_1822189.htm (accessed January 4, 2014).

Nye, J.S., Jr. (1990) 'Soft Power', *Foreign Policy*, 80: 153–71.

Obstfeld, M., Shambaugh, J.C. and Taylor, A.M. (2005) 'The Trilemma in History: Tradeoffs among Exchange Rates, Monetary Policies, and Capital Mobility', *Review of Economics and Statistics*, 87 (3): 423–38.

Office of the Secretary of Defense Annual Report (2014) 'Military and Security Developments Involving the People's Republic of China', U.S. Department of Defense, at: www.defense.gov/pubs/2014_DoD_China_Report.pdf.

O'Rourke, R. (2014) 'Maritime Territorial and EEZ Disputes Involving China: Issues for Congress', *Congressional Research Service*, Report R42784, December 24.

Oster, S. (2014) 'President Xi's Anti-Corruption Campaign Biggest since Mao', *Bloomberg Business*, March 4, at: www.bloomberg.com/news/articles/2014-03-03/china-s-xi-broadens-graft-crackdown-to-boost-influence.

Oxman, B.H. (1984) 'The Regime of Warships under the United Nations Convention on the Law of the Sea', *American Journal of International Law*, 24: 829–32.

Page, J. (2013) 'Xi Comes out on Top after Bo Verdict', *Wall Street Journal*, September 22, at: www.wsj.com/articles/SB10001424052702303983904579090811721854036.

Paik, Wooyeal and Lee, Kihyun (2012) 'I Want to Be Expropriated! The Politics of Xiaochanquanfang Land Development in Suburban China', *Journal of Contemporary China*, 21 (74): 261–79.

Patience, M. (2013) 'Charles Xue "Confession" Highlights China's Blogging Backlash', BBC, October 1, at: www.bbc.com/news/world-asia-pacific-24182336.

Pedrozo, R. (2010) 'Preserving Navigational Rights and Freedoms: The Right to Conduct Military Activities in China's Exclusive Economic Zone', *Chinese Journal of International Law*, 9 (1): 9–29.

Pedrozo, R. (2011) 'A Response to Cartner's and Gold's Commentary on "Is It Time for the United States to Join the Law of the Sea Convention?"', *Journal of Maritime Law and Commerce*, October, 42 (4): 487–510.

Peerenboom, R. (2011) 'Law, Wealth and Power in China', in J. Garrick (ed.), *Law, Wealth and Power in China: Commercial Law Reforms in Context*, London: Routledge.

Peerenboom, R. (2012) 'Economic and Social Rights: The Role of Courts in China', in J. Garrick (ed.), *Law and Policy for China's Market Socialism*, London: Routledge.

Peerenboom, R. (2014a) 'The Future of Legal Reforms in China: A Critical Appraisal of the Decision on Comprehensively Deepening Reform', *SSRN*, January, at: http://ssrn.com/abstract=2379161.

Peerenboom, R. (2014b) 'Fly High the Banner of Socialist Rule of Law with Chinese Characteristics! What Does the 4th Plenum Decision Mean for Legal Reforms in China?' *SSRN*, November 6, at: http://papers.ssrn.com/sol3/papers.cfm?abstract_id=2519917.

Peerenboom, R. and Ginsburg, T. (eds.) (2014) *Law and Development in Middle-Income Countries: Avoiding the Middle-Income Trap*, Cambridge: Cambridge University Press.

Peng, S. (2000) 'The WTO Legalistic Approach and East Asia: From the Legal Culture Perspective', *Asian-Pacific Law and Policy Journal*, 1: 78.

Peng, Zhen (1992) *On Political and Judicial Work in the New China* [*Lun Xinzhongguo De Zhengfa Gongzuo*], Beijing: Press of the Chinese Communist Party Documents.

People's Daily (2014a) 'China Intends to Resolve the Problems in Filing for Suit in Administrative Litigation and Expand Scope for Citizens to Sue Government', February 19, at: http://news.xinhuanet.com/legal/2014-02/19/c_126155103.htm (accessed February 19, 2014).

People's Daily (2014b) 'After 24 Years the Administrative Litigation Law Undertook a Substantive Revision' [*Renmin Ribao*], November 6, at: www.chinanews.com/fz/2014/11-06/6757401.shtml.

People's Daily (2015) 'Si ge quan mian', February 24, front-page editorial.

People's Daily Online (2013) 'Survey Shows 90% Female College Students Encounter Gender-Based Employment Discrimination' [citing a recent survey by the All China Women's Federation on Employment of Female College Students], May 15, at: www.chinapeace.gov.cn/2013-05/15/content_7642910.htm.

Pettis, M. (2014a) 'The Impact of Reform on Growth', at: http://blog.mpettis.com/2014/01/the-impact-of-reform-on-growth.

Pettis, M. (2014b) 'Will the Reforms Speed Growth in China?' At: http://blog.mpettis.com/2014/01/will-the-reforms-speed-growth-in-china.

Pi, Chunxi (1995) 'An Important Law That Needs Serious Implementation', *Administrative Law Review* [*Xingzhengfa Yanjiu*], 4: 12.

Pistor, K. and Xu, C. (2005) 'Governing Stock Markets in Transition Economies: Lessons from China', *American Law and Economics Review*, 7 (1): 1–27.

Pistor, K., Martin, R. and Gelfer, S. (2000) 'Law and Finance in Transition Economies', *Economics of Transition*, 8 (2): 325–68.

Posner, E.A. (2000) *Law and Social Norms*, Cambridge, MA: Harvard University Press.

Posner, E.A. and Sykes, A.O. (2009) 'Economic Foundations of the Law of the Sea', *SSRN*, at: http://ssrn.com/abstract=1524274.

Potter, P.B. (1994) 'The Administrative Litigation Law of the PRC: Judicial Review and Bureaucratic Reform', in P.B. Potter (ed.), *Domestic Law Reforms in Post-Mao China*, New York/London: M.E. Shaper.

Propaganda Department of Chinese Communist Party Central Committee (2014) *A Reader of General Secretary Xi Jinping's Important Speeches* [*xuexi xijinping zongshuji zhongyao jianghua duben*], Beijing: People's Press.

Qian, Y. and Xu, C. (1993) 'The M-form Hierarchy and China's Economic Reform', *European Economic Review*, 37: 541–8.

Qian, Zhu (2012) 'Post-reform Urban Restructuring in China: The Case of Hangzhou 1990–2010', *Town Planning Review*, 83 (4): 431–55.

Raice, S. and Dowell, A. (2011) 'Huawei Drops U.S. Deal Amid Opposition', *Wall Street Journal*, February 22, at: www.wsj.com/articles/SB10001424052748703407304576154121951088478.

Ralls Corp. v. Committee on Foreign Investment in the United States, et al., No. 13-5315 (D.C. Cir. July 15, 2014).

Ravallion, M. and Chen, S. (2007) 'China's (Uneven) Progress against Poverty', *Journal of Development Economics*, 82 (1): 1–42.

Research Group of Financial Survey and Statistics Department of PBoC (2012) 'Conditions Are Basically Ready for Accelerating China's Capital Account Liberlization', *China Finance* [*Zhongguo Jinrong*], 63: 5.

Riskin, C. (1987) *China's Political Economy: The Quest for Development since 1949*, Oxford: Oxford University Press.

Roach, J.A. and Smith, R.W. (2012) *Excessive Maritime Claims*, Dordrecht: Martinus Nijhoff.

Roberts, D. (2014a) 'Xi Jinping's Anti-corruption Paradox', *Businessweek*, January 15, at: www.bloomberg.com/bw/articles/2014-01-15/xi-jinpings-anti-corruption-paradox.

Roberts, D. (2014b) 'In China, Xi's Anti-corruption Drive Nabs Elite, Low Ranks Alike', *Bloomberg*, April 10, at: www.bloomberg.com/bw/articles/2014-04-10/in-china-xis-anticorruption-drive-nabs-elite-low-ranks-alike.

Rodrik, D., Subramanian, A. and Trebbi, F. (2004) 'Institutions Rule: The Primacy of Institutions over Geography and Integration in Economic Development', *Journal of Economic Growth*, 9 (2): 139–65.

Rosen, D.H. and Hanemann, T. (2012) 'Ralls vs. CFIUS: What Are the Implications for Chinese Investment?' At: http://rhg.com/articles/ralls-vs-cfius-what-are-the-implications-for-chinese-investment.

Ruskola, T. (2013) *Legal Orientalism: China, the United States and Modern Law*, Cambridge, MA: Harvard University Press.

Saha, S. (2012) 'CFIUS Now Made in China: Dueling National Security Review Frameworks as a Countermeasure to Economic Espionage in the Age of Globalization', *Northwestern Journal of International Law & Business*, 33: 199.

Sapio, F. (2008) 'Shuanggui and Extralegal Detention in China', *China Information*, 22: 7.

Scheffer, D. (1998) 'Is U.N. International Criminal Court in the U.S. National Interests?' Hearing before the Subcommittee on International Operations of the Committee on Foreign Relations, U.S. Senate, 105th Congress (July 23).

Schofield, C. and Storey, I. (2009) 'The South China Sea Dispute: Increasing Stakes and Rising Tensions', The Jamestown Foundation, Washington, DC, at: www.jamestown.org.

Schwartz, H. (2000) *The Struggle for Constitutional Justice in Post-Communist Europe*, London: University of Chicago Press.

SCNPC (2012) 'Decision to Revise the Civil Procedure Law of the PRC', adopted on August 31, 28th Session of the SCNPC of the 11th National People's Congress.

Scott, J. and Wilkinson, R. (2012) 'China in the WTO', in S. Kennedy and S. Cheng (eds.), *From Rule Takers to Rule Makers: The Growing Role of Chinese in Global Governance*, Bloomington: Indiana University and the International Centre for Trade and Sustainable Development, Switzerland.

Shambaugh, D. (2008) *China's Communist Party: Atrophy and Adaptation*, Washington, DC: Woodrow Wilson Center Press.

Shambaugh, D. (2015) 'The Coming Chinese Crackup: The Endgame of Communist Rule in China Has Begun, and Xi Jinping's Ruthless Measures Are Only Bringing the Country Closer to a Breaking Point', *Wall St Journal*, March 6.

Shen, Y., Shen, M., Xu, Z. and Bai, Y. (2009) 'Bank Size and Small and Medium-sized Enterprise (SME) Lending: Evidence from China', *World Development* (Special Issue on Law, Finance and Economic Growth in China), 37 (4): 800–11.

Sheng-ti Gau, M. (2011) 'The Commission on the Limits of the Continental Shelf as a Mechanism to Prevent Encroachment upon the Area', *Chinese Journal of International Law*, 10 (1): 3–33.

Shirk, S.L. (2008) *China: Fragile Superpower*, Oxford: University Press.

Siciliano, G. (2012) 'Urbanization Strategies, Rural Development and Land Use Changes in China: A Multiple-level Integrated Assessment', *Land Use Policy*, 29: 165–78.

Sidel, M. (2009) *The Constitution of Vietnam: A Contextual Analysis*, Oxford: Hart Publishing.

Sina News (2012) 'Legal Experts Interpret the Revision of the Criminal Procedure Law: Many Important Aspects Still Not Addressed', at: http://news.sina.com.cn/c/sd/2012-03-15/145824120642.shtml (accessed August 3, 2012).

South China Morning Post (2013) 'Supreme People's Court Judge Urges End to Wrongful Convictions', August 29, at: www.scmp.com/news/china/article/1232279/supreme-peoples-court-judge-urges-end-wrongful-convictions.

Southern Weekend (2002) 'Jiandu Fa: Minzhu Zhengzhi Shengzhang Dian' [Supervision Law: Growing Point for Democratic Politics], *Nanfang Zhoumo*, September 6, at: www.southcn.com/weekend/commend/200209050005.htm.

State Council of China (2014) 'Document on Further Promoting the Hukou System Reforms', at: www.gov.cn/zhengce/content/2014-07/30/content_8944.htm.

State Council of the People's Republic of China (1994) *Taiwan wenti wenxian ziliao xuanbian* [*Selected Works of the Literature on the Taiwan Issue*], Beijing: People's Press.

Sun, Guofeng and Lu, Dong (2012) 'Predictive Analysis on Mid-long Term Trend of Current Account Surplus in China: Based on a Perspective of Savings-investment Structural Change', *Comparative Studies* [*Bijiao*], 6: 6.

Sun, L. and Tobin, D. (2009) 'International Listing as a Means to Mobilize the Benefits of Financial Globalization: Micro-level Evidence from China', *World Development* (Special Issue on Law, Finance and Economic Growth in China), 37 (4): 825–38.

Sun, Wanning and Guo, Yingjie (eds.) (2012) *Unequal China: The Political Economy and Cultural Politics of Inequality*, Abingdon: Routledge.

Sun, Yi (2015) 'Basic-level Court Judges Thinks Pay Too Low, Work Load Too Heavy, and Dignity in Deficit, Now Showing Tide of Resignation', *Beijing Evening News*, January 7.

Suo, Husheng (2014) 'A Comparison of Logistics Cost between China and America', *Macroeconomic Management* [*Hongguan Jingji Guanli*], 30: 1.

Supreme People's Court (2000) 'Method for Administering the Publication of Judicial Opinions', *The SPC Gazette*, 4: 118.

Supreme People's Court Monitor (2015) 'Supreme People's Court President Says In-court Reforms in Deep Water', March 15, at: http://supremepeoplescourtmonitor.com.

Supreme People's Court of the PRC (2008) 'Stipulations on Causes of Actions in Civil Cases' (amended in 2011), at: www.npc.gov.cn/npc/xinwen/fztd/sfjs/2008-03/03/content_1425565.htm and www.lawinfochina.com/display.aspx?lib=law&id=8607.

Takeda, Jun'ichi (2014) 'China's Rise as a Maritime Power: Ocean Policy from Mao Zedong to Xi Jinping', The Centre for Island Studies, Sasakawa Peace Foundation, at: http://islandstudies.oprf-info.org/research/a00011 (accessed April 21, 2015).

Takeuchi, Hiroki (2013) 'Survival Strategies of Township Governments in Rural China: From Predatory Taxation to Land Trade', *Journal of Contemporary China*, 22 (83): 755–72.

Tan, S. (2003) 'Zhongguo yu guoji xingshi fayuan guanxi chutan' [An Analysis of the Relations between China and the ICC], in Bingzhi Zhao, Xiumei Wang and Sanjeewa Liyanage (eds.), *Guoji xingshi fayuan zhuanlun* [*Study on Major Issues Relating to the ICC*], Beijing: People's Court Press.

Tang, Y., Mason, R.J. and Sun, P. (2012) 'Interest Distribution in the Process of Coordination of Urban and Rural Construction Land in China', *Habitat International*, 36: 388–95.

Thomas, D. (2013) 'Huawei to Set up UK Finance Operation', *Financial Times*, August 5, p. 14.

Timberlake, M., Wei, Yehua Dennis, Ma, Xiulian and Hao, Jianmei (2014) 'Global Cities with Chinese characteristics', *Cities*, 41: 162–70.

Townsend, D.E. (1987–8) 'The Concept of Law in Post-Mao China: A Case Study of Economic Crime', *Stanford Journal of International Law*, 24: 227.

Traveskes, S. (2007) *Courts and Criminal Justice in Contemporary China*, New York/Toronto: Lexington Books.

UNCLOS (2011) 'Note Verbale', UNCLOS Commission on the Limits of the Continental Shelf, April, at: www.un.org/depts/los/clcs_new/commission_submissions.htm.

UNCLOS Part XVII Article 309 (1996) 'China's Official Statement on Ratification', at: www.un.org/depts/los/convention_agreements/convention_declarations.htm (June 7, 1996).

United Nations (1947) 'Resolution A/RES/174(II)', United Nations General Assembly Resolutions, November 21, at: www.worldlii.org/int/other/UNGARsn/1947.

United Nations (1969) 'Vienna Convention on the Law of Treaties', *U.N. Treaty Collection*, May 23, at: https://treaties.un.org/Pages/ViewDetailsIII.aspx?src=TREATY&mtdsg_no=XXIII~1&chapter=23&Temp=mtdsg3&lang=en.

United Nations (1984a) 'Convention against Torture and Other Cruel, Inhuman or Degrading Treatment or Punishment (CAT)', *UN Document* A/RES/39/46, New York: UN.

United Nations (1984b) 'Declarations and Reservations to the CAT', *U.N. Treaty Collection*, at: http://treaties.un.org/Pages/ViewDetails.aspx?mtdsg_no=IV-9&chapter=4&lang=en#EndDec (accessed March 9, 2015).

United Nations (1993) *UN Document* A/C.6/48/SR.19, New York: UN.

United Nations (1996) *UN Document* A/C.6/51/SR.28 New York: UN.
United Nations (1997) *UN Document* A/C.6/52/SR.11, New York: UN.
United Nations (1998a) *United Nations Diplomatic Conference of Plenipotentiaries on the Establishment of the International Criminal Court*, Vol. II, New York: UN.
United Nations (1998b) *UN Document* A/C.6/53/SR.9, New York: United Nations.
United Nations (2004) 'What Is the Rule of law?' United Nations Rule of Law, at: www.unrol.org/article.aspx?article_id=3.
United Nations Conference on Trade and Development (UNCTAD) (2006) *World Investment Report*, Washington, DC: UN Publications.
Upham, F.K. (1987) *Law and Social Change in Postwar Japan*, Cambridge, MA: Harvard University Press.
Veg, S. (2014) 'China's Political Spectrum under Xi Jinping', *The Diplomat*, August 11, at: http://thediplomat.com/2014/08/chinas-political-spectrum-under-xi-jinping.
Veugelers, R. (2011) 'A G2 for Science?' *Bruegel Policy Brief*, Issue 2011/03.
Von Stein, J. (2008) 'The International Law and Politics of Climate Change: Ratification of the United Nations Framework Convention and the Kyoto Protocol', *Journal of Conflict Resolution*, 52 (2): 243–68.
Wan, Exiang (1999) 'Deepening Judicial Reform, Guaranteeing Judicial Fairness', *Law Review*, 3: 1–2.
Wang, Chengguang (1998) 'Judicial Efficiency and the Reform of Internal Operating System of the Courts', *Jurisprudence*, 10: 46–51.
Wang, Hui, Wang, Lanlan, Su, Fubing and Tao, Ran (2012) 'Rural Residential Properties in China: Land Use Patterns, Efficiency and Prospects for Reform', *Habitat International*, 36: 201–9.
Wang, J.C.F. (1992) *Handbook on Ocean Politics and Law*, Westport, CT: Greenwood Press.
Wang, Lei (2014) 'Forging Growth by Governing the Market in Reform-era Urban China', *Cities*, 41: 187–93.
Wang, Tieya (1994) 'Status of Treaties in the Chinese Legal System', *Zhongguo Guojifa Niankan* [*Chinese Yearbook of International Law*], Beijing University Press.
Wang, Tieya (1998) *Introduction to International Law*, Beijing University Press.
Wang, X., Piesse, J. and Weaver, N. (2013) 'Mind the Gaps: A Political Economy of the Multiple Dimensions of China's Rural–Urban Divide', *Asian-Pacific Economic Literature*, 27 (2): 52–67.
Wang, Y. (2000) 'Shuli shiji zhijiaode xin zhuquanguan' ['Establish a New Sovereignty Perspective for the New Century'], *Liaowang xinwen zhoukan* [*Outlook Newsweek*], 17: 8–11.
Wang, Y. (2006) 'Zhuquan fanchou zaisikao' [Rethinking the Connotation of Sovereignty], *Ouzhou* [*Europe*], 6: 4–11.
Wang, Yongqing (2014) 'Better Use of Rule of Law Thought and Rule of Law Methods to Implement Legal Political Work: Deepening Study of the Spirit of a Series of Xin Jinping's Important Speeches', *People's Daily*, July 28, at: http://theory.people.com.cn/n/2014/0728/c40531-25351145.html.
Wang, Zhenyu and Wang, Jingcheng (1997) 'An Analysis on Problems in Our Administrative Litigation System and Their Solutions', *Jilin University Journal of Social Science* [*Jilin Daxue Shehui Kexue Xuebao*], 3: 79.
Wee, S. (2013) 'Lawyer Says Not Allowed to Represent China's Disgraced Bo Xilai', *Reuters*, August 8, at: www.reuters.com/article/2013/08/08/us-china-politics-bo-idUSBRE97708V20130808.

Wei, Dan (2014) 'On the Residual Rights in UNCLOS and Maritime Security' [海洋法上的剩餘權力與國際海洋安全], *Gongmin yu Fa*, 2.

Wei, Ye Hua Dennis (2012) 'Restructuring for Growth in Urban China: Transitional Institutions, Urban Development, and Spatial Transformation', *Habitat International*, 36: 396–405.

Weinberger v. Salfi, 422 U.S. 749 (1975).

Weisman, S.R. (2007) 'Little Headway with China on Finance', *New York Times*, at: www.nytimes.com/2007/12/13/business/13cnd-trade.html.

Wen, Jiabao (2012) *Government Work Report of 2012*, Beijing: People's Publishing House.

Wen, P. (2015) 'China's Ex-security Chief Zhou Yongkang Jailed for Life at Secret Trial', *SMH World*, June 12, at www.smh.com.au/world/chinas-exsecurity-chief-zhou-yongkang-jailed-for-life-at-secret-trial-20150612-ghm1jz.html.

Wen, P. and Garnaut, J. (2015) 'Chinese Police Chase Corruption Suspects in Australian Suburbs', *SMH World*, April 15, at: www.smh.com.au/world/chinese-police-chase-corruption-suspects-in-australian-suburbs-20150414-1mkwd2.html.

Wingfield, B. (2012) 'China Urges U.S. to End "Political" Vetting of Its Firms', *Bloomberg Business*, at: www.bloomberg.com/news/articles/2012-12-20/china-urges-u-s-to-end-political-vetting-of-its-firms.

Wise, M. (2013) 'Cuban Constitutionalism: Will There Be Changes?' *Duquesne Law Review*, 51: 467–85.

Wong, E. (2013) 'China Debates Effect of Trial's Rare Transparency', *New York Times*, September 3, at: www.nytimes.com/2013/09/03/world/asia/china-debates-effect-on-law-of-bo-xilais-trial.html?pagewanted=all&_r=0.

Worker's Daily (2012) 'First Equal Employment Promotion Commission Established: Combating Employment Discrimination as Measure of Government Performance', October 28, at: http://politics.people.com.cn/n/2012/1028/c70731-19412192.html.

Wu, Jinglian (2006) 'The Crux of Excessive Income Gap', *Finance and Economy* (CAIJING Magazine), 9: 21.

Wu, Qun, Li, Yongle and Yan, Siqi (2015) 'The Incentives of China's Urban Land Finance', *Land Use Policy*, 42: 432–42.

Wu, Shicun and Nong, Hong (eds.) (2014) *Recent Developments in the South China Sea Dispute: The Prospect of a Joint Development Regime*, London: Routledge.

Wuthnow, J. (2011) *Beyond the Veto: Chinese Diplomacy in the United Nations Security Council*, Ph.D. Dissertation, New York: Columbia University.

Xi, Jinping (2012) 'Xi Jinping nanxun jianghua zhaiyao' [Extracts of Xi Jinping's Southern Inspection Speeches], December, at: http://beijingspring.com/bj2/2010/140/2013127195801.htm.

Xi, Jinping (2013a) 'An Explanation of the Chinese Communist Party Central Committee Decision on Several Major Questions About Deepening Reform', *Xinhuanet.com*, November 19.

Xi, Jinping (2013b) 'Xi Jinping zai quanguo zuzhi gongzuo huiyi shang de jianghua' [Xi Jinping's Speech at the National Conference on Organization Work], October 27, at: www.caiyes.cn/forum.php?mod=viewthread&tid=40661.

Xi, Jinping (2013c) 'Xi Jinping zai quanguo xuanchuan sixiang gongzuo huiyi de jianghua jingshen xuanchuan tigang' [An Outline of Xi Jinping's Speech at the National Propaganda and Ideology Work Conference], August 19, at: www.boxun.com/news/gb/china/2013/11/201311042254.shtml#.U0RddPmSy8k.

Xi, Jinping (2014a) 'Juebu yunxu chi gongchandang de fan za gongchandang de guo' [Never Allow Eating the Communist Party's Food and Then Smashing the Communist Party's Cooking Pots], October 26, at: http://chinadigitaltimes.net/chinese/2014/10.

Xi, Jinping (2014b) 'Jiaqiang gaoxiao dangjian gongzuo' [Strengthening and Improving Party Building Work at Higher Education Institutions], December 29, at: http://news.xinhuanet.com/politics/2014-12/29/c_1113818177.htm.

Xi, Jinping (2014c) 'Explanation Concerning the "CCP Central Committee Decision Concerning Some Major Questions Comprehensively Moving Governing the Country According to Law Forward"', October, at: https://chinacopyrightandmedia.wordpress.com/2014/10/29.

Xi, Jinping (2014d) 'Carry Forward the Five Principles of Peaceful Coexistence to Build a Better World through Win–Win Cooperation', Address at Meeting Marking the 60th Anniversary of the Initiation of the Five Principles of Peaceful Coexistence, June 28, at: www.china.org.cn/world/2014-07/07/content_32876905.htm.

Xiang, Zexuan, Wu, Xiaocheng and Luo, Rui (2005) *On Legal Supervision and Remedies of Criminal Procedural Law* [*Falü Jiandu Yu Xingshi Susong Jiujilun*], Beijing: Beijing University Press.

Xiao, Xian and Luo, Jianbo (2002) 'Lengzhan hou dongmeng anquan hezuo de shenhua jiqi dui woguo zhoubian anquan huanjing de yingxiang' [The Strengthening of the Association of Southeast Asian Nations on Security Collaboration after the Cold War and Its Influence on China's Security Environment], *Journal of Yunnan Administration College*, 5.

Xiao, Xinxin (2014) 'Judicial Reform in Shanghai: The Central Reform Group Approves Pilot Project', *Twenty-First-Century Economic Times*, June 10.

Xiao, Xun (1991) 'Several Questions Concerning the Administrative Litigation Law', *People's Daily* [*Renmin Ribao*], March 10, at 5, English translation in FBIS-CHI-91-056, at 22–6.

Xinan Evening News (2014) 'China's First Residency Discrimination Case Won by Plaintiff: RMB11,000 in Compensation', August 8, at: http://news.qq.com/a/20140806/064939.htm.

Xinhua (2013a) 'Xi Jinping Qiangdiao: Yifa Zhiguo Yifa Zhizheng Yifa Xingzheng Gongtong Tuijin' [Xi Jinping Emphasizes: Promote Ruling the Country in Accordance with Law, Governing the Country in Accordance with Law, and Administration in Accordance with Law Together], *Xinhua Wang*, February 24, at: http://news.xinhuanet.com/politics/2013-02/24/c_114782088.htm.

Xinhua (2013b) 'Jiedu Laojiao Zhidu Feizhi: Dashi Suoqu Renxin Suoxiang' [Deciphering Abolition of the RTL System: Consistent with the General Trend and the People's Will], *Xinhua Wang*, November 20, at: http://news.xinhuanet.com/legal/2013-11/20/c_125727794.htm.

Xinhua Net (2005) 'Fan fenlie guojia fa' [The Anti-secession Law], March 14, at: http://news.xinhuanet.com/newscenter/2005-03/14/content_2694168.htm.

Xinhua Net (2013) 'Female Students in Eight Cities Report 267 Companies for Alleged Gender Discrimination: Only One Company Fined', January 26, at: http://news.xinhuanet.com/legal/2013-01/26/c_114510501.htm.

Xinhua News (2014) 'The Central Government Decided to Experiment Judicial Reform in Six Provinces and Municipalities, Including Shanghai and Guangdong', June 15, at: http://news.163.com/14/0615/17/9UQ1HJ9400014JB5.html.

Xinhua News Agency (2013) 'Xi Jinping Vows Unswerving Fight against Corruption', January 22, at: http://news.xinhuanet.com/english/china/2013-01/22/c_132119843.htm.

Xinhua News Agency (2014) 'CPC to Convene Key Meeting on Rule of Law Oct 20–23', *China Daily*, at: www.chinadaily.com.cn/china/2014-09/30/content_18689039.htm.

Xinhua News Agency (2015a) 'Education Minister Warns against "Western Values" in Colleges', January 30, at: http://news.xinhuanet.com/english/china/2015-01/30/c_133958419.htm.

Xinhua News Agency (2015b) 'Zhongyang zhengfa gongzuo huiyi zai jing zaokai Xi Jinping zuo zhongyao jianghua' [Party Centre Political and Legal Work Conference, Being, with Xi Jinping Making Important Speech], January 20, at: http://politics.people.com.cn/n/2015/0120/c70731-26419142.html.

Xiong, Qiuhong (2004) *The Changing Science of Criminal Procedural Law* [*Zhuanbianzhong De Xingshisusong Faxue*], Beijing: Beijing University Press.

Xu, Qiyuan (2013) 'Consensus and Divergence upon China's Financial Reforms: An Analysis Based on Questionnaire', *Research Center for International Finance*, Chinese Academy of Social Sciences, Policy Brief No. 2013.032.

Xu, Qiyuan (2009) 'China Should Rethink the International Trade Policy', *International Economic Review* [*Guoji Jingji Pinglun*], 17: 6.

Xu, Xin (2014) 'Judicial Reform in China', Cornell University Law School, at: http://meridian-180.org/node/1844 (accessed April 23, 2014).

Xue, Desheng and Wu, Fulong (2015) 'Failing Entrepreneurial Governance: From Economic Crisis to Fiscal Crisis in the City of Dongguan, China', *Cities*, 43: 10–17.

Xue, Hanqin and Jin, Qian (2009) 'International Treaties in the Chinese Domestic Legal System', *Chinese Journal of International Law*, 8: 299.

Yan, Guo'an (2013) 'After 23 Years the ALL Is up for First Revision, But Will It Promote the Independence of Adjudication?', *China Youth Daily* [*Zhognguo Qingnian Bao*], December 24, at: http://views.ce.cn/view/ent/201312/24/t20131224_1979254.shtml (accessed February 24, 2014).

Yan, Tian (2012) 'Rethinking the Modern Origins of China's Anti-Discrimination Legislation', *Peking University Law Journal*, 24 (3), at: http://journal.pkulaw.cn/ContentPDFType.aspx?isDL=rd&id=159373.

Yang, Tianyu (2009) *Income Distribution and Aggregate Consumption in China*, Peking: China Economic Publishing House.

Yao, Dongqing (2012) 'Insight into the Revision of the Criminal Procedure Law', *China Economic Weekly* [*Zhongguo Jingji Zhoukan*], March 26, at 27–9.

Yao, Y. and Yueh, L. (2009) 'Law, Finance and Economic Growth in China: An Introduction', *World Development* (Special Issue on Law, Finance and Economic Growth in China), 37 (4): 753–62.

Ye, Yumin, LeGates, Richard and Qin, Bo (2013) 'Coordinated Urban–Rural Development Planning in China', *Journal of the American Planning Association*, 79 (2): 125–37.

Yew, Chiew Ping (2012) 'Pseudo-Urbanization? Competitive Government Behavior and Urban Sprawl in China', *Journal of Contemporary China*, 21 (74): 281–98.

Ying, Songnian and Yang, Weidong (2011) 'Preliminary Thoughts on Revising the Administrative Litigation Law', November 11, at: www.aisixiang.com/data/46358.html (accessed February 24, 2014).

Young, A. (2000) 'The Razor's Edge: Distortions and Incremental Reform in the People's Republic of China', *Quarterly Journal of Economics*, 115 (4): 1091–135.

Yu, A.T.W., Wu, Yuzhe, Zheng, Bibo, Zhang, Xiaoling and Shen, Liyin (2014) 'Identifying Risk Factors of Urban–Rural Conflict in Urbanization: A Case of China', *Habitat International*, 44: 177–85.

Yu, Yongding (2009) 'Avoid the Dollar Trap and China's Selection', *Finance and Economy* (CAIJING Magazine), 12: 8.

Yuan, Dingbo (2014) 'Judicial Reform Needs Be Promoted', *Legal Daily*, July 18.

Yue, Ximing, Li, Shi and Sicular, T. (2012) 'Are the High Salaries of Employees in Monopoly Industries Justified?', *Social Sciences in China* [*Zhongguo Shehui Kexue*], 31: 3.

Yunliang, W. and Xiaoya, G. (2013) 'Plan of Two Thousand People Is an Innovative Model of Training the Talent', *Chinese Social Sciences Today*, August 19, at: www.csstoday.net/xueshuzixun/guoneixinwen/83918.html (accessed May 18, 2014).

Zang, Xiaowei (2016) *Understanding Chinese Society* (2nd edn.), Routledge: London.

Zejan, P. and Bartels, F.L. (2006) 'Be Nice and Get Your Money: An Empirical Analysis of World Trade Organization Trade Disputes and Aid', *Journal of World Trade*, 40 (6).

Zhan, J. (2014) 'Assessing Xi Jinping's Anti-Corruption Campaign', *World Policy Blog*, April 29, at: www.worldpolicy.org/blog/2014/04/29/assessing-xi-jinping%E2%80%99s-anti-corruption-campaign.

Zhang, Bin and He, Fan (2006) 'The Consequences of Currency Appreciation: A Theoretical Model Based on Chinese Stylized Facts', *Economic Research* [*Jingji Yanjiu*], 52: 5.

Zhang, Haiwen (2010) 'Is It Safeguarding the Freedom of Navigation or Maritime Hegemony of the United States? Comments on Raul (Pete) Pedrozo's Article on Military Activities in the EEZ', *Chinese Journal of International Law*, 9 (1): 31–47.

Zhang, Jiansheng (2013) 'Basic Points on the Revision of the ALL', March 4, at http://law.china.cn/features/2013-03/04/content_5773055_2.htm (accessed February 24, 2014).

Zhang, L. (2009) *Zhongguo yu guoji xingshi fayuan: Xianzhuang yu zhanwang* [*China and the ICC: Status and Prospects*], Beijing: People's Public Security University Press.

Zhang, Ming (2014) 'China's BOP Tends to be More Balanced', International Investment Studies (IIS), Institute of World Economy and Politics, Chinese Academy of Social Sciences, Quarterly Report No. 201402.

Zhang, P. (2013) 'Xi Jinping Maps out Anti-Graft Campaign', *South China Morning Post*, January 1, at: www.scmp.com/news/china/article/1117057/xi-jinping-maps-out-anti-graft-campaign.

Zhang, Qianfan (2003) 'The People's Court in Transition: The Prospects for Chinese Judicial Reform', *Journal of Contemporary China*, 12 (34): 69–101.

Zhang, Qianfan (2008) 'Judicial Populism Is a False Proposition', *Economic Observer Daily*, July 26.

Zhang, Qianfan (2011) 'Zhongguo Xianzheng de Lujing yu Kunjing' [The Paths and Difficulties of China's Constitutionalism], *Caijing Wang*, January 28, at: http://blog.caijing.com.cn/expert_article-151521-16381.shtml.

Zhang, Qianfan (2013) 'The Implementation of the Constitution and Long-term Governance', August 22, translated at China Copyright and Media, at: https://chinacopyrightandmedia.wordpress.com/2013/08/22/the-implementation-of-the-constitution-and-long-term-governance.

Zhang, X. (2012) 'Company Law Reform in China', in J. Garrick (ed.), *Law and Policy for China's Market Socialism*, London: Routledge.

Zhang, Yuanyan Sophia and Barnett, Steven (2014) 'Fiscal Vulnerabilities and Risks from Local Government Finance in China', International Monetary Fund, at: www.imf.org/external/pubs/ft/wp/2014/wp1404.pdf.

Zhao, Jianwen (2003) 'UNCLOS and China's South Sea Vested Interests', *Faxue Yanjiu*, 2.

Zhao, Lei (2010) 'The Li Zhuang Case: Contests in and outside the Court', *Southern Weekend*, January 6.

Zhao, Zhenjiang (ed.) (1990) *Forty Years of the Chinese Legal System* [*Zhongguo Fazhi Sishinian*], Beijing: Beijing University Press.

Zhejiang News (2014) 'Female College Student Sued Employer for Gender Discrimination: Court Awards Plaintiff RMB2,000 for Emotional Distress', November 14, at: http://zjnews.zjol.com.cn/system/2014/11/14/020357961.shtml.

Zhen, Zhongle (2013) 'The Revision of the Administrative Litigation Law Shall Seek Stability While Making Improvement', *Legal Daily*, December 25, at: www.legaldaily.com.cn/xwzx/content/2013-12/25/content_5154617.htm (accessed February 24, 2014).

Zheng, Shiping (1997) *Party vs. State in Post-1949 China: The Institutional Dilemma*, Cambridge: Cambridge University Press.

Zheng, Tianxiang (1999) *On Governing the State According to Law*, Beijing: People's Court Press.

Zheng, Wang (2013) 'How to Prevent Accidental Conflict in the East China Sea', *The Diplomat*, December 10, at: http://thediplomat.com/2013/12/how-to-prevent-accidental-conflict-in-the-east-china-sea.

Zhong, Sheng (2012) 中国在南海问题上自有定力 [China Is Self-restrained over Southern China Sea Issue], *People's Daily*, July 26, at: http://news.xinhuanet.com/comments/2012-07/26/c_112535906.htm (accessed May 28, 2015).

Zhou, Wei (2012) 'The Development of China's Anti-discrimination Law', *Tsinghua Law Journal*, 6 (2), at: http://166.111.104.103/homepage/uploads/files/zhouwei%281%29.pdf.

Zhou, Zhonghai (2006) *International Law*, Beijing: China University of Political Science and Law Press, May, 5: 119.

Zhu, Guobin (2010) 'Constitutional Review in China: An Unaccomplished Project or a Mirage?' *Suffolk University Law Review*, 43: 625–53.

Zhu, Guolin, Fan, Jianyong and Yan, Yan (2002) 'On China's Consumption Sag and Income Distribution', *Economic Research Journal* [*Jingji Yanjiu*], 48: 5.

Zhu, Jidong (2015) 'Sulian Wangdang Wangguo Guocheng Zhong de Jici Fazhi Gage Xianjing yu Jingshi' [Several Rule of Law Reform Pitfalls and Warnings in the Process of the Fall of the Soviet Party and State], *Hong Qi Wengao* [*Red Flag Manuscript*], May 11.

Zhu, Jingwen (2012) *Report on Legal Development in China 2011: Towards Plural Forms of Law Enforcement* [*Zhongguo Falü Fazhang Baogao 2011: Zouxiang Duoyuan de Falü Shishi*], Beijing: Renmin University Press.

Zimmermann, T.A. (2006) 'The DSU Review (1998–2004): Negotiations, Problems and Perspectives', in D. Georgiev and K. van der Borght (eds.), *Reform and Development of the WTO Dispute Settlement System*, London: Cameron May, pp. 443–72.

Zou, Yonghua, Zhao, Wanxia and Mason, R. (2014) 'Marketization of Collective-owned Rural Land: A Breakthrough in Shenzhen, China', *Sustainability*, 6: 9114–23.

Zuo, M. (2014) 'Four Chongqing Policemen to Face Trial for Alleged Torture under Bo Xilai's Crime Crackdown', *South China Morning Post*, April 25, at: www.scmp.com/news/china/article/1496733/four-chongqing-policemen-face-trial-alleged-torture-under-bo-xilais-crime.

Index

Page numbers in *italics* denote tables, those in **bold** denote figures.

3Leaf Systems (California-based company) 202
9/11 terrorist attacks 198

Administrative Litigation Law (ALL): adoption of 100; development of 99–105; enactment of 102; implementation of 100–1; scope of 101; statutory discretionary powers under 103
administrative managers 27–8, 53
administrative urbanization 127–8
aggression, crime of 153
Agricultural Bank of China 90
Agricultural Development Bank of China 90
agricultural operation system 129
alternative dispute resolution (ADR) 215
anti-corruption campaign 50, 56, 119, 121; Operation Fox Hunt 119, 221n6; 'Sky Net' campaign 119, 221n6; 'tigers and flies' campaign 10, 109, 117, 214
Anti-Monopoly Law (AML, 2008), China 202–3; Article 31 of 202
Anti-Secession Law (2005), China 161
anti-trust laws 135, 198
Arab Spring 4
assistant judges (*zhuli shenpanyuan*) 19

Bank of China 90
bianzhi system 144
Bo, Xilai 3, 109; crackdown on organized crime 110–11, 120; critical appraisal of trial of 114–17; downfall and trial 109, 112–14; embezzlement of public funds 112; historical perspective of trial 117–20; human rights violations 111; life sentence 116; Maoist-inspired policies in Chongqing 110; positive and negative aspects of trial 116–17; similarity with Gang of Four Trial 117–18; 'singing red' campaigns 110; unjust prosecutions in Chongqing 110
Brookings Institution 110
Budgetary Contracting System (BCS) 89

Cai, Dingjian 36
Caijing magazine 110
capital markets, liberalization of 86
Central Commission for Discipline Inspection (CCDI) 115–16
Central Internet and Informatization Leading Group 49
Central Leadership Group of Deepened Reforms 130
Central Politburo Standing Committee 23
Chen, Liangyu 119
Chen, Shiqiu 155
Chen, Youxi 110
Cheng, Li 110
China Banking Regulatory Commission (CBRC) 86
China Construction Bank 90
China Development Bank 90
China Disabled Persons Union 139
China Dream 55, 122, 219–20
China Insurance Regulatory Commission (CIRC) 86
China National Offshore Oil Corporation (CNOOC) 197
China paradox 80, 92
China Securities Regulatory Commission (CSRC) 86–7

China's maritime rights and interests: closing ranks around 186; concept of 186; control over contested maritime space 185; defining, protecting and expanding 185–6; EP-3 incident (2001) 191; geographic scope of state authority 188–90; *Impeccable* incident (2009) 191; jurisdictional content of state authority 187–8; law of the sea regime 185; Marine Environmental Protection Law (2002) 189; maritime law enforcement (MLE) agencies 191; National Maritime Development 186; position on 'archipelagic baselines' 189; roles of the state in maritime zones 190–2; standard list of zones 189; UNCLOS and 185–6
China's socialist market economy: aspects to boost domestic demand 62–3; contribution of net exports **60**; current account surplus 62; from demographic dividend to human capital bonus 67–9; export growth rate 62; from export-oriented to domestic demand-led 61–2; and household registration reforms 64–5; from investment-driven to consumption-driven 63–4; liberalized financial system 69–72; for reducing income disparities 65; in reshaping the industry structure 65–7; sequencing of financial reforms **71**; social welfare system 64; sustainable development of 73–4; from technological imitation to innovation 72–3; Twelfth Five-year Plan 62
China's socialist rule of law 1–3, 6, 11, 45, *81*; anti-corruption drive 46; decision on some major issues 46–50; democracy and 7; *Document No. 9* 51–6; forging of 3–6; Fourth Plenum decision 45–6; international implications of 216–19; law/growth nexus 212–13; major challenges for 212–16; role of the market in shaping 6–12; tenets of 50; Xi's approach to 50
Chongqing organized crime crackdown (2009–11) 110–12; corruption in 112–14; *see also* Bo, Xilai
Chongqing Public Security Bureau 113
circuit courts, establishment of 46
citizen constitutional activism 38
citizen–state constitutional disputes 5
civil and human rights legislation 140
Civil Procedure Law: code on 98; development of 98–9; implementation of 99; interpretation of 143; opinions of the Supreme Court on application of 98–9; reform of 98–9
Civil Rights Act (1964), US 141
Cohen, Jerome 115
collaborative governance 142–3, 216
collectively owned land, transfer rights of 124
Committee on Foreign Investment in the United States (CFIUS) 12, 197, 219; blockage of Japanese investment 198; and comparative regulatory frameworks in China 203–5; Court's jurisdiction over disputes regarding 200; decisions blocking Chinese investment projects 206; Due Process Clause 201; mandate and jurisdiction of 198–9; national security review in China and 202–3; post-Ralls national security review 200–1; Presidential Order based on 200
Communist Party of China (CPC) 84, 109; anti-corruption approaches 109; Eighteenth Central Committee 1, 8–9; Fourth Plenum of the Eighteenth Congress of 30, 42; leadership of 49; 'mass line' campaign 1; Political Bureau of the Central Committee 65; Third Plenum of the Eighteenth Congress of 25, 174
Company Law (1993) 85, 87–8
Congress of People's Deputies (CPD) 33
constitutional supervision committee: association with failed communist regimes 39–41; creation of 39; obstacles to 36–42; party's adaptive posture and 41–2; political sensitivity and capacity 37–9; precedent 37; Soviet Union 32–4, 39
constitutionality of legislation 9, 31, 39
Contract Law (1999) 85
Contract Responsibility System (CRS) 78, 89
Convention on the Law of the Sea (UNCLOS), United Nations 179, 218; Annex VII arbitration 180; China's domestic code and 181–6, 192; China's maritime rights and interests 185–6; China's ratification of 185; coastal state jurisdiction under 187; international arbitration under 8, 193; international law of the sea regime 180–1; interpretations of 180;

Convention on the Law of the Sea (UNCLOS) *continued*
lawful fisheries jurisdiction 190; provisions on archipelagic baselines 189; rules of conflict 183; *see also* China's maritime rights and interests
core crimes, definitions of 160–2
Corn Seed Case (2003) 20, 28
corporate governance 85–6, 198
corporate law, in China 85–6
corruption 65; anti-corruption campaign *see* anti-corruption campaign; property rights and freedom from *84*; in state-owned enterprises 50
Council on Constitutional Law 32
Court secretaries (*shujiyuan*) 19
crimes against humanity 153, 156, 160
Criminal Procedure Law 115; Criminal Procedure Law 1979 (CPL) 95; development of 95–7; 'due process' principles 95–7; enforcement of 97; procedures for criminal adjudication 95; reforms in 96; Western criminal procedure principles 96
cross-border transactions 85
Cultural Revolution (1966–76) 18, 27, 46, 53, 56, 95, 110, 112, 116–17, 210

danwei 86, 135
debt crisis in Europe 60
Deng, Xiaoping 161, 208, 211; Scientific Concept of Development 3; Three Represents 3; "two-hands" formula 1
Deng, Yujiao 24
Devillers, Patrick 113
difang baohu zhuyi 20, 210
disabled worker employment-guarantee funds 139
Dispute Settlement Mechanism (DSM), WTO 8, 167, 217; China's rising power, impact of 173–6; cost–benefit analysis 171–2; cross-jurisdictional tribunals 174; establishment of 169; frequency of litigation **171**; intersubjective model of 171; on Japan's recent lawsuits against China 176; literature review and a new norm-based theory 168–73; prisoner's dilemma problem 176; procedures to resolve trade disputes 173; for resolving international trade dispute 168, 172; social differentiation 170
Document No. 9 51–6
Document on Further Promoting the Hukou System Reforms (2014) 65
domestic armed conflicts 156, 161–2
domestic credit system 63
Duan, Jielong 156
Dubai Ports World 197, 199
Due Process Clause 201

East China Sea (ECS) 188, 218
economic crimes 50
Eighteenth Party Congress 8, 17, 64, 175
employment discrimination laws and policies 136; administrative claims process 142–3; administrative enforcement 137–8; anti-discrimination policy 139; China's challenges in enforcing 135–40; collaborative governance 143; equal rights protection 141–2; gender discrimination hiring practices 144; hiring practices 137; ineffective policy response on 138–40; labor contracts and labor relations 137; limited private enforcement 136–7; and market-based economic reforms 143; public interest litigation 143; public–private collaboration 144–5; 'social stability' function 143
employment, in the service sector **66**, **69**
Enforcement Bureau 22
EP-3 incident (2001) 191
Equal Employment Opportunity Commission (EEOC) 141; administrative claims proceedings 141; key features of 141
Equal Employment Promotion Law (EPL, 2008) 135; adoption of 136
equality and non-discrimination, principle of 134–5
ethnic and national unification 160
exchange rate controversies 198
exclusive economic zone (EEZ) 11, 185–6, 189; EEZ Law (1998), China 187; function of 12; restriction on military activities in 191
Exon–Florio provision (1988) 12, 198
export rebates 62–3
Export–Import Bank of China 90
extraterritoriality, principle of 5

Fan, Qihang 110
Fan, Yu 215
Feng, Chongyi 211–12
fiscal decentralization in China 90, 124
fixed-asset investments 67, 90
Foreign Corruption Practice Act, US 204
foreign direct investment (FDI) 12, 198, 202

Foreign Investment and National Security Act (FINSA, 2007), US 12, 197–9, 203–4; control, definition of 199; covered transactions under 198; enactment of 199; list of factors concerning national security 199
foreign-owned companies 71
Four Comprehensives 122, 208, 219–20

Gang of Four Trial (1981) 110, 117–20, 214
'gender and residency discrimination' cases 137
genocide 151, 153
Gini index of income 65
global financial crisis (2009) 59, 197
Goldman Sachs 205
Gorbachev, Mikhail 32, 39–40
Grameen Bank, Bangladesh 91
Gu, Kailai 113–15
Gu, Shengzu 100
guanxi (interpersonal relationships) 91
Guidance on Recognition of Hi-tech Enterprises 73
guizhang (departmental and governmental rules) 102
Guo, Yushan 210

Hand, Keith 210
Hanqin, Xue 181
He, Weifang 110
Heritage Foundation 81–2
Heywood, Neil 112–15
household consumption 64
household registration reforms 64–5
Household Responsibility System (HRS) 88–9
Hu, Jintao 56, 113, 119, 158
hukou (China's residence registration) system 39–40, 64, 128–9
human capital 61, 73, 126, 212; bonus 67–9
human rights: China's core sovereignty issues *versus* 158–9; Chinese socialization in 152; Chinese *versus* Western views on 158–9; concept of 158; PRC policy development with respect to 153; protection of 46; violation of 156–7, 160
human rights activists, criminal detention of 49

Impeccable incident (2009) 191
Industrial and Commercial Bank of China 90
Industrial Revolution 85
initial public offerings (IPOs) 87
institutional innovations 88–90, 153
intellectual property index 73
intellectual property rights (IPRs) 79, 93, 202
inter-regional development 129
International Court of Justice 181
International Covenant on Civil and Political Rights (ICCPR) 151, 163
International Covenant on Economic, Social and Cultural Rights (ICESCR) 151
International Criminal Court (ICC) 8, 151, 216; China's negotiations in the Rome Statute 154–7; China's rejection of the Rome Statute of 151; Convention against Torture (CAT) 163–4; on encroachment of state sovereignty 157; establishment of 161; 'human rights' perspective 156; implications for China of the Prosecutor's 'ex officio right' 162–3; jurisdiction of 156–7; Pre-Trial Chamber of the Court 154; Rome Statute, significance of 153–4; sovereignty costs 163–4; Taiwan Coalition for 162
international institutions, China's approach to 152
international law of the sea 179; in Chinese context 180–1
International Monetary Fund (IMF) 62, 132
Internet Cleaning-up Campaign 53
Internet sovereignty 49

Ji, Weidong 34
Jiang, Qing 119
Jiang, Zemin 46, 56, 119, 152, 216; discourses on human rights 158–9; Three Stresses Party Rectification 119
Joint Venture Law (1979), China 213
judges, financial condition of 28
judicial administration, centralization of 28–9, 210
judicial appointments 18–19, 28
judicial committee 20, 25–7, 97
judicial corruption 8, 17–18, 22, 28
judicial opinion-making, transparency in 21
judicial populism 23–5
judicial reasoning, quality of 21
judicial reform in China: during 1999–2013 21–5; on centralization of judicial power 27; *Corn Seed Case* 20;

judicial reform in China *continued*
courts of local governments 20; first and second outlines of 21–3; Five-Year Reform of the People's Court 21, 23; in judicial decisions 21; judicial syndrome 18–21; new reform (2014–present) 25–8; 'professionalization' reform 25; Shanghai project 26–7; third outline of 23–5; *see also* Supreme People's Court (SPC)

land acquisition 102, 131
'land finance' revenue 124, 128
land loss 131
land market reform 122; challenges and tensions 130–2; dual-track system for 123, 125; for industrialization and economic growth 128; land use system 123–6; urbanization, issue of 126–9
land trade 124
land transactions 128
land-based urbanization 126, 128–9, 131
Lardy, Nicholas 204
Law of the People's Republic of China on the Exclusive Economic Zone and the Continental Shelf (EEZ) 179
law of the sea, internalization of 11
Law on Individual Wholly-Owned Enterprises (1999) 85, 88
Law on Partnership Enterprises (1997) 85
Law on the Procedure of the Conclusion of Treaties (Treaty Law) 181
Law on the Territorial Sea and the Contiguous Zone (1992), China *see* Territorial Sea Law (1992), China
laws in China: comparative perspective of 83–8; complementarities between law and markets 88; corporate law and economic necessity 85–6; enforcement of 91–2; institutional development and 80; institutions and transition 88–91; for investor protection *83*; *versus* Japanese legal system 83; 'legal origins' school 80; markets and 79–83; regulatory quality *82*; and regulatory reform supporting markets 86–7; rule of law *81*
legal rights of citizens 47
Legislation Law (2000) 36–7, 182
Lenin, V. 49
Li, Keqiang 62, 73
Li, Shengxiong 162
Li, Xiaofeng 116
Li, Zhanshu 51
Li, Zhuang 22–3, 110–11, 121
Liu, Daqun 152
Liu, Yandong 215
Local People's Congress (LPC) 19

M&A Law and *Securities Investment Fund Law* (2003) 85
Mao, Zedong 49, 208
Maoist revolutionary movements 18
Marine Environmental Protection Law (2002) 189
marine scientific research (MSR) 191
maritime law enforcement (MLE) agencies 191
maritime legal system in China: domestic law reforms 179–80; formal sources of law in the PRC with respect to treaties 182; international law in the political continuum 183–4; National Maritime Development 186; politicization of 184; and ruling the country through law 184; Special Maritime Procedure Law (1999) 189; status of international law, in domestic legal hierarchy 182–3; *see also* China's maritime rights and interests
market socialism 54–5
market-based economic reforms 143
market-supporting institutions 80, 92
Marxism–Leninism–Mao Zedong Thought 54, 96; tenets of 55
Marxist–Leninist rule-by-law 4
Meiji Restoration 83
microfinance institutions 91
middle-income countries 5
middle-income trap 60, 209
Ministry of Commerce (MOFCOM), China 202; Regulation on Implementing of the Security Review System for Mergers and Acquisitions of Domestic Enterprises by Foreign Investors 202
Ministry of Human Resource and Social Security (MOHRSS) 137–8; office's labor supervision authority 144
Minnie, Chan 120
Minor Property Housing (MPH) 123
Model Format for Judicial Opinions in Criminal Trials (SPC, 1999) 22

National Maritime Functional Zones, China 190
National People's Congress (NPC) 30, 35, 112, 118, 181, 211; anti-crime campaigns 95; Standing Committee of 95
National Security Review Committee (NSRC), China 202–3, 219

national unification and regime security 159
'New Socialist Countryside' campaign 127–8
nomenklatura system 35
non-governmental organizations (NGOs) 153
North Korea 40, 49
NPC and its Standing Committee (NPCSC) 30, 34–5, 41–2; Filing and Review Office 36; Legislative Affairs Commission 36
Nye, Joseph 175

Office of Foreign Asset Control, US 204
'open door' policy 85, 95
Operation Fox Hunt 119, 221n6
Organic Law of the People's Courts 19–20
ownership bias, problem of 204

Paris Convention for the Protection of Industrial Property (1985) 221n3
Party-state–legal system nexus 46
Patent Cooperation Treaty (1994) 221n3
patents, structure of **72,** 73
Patriotic Education Campaign 55
People's Bank of China 71, 90
people's democratic dictatorship 6, 49, 55, 97
people's legislatures, supremacy of 31
People's Liberation Army (PLA) 50, 199, 214
People's Mediation Law (2010), China 215
personal rights, violation of 136, 138
Plenum decisions of 2013–14 7
Polish Constitutional Tribunal 33
'political and legal work' (*zhengfa gongzuo*) 18
political crime 49
political loyalty 2, 19, 38, 47
PRC Fisheries Law (2004) 190
PRC Foreign Investment Act (2015) 198, 202
predatory taxation 124
president responsibility system 20
private bank lending 90
private property: freehold ownership 79; leasehold 79; legal ownership of 79; rights of 77–8
privately owned enterprises (POEs) 204
proletarian dictatorship 18, 55
Property Law (2007) 79, 82, 90
property ownership and use rights 128
property right certificates 125
property rights 77–8; and freedom from corruption *84*; in intellectual property 88; of rural lands 125; security of 81
property rights management system 124
pseudo-urbanization 126–7
Pu, Zhiqiang 49, 210
public interest litigation 101, 143, 144
public thinking in China 55–6

Qi, Yuling 23, 38
Qian, Jin 181
Qianfan, Zhang 8, 34, 210
Qu, Wensheng 156

Ralls Corporation 197–8
Ralls Corporation v. CFIUS 200
re-education through labor (RTL) system 41–2
reform dividend 74
regional protectionism (*difang baohu zhuyi*) 20
Regulation for Strengthening Public Security during the Proletarian Culture Revolution (1967) 56
renminbi (RMB): exchange rate against US dollars 69; internationalization of 210; role in international trade and finance 210; undervaluation of 69–70
renquan 158–9
residential property 124–7
retail banking 90
risk assessment of banks 93
Rome Statute: Article 12 of 156; China's negotiations in 154–7; China's rejection of 151, 164, 216; definition of war crimes 162; potential impact of China's core sovereignty 160–4; significance of 153–4
rule of law *see* China's socialist rule of law
rural development 127–8
rural land contractual management 125
rural land market, liberalization of 125
rural land property right 124
rural migrants, citizenization of 129
rural tax reform 124–5
rural–urban disparity in China 64

Scheffer, David 157
scientific development, concept of 55
Securities and Exchange Commission (SEC) 204
Securities Law (1998) 87
Securities Law (1999) 78

Sejm statutes, constitutionality of 32
Selected Works of Jiang Zemin 158
Senkaku/Diaoyu islands dispute 192
separation of powers, doctrine of 6, 18, 30–1
Shanghai Free Trade Zone 73
Shanghai (judicial reform) project 26–7
Shirk, Susan 205
shuanggui 115–16, 213; detention and interrogation system of 50; extra-legal mechanism 105
Sino-foreign joint companies 71
Sino–Japanese relations 173
Sino–Japanese War (1894) 5
Six Articles for Public Security 56
'Sky Net' campaign 119, 221n6
social capital 91, 129, 132
social contract theory 55
social inequalities 64, 130
social welfare system 64, 66, 73, 212
socialist constitutional supervision models: application of 34–6; constitutional supervision committee 36–42; elements of 31–4
South China Sea (SCS) 188, 218
sovereignty costs 11, 152–4, 160, 163–4, 216
Soviet Union: collapse of 34, 39; Constitutional Supervision Committee 32–4; internal residence registration system 39; liberalization programs 34
Special Maritime Procedure Law (1999) 189; Article 7 of 189–90
Spratly Islands dispute 187
stability preservation, system of 50
Stalin 31, 55
stare decisis 77
State Asset Supervision and Administration Commission (SASAC) 87
state banking system 90
State Oceanic Administration (SOA) 190
state sovereignty, superiority of 158
state-controlled property system 79, 88, 92
state-owned banks 90; decentralization of 89
state-owned commercial banks (SCBs) 90
state-owned enterprises (SOEs) 65, 78, 204; corruption in 50; decline of 90; institutional innovations as incentives 90; privatization of 79; tax and profit remittances 89
state-owned housing 88
stock market, in China 87
'strike-mafia' (*dahei*) campaign 22
Sun, Chunlan 215
Supreme People's Court (SPC) 8, 17, 22, 98, 143; Fourth Five-Year Reform Plan of the People's Court (2014–18) 26; Model Format for Judicial Opinions in Criminal Trials (1999) 22; Notice on Gradual Expansion of Trial Work on Relatively Centralised Jurisdiction of Administrative Cases 104

Taiwan independence secessionist forces 161–2
Tan, Shigui 161
Tang, Xiaolin 112
tax and profit remittances 89
tax reimbursement, for exports 62
Territorial Sea Law (1992), China 186, 192
Theory of Three Represents 55
'Three Supremes' (*sange zhishang*) 8, 17
'three-together' (*santong*) phenomenon 22
'tigers and flies' anti-corruption campaign 10, 109, 117, 214
Tong, Zhiwei 115
torture, crime of 163
township and village enterprises (TVEs) 89
trade disputes, settlement of 167
TRIPS agreement 221n3
Twitter 49

UNCLOS *see* Convention on the Law of the Sea (UNCLOS), United Nations
United Nations (UN) 4, 45; Commission on Human Rights 161; Convention on the Law of the Sea (UNCLOS) *see* Convention on the Law of the Sea (UNCLOS), United Nations; peacekeeping operations 151; Security Council 152, 153
unity of state power, principle of 40
Unocal 197, 205
urban development, need for 126
urban governing capacity 128
urban planning 128
urban welfare system 64
urban–rural construction land market 125
urban–rural development planning 128–9
urbanization in China: administrative 127–8; government's role in 127–8; *hukou* system 128; 'human-centric' concept 129; land-based 126, 128–9; National New-type Urbanization Plan 129; 'New Socialist Countryside'

campaign 127; pseudo-urbanization 126; quality of 128; of rural residents 129; strategies for 126–9
US Court of Appeals 197, 200–1; decision on the Ralls case 206
US–Japan trade frictions 198

Vietnamese Communist Party (VCP) 40
Virtual Private Networks 49

Wang, Boming 110
Wang, Guangya 157
Wang, Jingcheng 100
Wang, Lijun 112, 114
Wang, Qishan 202
Wang, Quishan 197
Wang, Shengjun 18
Wang, Tieya 183
Wang, Yukai 116
Wang, Zhenyu 100
war crimes 153, 156, 161–2
Weibo 49, 115, 118
Wen, Jiabao 112, 116
Westphalian sovereignty 154
World Trade Organization (WTO) 4, 87; Appellate Body (AB) on issues of law 167; Dispute Settlement Mechanism (DSM) *see* Dispute Settlement Mechanism (DSM), WTO; impact of ongoing Chinese legal reform 173–6; international trade dispute 172; Worldwide Governance Indicators 80
World United Formosans for Independence 162

Xi, Jinping 1, 39, 41, 43, 116, 122, 161, 164, 174; approach to rule of law 50; ascension to power 117–18; Central Internet and Informatization Leading Group 49; China Dream 55; China's law reforms under 208; economic reform agenda 35; economic structural reform 7; equal employment opportunity and rights protection 215–16; ideological campaign 54; land and urbanization reforms 214–15; leadership of 45, 49; Operation Fox Hunt 119; power structure of China under 2; 'Sky Net' campaign 119; socialist ideological developments under 210–12; on supremacy of PRC Constitution 30; system of stability preservation 50; 'tigers and flies' anti-corruption campaign 10, 109, 117, 119, 214
Xiao, Yang 30
Xu, Ming 112–13
Xu, Ting 23–4
Xu, Xin 7
Xu, Zhiyang 49
Xu, Zhiyong 210
Xue, Charles 53

Yuhua, Wang 116

Zhang, Lifan 116
Zhang, Qianfan 115
Zhou, Yongkang 48, 120
Zhou, Zhonghai 187

For Product Safety Concerns and Information please contact our EU representative GPSR@taylorandfrancis.com
Taylor & Francis Verlag GmbH, Kaufingerstraße 24, 80331 München, Germany

www.ingramcontent.com/pod-product-compliance
Ingram Content Group UK Ltd.
Pitfield, Milton Keynes, MK11 3LW, UK
UKHW020014200926
475702UK00014B/1871
* 9 7 8 0 8 1 5 3 8 6 9 8 8 *